D1985529

The Ultimate Compendium of Sensor Projects

40+ Projects using Arduino, Raspberry Pi and ESP32

Dogan Ibrahim

elektor

LEARN DESIGN SHARE

This is an Elektor Publication. Elektor is the media brand of
Elektor International Media B.V.
78 York Street, London W1H 1DP, UK
Phone: (+44) (0)20 7692 8344

Acknowledgements
The author would like to express his thanks to Ferdinand te Walvaart of Elektor for the valuable suggestions he made throughout the duration of the preparation of this book. The author would like to thank also to his wife Nadire for her encouragement, motivation, and for being patient with me while working on this book.

British Library Cataloguing in Publication Data
A catalogue record for this book is available from the British Library

ISBN 978-1-907920-78-3

Prepress Production: D-Vision, Julian van den Berg
First published in the United Kingdom 2019
Printed in the Netherlands by Wilco

Preface

Sensors are devices or components that detect events or changes in their environments and send information to other electronics, frequently to microcontroller systems. Sensors are used in everyday life, to measure such things as temperature, humidity, pressure, wind and rain, touch, light levels, liquid levels, altitude, force, and many more.

Although some sensors have digital outputs, most sensors used in everyday life have analog outputs, usually in the form of voltages that are proportional to a measured quantity. This output voltage is normally fed to the input port of a microcontroller for processing. For example, the output of an analog temperature sensor is connected to an analog input port (an analog-to-digital converter) of a microcontroller. The microcontroller reads the temperature as a digital value and converts it into real physical temperature, which is then displayed or used to control the temperature of a machine or room.

This book is about using the sensors found in the sensor kit. Altogether, there are 40 sensors distributed with the kit. Some sensors provide analog outputs while others have digital outputs, and some have both analog and digital outputs. The kit includes sensors to measure temperature, humidity, atmospheric pressure, light intensity, and sound. There are also 2 and 3 colour LEDs, tilt switches, magnetic switches, relay, reed switches, piezo buzzer, button, joystick, obstacle detector, heartbeat sensor, analog-digital converter, voltage translator, vibrations switch, etc.

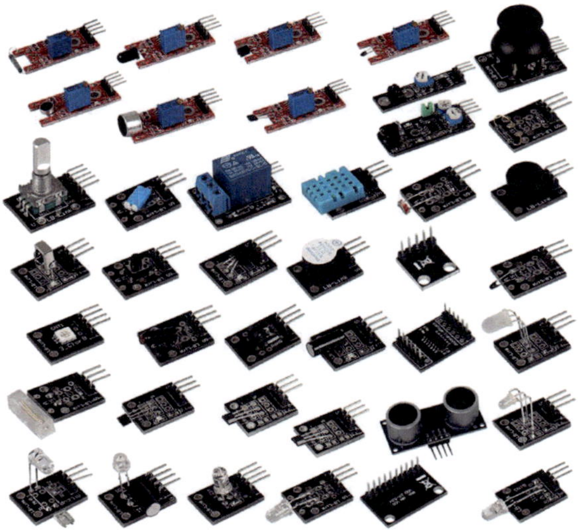

40 Sensors All-in-1 Kit

The book is intended to teach how to use sensors with the popular microcontroller development systems: Arduino Uno, ESP32 DevKitC, and Raspberry Pi. Example projects are given to show how to use the sensors with these microcontrollers. The programs can be modified for other microcontrollers, such as PIC, STM32, Banana Pi, CubieBoard, Beaglebone, etc. All the projects given in the book were built using a standard size breadboard, and they were fully tested and were all working. The projects are described with the following sub-headings:

- Project description
- Aim of the project
- Block diagram
- Circuit diagram
- Program listing

The operation of each sensor and each program listing are described in detail so that the readers will have no difficulty in either constructing or expanding a given project. Some projects make use of more than one sensor from the kit. It is recommended that readers follow the projects in the given order since some of the software tools used in some projects depend on the installation of these tools in an earlier project.

Full program listings of the projects with many comments are available at the Elektor website of the book and readers should be able to copy and use these programs without having to make modifications.

Arduino Uno and ESP32 DevKitC programs are based on using the Arduino IDE with the C language. Raspberry Pi projects use the Python programming language. Although the Arduino based projects specify Arduino Uno as the development board, these projects should also work with other Arduino development boards, such as Arduino Mega, Arduino Nano, etc.

I hope the readers find the book useful and enjoy experimenting with the various sensors.

Dogan Ibrahim
June 2019

Chapter 1 • Arduino Uno hardware interface and project development

1.1 Overview

In this book, we will use the Arduino Uno board in the Arduino based sensor projects. This Chapter shows the location of the various components on the Arduino Uno board and also describes the hardware interface to the external world. A simple project is given in this Chapter to make the reader familiar with developing programs with the Arduino Uno. The first program flashes a two colour LED alternately every second.

1.2 Arduino Uno board

Figure 1.1 shows the Arduino Uno board in close-up with the major components marked. The pin definitions are as follows (see Figure 1.2).

A0 – A5:	Analog input ports
0 – 13:	Digital input/output ports
~3,~5,~6,~9,~10,~11:	PWM output ports
0,1:	UART RX/TX pins. LEDs labelled TX, RX will flash when data is transmitted or received respectively
GND:	Power supply ground pin
5V:	Regulated +5V output
3.3V:	Regulated +3.3V output
Vin:	Voltage input (instead of using Power In or USB). The voltage must be in the range 7-12V. It is regulated to +5V internally. This pin can also be used as a voltage output (if power is supplied using Power In or USB port). The voltage is a copy of the voltage supplied through Power In or the USB port.
IORef:	Used by external shield boards to know if they should operate as +3.3V or as +5V devices
Power In:	Power supply Barrel Jack pin (6V to 12V)
USB port:	Power and data port (connect to computer)
User LED:	Onboard LED connected to output port 13 (can be used for testpurposes)

Notice that when the Arduino Uno is powered by the USB port (e.g. from a computer) the maximum current capacity is around 400mA for the +5V pin and 150mA for the +3.3V pin. When powered by an external source, the maximum current for the 5V pin is around 900mA and 150mA for the +3.3V pin. Any current drawn from the +3.3V goes through the +5V pin. Therefore, you have to take this into account when powering external devices.

The absolute maximum current for any I/O pin is specified as 40mA (it is however recommended not to exceed 20mA). The absolute total current from all the I/O pins is 200mA.

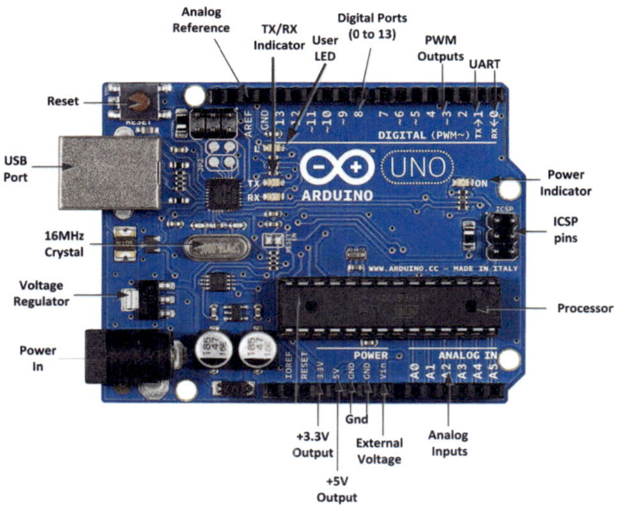

Figure 1.1 Arduino Uno board

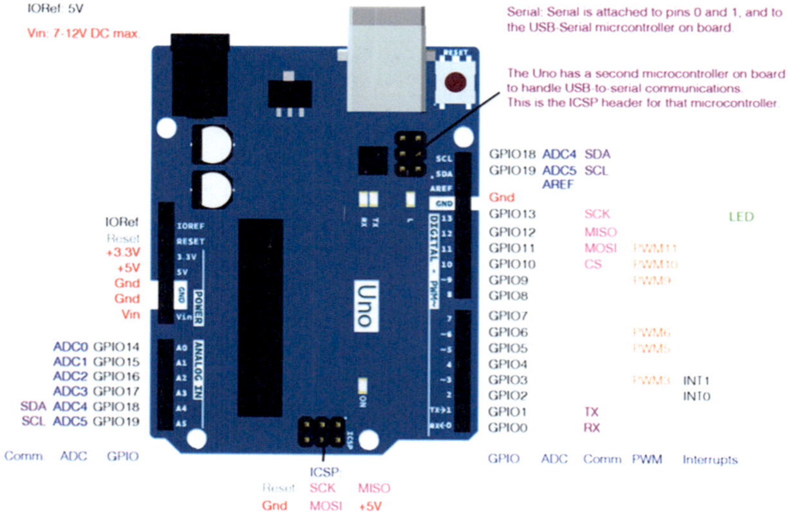

Figure 1.2 Arduino Uno pin layout

1.3 Arduino Uno program development

A nice feature of all Arduino boards is that they can all be programmed using the Arduino IDE. The latest version of Arduino IDE can be downloaded from the following web site. At the time of writing this book the latest version was 1.8.8:

https://www.arduino.cc/en/Main/Software

The steps to writing and upload a program to your Arduino Uno are as follows:

- Connect your Arduino Uno to the USB port of your computer
- Start the Arduino IDE on your computer
- Click **Tools -> Board** and select board type as **Arduino/Gerduino Uno**
- Click **Tools -> Port** and select the serial port that your Arduino Uno is connected to
- Write and then save your program
- Click **Sketch -> Verify/Compile** to compile your program. Make sure there are no compilation errors
- Click **Sketch->Upload** to upload the executable code to the program memory of your Arduino Uno

Two example projects are given in the following sections to make the reader familiar with the project development cycle using the Arduino Uno. It is assumed that the reader has some background in basic electronics and also some working knowledge of writing a high-level language.

1.4 Project – Flashing two colour LEDs

description: This is perhaps the easiest project you can design using your Arduino Uno. In this project, a two colour LED with common cathode is connected to the Arduino Uno. The LED colours are flashed alternately at a rate of one second.

Aim: The aim of this project is to show how to write, compile and upload a program to the Arduino Uno. The project additionally shows how to use some of the I/O and timing functions of the Arduino.

Sensor Used: Sensor KY-011 is used in this project. This sensor consists of a red and green colour LED housed in a package with a common cathode terminal. The sensor and its pins are shown in Figure 1.3. The sensor has 3 pins: red LED pin, green LED pin and GND pin. **The green LED pin is marked with letter S on the board for identification.** An LED is turned ON when logic 1 is applied to its pins. The basic specifications of this sensor are as follows:

Operating voltage:	2.0V to 2.5V
Operating current:	10mA (depends on the required brightness)
Wavelength:	green (571nm), red (644nm)
Luminous intensity (MCD):	green (20-40), red (40-80)

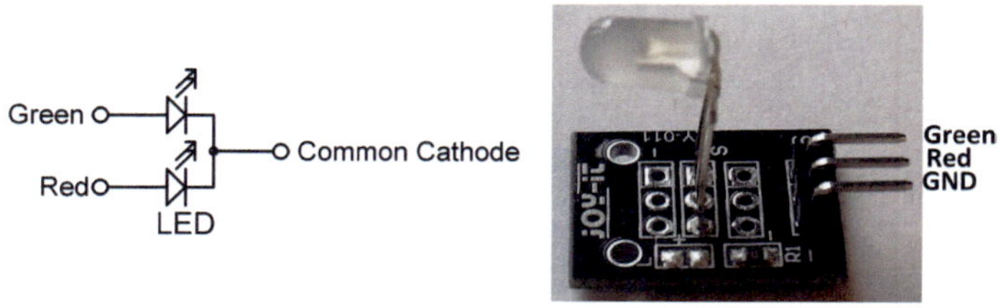

Figure 1.3 Sensor KY-011

Block diagram: The block diagram of the project is shown in Figure 1.4.

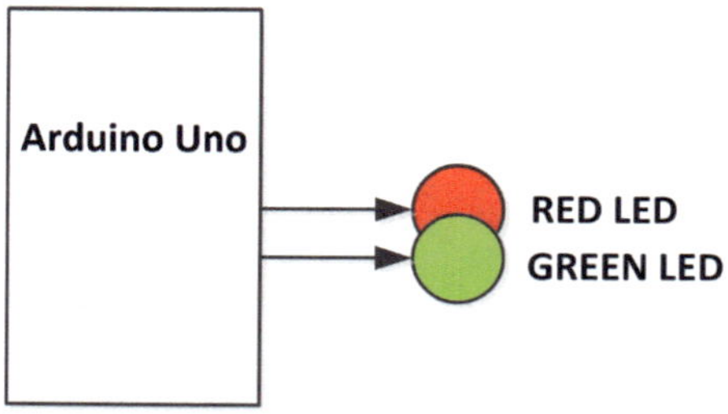

Figure 1.4 Block diagram of the project

Circuit diagram: The circuit diagram of the project is shown in Figure 1.5. The green and red LED pins are connected to port pins 2 and 3 of the Arduino Uno respectively through current limiting resistors. The GND pin is connected to Arduino Uno GND pin. The value of the current limiting resistor is calculated as follows:

The high voltage of an output pin is 5V. The forward voltage across an LED is approximately 2.0V (for the red LED this is 1.8V, and for the green LED this is 2.8V). Assuming that the forward current to the LED will be set to 10mA (reasonable brightness), then, the value of the current limiting resistor is:

R = (5V – 2V) / 10mA = 300 ohm, use 330 ohm resistor (you can use smaller value, e.g. 270 ohms for the green LED)

In Figure 1.5 the LED is operated in current sourcing mode where a high output from the I/O pin drives the LED. The LED can also be operated in current sinking mode where the other end of the LED is connected to +5V supply and not to the ground. In current sinking mode, the LED is turned ON when the I/O pin is at logic low.

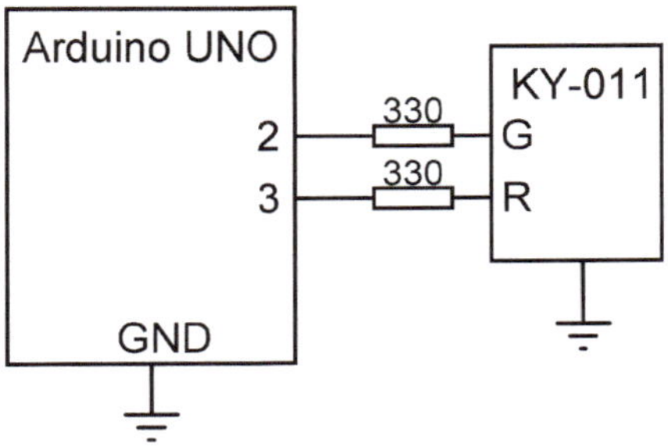

Figure 1.5 Circuit diagram of the project

Construction: The project is constructed on a breadboard as shown in Figure 1.6. Jumper wires are used to connect the KY-011 to digital port pins 2 and 3 and GND of the Arduino Uno.

Figure 1.6 The project constructed on a breadboard

Program listing: The program is called **TWOCOLOUR** and the listing is shown in Figure 1.7. At the beginning of the program, port pins 2 and 3 are assigned to the green LED and red LED pins respectively. Inside the setup routine, port pins 2 and 3 where the LED pins are connected to are configured as outputs. Inside the main program loop, the two colours are turned ON and OFF alternately with a one-second delay between each output. **Verify/ Compile** to make sure that there are no errors and then **Upload** the program code to your Arduino Uno. You should see the two colours flashing at a rate of one second.

It is highly recommended by the author to comment the lines in your program and describe the operation being performed as shown in Figure 1.7. You should also include a heading and describe what the program does briefly. This makes it easier to understand and maintain the program at a later date. It also makes it easier for anyone else to understand the logic of the program when they read it.

```
/******************************************************************
 *                FLASHING GREEN AND RED LEDs
 *                ===========================
 *
 * In this program the KY-011 sensor is used which has a green and
 * a red LED with a common cathode terminal. The green LED and the
 * red LED are connected to I/O pins 2 and 3 of the Arduino Uno
 * respectively. The program flashes the LEDs alternately at a rate
 * of one second.
 *
 * Author: Dogan Ibrahim
 * Date  : April 2019
 * File  : TWOCOLOUR
 ******************************************************************/
int GreenLED = 2;                                   // Green LED pin
int RedLED = 3;                                     // Red LED pin
#define ON HIGH
#define OFF LOW

void setup()
{
  pinMode(GreenLED, OUTPUT);                        // Set as output
  pinMode(RedLED, OUTPUT);                          // Set as output
}

void loop()
{
  digitalWrite(GreenLED, ON);                       // Turn ON green
  digitalWrite(RedLED, OFF);                        // Turn OFF red
  delay(1000);                                      // Wait 1 sec
  digitalWrite(GreenLED, OFF);                      // Turn OFF green
  digitalWrite(RedLED, ON);                         // Turn ON red
```

```
    delay(1000);                          // Wait 1 sec
}
```

Figure 1.7 Program listing of the project

What we have learned: In this project, we have learned how to use the following Arduino functions:

int:	declares an integer variable
#define:	assigns value or text to a string
pinMode (port pin, mode):	used to configure an I/O port pin as input or output
digitalWrite(port pin, value):	used to output digital value (logic LOW or HIGH) to a port pin
delay(n):	creates a delay of **n** milliseconds

1.5 Summary

In this Chapter, we have seen the various components and the pin definitions of the Arduino Uno microcontroller. Additionally, a simple project is given to demonstrate how to design simple projects and also how to compile upload the program code to the program memory of the Arduino Uno microcontroller.

In the next Chapter, we will be looking at how to use the Raspberry Pi microcontroller in projects.

Chapter 2 • Raspberry Pi hardware interface and project development

2.1 Overview

In this book, we will be using a Raspberry Pi 3 Model B in our Raspberry Pi projects. This Chapter shows the location of the various components on the Raspberry Pi board and also describes the hardware interface to the external world. Setting up Wi-Fi and remote access to your Raspberry Pi computer, and becoming familiar with the Python programming environment are also described briefly. A simple project is given to familiarize the reader with the steps of designing a project. In this book, when we write Raspberry Pi 3 we actually mean Raspberry Pi 3 Model B.

2.2 The Raspberry Pi 3 board

Figure 2.1 shows the Raspberry Pi 3 board with the major components marked. Some details on each component are given in this section.

Figure 2.1 Raspberry Pi 3 board

USB ports: Raspberry Pi 3 has 4 USB ports to connect a mouse, keyboard, webcam, etc.

Ethernet and Wi-Fi: Although the Raspberry Pi 3 has built-in Wi-Fi, it can also directly be connected to a router through an Ethernet cable connected to this socket.

Audio/Video Jack: A headphone or a speaker can be connected to this 3.5mm socket. This socket also carries a composite video interface.

CSI: This is the Camera Serial Interface where a compatible Raspberry Pi camera can be attached here.

HDMI: A suitable monitor can be connected to this port. The port carries both audio and video signals.

USB power: A +5V 2A power supply should be connected to this USB socket to provide power to the Raspberry Pi 3.

SD card slot: A micro SD card carrying the operating system must be attached to this slot.

DSI: A suitable display can be connected to this Display Interface connector.

SOC: This is the Broadcom BCM2837 System On Chip (SOC) which contains the 1.2GHz 64-bit quad-core ARM Cortex-A53 processor.

GPIO: The General Purpose Input-Output port is 40 pins wide.

BCM43438: This chip provides the Wi-Fi and Bluetooth to the Raspberry Pi 3.

2.3 Raspberry Pi 3 GPIO pin definitions

The Raspberry Pi 3 is connected to external digital electronic circuits and devices using its GPIO (General Purpose Input Output) port connector. This is a 2.54mm, 40-pin expansion header, arranged in a 2x20 strip as shown in Figure 2.2.

Figure 2.2 Raspberry Pi 3 GPIO pins

When the GPIO connector is at the far side of the board, the pins at the bottom, starting from the left of the connector are numbered as 1, 3, 5, 7, and so on, while the ones at the top are numbered as 2, 4, 6, 8 and so on.

The GPIO provides 26 general purpose bi-directional I/O pins. Some of the pins have multiple functions. For example, pins 3 and 5 are the GPIO2 and GPIO3 input-output pins respectively. These pins can also be used as the I^2C bus I^2C SDA and I^2C SCL pins respectively. Similarly, pins 9,10,11,19 can either be used as general purpose input-output, or as the SPI bus pins. Pins 8 and 10 are reserved for UART serial communication.

Two power outputs are provided: +3.3V and +5.0V. The GPIO pins operate at +3.3V logic levels (not like many other computer circuits that operate with +5V). A pin can either be an input or an output. When configured as an output, the pin voltage is either 0V (logic

0) or +3.3V (logic 1). Raspberry Pi 3 is normally operated using an external power supply (e.g. a mains adapter) with +5V output and minimum 2A current capacity. A 3.3V output pin can supply up to 16mA of current. The total current drawn from all output pins should not exceed the 51mA limit. Care should be taken when connecting external devices to the GPIO pins as drawing excessive currents or short-circuiting a pin can easily damage your Pi. The amount of current that can be supplied by the 5V pin depends on many factors such as the current required by the Pi itself, current taken by the USB peripherals, camera current, HDMI port current, and so on.

When configured as an input, a voltage above +1.7V will be taken as logic 1, and a voltage below +1.7V will be taken as logic 0. Care should be taken not to supply voltages greater than +3.3V to any I/O pin as large voltages can easily damage your Pi. The Raspberry Pi 3, like others in the family, has no over-voltage protection circuitry.

2.4 Setting up the Wi-Fi and remote access

It is very likely that you will want to access your Raspberry Pi 3 remotely from your desktop or laptop computer. The easiest option here is to enable Wi-Fi on your Pi computer and then access it from your computer using the SSH client protocol. This protocol requires a server and a client. The server is your Pi computer and the client is your desktop or laptop computer. In this section, we will see how to enable the Wi-Fi on your Pi computer and how to access it remotely.

Setting up Wi-Fi

To enable the Wi-Fi on your Pi, the steps are as follows:

- Click on the Wi-Fi icon which is a pair of red crosses at the top right-hand side of the screen

- Select your Wi-Fi router from the displayed list (see Figure 2.3)

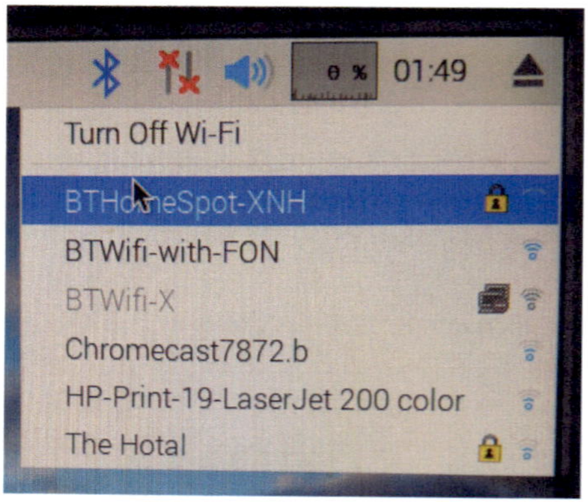

Figure 2.3 Select your Wi-Fi from the list

- Enter the password for your Wi-Fi router

- The WiFi icon should become a typical Wi-Fi image. If you click on the icon now you should see a green tick next to the selected router as shown in Figure 2.4.

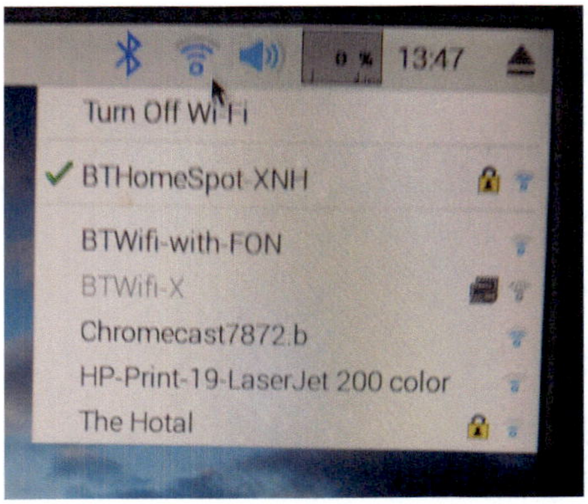

Figure 2.4 Connected to the Wi-Fi successfully

- To see the IP address of your Wi-Fi connection, place the mouse over the Wi-Fi icon as shown in Figure 2.5. In this example, the IP address was 192.168.1.84

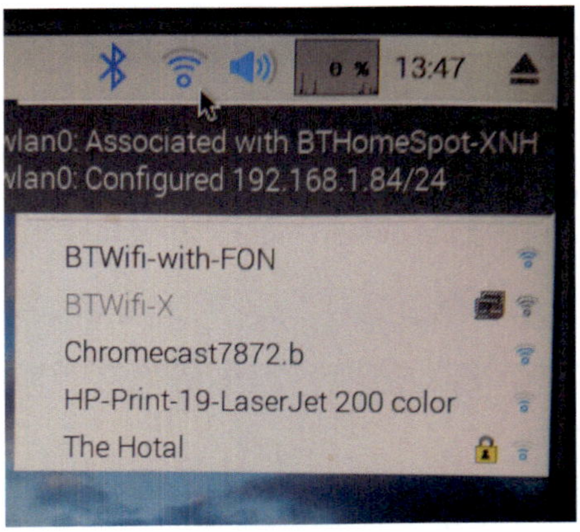

Figure 2.5 IP address of our connection

Remote Access

The program we will be using to access our Raspberry Pi 3 is called **Putty** with the SSH protocol. The steps to download and use Putty are as follows:

- Download Putty from the following link (or search Google for "Download Putty")

  http://www.chiark.greenend.org.uk/~sgtatham/putty/download.html

- For security reasons, the SSH protocol is disabled by default on a new operating system. To enable it, click on the **Applications** menu at the top left of the screen, click **Accessories**, and then click **Terminal** (see Figure 2.6)

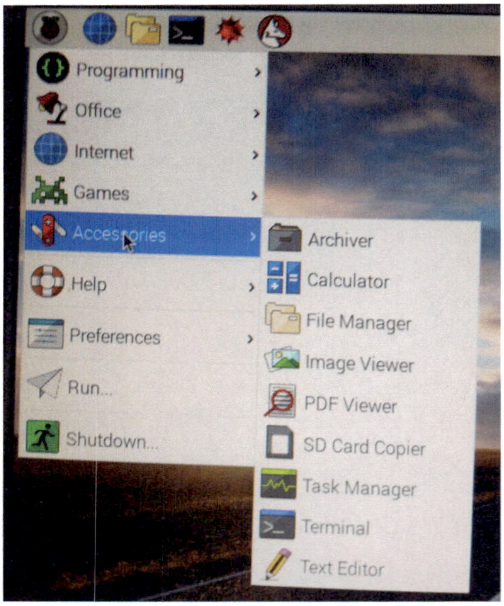

Figure 2.6 Access the Terminal menu

- You should now be in the Raspberry Pi 3 command prompt. Type:

```
sudo raspi-config
```

- to go into the configuration menu and select **Interface Options**. Go down to **P2 SSH** and enable SSH as shown in Figure 2.7

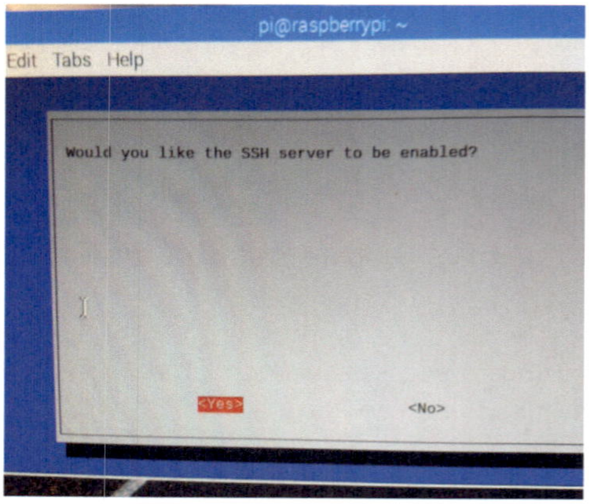

Figure 2.7 Enable the SSH server

- Click **<Finish>** to exit the configuration menu. You should now be back in the command mode, identified by the prompt:

```
pi@raspberrypi:~ $
```

- Putty is a standalone program and there is no need to install it. Simply double click to run it. You should see the Putty startup screen as in Figure 2.8.

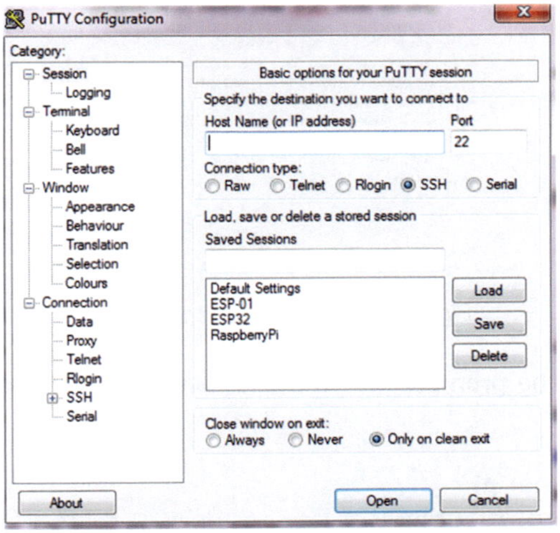

Figure 2.8 Putty startup screen

- Make sure that the Connection type is SSH and enter the IP address of your Raspberry Pi 3. Click Open as shown in Figure 2.9.

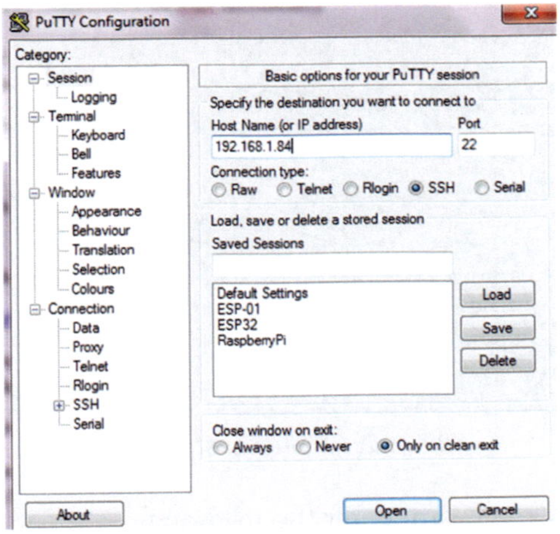

Figure 2.9 Enter the IP address

- The message shown in Figure 2.10 will be displayed on the PC screen the first time you access the Raspberry Pi 3. Click Yes to accept this security alert.

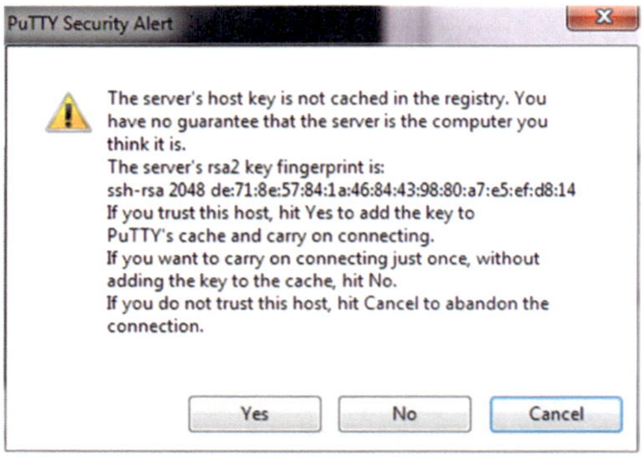

Figure 2.10 Click Yes to accept

- You will then be prompted for the username and password. The default values are:

  Username: **pi**
  Password: **raspberry**

- After a successful login, you should see the Raspberry Pi command prompt as in Figure 2.11.

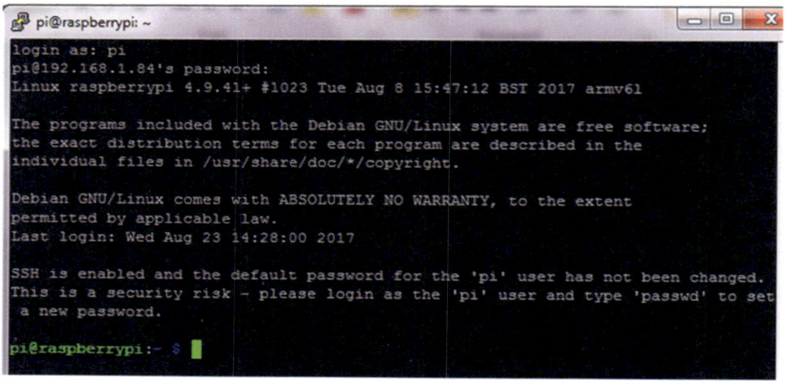

Figure 2.11 Successful login

- To change your password, enter the following command:

```
passwd
```

- To restart the Raspberry Pi ZW enter the following command:

```
sudo reboot
```

- To shut down the Raspberry Pi ZW enter the following command. Never shut down by pulling the power cable as this may result in the corruption or loss of files:

```
sudo shutdown -h now
```

2.5 Shutting down or rebooting in GUI mod

You must always shut down your Pi computer properly. To shut down while in the GUI mode, follow the steps given below:

- Click Applications menu (top left corner)
- Click Shutdown (see Figure 2.12)
- Click Shutdown (or Reboot as required)

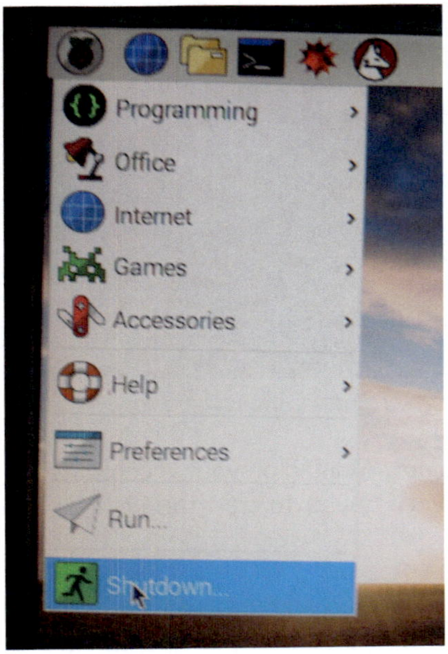

Figure 2.12 Shutdown or reboot in GUI mode

2.6 Remote access of the desktop

If you will be using your Raspberry Pi 3 with local keyboard, mouse, and monitor you can skip this section. If on the other hand, you want to access your Desktop remotely over the network, you will find that SSH services cannot be used. The easiest and simplest way to access your Desktop remotely from a computer is by installing the VNC (Virtual Network Connection) client and server. The VNC server runs on your Pi and the VNC client runs on your computer. The steps to install and use the VNC are given below:

- Connect to your Pi computer using SSH as explained earlier. Then enter the following command to install a program called **TightVNC** server on your Pi computer. You will see many lines of messages. Make sure there are no error messages:

```
sudo apt-get update
sudo apt-get install tightvncserver
```

- Run the VNC server on your Pi computer by entering the following command:

```
vncserver :1
```

- You will be prompted to enter and verify a password. This will be the password you will be using to access the Desktop remotely (see Figure 2.13).

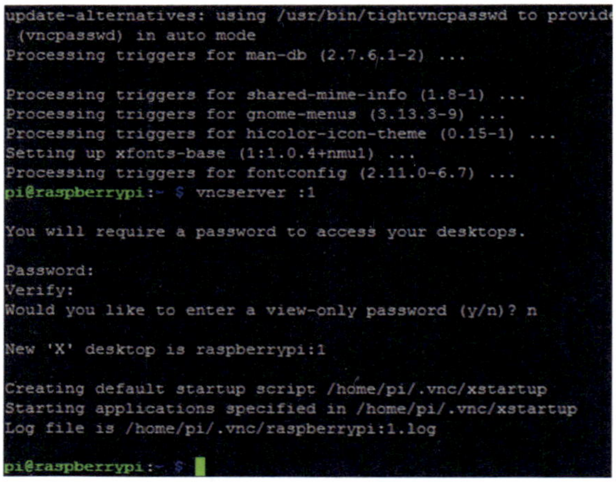

Figure 2.13 Enter a password for the VNC server

- The VNC server is now running on your Pi computer. The only command you need to enter on your Pi computer to start the VNC server is:

```
vncserver :1
```

- We must now set up a VNC client on our laptop (or desktop). There are many VNC clients available, but the recommended one which is compatible with Tight-VNC is the VNC Viewer, which can be downloaded from the following link. Notice that this program is not free of charge, but a 30-day free trial version is available. You should register to get a trial license and then apply this license to the software to use free of charge for 30 days:

  http://www.realvnc.com

Download the VNC Viewer program into a suitable directory on your computer.

Double click to install it and enter the required license. Start the **VNC Viewer** program by double-clicking its icon in your desktop. Enter the IP address of your Raspberry Pi 3 followed by **1** as shown in Figure 2.14 and click **Connect**.

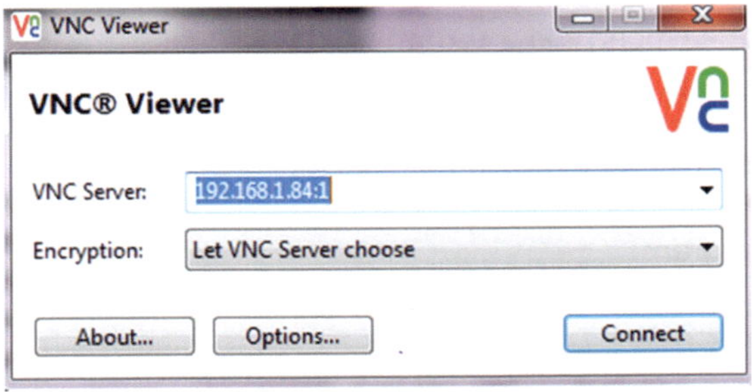

Figure 2.14 Enter the IP address

Enter the password selected previously. You should now see the Raspberry Pi 3 Desktop displayed on your laptop (or desktop) computer as in Figure 2.15 and you can access all of the Desktop applications remotely.

Figure 2.15 Raspberry Pi 3 Desktop displayed on the laptop

2.7 Creating and running a Python program

We will be programming our Raspberry Pi 3 using the Python programming language. It is worthwhile to look at the creation and running of a simple Python program on our Pi computer. In this section, we will display the message **Hello From Raspberry Pi 3** on our PC screen.

As described below, there are 3 methods that we can create and run Python programs on our Raspberry Pi 3:

Method 1 – Interactively from Command Prompt

In this method, we will log in to our Raspberry Pi 3 using the SSH and then create and run our program interactively. This method is excellent for small programs. The steps are as follows:

- Login to the Raspberry Pi 3 using SSH

- At the command prompt enter **python**. You should see the Python command mode which is identified by three characters **>>>**

- Type the program:

```
print ("Hello From Raspberry Pi 3")
```

- The required text will be displayed interactively on the screen as shown in Figure 2.16

```
pi@raspberrypi:~ $ python
Python 2.7.13 (default, Jan 19 2017, 14:48:08)
[GCC 6.3.0 20170124] on linux2
Type "help", "copyright", "credits" or "license" for more information.
>>> print("Hello From Raspberry Pi 3")
Hello From Raspberry Pi 3
>>>
```

Figure 2.16 Running a program interactively

Method 2 – Create a Python File in Command Mode
In this method, we will log in to our Raspberry Pi 3 using the SSH as before and then create a Python file. A Python file is simply a text file with the extension **.py**. We can use a text editor, e.g. the **nano** text editor to create our file. In this example, a file called **hello.py** is created using the **nano** text editor. Figure 2.17 shows the contents of file hello.py. This figure also shows how to run the file under Python. Notice that the program is run by entering the command:

```
>>> python hello.py
```

```
pi@raspberrypi:~ $ ls hello.py
hello.py
pi@raspberrypi:~ $ cat hello.py
print ("Hello From  Raspberry Pi Zero W")

pi@raspberrypi:~ $ python hello.py
Hello From  Raspberry Pi Zero W
pi@raspberrypi:~ $
```

Figure 2.17 Creating and running a Python file

Method 3 – Create a Python File in GUI mode
In this method, we will log in to our Raspberry Pi 3 using the VNC and create and run our program in GUI mode. The steps are given below:

- Click Applications menu

- Click Programming and select Python 2 or Python 3 (see Figure 2.18)

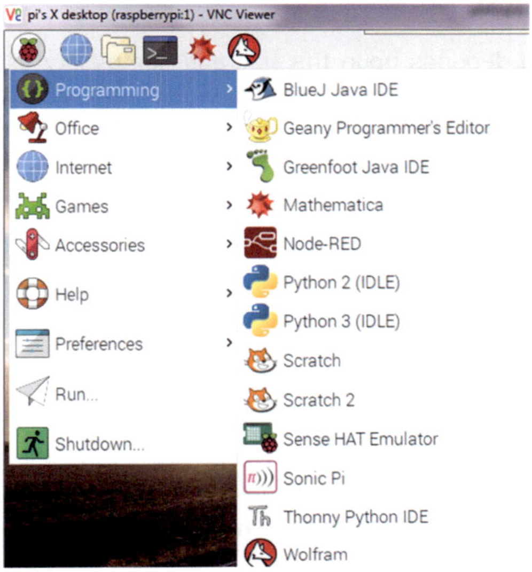

Figure 2.18 Select Python 2 programming

- You should see the Python command mode, identified by characters >>>
- Click **File** and then click **New File** and write your program
- Save the file by giving it a name (e.g. hello2)
- Run the program by clicking **Run** and then **Run Module** as shown in Figure 2.19

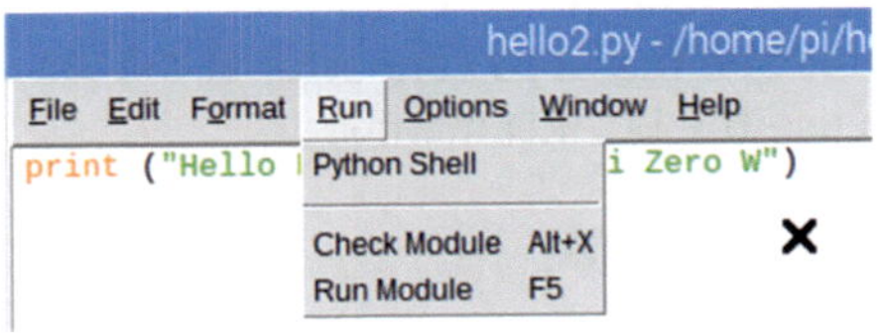

Figure 2.19 Run the program

- A new screen will be shown with the output of the program displayed as in Figure 2.20

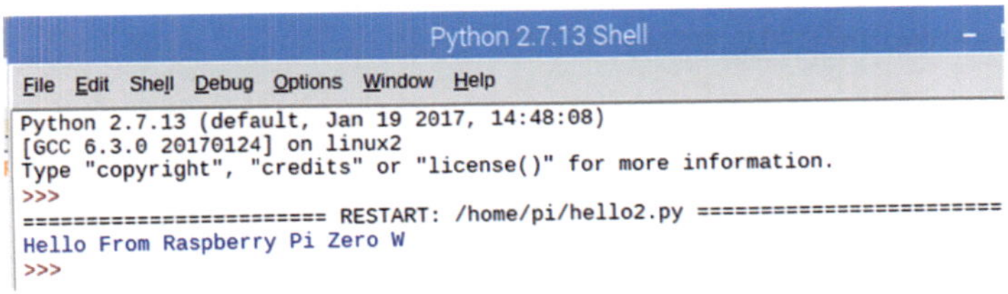

Figure 2.20 Output of the program

Which Method?

The choice of a method depends upon the size and complexity of a program. Small programs can be run interactively without creating a program file. Larger programs can be created as Python files and then they can run either in the command mode or in the GUI mode. In this book, program files are created for all the Python programs.

2.8 The GPIO library

The GPIO library is called RPi.GPIO and it should already be installed on your Raspberry Pi 3. This library must be included at the beginning of your Python programs if you will be using the GPIO functions. The statement to include this library is:

import RPi.GPIO as GPIO

If you get an error while trying to import the GPIO library then it is possible that the library is not installed. Enter the following commands while in the command mode (identified by the prompt **pi@raspberrypi:~ $**) to install the GPIO library (characters that should be entered by you are in bold):

pi@raspberrypi: ~ $ **sudo apt-get update**
pi@raspberrypi: ~ $ **sudo apt-get install python-dev**
pi@raspberrypi: ~ $ **sudo apt-get install python-rpi.gpio**

The GPIO provides a number of useful functions. The available functions are given in the next sections

2.8.1 Pin numbering

There are two ways that we can refer to the GPIO pins. The first is using the BOARD numbering, where the pin numbers on the GPIO connector of the Raspberry Pi 3 are used. Enter the following statement to use the BOARD method:

GPIO.setmode(GPIO.BOARD)

The second numbering system, also known as the BCM method is the preferred method and it uses the channel numbers allocated to the pins. This method requires that you know which channel number refers to which pin on the board. In this book, we will be using this second method. Enter the following statement to use the BCM method:

GPIO.setmode(GPIO.BCM)

The GPIO is a 40 pin header, mounted at one side of the board. Appendix A shows the Raspberry Pi 3 GPIO pin configuration.

2.8.2 Channel (I/O port pin) configuration

Input Configuration

You need to configure the channels (or port pins) you are using whether they are input or output channels. The following statement is used to configure a channel as an input. Here, channel refers to the channel number based on the **setmode** statement above:

GPIO.setup(channel, GPIO.IN)

When there is nothing connected to an input pin, the data at this input is not defined. We can specify additional parameters with the input configuration statement to connect pull-up or pull-down resistors by software to an input pin. The required statements are:

For pull-down:

GPIO.setup(channel, GPIO.IN, pull_up_down=GPIO.PUD_DOWN)

For pull-up:

GPIO.setup(channel, GPIO.IN, pull_up_down=GPIO.PUD_UP)

We can detect an edge change of an input signal at an input pin. Edge change is when the signal changes from LOW to HIGH (rising edge), or from HIGH to LOW (falling edge). For example, pressing a push-button switch can cause an edge change at the input of a pin. The following statements can be used to wait for an edge of the input signal. These are blocking functions. i.e. the program will wait until the specified edge is detected at the input signal. For example, if this is a push-button, the program will wait until the button is pressed:

To wait for a rising edge:

GPIO.wait_for_edge(channel, GPIO.RISING)

To wait for a falling edge:

GPIO.wait_for_edge(channel, GPIO.FALLING)

We can also wait until either a rising or a falling edge is detected by using the following statement:

GPIO.wait_for_edge(channel, GPIO.BOTH)

We can use event detection function with an input pin. This way, we can execute the event detection code whenever an event is detected. Events can be rising edge, falling edge, or change in either edge of the signal. Event detection is usually used in loops where we can check for the event while executing other code.

For example, to add rising event detection to an input pin:

GPIO.add_event_detect(channel, GPIO.RISING)

We can check whether or not the event occurred by the following statement:

```
If GPIO.event_detected(channel):
    ................................
    ................................
```

Event detection can be removed by the following statement:

```
GPIO.remove_event_detect(channel)
```

We can also use interrupt facilities (or callbacks) to detect events. Here, the event is handled inside a user function. The main program carries on its usual duties and as soon as the event occurs the program stops whatever it is doing and jumps to the event handling function. For example, the following statement can be used to add interrupt based event handling to our programs on rising edge of an input signal. In this example, the event handling code is the function named **MyHandler**:

```
GPIO.add_event_detect(channel, GPIO.RISING, callback=MyHandler)
........................................................................................
........................................................................................

def MyHandler(channel):
    ......................
    ......................
```

We can add more than one interrupt by using the add_event_callback function. Here the callback functions are executed sequentially:

```
GPIO.add_event_detect(channel, GPIO.RISING)
GPIO.add_event_callback(channel, MyHandler1)
GPIO.add_event_callback(channel, MyHandler2)
.................................................................
.................................................................

def MyHandler1(channel):
    ........................
    ........................

def MyHandler2(channel):
    ........................
    ........................
```

When we use mechanical switches in our projects we get what is known as the switch bouncing problem. This occurs as the contacts of the switch bounce many times until they settle to their final state. Switch bouncing could generate several pulses before it settles down. We can avoid switch bouncing problems in hardware or software. GPIO library provides a parameter called bouncetime that can be used to eliminate the switch bouncing problem. An example use of this parameter is shown below where the switch bounce time is assumed to be 10ms:

GPIO.add_event_detect(channel,GPIO=RISING,callback=MyHandler, bouncetime=10)

We can also use the callback statement to specify the switch bouncing time as@

GPIO.add_event_callback(channel, MyHandler, bouncetime=10)

To read the state of an input pin we can use the following statement:

GPIO.input(channel)

Output Configuration
The following statement is used to configure a channel as an output. Here, channel refers to the port number based on the **setmode** statement described earlier:

GPIO.setup(channel, GPIO.OUT)

We can specify a value for an output pin during its setup. For example, we can configure a channel as output and at the same time set its value to logic HIGH (+3.3V):

GPIO.setup(channel, GPIO.OUT, initial=GPIO.HIGH)

To send data to an output port pin we can use the following statement:

GPIO.output(channel, value)

Where value can be 0 (or GPIO.LOW, or False), or 1 (or GPIO.HIGH, or True)

At the end of the program, we should return all the used resources to the operating system. This is done by including the following statement at the end of our program:

GPIO.cleanup()

2.9 Raspberry Pi project development cycle

The project development cycle, in general, includes both hardware and software development. In simple projects where there is no external hardware used, we can simply use the Raspberry Pi board as it is and only software development is then required. Most projects, however, are more complex and require additional external components, such as LEDs, motors, displays, keypads, etc. The developer then has the tasks of making sure that the hardware is set up correctly and is in full working order before any software development is started. If the hardware is not set up correctly then time will be wasted trying to develop the software. Hardware development may require additional skills such as the familiarity with interfacing and correctly using various electronic components in microcontroller based systems.

The project development cycle, especially the software development cycle is an iterative process where the programmer may have to go back and keep making changes to the code until the required response is obtained from the system under development. There are various tools that can be helpful during the development of a project. For example, Flow Charts, Program Description Language (PDL), UML, State Machines, and many other tools can be used during the development cycle.

In Raspberry Pi projects in this book, we will be using the Python programming language. Python is a very powerful interactive programming language that is taught as the first programming language in many universities and colleges around the world. Python is available on the Raspberry Pi computers and it supports a large number of libraries that simplify the programming task considerably.

In the remainder of this Chapter, we will design a simple project using the KY-011 two colour LED board as in the previous Chapter.

2.10 Project – Flashing two colour LEDs

Description: This is perhaps the easiest project you can design using your Raspberry Pi. In this project, a two colour LED with common cathode is connected to the Raspberry Pi. The LED colours are flashed alternately at a rate of one second.

Aim: The aim of this project is to show how to write and run a program on the Raspberry Pi. The project additionally shows how to use some of the I/O and timing functions of the Raspberry Pi.

Sensor Used: Sensor KY-011 is used in this project as in the previous Chapter. The sensor and its pins are shown in Figure 1.3. The sensor has 3 pins: red LED pin, green LED pin, and GND pin, where **the green LED pin is marked with letter S on the board for identification.** An LED is turned ON when logic 1 is applied to its pins.

Block diagram: The block diagram of the project is shown in Figure 2.21.

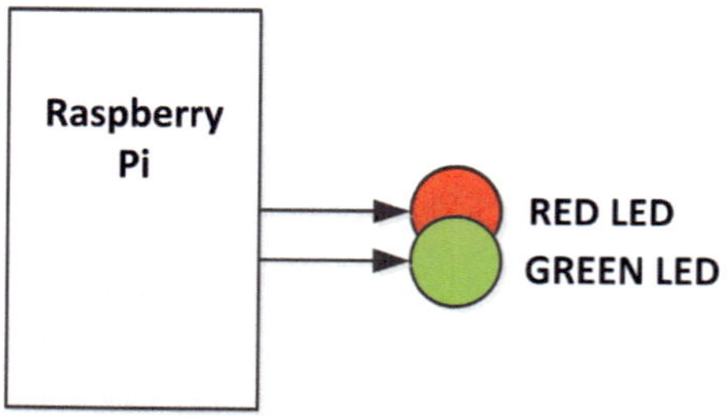

Figure 2.21 Block diagram of the project

Circuit diagram: The circuit diagram of the project is shown in Figure 2.22. The green and red LED pins are connected to port pin GPIO 2 (pin 3) and GPIO 3 (pin 5) of the Raspberry Pi respectively through current limiting resistors. The GND pin is connected to Raspberry Pi GND pin. The value of the current limiting resistor is calculated as follows:

The output high voltage of a GPIO pin is 3.3V. The voltage across an LED is approximately 2.0V (for red LED this is 1.8V, and for green LED 2.8V). The forward current through the LED depends upon the type of LED used and the amount of required brightness. Assuming that we choose 5mA of forward current, the value of the current limiting resistor is (the LED brightness can be increased by increasing the forward current):

> R = (3.3V - 2V) / 5mA = 260 ohm. We can choose 220-ohm resistors to give around 6mA forward currents for each LED (for green LED you can use smaller value, e.g. 150 ohms)

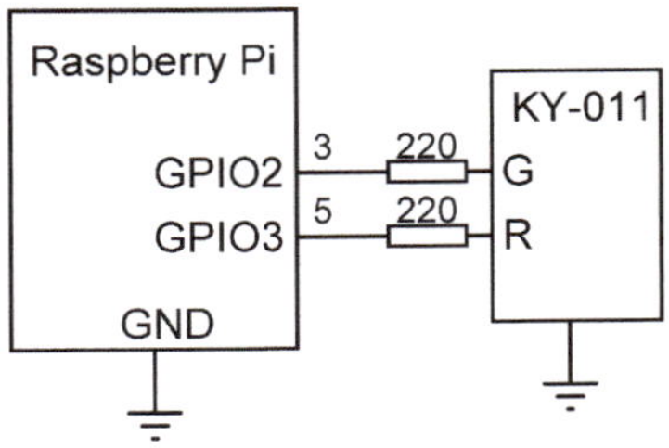

Figure 2.22 Circuit diagram of the project

Construction: The project is constructed on a breadboard as shown in Figure 2.23. Jumper wires are used to connect the KY-011 to digital port pins 2 and 3 and GND of Raspberry Pi.

Figure 2.23 Project constructed on a breadboard

Program listing: The program is called **rpitwoled.py** and the listing is shown in Figure 2.24. At the beginning of the program, libraries **RPi.GPIO** and **time** are imported into the program. Green and red LED pins are assigned to port GPIO port numbers 2 and 3 respectively. The LEDs are then configured as outputs. The remainder of the program runs in an endless loop. Inside this loop, the green and the red LEDs are flashed alternately with a one-second delay between each output.

You can run the program from the command line by entering the following command (characters entered by the user are in bold for clarity):

pi@raspberrypi:~ $ **python rpitwoled.py**

```
#-----------------------------------------------------------
#     TWO COLOUR LED FLASHING
#     =======================
#
# In thiS project the two colour LED KY-011 is used. The
# green and red LED pins are conncted to Raspberry Pi port
# pins GPIO2 and GPIO3. The LEDs flash alternately with a
# rate of one second
#
# Author: Dogan Ibrahim
# Date  : April 2019
# File  : rpitwoled.py
#----------------------------------------------------------
import RPi.GPIO as GPIO        # import Rpi library
import time                    # import time library
GPIO.setwarnings(False)        # disable warnings
GPIO.setmode(GPIO.BCM)         # set BCM mode

GreenLED = 2                   # green LED
RedLED = 3                     # red LED
ON = 1
OFF = 0

GPIO.setup(GreenLED, GPIO.OUT)    # Configure as output
GPIO.setup(RedLED, GPIO.OUT)      # configure as output

while True:                       # do forever
  GPIO.output(GreenLED, ON)       # green LED ON
  GPIO.output(RedLED, OFF)        # red LED OFF
  time.sleep(1)                   # wait 1 second
  GPIO.output(GreenLED, OFF)      # green LED ON
  GPIO.output(RedLED, ON)         # red LED ON
  time.sleep(1)                   # wait 1 secons
```

Figure 2.24 Program listing of the project

Note: You may find it easier to create and run your Python programs from the GUI desktop interface (IDLE 2) since the correct indentation is automatically placed in your code as you type the code.

What we have learned: In this project, we have learned how to use the following Raspberry Pi functions:

import:	import a library module to the program
GPIO.setmode(mode):	set the GPIO pin usage mode in the program
GPIO.setwarnings(mode):	disable (False) or enable (True) warning messages
GPIO.setup(port pin, mode):	set the pin mode as either input or output
GPIO.output(port pin, value):	send value (0 or 1) to specified port pin
time.sleep(n):	create a delay of **n** seconds

2.11 Summary

In this chapter we have looked at the pin configuration of the GPIO connector and how to enable the Wi-Fi module and access the Raspberry Pi remotely from a desktop computer or a laptop. Additionally, we have looked at the design of a simple KY-011 two colour LED-based project using the Python programming language.

In the next Chapter, we will be looking at how to install the firmware on the ESP32 microcontroller and how to use it in projects.

Chapter 3 • ESP32 hardware interface and project development

3.1 Overview

In the last chapter, we had a look at the hardware interface and project development of Raspberry Pi based projects. In this Chapter, we will be looking at the ESP32 processor hardware and the project development cycle. The installation of the Arduino IDE for the ESP32 processor is given in this Chapter. Additionally, a simple example project is given to illustrate how a program can be written and then uploaded to the ESP32 processor.

Currently, ESP32 DevKitC is one of the most popular development boards based on the ESP32 processor. In this book, all the ESP32 based projects use this development board. It is therefore important that we learn the architecture and the features of this board briefly.

3.2 ESP32 DevKitC hardware

ESP32 DevKitC is a small ESP32 processor based board developed and manufactured by Espressif. As shown in Figure 3.1, the board is breadboard compatible and has the dimensions 55 mm x 27.9 mm.

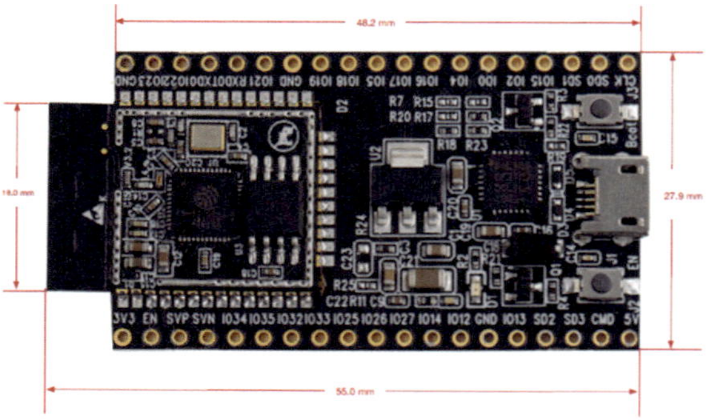

Figure 3.1 ESP32 DevKitC development board

The board has two connectors located along each side of the board for GPIO, clock, and power line interfaces. Each connector has 19 pins. As shown in Figure 3.2, the two connectors carry the following signals:

Left Connector	**Right Connector**
+3.3V	GND
EN	IO23
SVP	IO22
SVN	TXD0
IO34	RXD0
IO35	IO21
IO32	GND
IO33	IO19
IO25	IO18
IO26	IO5

IO27	IO17
IO14	IO16
IO12	IO4
GND	IO0
IO13	IO2
SD2	IO15
SD3	SD1
CMD	SD0
+5V	CLK

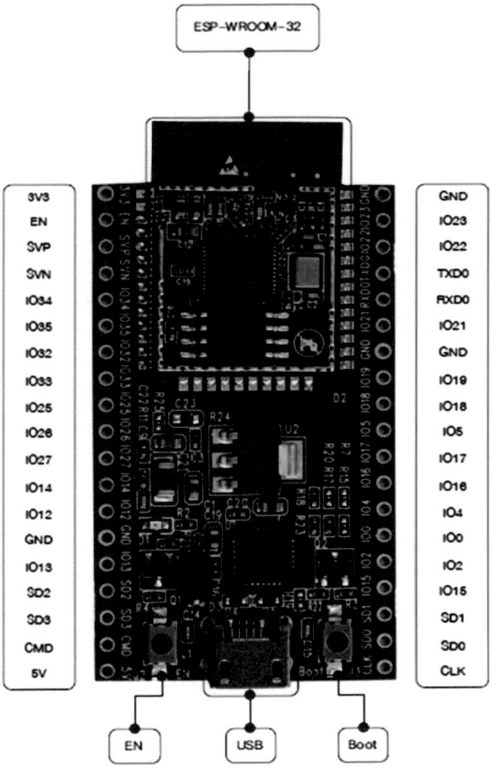

Figure 3.2 ESP32 DevKitC connectors

The board has a mini USB connector for connecting it to a PC. The board also receives its power from the USB port. Standard +5V from the USB port is converted into +3.3V on the board. In addition, two buttons are provided on the board named EN and BOOT, having the following functions:

EN: This is the reset button where pressing this button resets the board

BOOT: This is the download button. The board is normally in operation mode where the button is not pressed. Pressing and holding down this button and at the same time pressing the EN button starts the firmware download mode where firmware can be downloaded to the processor through the USB serial port.

The pins on the ESP32 DevKitC board have multiple functions. Figure 3.3 shows the functions of each pin. For example, pin 10 is shared with functions GPIO port 26, DAC channel 2, ADC channel 19, RTC channel 7, and RX01.

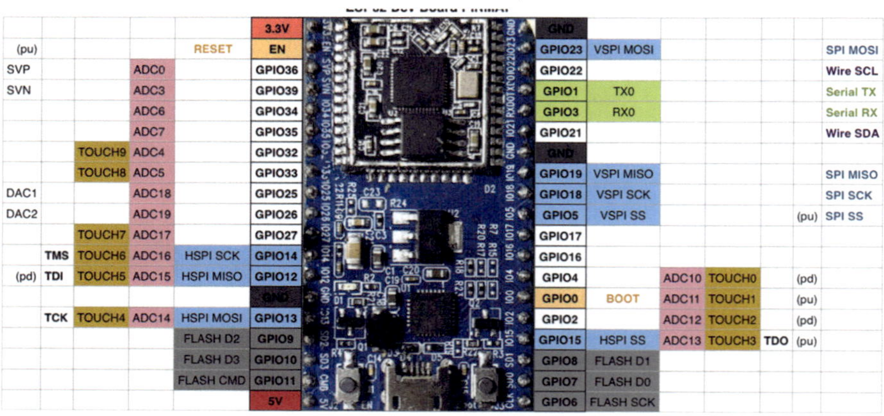

Figure 3.3 Multiple functions of each pin. Source: www.cnx-software.com

Note that GPIO34, GPIO35, GPIO36, GPIO37, GPIO38, and GPIO39 ports are input only and cannot be used as output ports (GPIO37 and GPIO38 are not available on the ESP32 board).

The board operates with a typical power supply of +3.3V, although the absolute maximum is specified as +3.6V. It is recommended that the current capacity of each pin should not exceed 6 mA, although the absolute maximum current capacity is specified as 12 mA. It is therefore important to use current limiting resistors while driving external loads such as LEDs. Depending upon the configuration the RF power consumption during reception is around 80 mA and it can be in excess of 200 mA during a transmission.

3.3 Arduino IDE for the ESP32 DevKitC

By default, the ESP32 DevKitC is distributed with no programming firmware installed. It is, therefore, necessary to install a programming language firmware on the processor so that user programs can be developed and uploaded to the processor. The ESP32 processor is compatible with various programming languages such as C, MicroPython and so on.

Arduino IDE is one of the most commonly used development environments for microcontrollers, especially for the Arduino family of microcontrollers. This IDE is easy to use, supports many microcontrollers, and includes a very rich library of functions that make the programming easier. Most electrical/electronic engineering students and people whose hobbies are electronics are familiar with using the Arduino IDE. In this section, we will be seeing how to install the ESP32 processor into the Arduino IDE on a Windows PC. It is important to note that using the Arduino IDE has some limitations and all features of the ESP32 cannot be programmed with this IDE.

3.3.1 Installing the Arduino IDE for the ESP32 DevKitC

The steps on installing the ESP32 support to the Arduino IDE on a Windows PC are given in this section. If you have already installed ESP32 on Arduino IDE then you must delete the **Espressif** folder from your Arduino directory before re-installing it.

The steps to install the ESP32 on Arduino IDE are as follows:

- Download and install the latest version of Arduino IDE from the following web site:

  https://www.arduino.cc/en/Main/Software

- Open your Arduino IDE and click **File -> Preferences** to open the Preferences window. Locate text box **Additional Board Manager URLs** at the bottom of the window and enter the following text as shown in Figure 3.4. If the text box contains another URL, add the new URL after separating it with a comma:

  https://dl.espressif.com/dl/package_esp32_index.json

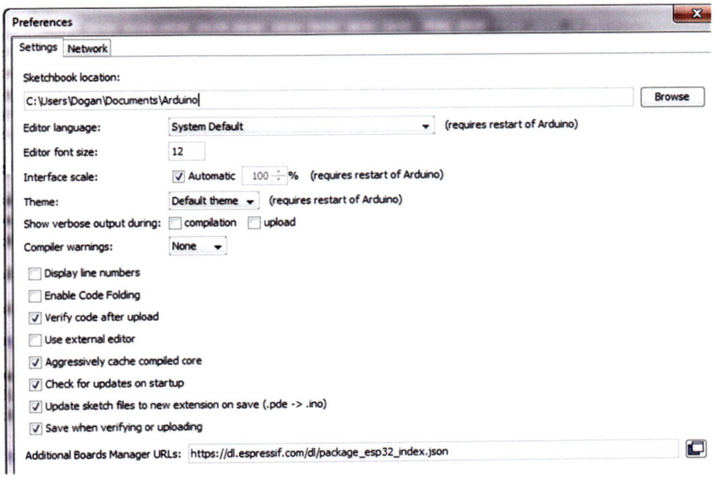

Figure 3.4 Preferences window

- Click **OK**

- Click **Tools -> Boards -> Board Managers** window and search for ESP32 as shown in Figure 3.5

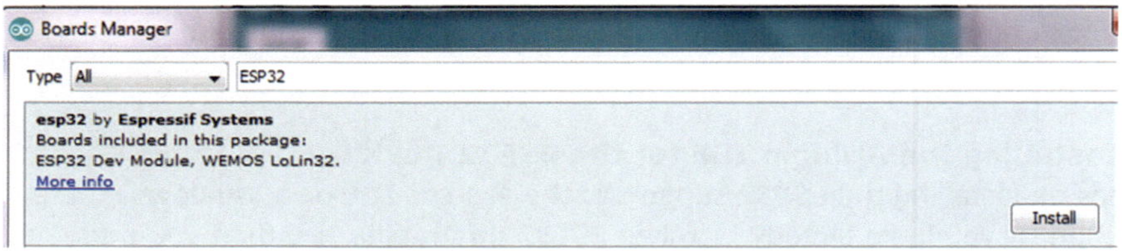

Figure 3.5 Search for ESP32

- Click the **Install** button. You should see the Installed message as shown in Figure 3.6. **Close** the window.

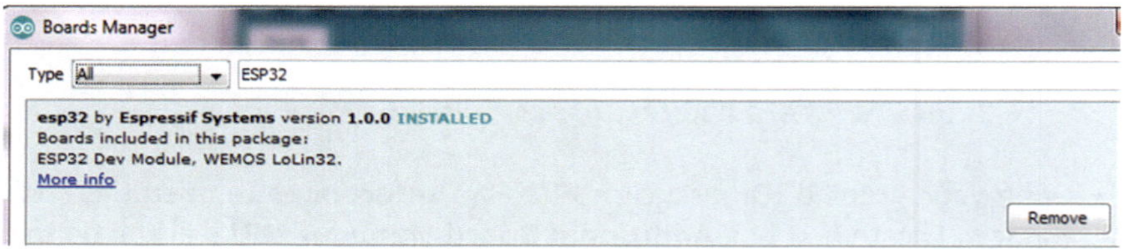

Figure 3.6 ESP32 installed

- We should now test the installation to make sure that all the necessary files have been loaded. We shall make use of one of the supplied example applications to make sure that our program can be uploaded to the ESP32 processor and is working correctly

- Plug in your ESP32 DevKitC to your PC and start the Arduino IDE

- Select **Tools -> Board ->ESP32 Dev Module** as shown in Figure 3.7.

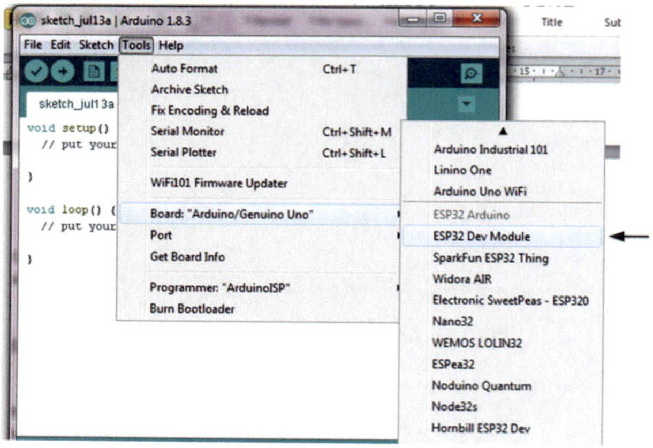

Figure 3.7 Select the ESP32 Dev Module

- Select the serial port number. In this example, this is COM47 as shown in Figure 3.8

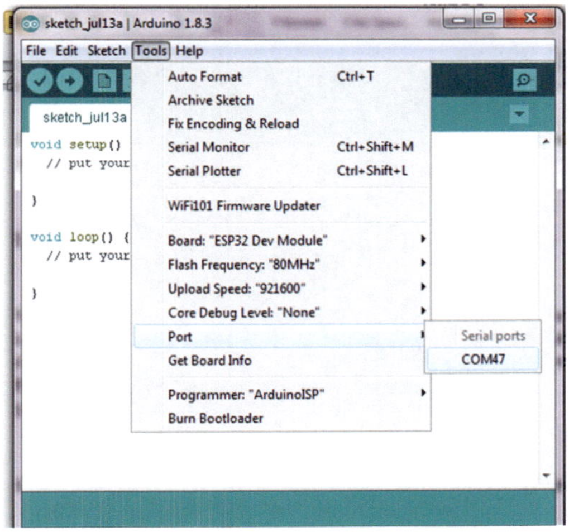

Figure 3.8 Select the serial port

- Open the example program in **File -> Examples -> WiFi (in ESP32) ->WiFi Scan** as shown in Figure 3.9

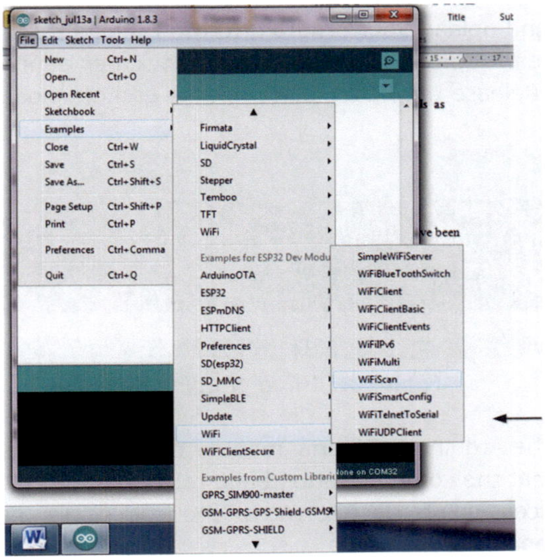

Figure 3.9 Open the example program WiFi Scan

- You should see the program as in Figure 3.10

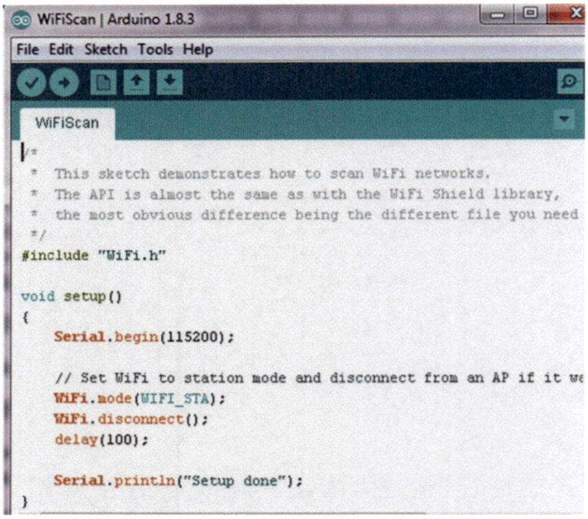

Figure 3.10 Example program to test the installation

- Now, we will upload the program to our ESP 32 DevKitC. First of all, we have to put the device into firmware upload mode. Press and hold the **BOOT** button (the one on the right-hand side). Press the **Sketch -> Upload** button in Arduino IDE to compile and upload your program to the ESP32 DevKitC. Wait until finished. After a successful process, you should see a screen similar to the one shown in Figure 3.11 Release the **BOOT** button at the end of uploading.

Figure 3.11 End of uploading

- Now, open the Arduino IDE Serial monitor by clicking **Tools -> Serial Monitor**. Make sure that the communication baud rate is set to 115200. You should see a list of the access points close to you as shown in Figure 3.12. The list is updated every 5 seconds.

- At this point, we have successfully installed the ESP32 processor into our Arduino IDE

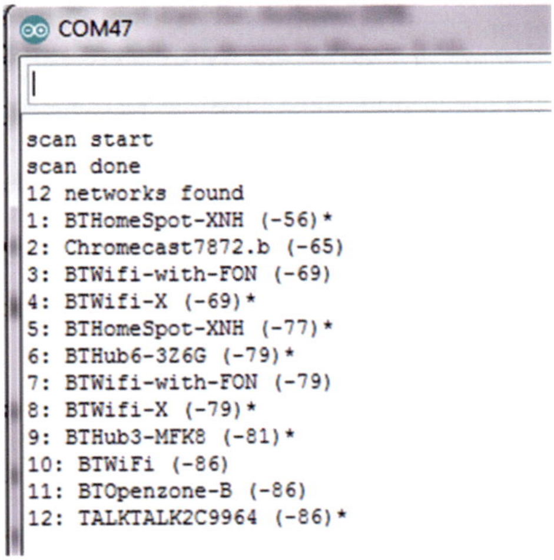

Figure 3.12 List of close access points

3.4 Project – Flashing two colour LEDs

Description: This is perhaps the easiest project you can design using your ESP32 DevKitC. In this project, a two colour LED with common cathode is connected to the ESP32 DevKitC. The LED colours are flashed alternately at a rate of one second.

Aim: The aim of this project is to show how to write and run a program on the ESP32 DevKitC. The project additionally shows how to use some of the I/O and timing functions.

Sensor Used: Sensor KY-011 is used in this project as in the previous two Chapters. The sensor and its pins are shown in Figure 1.3. The sensor has 3 pins: red LED pin, green LED pin, and GND pin, where **the green LED pin is marked with letter S on the board for identification.** An LED is turned ON when logic 1 is applied to its pins.

Block diagram: The block diagram of the project is shown in Figure 3.13.

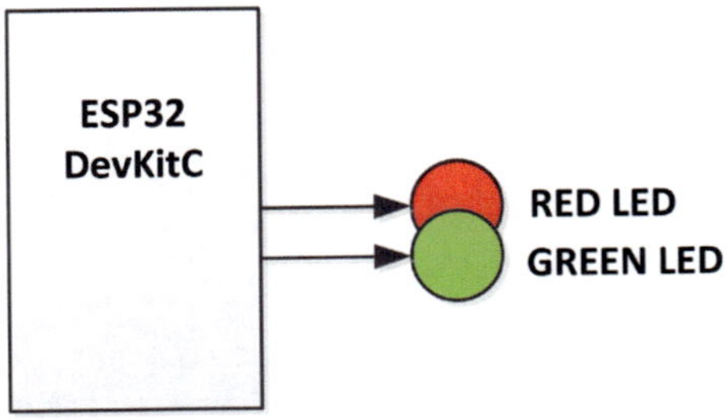

Figure 3.13 Block diagram of the project

Circuit diagram: The circuit diagram of the project is shown in Figure 3.14. The green and red LED pins are connected to port pin GPIO 22 and GPIO 23 of the ESP32 DevKitC respectively through current limiting resistors. The GND pin is connected to ESP32 DevKitC GND pin. The value of the current limiting resistor is calculated as follows:

The output high voltage of an ESP32 DevKitC GPIO pin is 3.3V. The voltage across an LED is approximately 2.0V. The forward current through the LED depends upon the type of LED used and the amount of required brightness. Assuming that we choose 5mA of forward current, the value of the current limiting resistor is (the LED brightness can be increased by increasing the forward current):

R = (3.3V – 2V) / 5mA = 260 ohm. We can choose 220-ohm resistors to give around 6mA forward currents for each LED.

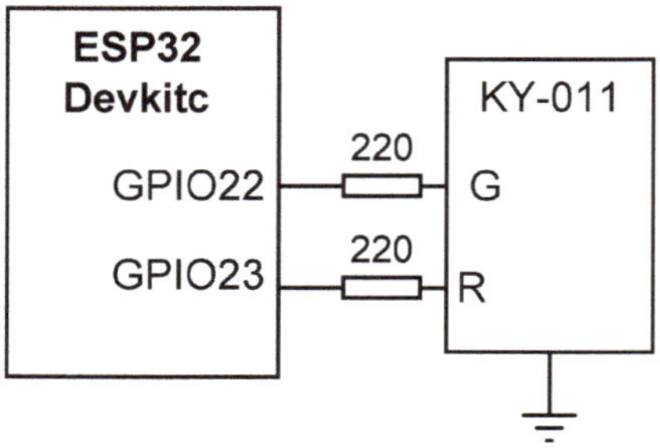

Figure 3.14 Circuit diagram of the project

Construction: The project is constructed on a breadboard as shown in Figure 3.15. Jumper wires are used to connect the KY-011 to digital port pins 22 and 23 and GND of ESP32 DevKitC.

Figure 3.15 Project constructed on a breadboard

Program listing: The program is called **esp32twoled** and the listing is shown in Figure 3.16. At the beginning of the program GPIO port pins, 22 and 23 are assigned to the green LED and red LED pins respectively. Inside the setup routine, port pins 22 and 23 where the

LED pins are connected to are configured as outputs. Inside the main program loop, the two colours are turned ON and OFF alternately with a one-second delay between each output. **Verify/Compile** to make sure that there are no errors. Press and hold the **BOOT** button (the one on the right-hand side). Press the **Sketch -> Upload** button in Arduino IDE to compile and upload your program to the ESP32 DevKitC, wait until finished. You should see the two colours flashing at a rate of one second.

```
/*****************************************************************
 *               FLASHING GREEN AND RED LEDs
 *               ===========================
 *
 * In this program the KY-011 sensor is used which has a green and
 * a red LED with a common cathode terminal. The red LED and the
 * green LED are connected to GPIO pins 23 and 22 of the ESP32
 * DevKitC respectively. The program flashes the LEDs alternately
 * at a rate of one second.
 *
 * Author: Dogan Ibrahim
 * Date  : April 2019
 * File  : esp32twoled
 ****************************************************************/
int GreenLED = 22;                              // Green LED pin
int RedLED = 23;                                // Red LED pin
#define ON HIGH
#define OFF LOW

void setup()
{
  pinMode(GreenLED, OUTPUT);                    // Set as output
  pinMode(RedLED, OUTPUT);                      // Set as output
}

void loop()
{
  digitalWrite(GreenLED, ON);                   // Turn ON green
  digitalWrite(RedLED, OFF);                    // Turn OFF red
  delay(1000);                                  // Wait 1 sec
  digitalWrite(GreenLED, OFF);                  // Turn OFF green
  digitalWrite(RedLED, ON);                     // Turn ON red
  delay(1000);                                  // Wait 1 sec
}
```

Figure 3.16 Program listing of the project

What we have learned: In this project, we have learned how to use the following ESP32 (or Arduino Uno) functions:

int:	declares an integer variable
#define:	assigns value or text to a string
pinMode (port pin, mode):	used to configure an I/O port pin as input or output
digitalWrite(port pin, value):	used to output digital value (logic LOW or HIGH) to a port pin
delay(n):	creates a delay of **n** milliseconds

Note: Notice that the ESP32 DevKitC program in Figure 3.16 is exactly the same as the Arduino Uno program given in Figure 1.7, except that the used port numbers are different. This is because we are using the same IDE for both processors.

3.5 Summary

In this chapter, we have seen how to install the ESP32 processor into the Arduino IDE so that we can develop programs using the Arduino IDE and then upload them to our ESP32 DevKitC. We have also seen how to develop a simple application and upload to the ESP32 DevKitC.

In the next chapter, we will be developing projects using the Arduino Uno, Raspberry Pi, and the ESP32 DevKitC.

Chapter 4 • Basic sensor projects: Arduino - Raspberry Pi - ESP32

4.1 Overview

In the previous Chapters, we have seen how to create projects for the Arduino Uno, Raspberry Pi, and ESP32, and also how to compile and upload the code to the program memory of the target processor.

In this Chapter and the remaining Chapters in this book, we will be developing various projects using the sensors in the sensor kit together with the Arduino Uno, Raspberry Pi, and the ESP32 DevKitC processors. Please note that although all the sensors in the sensor kit will be used, not all three processors will be used with all sensors.

It is important to realize that the Arduino and ESP32 processors use the Arduino IDE for the programming environment. The main differences between the codes developed for the two processors are that different GPIO ports are used, and also some of the functions are different between the two processors. Because of this, most of the projects in this book are based on using the Arduino Uno and the Raspberry Pi processors. Small notes, however, will be given at the end of every project to describe how a given Arduino Uno project can be modified and implemented on the ESP32 DevKitC.

The projects in the book are given in different sections, where similar sensors are used in each section. Some sections make use of the combination of two or more sensors. Information is given for each project to make it easy for the reader to understand and learn the aim of the projects, their hardware details, and explanations of the program codes, etc. The following sub-headings will be given for each project where necessary:

- Project title
- Brief description of the project
- Aim of the project
- Sensor(s) used
- Background information
- Block diagram
- Circuit diagram
- Construction (where necessary)
- Program listing with full description (Arduino/ESP32 and/or Raspberry Pi)

4.2 Light Projects

In this section, we will be developing light projects.

4.2.1 Project 1 – Changing the LED brightness

Description: In this project, a two colour (red+green) LED module is used and the brightness of the two LEDs are varied. By changing the brightness of the red and green LEDs fast enough our eye will see different tones of the yellow colour generated.

Aim: The aim of this project is to show how the PWM (Pulse Width Modulation) function can be used to change the brightness of an LED.

Sensor Used: The 3-pin KY-011 module with green and red LEDs and common cathode is used in this project.

Background Information: PWM is basically a square waveform with positive only pulses, used commonly to control the average voltage delivered to a load, for example to a motor. The duty cycle of this waveform is varied in order to change the average voltage applied to the load (e.g. to a motor or an LED). The duty cycle of a PWM waveform is normally expressed as a percentage:

$$\text{Duty Cycle} = \text{ON time} / (\text{ON time} + \text{OFF time}) \times 100\ \% \qquad (4.1)$$

or, since Period, T = ON time + OFF time

$$\text{Duty Cycle} = (T_{ON} / T) \times 100\ \% \qquad (4.2)$$

Where, T_{ON} is the ON time.

Figure 4.1 shows PWM waveforms with different duty cycles.

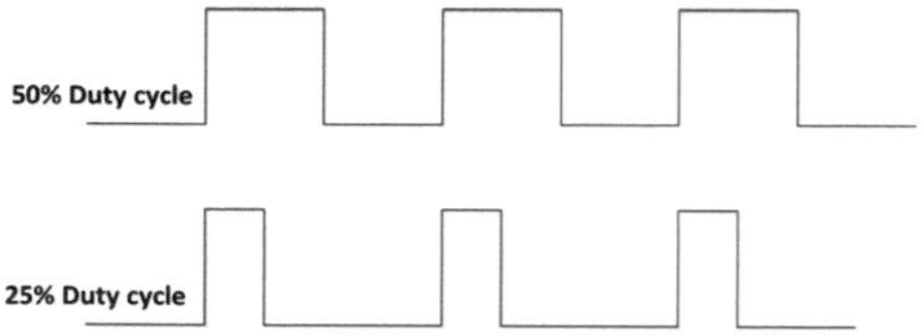

Figure 4.1 PWM waveforms

The average value of the voltage applied to the load can be calculated by considering a general PWM waveform shown in Figure 4.2. The average value A of waveform f(t) with period T and peak value y_{max} and minimum value y_{min} is calculated as:

$$A = \frac{1}{T}\int_0^T f(t)\,dt \qquad (4.3)$$

or,

$$A = \frac{1}{T}\left(\int_0^{T_{ON}} y_{\max}\,dt + \int_{T_{ON}}^{T} y_{\min}\,dt\right) \qquad (4.4)$$

In a PWM waveform $y_{min} = 0$ and the above equation becomes

$$A = \frac{1}{T}\left(T_{ON}\,y_{\max}\right) \qquad (4.5)$$

or, $$A = D\,y_{max} \tag{4.6}$$

where D is the duty cycle. As can be seen from equation (4.6), the average value of the voltage applied to the load is directly proportional to the duty cycle of the PWM waveform. If the peak value of the applied voltage is y_{max}, then as the duty cycle varies from 0% to 100%, the average voltage at the load varies from 0V to y_{max}.

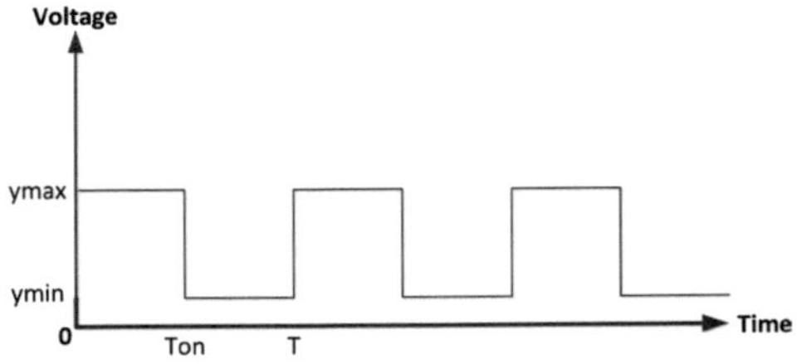

Figure 4.2 PWM waveform with y_{max} and y_{min}

Block Diagram: The block diagram of the project is as in Figure 1.4

Arduino Uno Circuit Diagram: In Arduino Uno board the following pins can be used to generate PWM waveform: 3, 5, 6, 9, 10, and 11. The circuit diagram of the project is shown in Figure 4.3 where pins 9 and 10 of the Arduino Uno are used for the green and red LEDs respectively through two current limiting resistors. In Arduino Uno, the frequency of the generated PWM waveform is approximately 490Hz for most PWM pins. The frequency is 980Hz if pins 5 and 6 are used for PWM.

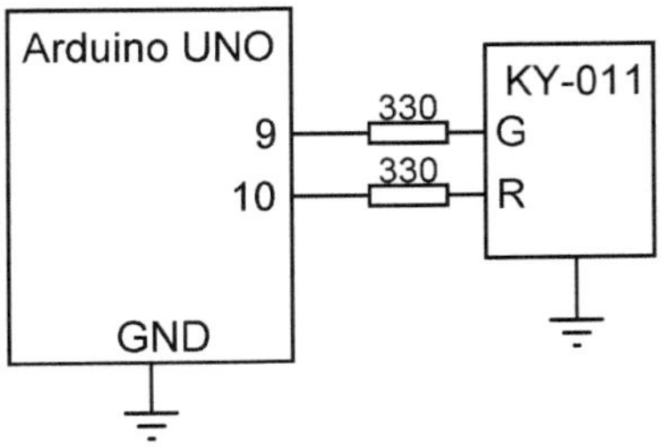

Figure 4.3 Arduino Uno circuit diagram of the project

Arduino Uno Construction: The project construction is similar to the one given in Figure 1.6 except that here different I/O pins are used.

Arduino Uno Program Listing: The program is called **ardpwm** and its listing is shown in Figure 4.4. At the beginning of the program, the LED pins and the duty cycle variable are declared as integers. Inside the setup routine, the LED pins are configured as outputs. The remainder of the program runs in an endless loop. Inside this loop two for loops are used. The first for loop starts with the green LED fully ON and the red LED OFF. The brightness of the green LED is reduced gradually by lowering its PWM duty cycle and that of the red LED is gradually increased by increasing its duty cycle. This happens so fast (repeated at a rate of 20ms) that the net effect is that the eye sees different tones of the yellow colour generated. In the second for loop, the reverse happens where initially the red LED is fully ON and the green LED is OFF. The duty cycle and hence the brightness of the red LED is gradually reduced and that of the green LED is gradually increased.

```
/*******************************************************************
 *               VARYING THE LED BRIGHTNESS
 *               ==========================
 *
 * In this program the KY-011 sensor is used which has a green and
 * a red LED with a common cathode terminal. The green LED and the
 * red LED are connected to I/O pins 9 and 10 of the Arduino Uno
 * respectively. The program sends PWM waveform to the LEDs to
 * change their brightness. At the same time, different tones of
 * yellow are produced by the combination of the red and green LEDs.
 *
 * Author: Dogan Ibrahim
 * Date  : April 2019
 * File  : ardpwm
 *******************************************************************/
int GreenLED = 9;                              // Green LED pin
int RedLED = 10;                               // Red LED pin
int DutyCycle;                                 // Duty cycle

void setup ()
{
  pinMode (GreenLED, OUTPUT);                  // LED is output
  pinMode (RedLED, OUTPUT);                    // LED is output
}

//
// This is the main program loop. Vary the Duty cycle of the voltage
// send to the LEDs which will change their brightness accordingly
// and also produce different colours. Notice that the green LED is
// first ON and the red LED is OFF. Gradually, the green LED is faded
// and the brightness of the red LED is increased. This is reversed
// in the second loop
//
void loop ()
{
   for (DutyCycle = 255; DutyCycle > 0; DutyCycle--)
   {
      analogWrite (GreenLED, DutyCycle);
      analogWrite (RedLED, 255-DutyCycle);
      delay(20);
   }
```

```
    for (DutyCycle = 0; DutyCycle < 255; DutyCycle++)
    {
       analogWrite (GreenLED, DutyCycle);
       analogWrite (RedLED, 255-DutyCycle);
       delay(20);
    }
}
```

Figure 4.4 Program listing

What we have learned: In this project, we have learned how to use the following Arduino function:

analogWrite(port pin, duty cycle): Generates PWM waveform at the specified port pin with the specified duty cycle. The duty cycle can take values between 0 and 255. 0 corresponds to OFF (0 voltage output), and 255 corresponds to ON (full voltage output).

Using the BiColor Arduino Library

An Arduino library, called **Bicolor LED Library**, is available (see link: **https://playground.arduino.cc/Code/BiColorLED/**) that can be used to simplify the control of two colour LEDs. This library can be downloaded to the Arduino workplace as follows:

- Go to link:

  https://github.com/wolfgang42/bicolorled

- Click on button **Clone or download** as shown in Figure 4.5 and save the ZIP file (named **bicolorled-master.zip**) in a folder

Figure 4.5 Clone or download

- Start new Arduino IDE session and click **Sketch -> Include library -> Add .ZIP library...**

- Browse to and click on the saved ZIP file

You can now use the bicolor library functions in your programs after including the header file **BicolorLED.h** at the beginning of the programs. Before using the functions, you must define the LED pins using a declaration of the following format:

```
BiColorLED led=BiColorLED(pin1, pin2);
```

Where pin1 and pin2 are the green and the red LED pins.

The Bicolor LED library has the following functions:

led.setColor(colour number): this function sets the LED colour. Valid colour numbers are:

0	LEDs OFF
1	Red
2	Green
3	Yellow

led.setColor(colour number1, colour number2): alternate with a colour other than black (OFF) when only one colour is specified in the program

led.getColor(): retruns the LED colour at any time.

led.setBlinkSpeed(speed): set blinking speed in milliseconds

led.getBlinkSpeed(): returns the blink speed

led.setBlinkSpeed(speed1 speed2): set separate delays for each colour

For blinking, we have to call function **led.drive()**. This function must be called at least every 9ms for the yellow LED to work.

An example of using the Bicolor library is given in the program (**ardpwm2**) in Figure 4.6. In this example, the colours flash at a rate of 2 seconds.

```
/*****************************************************************
*                         USING THE BICOLOR LED LIBRARY
*                         =============================
*
* In this program the Bicolor LED library is used to flash the
* red and the green LEDs every 2 seconds, using the KY-011 module.
* In this program the green and the red LED pins are connected to
* GPIO pins 9 and 10 respectively (any other digital pins could
* also be used).
```

```
*
* Author: Dogan Ibrahim
* Date  : April, 2019
* File  : ardpwm2
*****************************************************************/
#include <BiColorLED.h>                     // Include the library

BiColorLED led=BiColorLED(9,10);            // LEDs on pins 9 and 10

void setup()
{
  led.setColor(1);                          // Set red colour
  led.setColor2(2);                         // Set green colour
  led.setBlinkSpeed(2000);                  // Blink every 2 second
}


void loop()
{
  led.drive();                              // Call for blinking
}
```

Figure 4.6 Program listing

Another example is given in the program (**ardpwm3**) in Figure 4.7 where the green and the red LEDs flash at different rates. The green LED is ON for 500ms and the red LED is ON for one second.

```
/*****************************************************************
*                      USING THE BICOLOR LED LIBRARY
*                      =============================
*
* In this program the Bicolor LED library is used to flash the
* red and the green LEDs. The green LED is ON for 500ms and the
* red LED is ON for 1 second.
*
* Author: Dogan Ibrahim
* Date  : April, 2019
* File  : ardpwm3
*****************************************************************/
#include <BiColorLED.h>                     // Include the library

BiColorLED led=BiColorLED(9,10);            // LEDs on pins 9 and 10

void setup()
{
  led.setColor(1);                          // Set red colour
```

```
    led.setColor2(2);                    // Set green colour
    led.setBlinkSpeed(500, 1000);        // blink at different rates
  }


  void loop()
  {
    led.drive();                         // Call for blinking
  }
```

Figure 4.7 Program listing

ESP32 DevKitC Program Listing: The circuit diagram of the ESP32DevkitC version of this project is as in Figure 3.14. The program listing (**esp32pwm**) is shown in Figure 4.8. Although the Arduino IDE is used to program the ESP32, the program is different because the PWM **analogWrite** function is not supported on the ESP32. On ESP32 there are 16 PWM channels from 0 to 15. The resolution of the PWM can be select either as 8 or 16 bits. Selecting 8 bits allows us to set the duty cycle from 0 to 255. The frequency of the required PWM channel is also selected by the user. The PWM channel, resolution, and the frequency are selected using the following function:

ledcSetup(channel, frequency, resolution)

In this program, channels 0 and 1 are used with 8 bits of resolution and the frequency of the PWM waveforms are set to 500Hz. After configuring the PWM parameters we have to attach an output pin to the selected PWM channel. This is done using the function:

ledcAttachPin(port pin, channel)

In this program, both port pins 22 and 23 are set to generate PWM waveforms. The duty cycle of the generated waveform is changed using the function:

ledcWrite(channel, duty cycle)

Note that any output pin of the ESP32 DevKitC can be programmed to generate PWM waveform.

At the beginning of the program, the green and red LED pins, the channel used, and the frequency of the required PWM waveform is defined and set as required. Inside the setup routine, two PWM channels named **GreenChannel** and **RedChannel** are created and are attached to port pins 22 and 23 respectively. The remainder of the program runs in an endless loop. Inside this loop two **for** loops are used. First **for** loop starts with the green LED fully ON and the red LED OFF by setting the duty cycle of green LED to 255, and that of the red LED to 0. The duty cycle of the green LED is then decreased and that of the red LED is increased every 15 milliseconds. Inside the second **for** loop, the reverse operations are done where the brightness of the red LED is decreased and that of the green one is increased.

```
/****************************************************************
 *              VARYING THE LED BRIGHTNESS
 *              ==========================
 *
 * In this program the KY-011 sensor is used which has a green and
 * a red LED with a common cathode terminal. The green LED and the
 * red LED are connected to I/O pins 22 and 23 of the ESP32 DevKitC
 * respectively. The program sends PWM waveform to the LEDs to
 * change their brightness. At the same time, different tones of
 * yellow are produced by the combination of the red and green LEDs.
 *
 * Author: Dogan Ibrahim
 * Date  : April 2019
 * File  : esp32pwm
 ****************************************************************/
int GreenLED = 22;                          // Green LED pin
int RedLED = 23;                            // Red LED pin
int DutyCycle;                              // Duty cycle
const int GreenChannel = 0;                 // Green LED channel
const int RedChannel = 1;                   // Red LED channel
const int resolution = 8;                   // PWM Resolution
const int frequency = 500;                  // PWM Frequency

//
// Setup two PWM channels, one for the green and one for the red
// LED. Atatch these channels to port pins 23 and 22 respectively
//
void setup ()
{
  ledcSetup(GreenChannel, frequency, resolution);
  ledcSetup(RedChannel, frequency, resolution);
  ledcAttachPin(GreenLED, GreenChannel);
  ledcAttachPin(RedLED, RedChannel);
}

//
// Send the generated PWM waveforms to the two LEDs with varying
// duty cycles. As the brightness of one LED is decreased, the
// brightness of the other one is increased. Tones of yellow are
// generated when this process is done fast
//
void loop ()
{
   for (DutyCycle = 255; DutyCycle > 0; DutyCycle--)
   {
      ledcWrite(GreenChannel, DutyCycle);
```

```
        ledcWrite(RedChannel, 255-DutyCycle);
        delay(15);
    }

    for (DutyCycle = 0; DutyCycle < 255; DutyCycle++)
    {
        ledcWrite(GreenChannel, DutyCycle);
        ledcWrite(RedChannel, 255-DutyCycle);
        delay(15);
    }
}
```

Figure 4.8 Program listing

Raspberry Pi Program Listing: The circuit diagram of the Raspberry Pi version of this project is as in Figure 2.22. The program listing (**rpipwm**) is shown in Figure 4.9. In order to generate PWM waveforms on the Raspberry Pi we need to use the following functions: Function **x = GPIO.PWM(port pin, frequency)** is used to create a PWM channel on the specified port pin and with the specified frequency, where **x** is a variable. Then, function **x.start(duty cycle)** is used to start generating PWM waveform on the specified port pin. The initial value of the duty cycle is set to **duty cycle**. Function **x.ChangeDutyCycle(new duty cycle)** can then be used to change the duty cycle of the generated waveform at any time. It is also possible to use function **x.ChangeFrequency(new frequency)** to change the frequency of the generated waveform at any time.

At the beginning of the program, modules **RPi.GPIO** and **time** are imported into the program, the interface between the Raspberry Pi and KY-011 are defined and the frequency of the PWM waveform is set to 500Hz. Port pins where the LEDs are connected to are then configured as outputs and two PWM channels are created with the names **RedChannel** and **GreenChannel**. PWM waveforms then output from these channels with the duty cycles set to 0 (i.e. both LEDs are OFF to start with). Inside the main program loop two **for** loops are used, wherein the first **for** loop the duty cycle of the green LED is decreased and that of the red LED is increased. In the second **for** loop, the inverse is done. The net effect is that the brightness of the two LEDs vary and at the same time different tones of yellow are generated.

```
#-----------------------------------------------------------
#     VARY LED BRIGHTNESS
#     ===================
#
# In thiS project the two colour LED KY-011 is used. The
# green and red LED pins are conncted to Raspberry Pi port
# pins GPIO2 and GPIO3. The brightness of the two LEDs are
# varied by sending PWM waveform to them. Also, different
# tones of yellow are generated
#
# Author: Dogan Ibrahim
```

```
# Date  : April 2019
# File  : rpipwm.py
#--------------------------------------------------------
import RPi.GPIO as GPIO                   # import Rpi library
import time                               # import time library
GPIO.setwarnings(False)                   # disable warnings
GPIO.setmode(GPIO.BCM)                    # set BCM mode

GreenLED = 2                              # green LED
RedLED = 3                                # red LED
freq = 500                                # PWM frequency

GPIO.setup(GreenLED, GPIO.OUT)            # Configure as output
GPIO.setup(RedLED, GPIO.OUT)              # configure as output

RedChannel = GPIO.PWM(RedLED, freq)       # initialize red channel
GreenChannel = GPIO.PWM(GreenLED, freq)   # initialzoe green channel
RedChannel.start(0)                       # generate PWM on red channel
GreenChannel.start(0)                     # generate PWM on green channel


while True:                               # do forever
  for DutyCycle in range(100, 0, -1):
     GreenChannel.ChangeDutyCycle(DutyCycle)
     RedChannel.ChangeDutyCycle(100-DutyCycle)
     time.sleep(0.020)

  for DutyCycle in range(0, 101):
     GreenChannel.ChangeDutyCycle(DutyCycle)
     RedChannel.ChangeDutyCycle(100-DutyCycle)
     time.sleep(0.020)
```

Figure 4.9 Program listing

Notice that the program in Figure 4.9 is in a loop and the only way to stop the program is to enter Cntl+C characters from the keyboard. This, however, does not stop the program in an orderly manner and does not clear the GPIO ports that we have used. It is recommended to modify the program loop as shown below using **try-except** statements so that the program is terminated orderly when the Cntrl+C characters are entered

```
try:

  while True:
     for DutyCycle in range(100, 0, -1):
     GreenChannel.ChangeDutyCycle(DutyCycle)
     RedChannel.ChangeDutyCycle(100-DutyCycle)
```

```
            time.sleep(0.020)

            for DutyCycle in range(0, 101):
            GreenChannel.ChangeDutyCycle(DutyCycle)
            RedChannel.ChangeDutyCycle(100-DutyCycle)
            time.sleep(0.020)
    except KeyboardInterrupt:
      GPIO.cleanup()
```

4.2.2 Project 2 – Using an RGB LED – Rainbow colours

Description: In this project, a three colour RGB LED module is used. The project displays all the 7 rainbow colours for one second, repeating the display every 5 seconds.

Aim: The aim of this project is to show how the three colour RGB LED module can be used in a project to display all 7 colours of the rainbow. This project makes use of the PWM channels of the processor.

Sensor Used: The 4-pin KY-009 SMD RGB module is used in this project. Figure 4.10 shows the pin layout of this module. The module basically consists of three LEDs in a package with red, green and blue colours, where the cathode terminals are all connected together to form a common terminal (denoted by the – character). An LED is turned ON when a logic HIGH is applied to its terminal. Notice that the colours are marked wrongly on the module. The correct marking should be GND, GREEN, RED, BLUE, where GND is the pin marked with the - character.

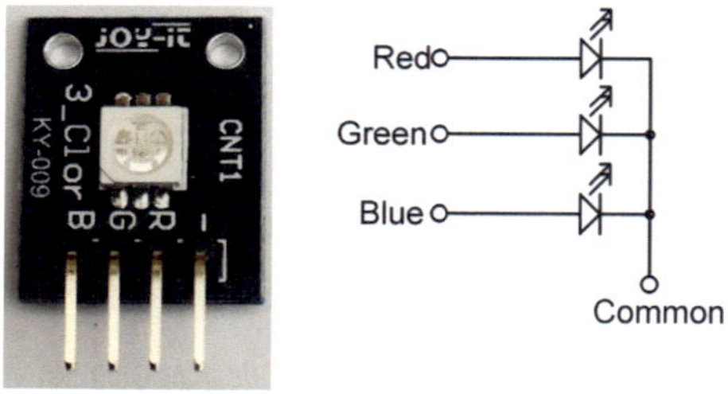

Figure 4.10 KY-009 RGB SMD module

The basic specifications of the KY-009 module are:

- LED type: SMD
- Common cathode
- Vf (red): 1.8V, Vf(green):2.8V, Vf(blue): 2.8V
- Luminous intensity(McD): red: (100), green: (400), blue: (100)

Background Information: It is well known that the rainbow is made up of 7 colours. Using the red, green, and blue (RGB) colours in various combinations we can generate any colour that we like. Assuming that each colour is represented with an 8-bit value from 0 to 255, the rainbow colours and the RGB values to obtain these colours are shown in Table

4.1. Although not relevant here, the approximate wavelength of each colour is also shown in this table in nanometres. These colours are usually remembered with the word ROYGBIV which is made up of the first letter of each colour.

Colour	R	G	B	Wavelength
Red	255	0	0	623
Orange	255	127	0	596
Yellow	255	255	0	571
Green	0	255	0	547
Blue	0	0	255	480
Indigo	75	0	130	460
Violet	148	0	211	440

Table 4.1 Rainbow colours

Block Diagram: The block diagram of the project is shown in Figure 4.11.

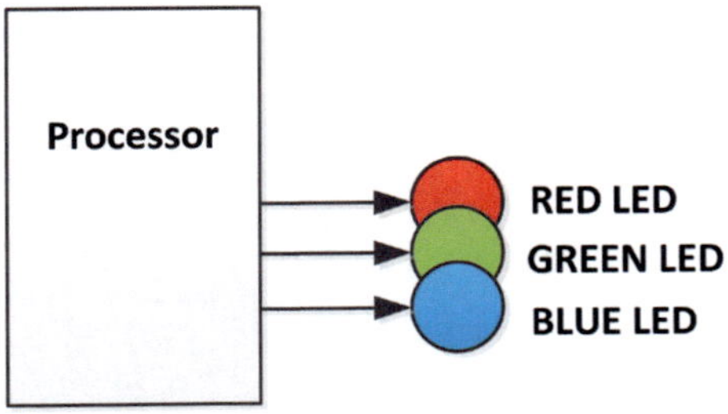

Figure 4.11 Block diagram of the project

Arduino Uno Circuit Diagram: The circuit diagram of the project is shown in Figure 4.12 where the PWM pins 10, 9, and 11 of the Arduino Uno are used for the red, green, and blue LEDs respectively. 220-ohm current limiting resistors are connected in series with the LED pins. The current through each LED is then given by:

- Red LED: (5V – 1.8V) / 220 = 14.5mA
- Green LED: (5V – 2.8V) / 220 = 10mA
- Blue LED: (5V – 2.8V) / 220 = 10mA

The actual current through each LED was measured with a digital ammeter to be as follows:

- Red LED: 12.15mA
- Green LED: 7.35mA
- Blue LED: 8.26mA

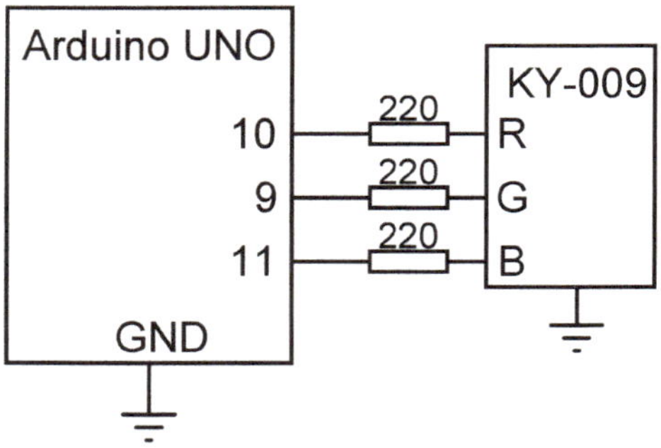

Figure 4.12 Arduino Uno circuit diagram of the project

Arduino Uno Construction: The project is constructed on a breadboard and is shown in Figure 4.13.

Figure 4.13 Project construction

Arduino Uno Program Listing: Although the same current limiting resistors were used in the design, the current through each LED and hence the brightness of each LED is different even if the same voltage is applied to their terminals. This is further complicated by the fact that the brightness of the green LED is 4 times the brightness of the read and the blue

LEDs even if the same current is drawn by each LED. As a result of this, we cannot simply apply the colour combinations given in Table 1 and expect to get the correct colours. What is required here is to modify the values given in Table 1 by considering the currents through each LED and also the fact that the green LED is 4 times brighter than the other two for the same forward current. The required modifications are given below:

- Divide the green values by 4 so that all 3 LEDs are equal
- Divide the red values by 12.15/7.25 = 1.65 to make for the current difference
- Divide the blue values by 8.26/7.35 = 1.12 to make for the current difference

The new Table 4.2 should give the correct values to generate the required rainbow colours.

Colour	R	G	B	Wavelength
Red	154	0	0	623
Orange	154	32	0	596
Yellow	154	64	0	571
Green	0	64	0	547
Blue	0	0	227	480
Indigo	45	0	116	460
Violet	89	0	188	440

Table 4.2 Corrected colour values

The program is called **ardrgb** and its listing is shown in Figure 4.14. At the beginning of the program, the LED pins are defined. Then three integer arrays called **Red**, **Green,** and **Blue** are created to store the colour values for the red, green and the blue colours as in Table 4.2. Inside the setup routine, the LED ports are configured as outputs and all the LEDs are turned OFF to start with by calling function **AllOFF**. The remainder of the program runs in a loop continuously. Inside this loop, the values shown in Table 4.2 are given to each LED for the duration of one second. All the LEDs are turned OFF for 5 seconds and then the above process repeats again.

```
/*****************************************************************
 *                         RAINBOW COLOURS
 *                         ===============
 *
 * In this program the KY-009 LED module is used which has a red,
 * green, and blue LED with a common cathode terminal. The red,
 * green, and blue LEDs are connected to I/O pins 10, 9, and 11
 * of the Arduino respectively. The program sends PWM waveforms
 * to the LEDs to display the 7 rainbow colours. Each colour is
 * displayed for one second and teh process is repeated after 5
 * seconds delay.
 *
```

```
 * Author: Dogan Ibrahim
 * Date   : April 2019
 * File   : ardrgb
 ****************************************************************/
int GreenLED = 9;                                   // Green LED pin
int RedLED = 10;                                    // Red LED pin
int BlueLED = 11;                                   // Blue LED pin

int Red[] = {154, 154, 154, 0, 0, 45, 89};          // Red values
int Green[] = {0, 32, 64, 64, 0, 0, 0};             // Green values
int Blue[] = {0, 0, 0, 0, 227, 116, 188};           // Blue values

//
// Turn OFF all LEDs
//
void AllOFF()
{
   digitalWrite(GreenLED, 0);
   digitalWrite(RedLED, 0);
   digitalWrite(BlueLED, 0);
}


void setup ()
{
  pinMode(GreenLED, OUTPUT);                       // G LED is output
  pinMode(RedLED, OUTPUT);                         // R LED is output
  pinMode(BlueLED, OUTPUT);                        // B LED is output
  AllOFF();                                        // All LEDS OFF
}

//
// This is the main program loop. RED+GREEN+BLUE colours are mixed
// together to generate the 7 colours of the rainbow, where each
// colour is displayed for one second
//
void loop ()
{
   for(int k = 0; k < 7; k++)                      // Do for all colours
   {
     analogWrite(RedLED, Red[k]);                  // Display red
     analogWrite(GreenLED, Green[k]);              // Display green
     analogWrite(BlueLED, Blue[k]);                // Display blue
     delay(1000);                                  // Wait 1 sec
   }
   AllOFF();                                       // Turn all LEDs OFF
```

```
        delay(5000);                                    // Wait 5 secs
    }
```

Figure 4.14 program listing

ESP32 DevKitC Program Listing: The circuit diagram of the ESP32 DevKitC version of the program is similar to Figure 4.12, but different I/O port pins are used with the ESP32 DevKitC. The required program listing is not given here and it can be derived from Figure 4.8 and Figure 4.14.

Raspberry Pi Program Listing: The circuit diagram of the Raspberry Pi version of the program is similar to Figure 4.12, but different I/O port pins are used with the Raspberry Pi. The required program listing is not given here and it can be derived from Figure 4.9 and Figure 4.14. *Hint: Lists can be used in Python to store array elements.*

4.2.3 Project 3 – Magic wand

Description: In this project, a three colour RGB LED and a tilt switch module is used. The RGB LED is placed at the tip of a wand, while the tilt switch is placed at the body of the wand. When the wand is pointed down to an object the LED is turned ON which displays random colours as if it is a magic wand.

Aim: The aim of this project is to show how the three colour RGB LED module and a tilt switch module can be used together to form a magic wand. The project shows how to create and use integer random numbers.

Sensors Used: Two modules are used in this project from the sensor kit: The 4-pin KY-016 RGB module, and the 3-pin KY-017 (or KY-020) tilt switch. Figure 4.15 shows a picture of KY-016 module which is similar to KY-009 SMD RGB module used in the previous project, but additionally, it has onboard 150-ohm current limiting resistors.

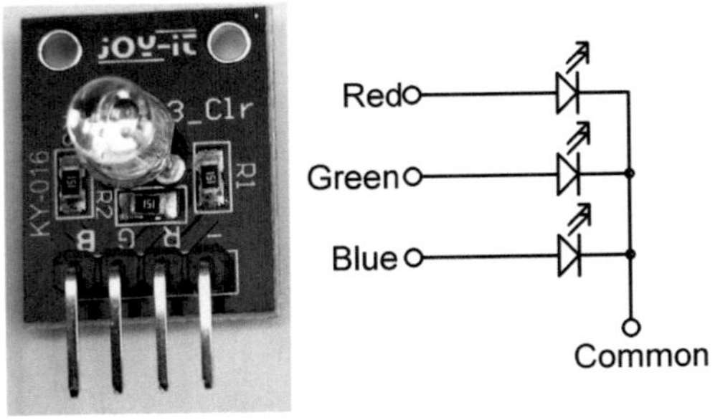

Figure 4.15 KY-016 RGB module

KY-017 has a mercury-based switch where the mercury closes the switch contacts when the module is not tilted. Additionally, there is an LED with a serial current limiting resistor on the board. When the module is not tilted, the switch contact is closed and the output is LOW with the LED being ON. When tilted, the switch contacts open and the output is forced to logic HIGH. At the same time, the onboard LED turns OFF. Figure 4.16 shows a picture of the KY-017 together with its internal circuit diagram. The tilted/not tilted position of the module is shown in Figure 4.17.

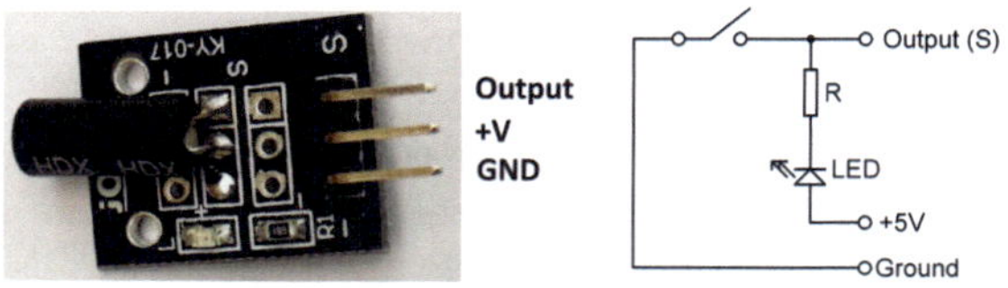

Figure 4.16 KY-017 tilt switch module

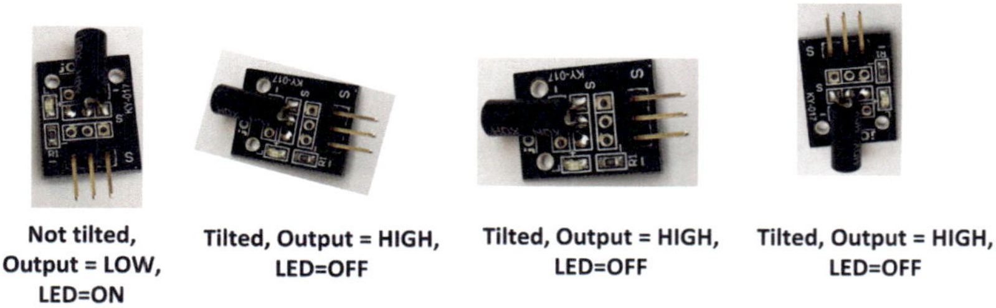

Figure 4.17 Tilt switch positions

Background Information: Tilt switches are usually made of two electrical electrodes housed in a small amount of liquid mercury. These switches are in one state when tilted with respect to horizontal, and in another state when no tilted. With the help of gravity, the mercury inside the switch assembly moves to make or break the contacts. Tilt switches are used in many domestic and industrial applications, such as in aircraft attitude indicators, fall sensors, pressure switches, thermostats and so on. Mercury tilt switches have the advantages that they are clean, quiet, and because the contacts are enclosed there is no risk of oxidation of the contacts. Their biggest disadvantage is that they are slow and also mercury is a highly toxic element.

Block Diagram: The block diagram of the project is shown in Figure 4.18.

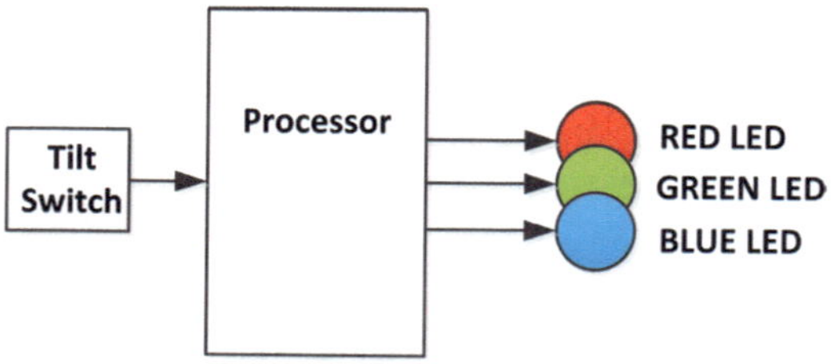

Figure 4.18 Block diagram of the project

Arduino Uno Circuit Diagram: The circuit diagram of the project is shown in Figure 4.19. The red, green, and blue LEDs are connected to Arduino Uno I/O pins 9, 10 and 11 respectively. Additionally, the output of the tilt switch is connected to I/O pin 2. Normally the output of the tilt switch is at logic 0 and tilting it forces the output too logic 1. +V pin of the tilt switch is connected to pin +5V of the Arduino Uno.

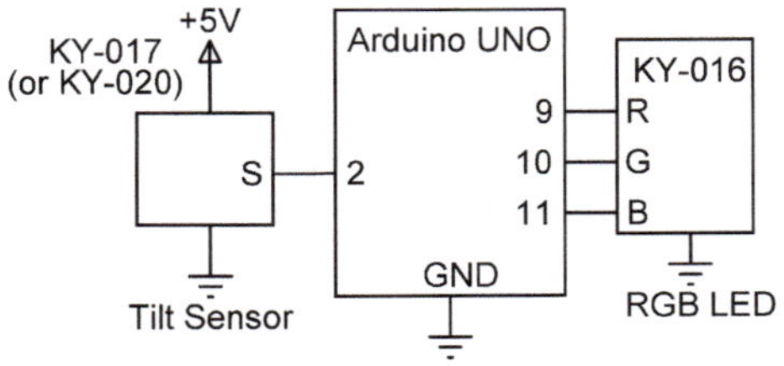

Figure 4.19 Arduino Uno circuit diagram

Construction: As shown in Figure 4.20, the RGB LED is mounted at the tip of the wand, and the tilt switch is mounted at the body of the wand such that pointing the wand downwards activates the switch.

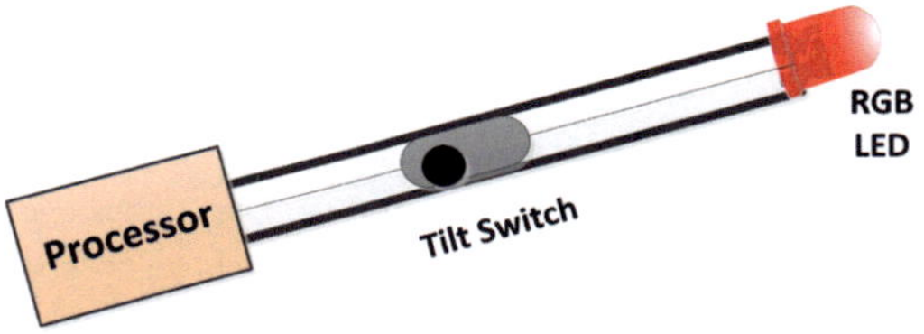

Figure 4.20 The wand

Arduino Uno Program Listing: The program listing (**ardwand**) is shown in Figure 4.21. At the beginning of the program, the connections to the RGB module are defined. Inside the setup routine, the LED pins are configured as outputs and the tilt switch pin is configured as an input. The remainder of the program runs in an endless loop. Inside this loop, the program reads the state of the tilt switch. If the switch is tilted (i.e. switch output is HIGH) then random numbers are generated between 0 and 255 for each LED and are stored in variables **NoR**, **NoG**, and **NoB**. These random numbers are then used as the duty cycles of PWM waveforms sent to each LED. The result is that the LEDs flash randomly in different colours. This process continues after 200ms delay. If on the other hand the switch is not tilted (i.e. switch output is LOW) then all the LEDs are turned OFF.

```
/*****************************************************************
 *                        MAGIC WAND
 *                        ==========
 *
 * In this program the KY-016 RGB LED module is used together with
 * the KY-017 tilt switch to create a magic wand. When the wand is
 * pointed down the tilt switch becomes activated which turns ON
 * the RGB LED which in turn displays random colours to simulate a
 * magic wand
 *
 * Author: Dogan Ibrahim
 * Date  : April 2019
 * File  : ardwand
 *****************************************************************/
```

```
int RedLED = 9;                             // Red LED pin
int GreenLED = 10;                          // Green LED pin
int BlueLED = 11;                           // Blue LED pin
int Tilt = 2;                               // Tilt switch
int TiltMode;
long NoR, NoG, NoB;

void setup ()
{
  pinMode(GreenLED, OUTPUT);                // G LED is output
  pinMode(RedLED, OUTPUT);                  // R LED is output
  pinMode(BlueLED, OUTPUT);                 // B LED is output
  pinMode(Tilt, INPUT);                     // Tilt is input
}

//
// This is the main program loop. Normally the output of the tilt
// switch is at logic 0 and it goes to logic 1 when the switch is
// tilted (i.e. the wand is tilted). When tilted, the RGB lights
// flash randomly
//
void loop ()
{
     TiltMode = digitalRead(Tilt);          // Read tilt switch
     if(TiltMode == 1)                      // If switch tilted
     {
        NoR = random(256);                  // Random number 0-255
        NoG = random(256);                  // random number 0-255
        NoB = random(256);                  // Random number 0-255
        analogWrite(RedLED, NoR);           // Generate red
        analogWrite(GreenLED, NoG);         // Generate green
        analogWrite(BlueLED, NoB);          // Generate blue
        delay(200);
     }
     else                                   // Turn OFF all LEDs
     {
        digitalWrite(RedLED, 0);            // Red OFF
        digitalWrite(GreenLED, 0);          // Green OFF
        digitalWrite(BlueLED, 0);           // Blue OFF
     }
}
```

Figure 4.21 Arduino Uno program listing

What we have learned: In this project, we have learned how to use the following Arduino functions:

random(n): Generates integer random numbers between 0 and **n-1**. We can also generate integer random numbers between **m** and **n-1** with the function **random(m, n)**.

x = digitalRead(port pin): This function reads the state of the specified port pin. Logic 0 or 1 is returned.

ESP32 DevKitC Program Listing: The circuit diagram of the DevKitC version of the program is similar to Figure 4.19, but the following pins are used for the DevKitC version (there is no need for external current limiting resistors):

ESP32 DevKitC Pin	KY-016 or KY-017 pin(s)
23	connect to pin R of KY-016 RGB module
22	connect to pin G of KY-016 RGB module
21	connect to pin Y of KY-016 RGB module
19	connect to pin S of KY-017 Tilt switch
GND	connect to GND of KY-016 and to GND of KY-017

ESP32 DevKitC version of the program (**esp32wand**) is shown in Figure 4.22. This program is similar to the one given in Figure 4.8, but here three colour LEDs are used and also a tilt switch is used.

```
/*****************************************************************
 *                         MAGIC WAND
 *                         ==========
 *
 * In this program the KY-016 RGB LED module is used together with
 * the KY-017 tilt switch to create a magic wand. When the wand is
 * pointed down the tilt switch becomes activated which turns ON
 * the RGB LED which in turn displays random colours to simulate a
 * magic wand
 *
 * Author: Dogan Ibrahim
 * Date  : April 2019
 * File  : esp32wand
 *****************************************************************/
int RedLED = 23;                                // Red LED pin
int GreenLED = 22;                              // Green LED pin
int BlueLED = 21;                               // Blue LED pin
int Tilt = 19;                                  // Tilt switch pin
const int RedChannel = 0;                       // Red channel
const int GreenChannel = 1;                     // Green channel
const int BlueChannel = 2;                      // Blue channel
const int resolution = 8;                       // PWM resolution
const int frequency = 500;                      // PWM frequency
int TiltMode;
long NoR, NoG, NoB;
```

```
//
// Create three PWM channels for the 3 LEDs and attach them to
// the ESP32 DevKitC pins
//
void setup ()
{
  ledcSetup(RedChannel, frequency, resolution);
  ledcSetup(GreenChannel, frequency, resolution);
  ledcSetup(BlueChannel, frequency, resolution);
  ledcAttachPin(RedLED, GreenChannel);
  ledcAttachPin(GreenLED, RedChannel);
  ledcAttachPin(BlueLED, BlueChannel);
  pinMode(Tilt, INPUT);                         // Tilt is input
}

//
// This is the main program loop. Normally the output of the tilt
// switch is at logic 0 and it goes to logic 1 when the switch is
// tilted (i.e. the wand is tilted). When tilted, the RGB lights
// flash randomly
//
void loop ()
{
     TiltMode = digitalRead(Tilt);              // Read tilt switch
     if(TiltMode == 1)                          // If switch tilted
     {
        NoR = random(256);                      // Random number 0-255
        NoG = random(256);                      // random number 0-255
        NoB = random(256);                      // Random number 0-255
        ledcWrite(RedChannel, NoR);             // Generate PWM
        ledcWrite(GreenChannel, NoG);           // Generate PWM
        ledcWrite(BlueChannel, NoB);            // Generate PWM
        delay(200);                             // 200ms delay
     }
     else                                       // Turn OFF all LEDs
     {
        ledcWrite(RedChannel, 0);               // Red OFF
        ledcWrite(GreenChannel, 0);             // Green OFF
        ledcWrite(BlueChannel, 0);              // Blue OFF
     }
}
```

Figure 4.22 ESP32 DevKitC program listing

At the beginning of the program, the I/O pins are assigned to the KY-016 and KY-017 pins. Then, three PWM channels, PWM frequency, and the PWM resolution are defined. Inside the setup routine three PWM channels **RedChannel**, **GreenChannel,** and **BlueChannel** are created and are attached to the specified I/O pins. Also, the tilt switch output is configured as a digital input. Inside the program loop, the state of the tilt switch is checked and if the switch is tilted (i.e. switch output HIGH) then three random numbers are generated between 0 and 255 and these numbers are used as the duty cycles for the PWM waveforms. The LEDs are turned OFF when the switch is not tilted.

Raspberry Pi Program Listing: The circuit diagram of the Raspberry Pi version of the program is similar to Figure 4.19, but the following pins are used for the Raspberry Pi version (there is no need for external current limiting resistors):

Raspberry Pi GPIO Pin	KY-016 or KY-017 pin(s)
17	connect to pin R of KY-016 RGB module
27	connect to pin G of KY-016 RGB module
22	connect to pin Y of KY-016 RGB module
10	connect to pin S of KY-017 Tilt switch
GND	connect to GND of KY-016 and to GND of KY-017

Raspberry Pi version of the program (**rpiwand.py**) is shown in Figure 4.23. This program is similar to the one given in Figure 4.9, but here three colour LEDs are used and also a tilt switch is used. At the beginning of the program, library modules **RPi.GPIO**, **time**, and **random** are included in the program, the LED pins are assigned to variables **RedLED**, **GreenLED**, and **BlueLED**, and the frequency and resolution of the PWM are set. The LED pins are then configured as outputs and the tilt switch pin is configured as input. Three PWM channels are then created, one for each LED. The main program loop checks the state of the tilt switch and if the switch is tilted then integer random numbers are created between 0 and 100 and these numbers are used to set the duty cycles of each PWM output waveform. If the switch is not tilted then the duty cycles of all the LEDs are set to 0 to turn OFF the LEDs. The program terminates when the Cntrl+C keys are entered where the PWM channels are stopped, the GPIO ports are cleared and the program exits.

```
#-----------------------------------------------------------
#    MAGIC WAND
#    ==========
#
# In this project the three colour RGB LED KY-016 is used.
# The red, green, and blue LEDs are connected to RPi GPIO
# pins 17,27,22 respectively. A KY-017 tilt switch module is
# connected to GPIO pin 10. When the tilt switch is tilted,
# random numbers are generated and the RGB LEDs are lit
# randomly, giving the visual effect of a magic wand.
#
# Author: Dogan Ibrahim
# Date  : April 2019
```

```
# File   : rpiwand.py
#-----------------------------------------------------------
import RPi.GPIO as GPIO                    # import Rpi library
import time                                # import time library
import random                              # import random library
GPIO.setwarnings(False)                    # disable warnings
GPIO.setmode(GPIO.BCM)                     # set BCM mode

RedLED = 17                                # green LED
GreenLED = 27                              # red LED
BlueLED = 22                               # blue LED
Tilt = 10                                  # tilt switch pin
freq = 500                                 # PWM frequency

GPIO.setup(RedLED, GPIO.OUT)               # Configure as output
GPIO.setup(GreenLED, GPIO.OUT)             # configure as output
GPIO.setup(BlueLED, GPIO.OUT)              # configure as output
GPIO.setup(Tilt, GPIO.IN)                  # configure as input

RedChannel = GPIO.PWM(RedLED, freq      )  # initialize red channel
GreenChannel = GPIO.PWM(GreenLED, freq)    # initialzoe green channel
BlueChannel = GPIO.PWM(BlueLED, freq)      # initialize blue channel
RedChannel.start(0)                        # generate PWM on red channel
GreenChannel.start(0)                      # generate PWM on green channel
BlueChannel.start(0)                       # generate PWM on blue channel

#
# Turn OFF all LEDs
#
def AllZero():
  RedChannel.ChangeDutyCycle(0)
  GreenChannel.ChangeDutyCycle(0)
  BlueChannel.ChangeDutyCycle(0)

try:
  while True:
     t = GPIO.input(Tilt)                  # Check tilt switch state
     if t == 1:                            # if tilted
        NoR = random.randint(0, 100)       # generate random no
        NoG = random.randint(0, 100)       # generate random no
        NoB = random.randint(0, 100)       # generate random no
        RedChannel.ChangeDutyCycle(NoR)
        GreenChannel.ChangeDutyCycle(NoG)
        BlueChannel.ChangeDutyCycle(NoB)
        time.sleep(0.20)
     else:
```

```
            AllZero()

    except KeyboardInterrupt:
      RedChannel.stop()
      GreenChannel.stop()
      BlueChannel.stop()
      GPIO.cleanup()
```

Figure 4.23 Raspberry Pi program listing

Note that the state of GPIO pins 0, 1, 7, 8, 14 and 15 are all HIGH after a system reboot or after a program exits. You should avoid using these pins if it is required for them to be LOW after a system reboot.

4.2.4 Project 4 – Silent door alarm

Description: In this project, a mini reed switch module is used together with a 7-colour flashing LED module. A small magnet is mounted on the door frame such that this magnet is very close to the reed switch and as a result the reed switch contacts are closed. When the door opens, the reed switch moves away from the magnet and as a result, the reed switch contacts open and this activates a 7-colour flashing LED module which flashes to indicate that the door is opened.

Aim: The aim of this project is to show how a mini reed switch module can be used together with a 7-colour flashing LED module to create a silent door alarm.

Sensors Used: Two sensor modules are used in this project from the sensor kit: The KY-021 mini reed switch module and the KY-034 7-colour flashing LED module. Figure 4.24 shows a picture of KY-021 module. This is a 3-pin module with the connections GND, +V, and Signal. GND and +V pins are connected to the ground and power pins of the processor respectively. If you are using the Arduino Uno then connect the +V pin to +5V on the processor card. If you are using the ESP32 DevKitC or the Raspberry Pi then connect this pin to +3.3V on the processor card. The Signal pin can be connected to any general purpose input/output pin. An onboard 10K resistor is connected between the +V and the S pins as shown in Figure 4.24.

Figure 4.24 KY-021 mini reed switch module

Figure 4.25 shows a picture of the KY-034 7-colour LED module. This is a 3-pin module where two GND pins are connected together. The other pin is the Signal pin. A 10K resistor is connected to onboard pin V but is not used here. The module generates 7-colours when the Signal pin is connected.

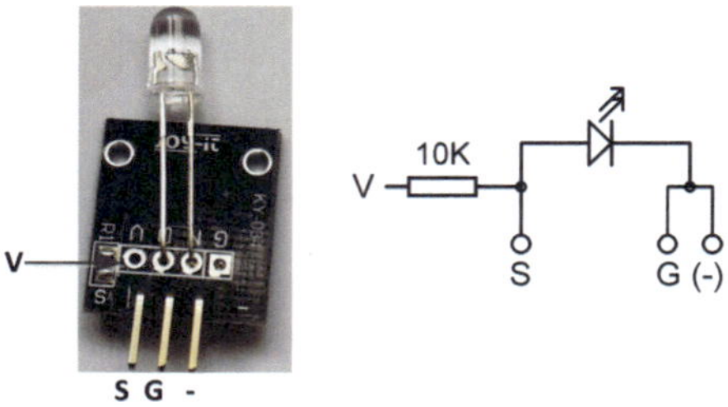

Figure 4.25 KY-034 7-colour LED module

Background Information: Reed switches are electrical switches operated by an applied magnetic field. These switches consist of a pair of ferromagnetic flexible metal contacts in a sealed glass envelope (see Figure 4.26). The contacts are normally open, closing when magnetic field (e.g. a magnet) is present near the contacts, and re-open i.e. return to their normal state when the magnetic field is removed. Reed switches are used in door and window mechanisms to detect when they are open or closed, and in many other security applications.

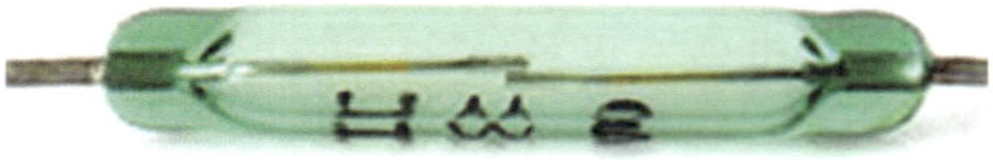

Figure 4.26 Typical reed switch in glass enclosure

The 7-colour LED module has a built-in chip that controls the LED so that it flashes and cycles through 7 colours when power is applied to the LED. The operating voltage of the module is +3.3V to +5V. The module has pink, yellow, and green high brightness lights. Flash module generates light of high brightness. By setting the LED ON and OFF with different durations we can get interesting flashing effects.

Block Diagram: The block diagram of the project is shown in Figure 4.27.

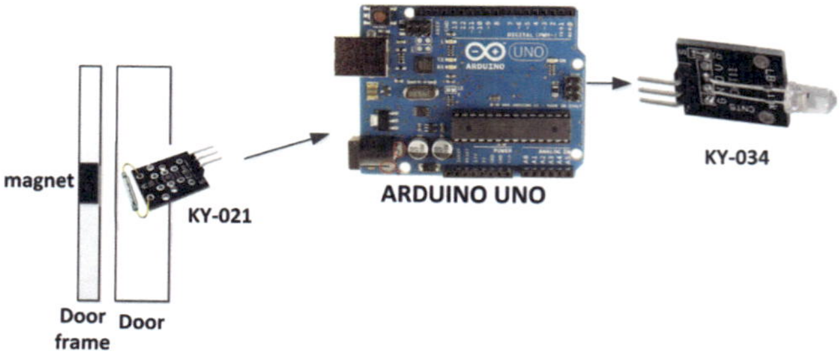

Figure 4.27 Block diagram of the project

Arduino Uno Circuit Diagram: The circuit diagram of the project is shown in Figure 4.28 for the case when the door is closed. Here, pin 2 and pin 3 of the Arduino are connected to the KY-021 reed switch and KY-034 7-color LED. The reed switch output is pulled HIGH through a pull-up resistor and because the magnet is near the reed switch when the door is closed, pin 2 is normally at logic LOW. As shown in Figure 4.29, this pin goes to logic HIGH when the door is opened (i.e. when the reed switch contacts open). The LED module is connected to the Arduino through a 220-ohm current limiting resistor.

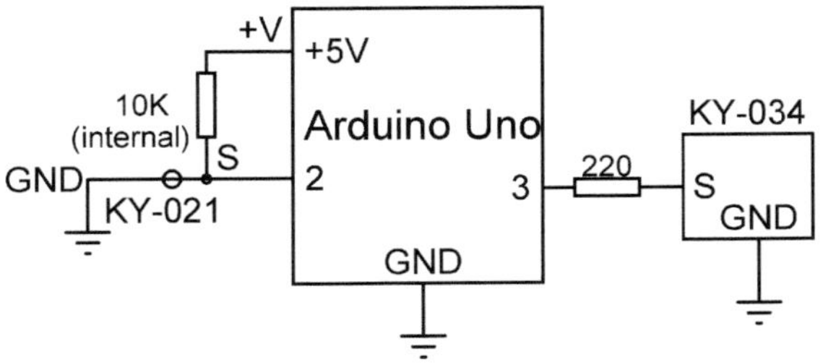

Figure 4.28 Door is closed

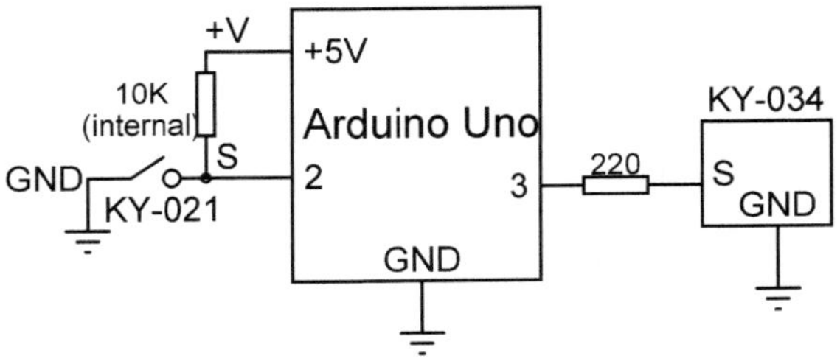

Figure 4.29 Door is open

Arduino Uno Program Listing: The program listing (**reeddoor**) is shown in Figure 4.30. At the beginning of the program, the connections to KY-021 and KY-034 are defined. Inside the setup routine, pin 2 and pin 3 are configured as digital input and output respectively. The remainder of the program runs in an endless loop. Inside this loop, the state of the reed switch is checked and if pin 2 is at logic HIGH then it is assumed that the reed switch contacts are open i.e. the door is opened. As a result of this, the 7-color LED is activated to give a visual indication that the door is opened.

```
/****************************************************************
 *                        SILENT DOOR ALARM
 *                        =================
 *
 * In this program the KY-021 reed switch and the KY-034 7-colour
 * flashing LED module re used. The switch and the LED module
 * are connected to pins 2 and 3 of the Arduino Uno respectively.
 * The reed switch is mounted on a door and a magnet is mounted
 * opposite the switchs such that when the door is closed the reed
 * switch contacts are closed. When the door is opened the reed
```

```
 * switch contacts open and this activates the 7-colour LED which
 * flashes in 7 colours to indicate silently that the door is
 * opened.
 *
 * Author: Dogan Ibrahim
 * Date  : April 2019
 * File  : reeddoor
 ****************************************************************/
#define ON HIGH
#define OFF LOW
#define OPEN HIGH
int ReedSwitch = 2;                                // Reed switch pin
int LED = 3;                                       // LED pin

//
// Configure pins 2 and 3 as inputs and outputs respectively.
// Also, turn OFF the LED to start with
//
void setup ()
{
  pinMode(ReedSwitch, INPUT);                      // Input
  pinMode(LED, OUTPUT);                            // Output
  digitalWrite(LED, OFF);                          // LED OFF
}

//
// This is the main program loop. Check the state of the reed switch
//
void loop ()
{
     int door = digitalRead(ReedSwitch);           // Read reed switch
     if(door == OPEN)                              // If door opened
        digitalWrite(LED, ON);                     // LED ON
     else
        digitalWrite(LED, OFF);                    // LED OFF
}
```

Figure 4.30 Arduino Uno program listing

Figure 4.31 shows the project built on a breadboard

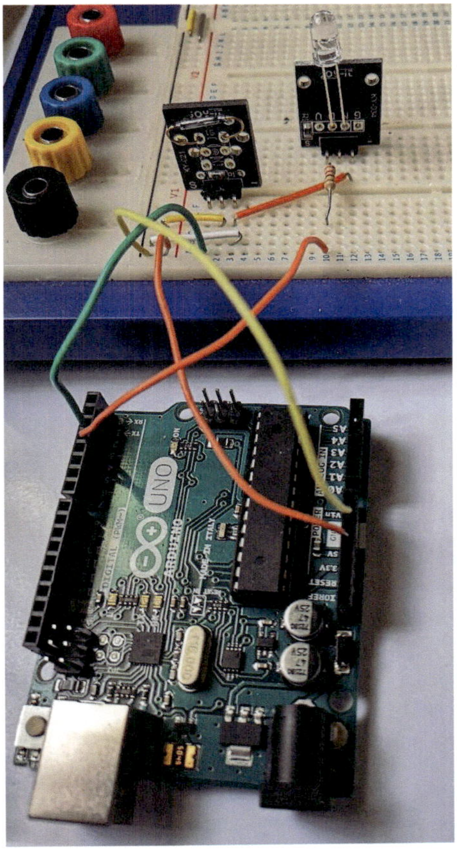

Figure 4.31 Project built on a breadboard

Raspberry Pi Program Listing: The circuit diagram of the Raspberry Pi version of the program is similar to Figure 4.28 and Figure 4.29, but the following pins are used for the Raspberry Pi version:

Raspberry Pi GPIO Pin	KY-021 or KY-034 pin(s)
23	connect to pin S of KY-021
22	connect to pin S of KY-034
GND	connect to GND of KY-021 and to GND of KY-034
+3.3V	connect to +V of KY-021

Raspberry Pi version of the program (**esp32reeddoor.py**) is shown in Figure 4.32. At the beginning of the program, the I/O pins are assigned to the KY-021 and KY-034 pins. These pins are then configured as input and output respectively. Inside the program loop, the state of the reed switch is checked and if pin 23 is at logic 1 then it is assumed that the reed switch contacts are open i.e. the door is opened. As a result of this, the 7-color LED is activated to give a visual indication that the door is opened.

```
#-----------------------------------------------------------
#    SILENT DOOR ALARM
#    =================
#
# In this program the KY-021 reed switch and the KY-034 7-colour
# flashing LED module are used. The switch and the LED module
# are connected to pins 23 and 2 of the Arduino Uno respectively.
# The reed switch is mounted on a door and a magnet is mounted
# opposite the switchs such that when the door is closed the reed
# switch contacts are closed. When the door is opened the reed
# switch contacts open and this activates the 7-colour LED which
# flashes in 7 colours to indicate silently that the door is
# opened.
#
#
# Author: Dogan Ibrahim
# Date  : April 2019
# File  : esp32reeddoor.py
#----------------------------------------------------------
import RPi.GPIO as GPIO              # import Rpi library
import time                          # import time library
import random                        # import random library
GPIO.setwarnings(False)              # disable warnings
GPIO.setmode(GPIO.BCM)               # set BCM mode

ReedSwitch = 2                       # Reed switch
LED = 3                              # LED module

GPIO.setup(LED, GPIO.OUT)            # Configure as output
GPIO.setup(ReedSwitch, GPIO.IN)      # configure as input
GPIO.output(LED, 0)                  # LED OFF to start with

while True:
     door = GPIO.input(Door)         # Check door state
     if door == 1:                   # Door is open
       GPIO.output(LED, 1)           # Turn ON LED module
     else:
       GPIO.output(LED, 0)           # Turn OFF LED module
```

Figure 4.32 Raspberry Pi program listing

ESP32 DevKitC Program Listing: The circuit diagram of the DevKitC version of the program is similar to Figure 4.28 and Figure 4.29, but the following pins are used for the DevKitC version:

ESP32 DevKitC Pin	KY-021 or KY-034 pin(s)
23	connect to pin S of KY-021
22	connect to pin S of KY-034
GND	connect to GND of KY-021 and to GND of KY-034
+3.3V	connect to +V of KY-021

The program listing is the same as in Figure 4.30 except that different GPIO pins are used in this version of the program.

4.2.5 Project 5 – Dark sensor with timed relay – Arduino Uno project

Description: In this project, a photoresistor is used to sense the environmental light conditions and a relay is activated when it is dark. The relay, for example, can be connected to lights to turn them ON for a specified period of time, e.g. for 30 seconds.

Aim: The aim of this project is to show how the photosensor and the relay modules can be used in a simple project. The project also shows how to use an analog input of the Arduino Uno.

Sensors Used: Two sensor modules are used in this project from the sensor kit: The KY-018 photoresistor and the KY-019 5V relay module. Figure 4.33 shows a picture of KY-018 photoresistor module. This is a 3-pin module with the connections GND, +V, and Signal. GND and +V pins are connected to the ground and power pins of the processor respectively. Connect the +V pin to +5V on the Arduino Uno processor board. The resistance of the photoresistor will decrease in the presence of light and increase in the absence of it. A 10K resistor is used in series with the photoresistor as shown in Figure 4.33. If the applied voltage is 5V then the voltage across the LDE is given by:

$$V_{LDR} = (5 \times R_{LDR}) / (R_{LDR} + 10)$$

Where R_{LDR} is the resistance of the LDR in Kohms.

Figure 4.33 KY-018 photoresistor module

KY-019 is a 3-pin 5V relay module that can be used as a switch to control AC loads. The pins are GND (-), +V, and S. The contacts of the relay are capable of handling up to 250VAC at 10A. The relay module has two output terminals: Normally Closed (NC) where the contacts are closed by default and Normally Open (NO) where the contacts are open by default. The relay contacts operate with +5V.

Figure 4.34 KY-019 relay module

Background Information: Photoresistors, also known as Light Dependent Resistors (LDR) are light sensitive 2-pin resistors that can be used to indicate the presence or absence of light. Their dark resistances are very high (up to 1Mohm), but when they are exposed to light their resistances can drop down to several ohms depending on the light intensity (Figure 4.35). Modern LDRs are made up of cadmium selenide (CdS), where a light-sensitive tract is created using CdS (Figure 4.36). The sensitivity of a photoresistor varies with the light wavelength (Figure 4.37). In general, they have lower sensitivities than photodiodes or phototransistors. LDRs are also sensitive to temperature changes and because of this, they are not suitable for precise light intensity measurements. LDRs are slow devices where it can take up to 10ms for their resistance to change when the light intensity changes. For this reason, LDRs cannot be used in applications where the light intensity changes fast. LDRs are normally used with a series resistor where a voltage is applied to the resistor. The voltage across the LDR is related to the light intensity striking on the LDR.

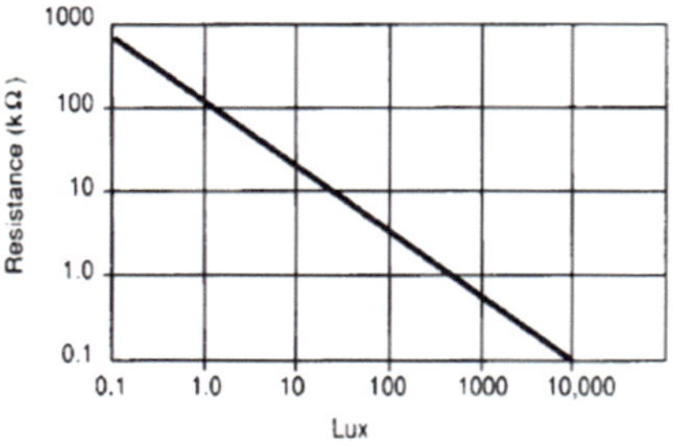

Figure 4.35 Light intensity-resistance characteristic of an LDR

Figure 4.36 Typical LDR

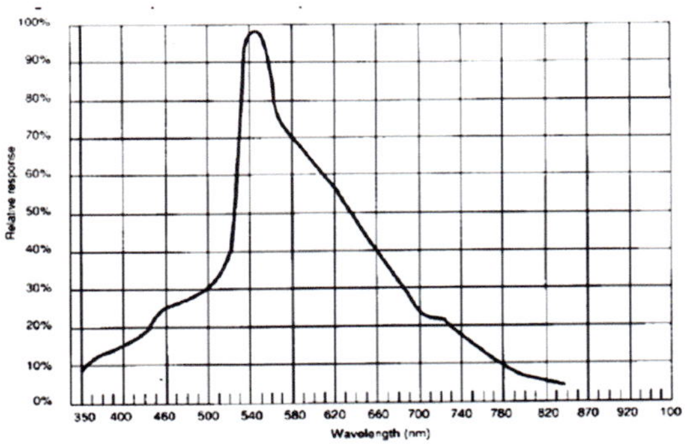

Figure 4.37 LDR sensitivity to light wavelength

Relays are used to switch high current AC loads. The operating voltage of the KY-019 relay is specified as +5V and it may not work properly if connected directly to an ESP32devKitC or a Raspberry Pi where the output voltage of an output pin is only +3.3V. A voltage translator module KY-051 will be used in ESP32 DevKitC and Raspberry Pi versions of this project to boost up the pin output voltage from +3.3V to +5V. More details on KY-051 will be given later in the next project.

Block Diagram: The block diagram of the project is shown in Figure 4.38.

Figure 4.38 Block diagram of the project

Circuit Diagram: The circuit diagram of the project is shown in Figure 4.39. S pin of the photoresistor module is connected to analog input A0 of the Arduino Uno. KY-019 Relay S pin is connected to port pin 3 of the Arduino Uno. The voltage across the KY-018 LDR module is around 500mV in light and around 2V when dark. The software will measure the voltage across the LDR and dark will be assumed if the voltage is greater than 1.5V.

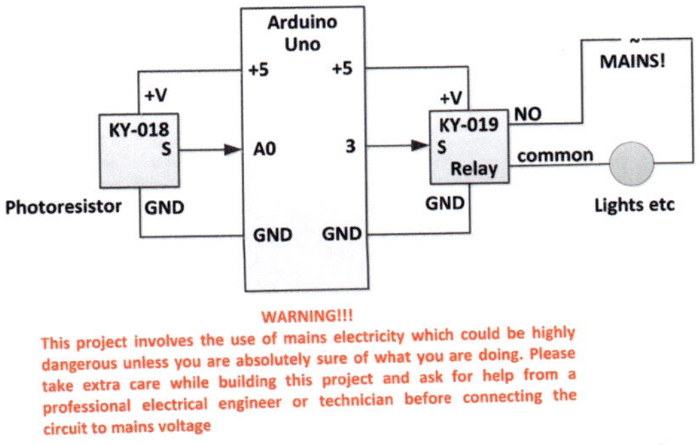

Figure 4.39 Circuit diagram of the project

Program Listing: Figure 4.40 shows the program listing (program **LDR1**). At the beginning of the program, the LDR and relay connections are defined. Inside the setup routine, the relay is configured as an output and it is de-activated to start with. Inside the main program loop, the analog voltage across the LDR is read and stored in a variable called **resistor**. The Arduino Uno processor has a 10-bit ADC with the quantization levels between 0 and 1023 with a reference voltage of 5V (5000mV). Therefore, in order to convert the read ADC value into physical voltage in millivolts, we have to multiply it by 5000 and divide by 1024. This is done as a floating point calculation for accuracy, and the voltage is stored in a floating point variable called **mV**. The voltage across the LDR is then compared with the dark voltage which is assumed to be 1500mV. If it is dark then the relay is activated for 30 seconds. At the end of this time, the relay is de-activated and the above process is repeated.

```
/****************************************************************
 *                 DARK SENSOR WITH TIMED RELAY
 *                 ============================
 *
 * In this program the KY-018 photoresistor is connected to analog
 * input A0 of the Arduino Uno. Additionally, KY-019 relay module
 * is connected as an output to port pin 3. The project detects
 * when it is dark and activates the relay for 30 seconds. At the
 * end of 30 seconds the relay is de-activated. the relay could be
 * connected for example to mains lights etc.
 *
 * Author: Dogan Ibrahim
 * Date  : April 2019
 * File  : LDR1
 ****************************************************************/
#define OFF LOW
#define ON HIGH
int LDR = 0;                                    // Photosensor
int Relay = 3;                                  // Relay pin
int DARK = 1500;

//
// Configure Relay as output and de-activate it to start with
//
void setup ()
{
  pinMode(Relay, OUTPUT);                       // Relay output
  digitalWrite(Relay, OFF);                     // Relay OFF
}

//
// This is the main program loop. Check if its dark by reading the
// volatge across the LDR. If its greater than 1500mV then it is
```

```
// assumed that it is dark. If so activate the relay fo 30 secs
//
void loop ()
{
    int resistor = analogRead(LDR);              // Read LDR
    float mV = resistor * 5000.0 / 1024.0;       // LDR voltage
    if(mV > DARK)                                // If its is dark
    {
      digitalWrite(Relay, ON);                   // Relay ON
      delay(30000);                              // 30 secs delay
      digitalWrite(Relay, OFF);                  // Relay OFF
    }
    else
      digitalWrite(Relay, OFF);                  // Relay OFF
}
```

Figure 4.40 Program listing

Figure 4.41 shows the project built on a breadboard

Figure 4.41 Project built on a breadboard

4.2.6 Project 6 – Dark sensor with timed relay – Raspberry Pi project

Description: This project is the same as the previous project where a photoresistor is used to sense when it is dark and then a relay is activated. The differences in this project are that because the Raspberry Pi does not have an ADC, the external ADC module KY-053 is used to read the analog voltage across the LDR. Also, because the KY-019 relay operates with +5V, the KY-051 voltage translator module is used to boost up the +3.3V pin output voltage of Raspberry Pi to +5V.

Aim: The aim of this project is to show how the photosensor module, relay module, ADC module, and the voltage translator modules can be used in a Raspberry Pi based project.

Sensors Used: Four modules are used in this project from the sensor kit: KY-018 photoresistor module, KY-053 ADC module, KY-051 voltage translator module, and KY-019 5V relay module. KY-018 and KY-019 were described in the previous project. In this project, we will be learning about KY-053 and KY-051.

Figure 4.42 shows a picture of KY-053 ADC module (pins are named on the module). This module is a 16-bit 4-channel ADC that is connected to the host computer via the I^2C bus. KY-053 makes use of the ADS1115 ADC converter chip. This converter has a programmable gain feature so that small signals can be amplified and read with higher precision. The analog voltage to be converted into digital is applied to one of the A0-A3 input pins. The converter produces 16-bit data in 2's complement form where the highest positive number is 7FFFh and the highest negative number is 8000h. The basic features of the KY-053 ADC module are as follows:

- 16-bit conversion
- 2.0V to 5.0V operation
- Continuous or single-shot modes
- Low current operation (150µA)
- Internal voltage reference
- 4-single-ended or 2-differential input channels

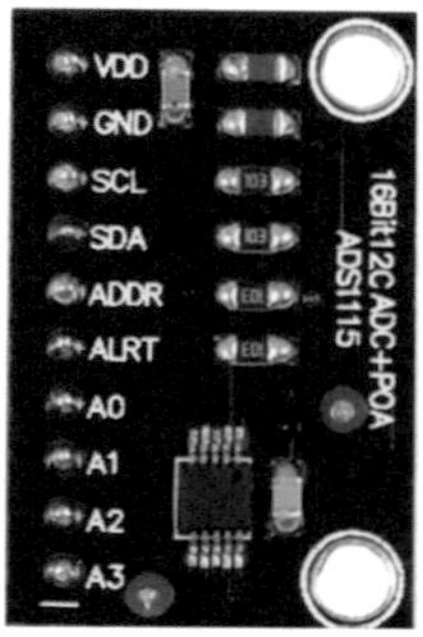

Figure 4.42 KY-053 ADC module

KY-053 has the following pins:

Pin	**Description**
VDD	power
GND	ground
SCL	I^2C clock
SDA	I^2C data
ADDR	no connection
ALRT	no connection
A0	analog in 0
A1	analog in 1
A2	analog in 2
A3	analog in 3

As we shall see later in this section, it is required to download and use library functions to read analog data from the KY-053.

Figure 4.43 shows the KY-051 voltage translator module. This is a 4-channel module that can be used to convert between 3.3V/5V and 5V/3.3V systems. Two voltage ranges are provided on the board. VCCa can be between 1.2V – 3.6V, while VCCb can be between 1.7V – 5.5V. It is important that VCCb must be higher or equal to VCCa. After applying VCCa and VCCb we can use pins A1-A4 or B1-B4 to make the required voltage conversion. For example, if we wish to boost the Raspberry Pi GPIO 2 output to +5V, we have to connect VCCa and VCCb to +3.3V and +5V respectively. Then, connect GPIO 2 to pin A1. The signal will then be boosted to +5V level at pin B1 of KY-051. Notice that the OE pin is not used. Also, KY-051 does not require any software to work.

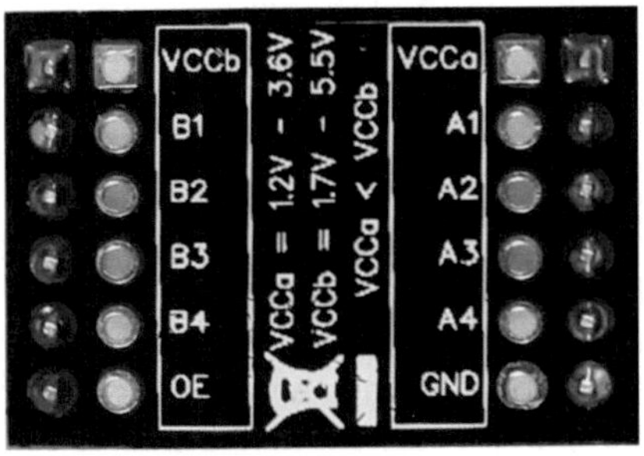

Figure 4.43 KY-051 voltage translator module

Background Information: Almost all signals in the environment, such as sound, temperature, pressure, light, etc are analog in nature. Because computers work with digital signals, it is not possible to connect an analog signal directly to a computer. An analog-to-digital converter, or ADC for short, receives an analog signal and converts into a digital format that can be read and understood by a computer. ADCs come in different resolutions, such as 8-bit, 10-bit, 12-bit, 16-bit, etc. The higher the resolution, the more precise is the converted signal. For example, in a 10-bit converter, we have 0-1023 quantization levels and thus the converted digital signal will have 10-bits. If the reference voltage of the ADC is +5V then each quantization level corresponds to 5000/1024 = 4.88mV. Thus, 4.88mV input signal will be represented in binary as "00 00000001", 9.76mV as "00 00000010" and so on. In general, after reading the ADC data we can calculate the actual physical voltage using the following formula:

$$V = ADC_V * Ref / 2^n$$

Where **V** is the actual physical voltage, **ADC_V** is the binary data read by the ADC, **Ref** is the ADC reference voltage, and **n** is the number of bits used in the ADC. For an 8-bit converter, **n** is 8, for a 10-bit converter **n** is 10, etc.

The gain of the KY-053 ADC can be selected from 2/3x to 16x. Depending on the gain selection, the corresponding physical voltages corresponding to 1 bit are as follows:

GAIN	**1-bit (mV)**
2/3	0.1875
1	0.125
2	0.0625
4	0.03125
8	0.01562
16	0.007812

In this project, we will set the gain to 1 where each bit corresponds to 0.125mV. Therefore, at full scale of 3300mV, the output of the ADC will be 3300/0.125 = 26400. To convert the ADC output to physical voltages in millivolts, we have to multiply it with 0.125.

The KY-053 ADC operates with the I^2C (Inter-integrated circuit) bus interface. This is a 2-wire serial protocol invented by Philips and is now used by many manufacturers. I^2C devices operate mainly as slaves (although it is also possible to have master I^2C devices) where each device usually has a unique 7-bit address. The interface uses two signals: SDA and SCL. SDA is the bi-directional data line where SCL is the bus clock. The bus clock is always generated by the bus master. I^2C bus allows many devices to be connected and to communicate over these two signal lines. Both of the signal lines must be pulled high to VCC for proper operation of the bus. For 7-bit address, the address is clocked out with the most significant bit (MSB) first, followed by an R/W bit to indicate whether this is a read (1) or a write (0) operation. Interested readers can find further information on the I^2C bus at the following tutorial link:

https://learn.sparkfun.com/tutorials/i2c/all

Block Diagram: Figure 4.44 shows the block diagram of the project.

Figure 4.44 Block diagram of the project

Circuit Diagram: The circuit diagram of the project is shown in Figure 4.45. The connections between the Raspberry Pi and the KY-053 ADC are as follows:

KY-053	**Raspberry Pi**
VDD	+3.3V
GND	GND
SCL	GPIO 3 (SCL)

SDA	GPIO 2 (SDA)
ADDR,ALRT	no connection
A0	KY-018 photo sensor output

GPIO 17 of the Raspberry Pi is configured as an output pin to drive the KY-019 relay module through the KY-051 voltage translator module. It was found by experimentation that when the KY-018 photoresistor is connected to +3.3V, the voltage across the LDR is greater than about 1500mV when it was dark.

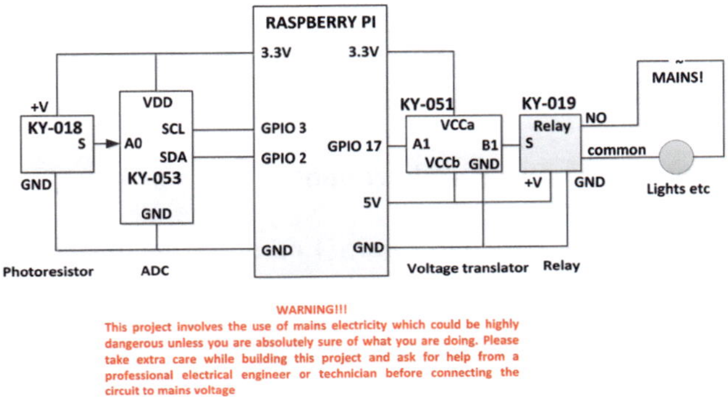

Figure 4.45 Circuit diagram of the project

Program Listing: Before using the ADC, we have to enable the I²C interface on our Raspberry Pi and also download the KY-053 ADC library for Python. The steps are as follows:

- Start the configuration menu from the command prompt:

  pi@raspberrypi:~ $ **sudo raspi-config**

- Go down the menu to **Interface Options**
- Go down and select **I²C**
- Enable the I²C interface
- Select **Finish** to complete

Now we have to install the I²C library on our Raspberry Pi 3. The steps are as follows:

- Enter the following commands from the command menu:

```
pi@raspberrypi:~ $ sudo apt-get update
pi@raspberrypi:~ $ sudo apt-get install -y python-smbus i2c-tools
pi@raspberrypi:~ $ sudo reboot
```

Modify the following configuration file, e.g. using the nano text editor:

pi@raspberrypi:~ $ **sudo nano /etc/modules**

- Add the following lines (if they are not already there):

22

- Exit from nano by typing Ctrl X and Y to save the file. You can check the contents of this file by entering the command:

pi@raspberrypi:~ $ **cat /etc/modules**

- Reboot the Raspberry Pi by entering:

pi@raspberrypi:~ $ **sudo reboot**

- Build your circuit as shown in Figure 4.45 and enter the following command to check whether or not the KY-052 ADC module is recognized by the Raspberry:

pi@raspberrypi:~ $ **sudo i2cdetect –y 1**

You should see a table similar to the one shown below. A number in the table means that the ADC has been recognizing correctly and the I²C slave address of the ADC is shown in the table. In this example the ADC address is 0x48:

```
pi@raspberrypi:~ $ sudo i2cdetect -y 1
     0  1  2  3  4  5  6  7  8  9  a  b  c  d  e  f
00:          -- -- -- -- -- -- -- -- -- -- -- -- --
10: -- -- -- -- -- -- -- -- -- -- -- -- -- -- -- --
20: -- -- -- -- -- -- -- -- -- -- -- -- -- -- -- --
30: -- -- -- -- -- -- -- -- -- -- -- -- -- -- -- --
40: -- -- -- -- -- -- -- -- 48 -- -- -- -- -- -- --
50: -- -- -- -- -- -- -- -- -- -- -- -- -- -- -- --
60: -- -- -- -- -- -- -- -- -- -- -- -- -- -- -- --
70: -- -- -- -- -- -- -- --
pi@raspberrypi:~ $
```

We should now install the KY-053 Python library so that we can send commands and data to our ADC. The library chosen here is the Adafruit ADS1x15. This library is installed as follows:

- pi@raspberrypi:~ $ **sudo apt-get update**

- pi@raspberrypi:~ $ **sudo apt-get install build-essential python-dev python-smbus python-pip**

- pi@raspberrypi:~ $ **sudo pip install adafruit-ads1x15**

We are now ready to use the ADC library in our Python programs. It is worthwhile to look at some of the library functions before we write our program. Library file **Adafruit_ADS1x15** must be imported at the beginning of the program. The default I^{2}C address is 048, but this can be changed when an instance of ADS1115 is created. For example, to change the I^{2}C address to 0x47, use with the following statement:

adc = Adafruit_ADS1x15.ADS1115(address=0x47, busnam=1)

ADC values can be read into variable **v** with the statement of the form:

v = adc.read_adc(ch, gain=GAIN)

where **ch** is the ADC channel number (0 to 3). Note that we can also pass an optional data_rate parameter to control the ADC conversion time in samples/second. For example, to set to 128 samples/second, use the following statement:

v = adc.read_adc(ch, gain=GAIN, date_rate=128)

Since we are using the ADS1115 chip, the converted digital value is 16-bits wide

The program listing (program: **rpildr1.py**) is shown in Figure 4.46. At the beginning of the program, GPIO, time, and ADC libraries are imported to the program. The gain of the ADC (**GAIN**) and the channel to be used (**ch**) are defined and variable **DARK** is set to 1500 as this is the voltage in millivolts which determines when it is dark. The relay is then turned OFF to start with. Inside the main program loop, the output voltage of the photoresistor is read into variable **photoR** and is then converted into physical voltage in millivolts and stored in variable **mV**. If this voltage is greater than **DARK**, i.e. 1500mV, then it is assumed that it is dark and the relay is activated for 30 seconds, otherwise, the relay is de-activated.

```
#--------------------------------------------------------------
#
#               DARK SENSOR WITH TIMED RELAY
#               ============================
#
# In this program a phoresistor (KY-018) is used to detect the
# light level. When the light level falls to a certain point
# then a relay (KY-019) is operated for 30 seconds. In this
# program, additionally, an ADC module (KY-053), and a voltage
# translator module (KY-051) is used since the GPIO output
# voltage of Raspberry Pi is not high enough to activate the
# relay module
#
# Program: rpildr1.py
# Date   : July 2018
# Author : Dogan Ibrahim
#---------------------------------------------------------------
import RPi.GPIO as GPIO          # Import GPIO
import time                      # Import time
```

```
import Adafruit_ADS1x15       # import ADC

adc = Adafruit_ADS1x15.ADS1115()
GAIN = 1                      # Set ADC gain
ch = 0                        # Channel 0

DARK = 1500
Relay = 17                    # Relay at GPIO17
GPIO.setmode(GPIO.BCM)
GPIO.setwarnings(False)
GPIO.setup(Relay, GPIO.OUT)
GPIO.output(Relay, GPIO.LOW)

#
# Program loop. Read the photoresistor output and activate the
# relay for 30 seconds if it is dark
#
while True:
    photoR = adc.read_adc(ch, gain=GAIN)
    mV = photoR * 0.125
    if mV > DARK:
      GPIO.output(Relay, GPIO.HIGH)
      time.sleep(30)
      GPIO.output(Relay, GPIO.LOW)
    else:
      GPIO.output(Relay, GPIO.LOW)
```

Figure 4.46 Program listing

Figure 4.47 shows the project constructed on a breadboard.

Figure 4.47 Project constructed on a breadboard

You may want the program to start automatically after system restart. The steps are given below:

- Use the **nano** editor and edit file **/etc/rc.local**

  pi@raspberrypi:~ $ **sudo nano /etc/rc.local**

- Enter the following line to the file:

  sudo python /home/pi/rpildr1.py

- Exit the editor by entering **Cntrl+X** followed by **Y**

Do not forget to remove the above lines if you do not want to re-start the program automatically.

4.2.7 Project 7 – Dark sensor with timed relay – ESP32 DevKitC project

Description: This project is the same as the previous project where a photoresistor is used to sense when it is dark and then a relay is activated. The differences in this project are that because the ESP32 DevkitC has a built-in ADC, there is no need to use the KY-053 module. It is, however, necessary to use the KY-051 voltage translator module to boost the pin output signal level to +5V to activate the relay reliably.

Aim: The aim of this project is to show how the photosensor module, relay module, and the voltage translator modules can be used in an ESP32 DevKitC based project.

ESP32 DevKitC ADC Channels: The ESP32 DevKitC has 18 ADC channels with 12-bit resolution, configured as follows:

ADC1_CH0 (GPIO 36)
ADC1_CH1 (GPIO 37)
ADC1_CH2 (GPIO 38)
ADC1_CH3 (GPIO 39)
ADC1_CH4 (GPIO 32)
ADC1_CH5 (GPIO 33)
ADC1_CH6 (GPIO 34)
ADC1_CH7 (GPIO 35)
ADC2_CH0 (GPIO 4)
ADC2_CH1 (GPIO 0)
ADC2_CH2 (GPIO 2)
ADC2_CH3 (GPIO 15)
ADC2_CH4 (GPIO 13)
ADC2_CH5 (GPIO 12)
ADC2_CH6 (GPIO 14)
ADC2_CH7 (GPIO 27)
ADC2_CH8 (GPIO 25)

ADC2_CH9 (GPIO 26)

Notice that the ESP32 ADC channels do not have a linear behaviour and is not very accurate. Also, ADC2 channels cannot be used when the Wi-Fi is used.

Block Diagram: Figure 4.48 shows the block diagram for the ESP32 DevKitC based project.

Figure 4.48 Block diagram of the project

The Circuit Diagram: The circuit diagram of the DevKitC version of the project is shown in Figure 4.49. ADC2_CH0 (GPIO 4) is used to read the photoresistor analog voltage. Notice the use of the voltage translator module to drive the relay module, where the GPIO 0 port pin is connected to A1 pin of the voltage translator module. VCCa and VCCb pins of the voltage translator module are connected to +3.3V and +5V respectively. B1 output of the voltage translator module drives the relay directly. It was found with experimentation that the output voltage of the photoresistor module is greater than about 1500mV when dark.

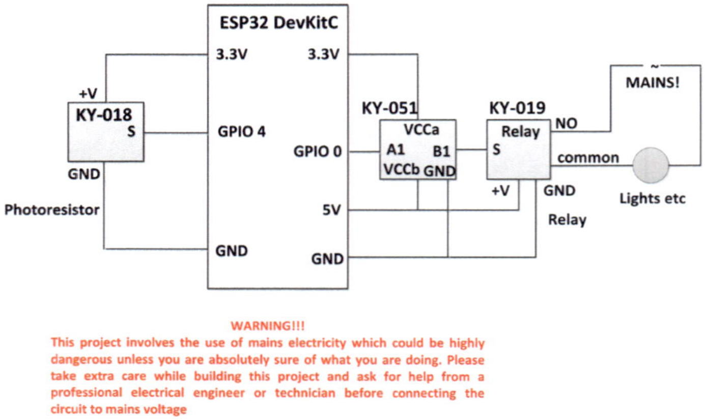

Figure 4.49 Circuit diagram of the project

Program Listing: The program listing is shown in Figure 4.50 (program: **espldr1**). At the beginning of the program, the relay and photoresistor connections are defined. Inside the setup routine, the relay is turned OFF to start with. The main program loop runs continuously. Inside this loop, the analog output voltage of the photoresistor module is read through ADC channel ADC2_CH0 (GPIO 4) and stored in the variable **resistor**. The ADC on ESP32 DevKitC is 12 bits wide, having 4096 quantization levels with a reference voltage of 3.3V. This reading is then converted into physical millivolts by multiplying with 3300mV and dividing by 4096. If the reading is greater than 1500mV then dark is assumed and the relay is activated for 30 seconds.

```
/****************************************************************
 *                  DARK SENSOR WITH TIMED RELAY
 *                  ============================
 *
 * In this program the KY-018 photoresistor is connected to analog
 * input A0 of the ESp32 DevKitC. Additionally, KY-019 relay module
 * is connected to the processor through a voltage translator module.
 * The project detects when it is dark and activates the relay for
 * 30 seconds. At the end of 30 seconds the relay is de-activated.
 * The relay could be connected for example to mains lights etc.
 *
 * Author: Dogan Ibrahim
 * Date  : April 2019
 * File  : espldr1
 ****************************************************************/
#define OFF LOW
#define ON HIGH
int LDR = 4;                                    // Photoresistor
int Relay = 0;                                  // Relay pin
int DARK = 1500;

//
// Configure Relay as output and de-activate it to start with
//
void setup ()
{
  pinMode(Relay, OUTPUT);                       // Relay output
  digitalWrite(Relay, OFF);                     // Relay OFF
}

//
// This is the main program loop. Check if its dark by reading the
// volatge across the LDR. If its greater than 1500mV then it is
// assumed that it is dark. If so activate the relay fo 30 secs
//
void loop ()
{
     int resistor = analogRead(LDR);            // Read LDR
     float mV = resistor * 3300.0 / 4096.0;     // LDR voltage
     if(mV > DARK)                              // If its is dark
     {
        digitalWrite(Relay, ON);                // Relay ON
        delay(30000);                           // 30 secs delay
```

```
            digitalWrite(Relay, OFF);             // Relay OFF
        }
        else
            digitalWrite(Relay, OFF);             // Relay OFF
    }
```

Figure 4.50 Program listing

Figure 4.51 shows the project constructed on a breadboard

Figure 4.51 Project constructed on a breadboard

4.2.8 Project 8 – Turn ON lights when it is dark and the door is opened – Arduino Uno project

Description: This project is similar to the one given in section 4.2.5 where a photoresistor is used to sense when it is dark and then a relay is activated. In this project, additionally, a Hall magnetic field sensor module is used to detect the state of the door. When the door is opened the lights are turned ON for 30 seconds if it is dark, otherwise, no action is taken.
Aim: The aim of this project is to show how the photosensor module, relay module, and the Hall magnetic field sensor module are used in an Arduino Uno project.

Sensors Used: Three modules are used in this project from the sensor kit: KY-018 photoresistor module, KY-019 5V relay module, and the KY-003 Hall magnetic field sensor module. KY-018 and KY-019 have been described in earlier projects and therefore only the KY-003 will be described here.

Figure 4.52 shows a picture of the KY-003 Hall magnetic field sensor module. This module is similar to the KY-021 magnetic reed module used earlier, but KY-003 is more sensitive to magnetic fields and its response is much faster than the KY-021, operating at frequencies of 100kHz. KY-003 is based on semiconductor technology has no contacts and is therefore much more reliable and has a longer lifetime than the KY-021. KY-003 is a 3-pin device based on the 3144EUA-S Hall effect magnetic switch and it can operate at up to +150ºC. The module has an onboard 680-ohm resistor in series with an LED. The LED is turned ON when the magnetic field is detected. The operating voltage is +4.5V to 24V and its pins are GND, +V, and the output (S). The module output is open-collector and the output is normally at logic HIGH when there is no magnetic field. It goes to logic LOW when the module is close to a magnetic field (e.g. a magnet).

Figure 4.52 KY-003 Hall magnetic field sensor module

Block Diagram: The block diagram of the project is shown in Figure 4.53.

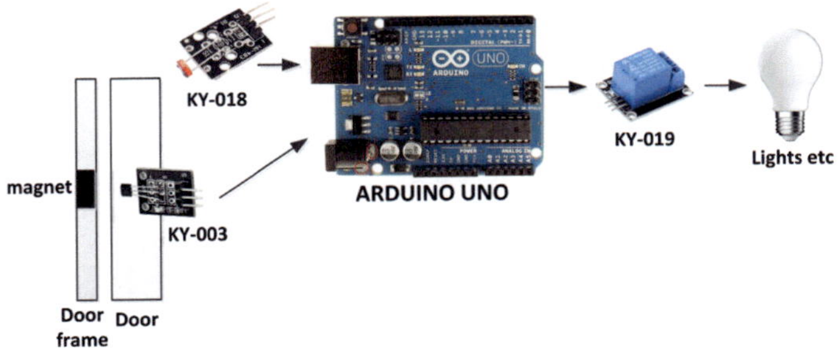

Figure 4.53 Block diagram of the project

Circuit Diagram: Figure 4.54 shows the circuit diagram of the project. S pin of the KY-018 photoresistor module is connected to analog input A0 of the Arduino Uno. KY-019 Relay S pin is connected to port pin 3 of the Arduino Uno. S pin of the KY-003 Hall magnetic field sensor module is connected to port pin 4 of the Arduino Uno. The voltage across the KY-018 LDR module is around 500mV in light and around 2V when dark. The software will measure the voltage across the LDR and dark will be assumed if the voltage is greater than 1.5V.

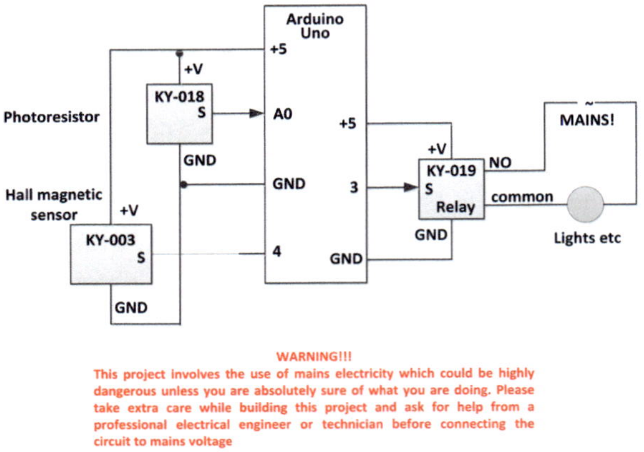

Figure 4.54 Circuit diagram of the project

Program Listing: Figure 4.55 shows the program listing (program **LDR2**). At the beginning of the program, the connections to the photoresistor, relay, and the Hall magnetic sensor are defined. Inside the setup routine, the relay and the Hall magnetic sensor are configured as output and input respectively. The relay is de-activated at the beginning of the program. Inside the program loop, the analog voltage across the LDR is read and stored in a variable called **ldrv**. Also, the state of the Hall magnetic sensor is read and stored in a variable called **hallswitch**. After converting the voltage across the LDR into millivolts, this voltage is compared with the dark voltage called **DARK**. If it is dark and the output of the Hall magnetic sensor is at logic LOW (the i.e. door is opened), then the relay is activated for 30 seconds, otherwise, the door relay remains de-activated.

```
/*****************************************************************
 *      TURN ON LIGHTS WHEN IT IS DARK AND DOOR IS OPENED
 *      =================================================
 *
 * In this program the KY-018 photoresistor is connected to analog
 * input A0 of the Arduino Uno. Additionally, KY-019 relay module
 * is connected as an output to port pin 3, and KY003 Hall magnetic
 * field sensor module is connected to port pin 4. The project detects
 * when it is dark and also when the door is opened and then activates
 * the relay for 30 seconds. At the end of 30 seconds the relay is
 * de-activated. The relay could be connected for example to mains
 * lights or to some other equipment.
 *
 * Author: Dogan Ibrahim
 * Date  : April 2019
 * File  : LDR2
 *****************************************************************/
#define OFF LOW
#define ON HIGH
int LDR = 0;                                    // Photosensor
```

```
int Relay = 3;                                          // Relay pin
int Hall = 4;                                           // Hall effect sensor
int DARK = 1500;

//
// Configure Relay as output and de-activate it to start with
//
void setup ()
{
  pinMode(Relay, OUTPUT);                               // Relay output
  pinMode(Hall, INPUT);                                 // Hall is input
  digitalWrite(Relay, OFF);                             // Relay OFF
}

//
// This is the main program loop. Check if its dark by reading the
// voltage across the LDR. If its greater than 1500mV then it is
// assumed that it is dark. If also the door is opened then activate
// the relay for 30 secs
//
void loop ()
{
     int ldrv = analogRead(LDR);                        // Read LDR
     int hallswitch = digitalRead(Hall);                // Hall switch
     float mV = ldrv * 5000.0 / 1024.0;                 // LDR voltage
     if(mV > DARK && hallswitch == LOW)                 // If dark and door opened
// If its is dark
     {
        digitalWrite(Relay, ON);                        // Relay ON
        delay(30000);                                   // 30 secs delay
        digitalWrite(Relay, OFF);                       // Relay OFF
     }
     else
        digitalWrite(Relay, OFF);                       // Relay OFF
}
```

Figure 4.55 program listing

Raspberry Pi Program Listing: The minimum operating voltage of the KY-003 module is specified as 4.5V. Because of this, it will be necessary to use the KY-051 voltage translator module to boost the Raspberry Pi pin output voltage to +5V. The Raspberry Pi program is not given here as it can easily be derived from the last two projects.

ESP32 DevKitC Program Listing: As with the Raspberry Pi version of the project, we need to use the KY-051 voltage translator module to boost the ESP32 DevKitC pin output voltage to +5V. The ESP32 DevKitC program is very similar to the program given in the previous project and it can easily be derived by the readers.

4.2.9 Project 9 – Secret Key using the photo interrupter (light barrier) module

Description: In this project, a photo interrupter module is used to detect a code and activate a buzzer if the code is correct. A pre-defined secret key is stored inside the processor. Parts of a long transparent plastic in the form of tape are covered by opaque regions and these constitute the key. This plastic tape is passed between the sensors of the photo interrupter module at a slow speed. The module detects the transparent and opaque regions of the tape where the opaque regions are given code 1 and transparent regions are given code 0. If the code of the key matches the stored secret key then the active buzzer sounds (you may like to use a relay instead of a buzzer and for example open a door if the code is correct) for 10 seconds. Figure 4.56 shows the plastic key tape used in this project.

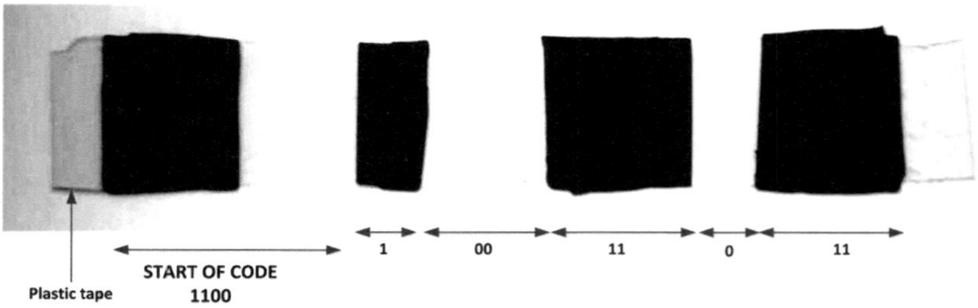

Figure 4.56 Plastic key tape used in the project

Aim: The aim of this project is to show how the photo interrupter module and the active buzzer module can be used in a project.

Sensors Used: Two modules are used in this project from the sensor kit: KY-010 photo interrupter (light barrier) module, and the KY-012 active piezo buzzer module. Figure 4.57 shows a picture of the KY-010 photo interrupter module. Basically, this module consists of an LED light emitter and a light activated transistor light detector with a gap between them. Normally, the emitted light falls on the base of the transistor thus turning the transistor ON and as a result, the output of the module is at logic LOW. When the light between the emitter and the detector is blocked (e.g. by placing an opaque object between them) then the transistor is cut-off and the output of the module goes to logic HIGH. KY-010 operates with a voltage +3.3V to +5V and it is a 3-pin module with the pins: GND, +V, and output (S).

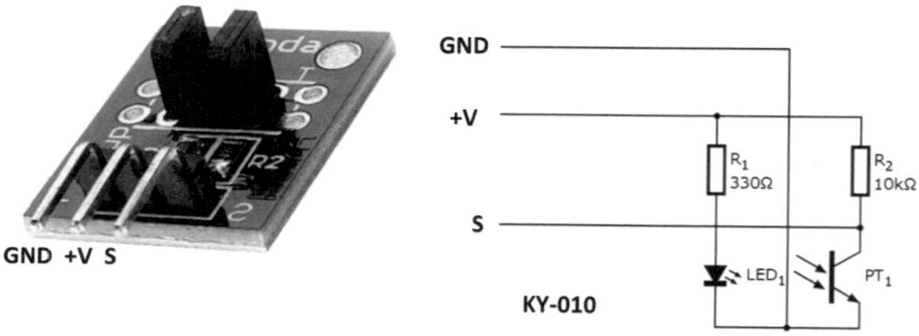

Figure 4.57 KY-010 photo interrupter module

KY-012 is an active piezo buzzer module as shown in Figure 4.58. Although there are 3-pins, the module has only 2-pins in use: GND and input (S). When the input is at logic HIGH the module produces a single tone sound with a frequency of approximately 2.5kHz. The basic specifications of this module are:

- Operating voltage: +3.3V to +5V
- Operating current: 30mA (at +5V)
- Sound output frequency: 2500Hz ± 300Hz
- Sound output: 85dB (at 10cm)

Figure 4.58 KY-012 active buzzer module

Background Information: Photo interrupter circuits basically consists of a light emitting part and a light receiving part, aligned facing each other in a single package (see Figure 4.59). The circuit detects light blockages when an object comes between both parts of the circuit. Some photo interrupter circuits employ visible light LEDs, although most of them use infrared light so that the operation of the circuit is not affected by ambient lighting.

Figure 4.59 A typical photo interrupter

As we shall see in a later Chapter, basically, there are two types of piezo buzzers used in electronic circuits: active buzzers, and passive buzzers. The difference between the two types of buzzers is that the active buzzers produce sound at a single frequency and this cannot be changed. Applying a logic HIGH voltage to the active buzzer will produce the sound. Passive piezo buzzers, on the other hand, can generate sounds in the frequency range of 1kHz to 3kHz. These buzzers are normally driven using PWM waveforms such that the produced sound frequency depends on the frequency of the input waveform.

Key Tape: As shown in Figure 4.56, parts of a plastic tape were covered by opaque material so that passing the tape through the photo-interrupter will generate different codes. An opaque region will block the light and therefore generate a logic 1. A transparent region, on the other hand, does not block the light and it will generate a logic 0. In this project, the width of a unit region on the tape is taken to be 1cm. Therefore, an opaque region 2cm wide will generate 11, a 1cm transparent region will generate 0 and so on. At the beginning of the tape 2cm wide opaque region was made, followed by 2cm wide transparent region and this is assumed to be the START of the key code, which translates to 1100. This is followed by 8 bits of key code. Overall, the following code is generated by the tape (if the speed of sliding the tape is correct!):

1100	10011011
START	KEY

The photo interrupter module constantly looks for the START code and once this is detected the remaining 8 bits of the key code are read. By sliding the tape inside the photo interrupter module, it is expected to generate the above code. This will require some training since the success of generating the correct key code depends entirely on the speed that the tape is slid inside the photo interrupter module. This is controlled by a delay function in the program.

Block Diagram: Figure 4.60 shows a block diagram of the project.

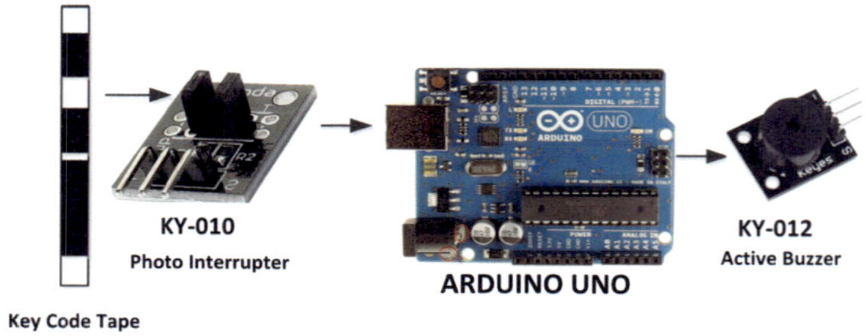

Figure 4.60 Block diagram of the project

Arduino Uno Circuit Diagram: The circuit diagram of the project is shown in Figure 4.61. S pin of the photo interrupter and the active buzzer are connected to port pins 2 and 3 of the Arduino Uno respectively. The other pins are connected to GND and +5V as shown in Figure 4.210.

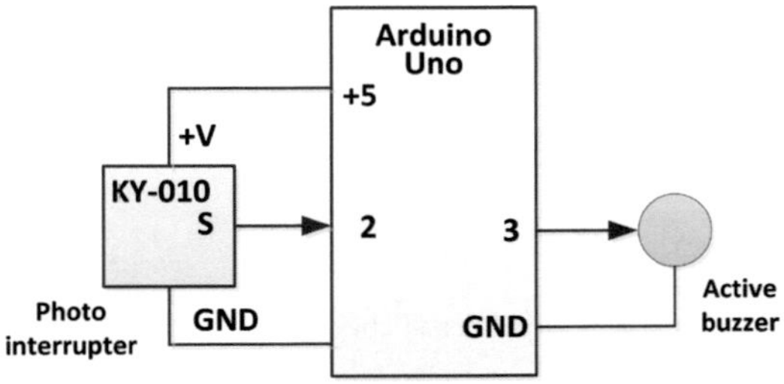

Figure 4.61 Circuit diagram of the project

Arduino Uno Program Listing: The program is shown in Figure 4.62 (program: **photoint**). At the beginning of the program, the connections between the passive buzzer and the photo interrupter module are defined. Inside the setup routine, buzzer and the photo interrupter module are configured as output and input respectively. Also, the buzzer is turned OFF at the start of the program. Notice that the serial monitor is also enabled as it can be helpful while adjusting the delay in the program. This can, however, be removed if required. Inside the main program loop, the START bits are read and if this is successful then the remaining 8 key bits are read and stored in integer array **ReceivedCode**. The received code is then compared with the secret code in integer array **SecretCode**, and if there is a match then the buzzer is activated for 10 seconds.

```
/*****************************************************************
 *             PHOTO INTERRUPT SECRET KEY
 *             ==========================
 *
 * In this program the KY-010 photo interrupter module is used. A
 * tape with a key code on it is passed through the photo interrupter
 * slot and the generated code is compared with a secret key code
 * stored in Arduino Uno. If the correct key is geenrated then the
 * active buzer is activated for 10 seconds.
 *
 * Author: Dogan Ibrahim
 * Date  : April 2019
 * File  : photoint
 *****************************************************************/
int PhotoInterrupt = 2;                    // Photo interrupt
int Buzzer = 3;                            // Buzzer
int SecretCode[] = {1,0,0,1,1,0,1,1};      // Secret code
int ReceivedCode[8];
int flag, k;


//
// Configure active buzzer as output and de-activate it to start with
//
void setup ()
{ Serial.begin(9600);
```

```
  pinMode(Buzzer, OUTPUT);                      // Buzzer output
  pinMode(PhotoInterrupt, INPUT);               // Photo interrupt input
  digitalWrite(Buzzer, LOW);                    // Buzzer OFF
}

//
// This function reads a bit from the photo interrupt module
//
int Read()
{
    int r = digitalRead(PhotoInterrupt);        // Read a bit
    return r;
}

//
// This function generates delay (you should adjust this delay until
// correct speed is obtained)
//
void del()
{
    delay(300);                                 // 300ms delay
}

//
// This is the main program loop. Read the code on the tape. First,
// read the START bits and if successful, carry on reading the key
// code bits. Then compare the received bits with the secret key.
// If there is a match, sound the buzzer for 10 seconds
//
void loop ()
{
  back:
    Serial.println("START");                  // Display message
    while(Read() == 0);                       // Wait to rcv 1
    del();                                    // Small delay
    if(Read() == 0) goto back;                // Go if not 1
    del();                                    // Small delay
    if(Read() == 1) goto back;                // Go if not 0
    del();                                    // Small delay
    if(Read() == 1) goto back;                // Go if not 0
    del();                                    // Small delay

    Serial.println("START Received OK");
    for(int k = 0; k < 8; k++)                // Read remaining 8 bits
     {
       ReceivedCode[k] = Read();              // Save rcvd bits
```

```
            del();                                    // Small delay
         }

    //
    // Compare the received code and Secret Code. If flag=0 at the end
    // the it means that there is match. i.e. the key code is ok
    //
          flag = 0;
          for(k = 0; k < 8; k++)
          {
            if(ReceivedCode[k] != SecretCode[k]) flag = 1;
          }

          if(flag == 0)                               // If code rcvd ok
          {
            Serial.println("CODE RECEIVED OK");       // Display message
            digitalWrite(Buzzer, HIGH);               // Turn ON Buzzer
            delay(10000);                             // 10 secs delay
            digitalWrite(Buzzer, LOW);                // Buzzer OFF
          }
          else
            digitalWrite(Buzzer, LOW);                // Buzzer OFF
    }
```

Figure 4.62 Program listing

Suggestions: You may find it difficult to adjust the speed at which you slide the tape inside the photo interrupter module. It might be worthwhile to change the delay time and try until the correct code is generated. Also, you could replace the buzzer with a relay and for example open a door if the correct key code is received. You can also change the length of the code to make it more difficult.

Figure 4.63 shows the project built on a breadboard

Figure 4.63 Project built on a breadboard

ESP32 DevKitC Project: The ESP32 DevKitC project block diagram is the same as in Figure 4.60, but Arduino should be replaced with ESP32 DevKitC. Also, the circuit diagram of the ESP32 DevKitC version is similar to Figure 4.61, but port pins 2 and 3 should be replaced with ESP32 DevKitC pins (e.g. 22 and 23), and KY-010 should be powered from the +3.3V on ESP32 DevKitC. The same program as in Figure 4.62 can be used after making the above changes and also setting the board type to ESP32 Dev Module.

Raspberry Pi Project: The Raspberry Pi project block diagram is the same as in Figure 4.60, but Arduino should be replaced with Raspberry Pi. Also, GPIO pins 17 and 3 are used for photo interrupter and relay interface respectively, and KY-010 should be powered from the +3.3V on Raspberry Pi. The program listing (program: **rpiphotoint.py**) is shown in Figure 4.64. The program initially waits to receive the START code (1100) and then reads the code stored on the tape. If this code matches the secret code then the buzzer is activated for 10 seconds.

```
#--------------------------------------------------------------
#
#              SECRET KEY USING THE PHOTO INTERRUPTER
#              ======================================
#
# In this project the KY-010 photo interrupter module and the
# active buzzer module are used. When the secret key is detected
# the buzzer is activated for 10 seconds
#
# Program: rpiphotoint.py
# Date   : April 2019
# Author : Dogan Ibrahim
#---------------------------------------------------------------
import RPi.GPIO as GPIO
import time

Buzzer = 3                                    # Buzzer interface
PhotoInterrupt = 17                           # Photo interrupt

GPIO.setmode(GPIO.BCM)
GPIO.setwarnings(False)
GPIO.setup(Buzzer, GPIO.OUT)                  # Buzzer is output
GPIO.setup(PhotoInterrupt, GPIO.IN)
GPIO.output(Buzzer, GPIO.LOW)                 # Buzzer OFF

SecretCode = [1,0,0,1,1,0,1,1]                # Secret code
ReceivedCode = [None]*10

#
# This function reads a bit from the photo interrupt module
#
```

```
def Read():
   r = GPIO.input(PhotoInterrupt)
   return r

#
# This function generates delay (you should adjust this delay)
#
def Del():
     time.sleep(0.3)                          # 300ms delay

#
# Program loop. Read the code on teh tape. First, read the START
# bits (1100) and if successful, carry on reading the key code bits.
# Then, compare the received bits with the secret key. If there
# is a match, sound the buzzer for 10 seconds
#
while True:
  flag = 0
  while(flag == 0):
     print("START")
     while(Read() == 0):
        pass
     Del()

     if Read() == 1:
       Del()
       if Read() == 0:
         Del()
         if Read() == 0:
            Del()
            print("START Received OK")
            flag = 1

  for k in range(8):                          # Receive the code
    ReceivedCode[k] = Read()
    Del()

#
# Compare the received code and Secret Code. If flag=0 then
# correct code is received
#
  flag = 0
  for k in range(8):
    if(ReceivedCode[k] != SecretCode[k]):
         flag = 1
```

```
if flag == 0:
   print("CODE RECEIVED OK")
   GPIO.output(Buzzer, GPIO.HIGH)
   time.sleep(10)
   GPIO.output(Buzzer, GPIO.LOW)
else:
   GPIO.output(Buzzer, GPIO.LOW)
```

Figure 4.64 Raspberry Pi program listing

Figure 4.65 shows the project built on a breadboard

4.2.10 Project 10 – Using the magic light cup module

Description: In this project the KY-027 Magic Light Cup module is used. This module consists of a set of two small boards. Each board is mounted with a mercury tilt switch and an independent LED. The boards can be used on their own in tilt-sensing applications, where the LED becomes activated when the board is tilted. The boards can also be used as a pair in special effects projects such as magic light cup projects, where the LEDs are driven using PWM and we can achieve the effect of light being **magically** transferred from one module to the other one when both modules are tilted together. As one LED fades the other one gets brighter and vice versa.

Aim: The aim of this project is to show how the magic light cup effect can be achieved using the KY-027 set of modules.

Sensors Used: Only the KY-027 set of two modules is used in this project. Since both sets are identical, only the operation of one of the modules is described here. As shown in Figure 4.66, each set of the module has 4-pins and they consist of a mercury switch mounted horizontally to the board, an LED which is mounted vertically, and a 10K pull-up resistor for the switch:

L (LED pin)
S (Switch pin)
+V
GND

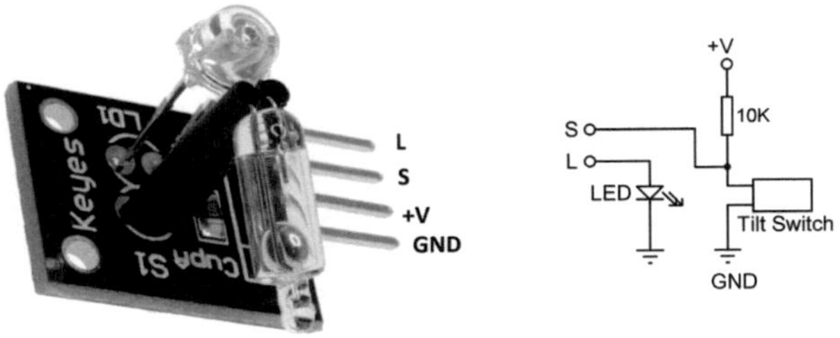

Figure 4.66 One of KY-027 boards

Block Diagram: Figure 4.66 shows the block diagram of the project.

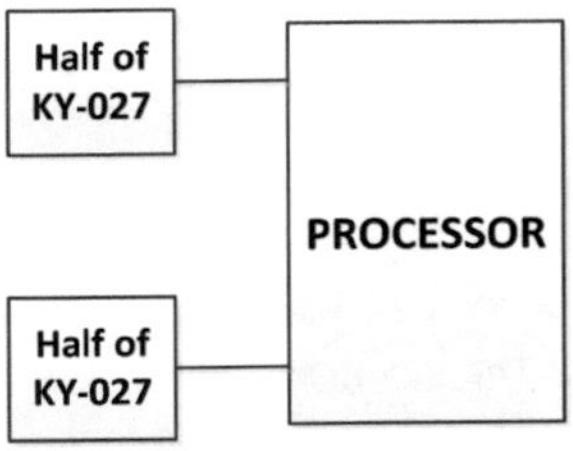

Figure 4.67 Block diagram of the project

Arduino Uno Circuit Diagram: The circuit diagram is shown in Figure 4.68. Notice that current limiting resistors are required in the LED circuits to limit the current through the LEDs and also to limit the processor output current.

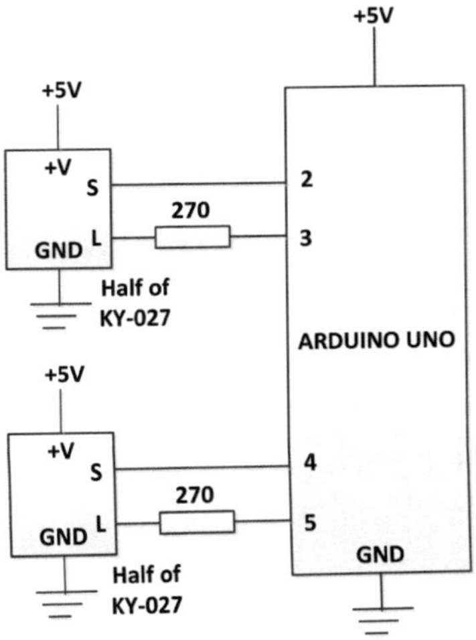

Figure 4.68 Arduino Uno circuit diagram

Arduino Uno Program Listing: The program listing is shown in Figure 4.69 (program: **magiclight**). At the beginning of the program, the connections to the module are specified. MAX and MIN are set to 255 and 0 respectively. Inside the setup routine, the switch pins are configured as inputs and the LED pins are configured as outputs. Normally, when a board is held horizontally the switch output is 0. The switch output goes to 1 if the board is tilted towards the switch, otherwise, the switch state remains at 0. Inside the main program loop, the state of a switch is read. If the board is tilted towards the switch (output HIGH) then the brightness of the corresponding LED is incremented, otherwise, it is decremented. The same applies to both switches and LEDs. The brightness of an LED is changed by changing the Duty Cycle of the PWM waveform sent to the LED using the built-in statement **analogWrite**. The Duty cycle can take an integer value between 0 and 255, where 255 corresponds to full voltage, and 0 corresponds to zero voltage.

It is important that both boards must be positioned such that the switches are at opposite sides and both boards must be tilted in the same direction at the same time. The net result is that as the brightness of one LED fades, the other one gets brighter.

```
/*****************************************************************
 *                   MAGIC LIGHT CUP
 *                   ===============
 *
 * In this program a KY-027 magic light cup module is connected to
 * the Arduino Uno. The program generates the effect that light falls
 * from one LED to the other LED. As one LED fades, the other LED
 * gets brighter and so on.
 *
 * Normally the switch output is 0. When the board is tilted towards
 * the switch (holding the board such that the connector is at the right
 * hand or laft hand side of the board) then the switch output becomes 1.
 * If the board is tilted away from the switch then the switch output
 * remains at 0
 *
 * Author: Dogan Ibrahim
 * Date  : May 2019
 * File  : magiclight
 *****************************************************************/
int Switch1 = 2;                                  // Switch1 pin
int LED1 = 3;                                     // LED1 pin
int Switch2 = 4;                                  // Switch2 pin
int LED2 = 5;                                     // LED2 pin
int Switch1State = 0;                             // Switch1 state
int Switch2State = 0;                             // Switch2 state
int Brightness1 = 0;                              // LED1 brightness
int Brightness2 = 0;                              // LED2 brightness

#define TiltedTowardsSwitch HIGH
#define MAX 255                                   // Duty cycle=255
```

```
#define MIN 0                                          // Duty cycle=0

void setup ()
{
  pinMode(LED1, OUTPUT);                               // LED1 is output
  pinMode(LED2, OUTPUT);                               // LED2 is output
  pinMode(Switch1, INPUT);                             // Switch1 is input
  pinMode(Switch2, INPUT);                             // Switch2 is inpu
}


//
// Read the state of Switch1 and if it is tilted towards the switch
// then increase its brightness. At the same time read state of Switch2
// and if it is tilted towards the switch then decrease its brightness
//
void loop ()
{
  Switch1State = digitalRead(Switch1);                 // Read Switch1
  if(Switch1State == TiltedTowardsSwitch)              // If tilted
  {
      Brightness1++;                                   // Increase brightness
      if(Brightness1 > MAX)Brightness1 = MAX;
  }
  else
  {
      Brightness1--;                                   // Decrease brightness
      if(Brightness1 < MIN)Brightness1 = MIN;
  }

  Switch2State = digitalRead(Switch2);                 // Read Switch2
  if(Switch2State == TiltedTowardsSwitch)              // If tilted
  {
      Brightness2++;                                   // Increaase brightness
      if(Brightness2 > MAX)Brightness2 = MAX;
  }
  else
  {
      Brightness2--;                                   // Decrease brightness
      if(Brightness2 < MIN)Brightness2 = MIN;
  }

  analogWrite(LED1, Brightness1);                      // Set LED1 brightness
  analogWrite(LED2, Brightness2);                      // Set LED2 brightness
  delay(10);
}
```

Figure 4.69 Arduino Uno program listing

Figure 4.70 to Figure 4.72 show the two boards being tilted at the same time.

Figure 4.70 Boards held together before tilting

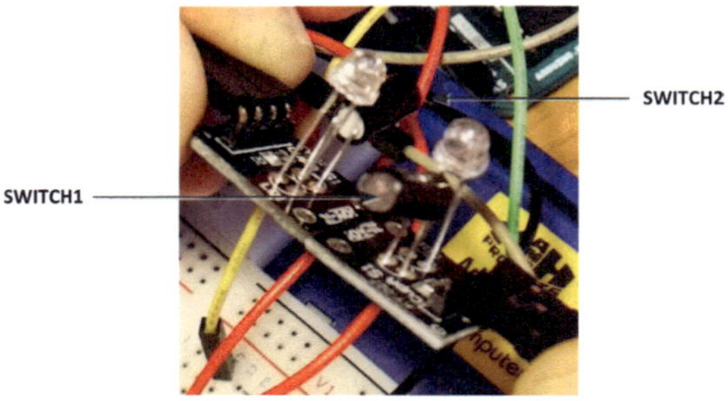

Figure 4.71 Boards tilted towards Switch2

Figure 4.72 Boards tilted towards Switch1

ESP32 DevKitC Project: The ESP32 DevKitC project is similar to the Arduino Uno version, but the +V pins of the sensor module should be connected to +3.3V. Also, the ADC and PWM functions described in Sections 4.2.1 and 4.2.7 should be used.

Raspberry Pi Project: The +V pins of the sensor module should be connected to +3.3V. Raspberry Pi does not include an ADC. The functions described in Sections 4.2.1 and 4.2.6 should be used for analog functions.

4.3 Summary

In this Chapter, we have developed 10 projects using the light modules in the sensor kit. Some of the projects also use the tilt sensor, relay, and active buzzer.

In the next Chapter, we will be developing projects using the Infrared transmitter/receiver pair of the sensor kit.

Chapter 5 • Infrared receiver-transmitter projects

5.1 Overview

In the previous Chapter, we have seen how to develop projects for the Arduino Uno, Raspberry Pi, and ESP32 using the light modules and some other modules in the sensor kit.

In this Chapter, we will be developing projects using the infrared receiver and transmitter modules distributed with the sensor kit.

5.2 Project 1 – Receiving and decoding the codes of commercial IR handsets

Description: In this project, we will receive codes from a commercial IR handset and decode and display them.

Aim: The aim of this project is to show how we can receive IR codes from a commercial handset using the library functions.

Sensor Used: In this project, the KY-022 sensor is used. This is a 3-pin IR LED type sensor chip with the following basic specifications:

- Type: 1838 IR LED sensor with built-in IC
- 38kHz carrier frequency
- Operating voltage: 2.7V to 5.5V
- Operating current: 0.4mA to 1.5mA
- Reception distance: 18 meters

As shown in Figure 5.1, the pins are GND, +V, and output (S). The sensor can easily be connected to Arduino, ESP32 DevKitC, and Raspberry Pi processors without any additional components. A 1K pull-up resistor together with an LED is used on the board.

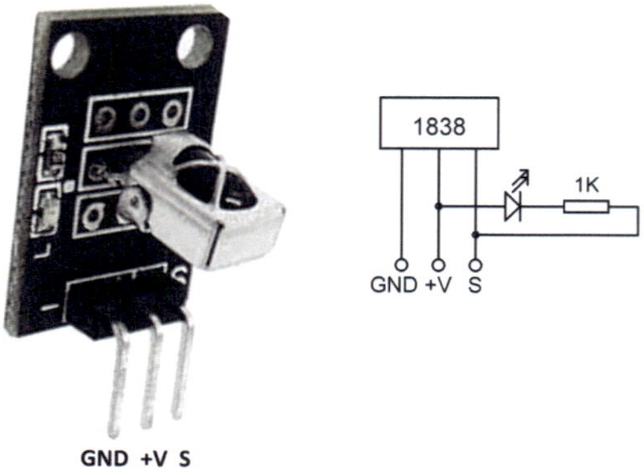

Figure 5.1 KY-022 IR LED sensor

Background Information: Infrared (IR) protocols use an IR LED to transmit infrared light to a receiver by switching the LED ON and OFF at certain frequencies, usually in the form of PWM waveforms. Most commonly used IR frequencies are 36kHz, 38kHz, or 40kHz, although there are some systems that use lower or higher frequencies. In most IR operations only a small number of data rate is used since the required control functions are very simple, e.g. turn the volume up/down, change the TV channel up/down, etc. Several different modulation techniques are used in IR transmitter/receiver protocols (see: http://www.vishay.com/docs/80071/dataform.pdf). In **Bi-Phase Coding**, a rising edge within a time window is equivalent to logic 1, a falling edge is equivalent to logic 0. In **Pulse Distance Coding**, the time between the bursts depends on the value of the bit, but all bursts have the same length. In **Pulse Length Code**, two kinds of burst lengths are used depending on the bit value.

Different appliances controlled with remote IR handsets have different IR codes for different control functions. When a button is pressed on the handset, the processor inside the handset sends the corresponding modulated signal (i.e. code) to the IR LED mounted in front of the appliance. The receiver processor then decodes the code and implements the required control action.

There are many IR codes as shown in Table 5.1. Most commonly used IR codes are the RC5 and NEC. RC5 operates with a carrier frequency of 36kHz and is based on bi-phase coding. It was developed by Philips and has been adopted by many European and US manufacturers. RC5 can be used to send 2048 different commands, organized in the form of 32 addressable groups, each having up to 64 commands. Every equipment has its own address so that for example increasing the volume of your TV does not affect the volume of your Hi-Fi equipment. Some of the RC5 codes are shown in Table 5.2 (see: http://read.pudn.com/downloads157/sourcecode/embed/701593/docs/IR%20Formats%201.PDF for more information).

Code	Manufacturer
RC5	Philips, Grundig, Loewe, Marantz
NEC	Canon, Yamaha, Harman-Kardon
SIRCS	Sony
SAMSUNG	Samsung
JAPAN	Loewe, Panasonic
RECS80	Nordmende, Thomson

Table 5.1 Some popular IR codes and manufactures using them

Handset key	Key function
Volume +	16
Volume -	17
Brightness +	18
Brightness -	19

Table 5.2 Some RC5 TV codes

NEC code operates at 38kHz and is mainly used by Japanese manufacturers. The advantage of the RC5 protocol is that any handset can be used to control any brand of equipment that is compatible with the RC5 protocol. The advantage of the NEC protocol is that there is no interference between handsets made by different manufacturers.

We do not need to know the details of these codes since there are library functions that can be used to transmit, receive, and decode the IR codes easily. In this and the following sections, we will be developing projects using the IR receiver and transmitter modules distributed in the sensor kit.

Figure 5.2 shows some commercial IR handsets.

Figure 5.2 Some commercial IR handsets

Block Diagram: Figure 5.3 shows the block diagram of the project. A commercial TV handset is used in this project (the reader can use any model IR handset in this project).

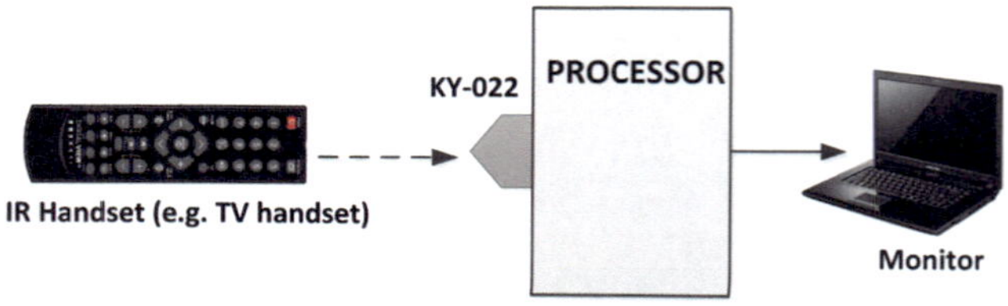

Figure 5.3 Block diagram of the project

Arduino Uno Circuit Diagram: The circuit diagram of the project is shown in Figure 5.4. S pin of the KY-022 is connected to port pin 2 of the Arduino Uno, while the GND and +V pins are connected to the ground and +5V pins respectively.

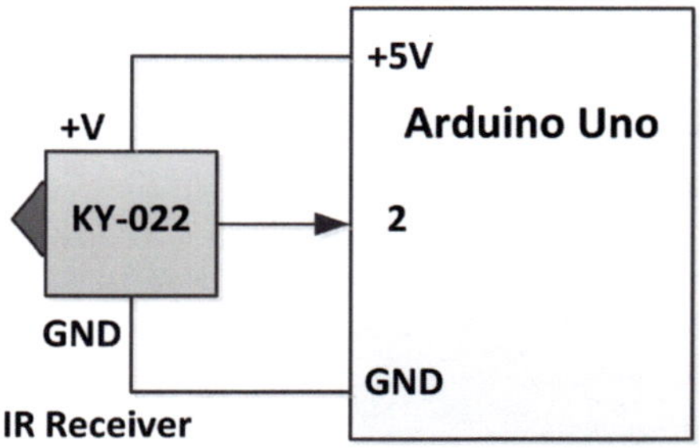

Figure 5.4 Circuit diagram of the project

Arduino Uno Program Listing: The IR library must be downloaded and included in the program before we can use the IR functions. There are several IR libraries available for the Arduino. In this project, we will be using the library by **z3t0** which can decode a large number of IR codes. The steps are as follows:

- Go to the following GitHub site:

  https://github.com/z3t0/Arduino-IRremote

- Click the green **Clone or download** button at the right-hand side (Figure 5.5), and then click download ZIP. You should copy the downloaded file **Arduino-IR-remote.master.zip** to a folder on your PC.

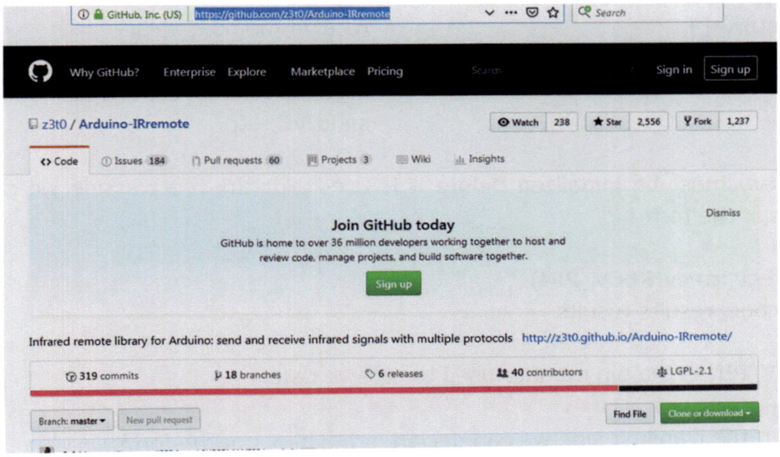

Figure 5.5 Click the Clone or download button

- Start your Arduino IDE and click **Sketch -> Include Library -> Add .ZIP Library** (Figure 5.6). Browse the library file you have downloaded.

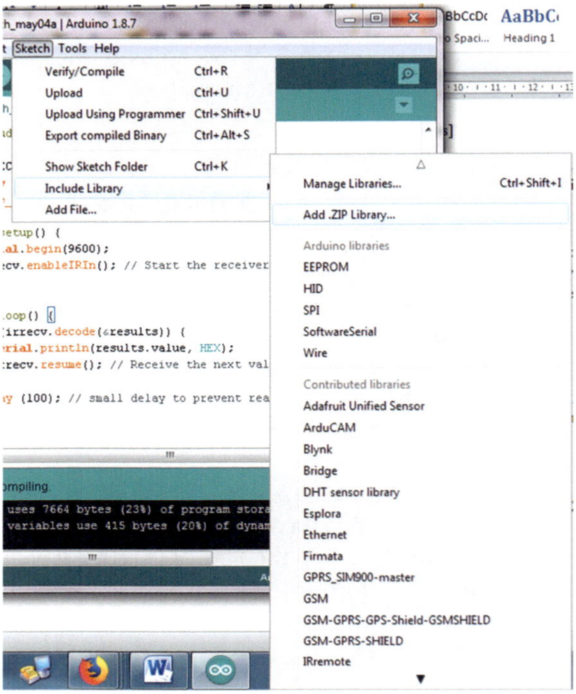

Figure 5.6 Add the .ZIP library

The functions supported by the IR library are summarized below:

enableIRIn():	enable the IR receiver
decode(&results):	decode the received code
resume():	receive the next value
sendmmm(code value, code len):	sends data in the code specified by **mmm**, e.g. sendSony, sendPanasonic, sendNEC, sendJVC, etc.

The IR library must be initialized before it is used. For the receive side we can declare statements of the form:

```
IRrecv irrecv(RECV_PIN)
decode_results results
```

where RECV_PIN is the pin number used to receive data

Similarly, for the transmit side we can declare statements of the form:

```
IRsend irsend
```

Different models of Arduino use different pins to transmit the IR code (check the web site: http://z3t0.github.io/Arduino-IRremote/). For the Arduino Uno, port pin 3 must be used.

Figure 5.7 shows the Arduino Uno program listing (program: **IRhandset**). The IR header file **IRremote.h** is included at the beginning of the program. Connection of the KY-022 to Arduino is then defined as port pin 2. Inside the setup routine, the IR receiver is enabled. The commands sent by the IR handset are received, decoded and displayed on the serial monitor.

```
/*********************************************************************
 *            DISPLAY CODES OF A COMMERCIAL IR HANDSET
 *            ========================================
 *
 * In this program the KY-022 IR LED receiver module is connected
 * to port pin 2 of the Arduino Uno. The program receives codes from
 * a commercial IR handset and displays these codes on serial monitor
 *
 * Author: Dogan Ibrahim
 * Date  : April 2019
 * File  : IRhandset
 ********************************************************************/
#include <IRremote.h>                          // Include IR header file

int RECV_PIN = 2;                              // KY-022 S pin at pin 2
IRrecv irrecv(RECV_PIN);                       // Initialize library
decode_results results;

void setup()
{
  Serial.begin(9600);                          // Start serial monitor
  irrecv.enableIRIn();                         // Enable the IR receiver
}

//
// Inside the main program loop, decode and display the received
// IR codes from the handset
//
void loop()
{
  if (irrecv.decode(&results))
  {
    Serial.println(results.value, DEC);        // Display in decimal
    irrecv.resume();                           // Rcv next code
  }
}
```

Figure 5.7 Arduino Uno program listing

The handset used in this project was a Panasonic smart TV handset (Figure 5.8). A list of some of the key presses and the resulting codes are shown in Table 5.3 in both decimal and hexadecimal format (the program displays in decimal, to display in hexadecimal, change DEC to HEX in **Serial.println** statement.

Handset key pressed	Received code (DEC)	Received code (HEX)
1	4146609271	F7283C77
2	1971303647	757FB4DF
3	3007006103	B33B4597
4	1006888199	3C03E507
5	3875886367	E705551F
6	2762313415	A4A58EC7
7	3806617471	E2E45F7F
8	1806499567	6BACFEEF
9	243853599	E88E91F
0	2098629583	E88E91F
Channel up	1307002951	4DE74847
Channel down	193429999	B8781EF
Volume up	199473975	BE3BB37
Volume down	3571053223	D4D9F2A7

Table 5.3 Key presses and received codes

Figure 5.8 Handset used in the project

KY-022 infrared receiver module was connected to Arduino Uno using jumper wires as shown in Figure 5.9.

Figure 5.9 Connecting KY-022 to Arduino Uno

ESP32 DevKitC Program Listing: The ESP32 DevKitC version of the project is very similar to the Arduino Uno version, where KY-022 is connected to GPIO 2 of ESP32 DevKitC. Also, the +V pin of KY-022 should be connected to +3.3V pin of the ESP32 DevKitC. The same program as in Figure 5.7 can be used for the ESP32 DevKitC version, but before compiling the program make sure that you change the Board type from **Arduino/Genuino Uno** to **ESP32 Dev Module**, using **Tools -> Board** in the Arduino IDE.

Raspberry Pi Program Listing: Before developing the Raspberry Pi program, we have to install the IR library for Python. In this project, we will be using the LIRC (Linux Infrared Remote Control) library which allows us to decode and send IR signals. The installation process is as follows:

- Install the LIRC library and its dependencies:

  pi@raspberrypi:~$ **sudo apt-get install lirc liblircclient-dev**

- Setup LIRC by editing file **/etc/modules**:

  pi@raspberrypi:~$ **sudo nano /etc/modules**

- add the following lines to the end of this file (Figure 5.10) and save changes by entering Cntrl+X followed by Y. In this setup, GPIO 23 is configured as input and GPIO 22 as output:

lirc_dev
lirc_rpi gpio_in_pin=23 gpio_out_pin=22

```
pi@raspberrypi:~ $ cat /etc/modules
# /etc/modules: kernel modules to load at boot time.
#
# This file contains the names of kernel modules that should be loaded
# at boot time, one per line. Lines beginning with "#" are ignored.
i2c-bcm2837
i2c-dev
#
# LIRC infrared files
#
lirc_dev
lirc_rpi gpio_in_pin=23 gpio_out_pin=22

pi@raspberrypi:~ $
```

Figure 5.10 Edit file /etc/modules

- Create file **/etc/lirc/hardware.conf**:

pi@raspberrypi:~$ **sudo nano /etc/lirc/hardware.conf**

- Enter the statements as shown in Figure 5.11 and then save and exit by entering Cntrl+X followed by Y

```
pi@raspberrypi:~ $ cat /etc/lirc/hardware.conf
LIRCD_ARGS="--uinput"
LOAD_MODULES=true
DRIVER="default"
DEVICE="/dev/lirc0"
MODULES="lirc_rpi"
LIRCD_CONF=""
LIRCMD_CONF=""
```

Figure 5.11 File /etc/lirc/hardware.conf

- Edit file **/etc/lirc/lirc_options.conf**:

pi@raspberrypi:~$ **sudo nano /etc/lirc/lirc_options.conf**

- change the following lines:

driver = default
device = /dev/lirc0

- Save and exit the editor

- Edit file **/boot/config.txt:**

pi@raspberrypi:~$ **sudo nano /boot/config.txt**

- add the following line to the end of file, save and exit the file:

dtoverlay=lirc-rpi,gpio_in_pin=23,gpio_out_pin=22

- Restart your Raspberry Pi:

  pi@raspberrypi:~$ **sud24o reboot**

- Restart LIRC:

  pi@raspberrypi:~$ **sudo systemctl stop lircd.service**
  pi@raspberrypi:~$ **sudo systemctl start lircd.service**

- Check LIRC status:

  pi@raspberrypi:~$ **sudo systemctl status lircd.service**

Testing the IR Receiver
To test the IR receiver, connect the KY-022 S pin to GPIO 23 of Raspberry Pi and also connect +V and GND to the +3.3V and GND pins respectively. Run the following command to stop **lircd** and start outputting raw data from the IR receiver:

- pi@raspberrypi:~$ **sudo systemctl stop lircd.service**
- Use the **mode2** command to test the IR receiver:
- pi@raspberrypi:~$ **mode2 –d /dev/lirc0**
- Now, point your IR handset to KY-022 module and press some buttons. If everything is ok, you should see something similar to Figure 5.12.

```
pi@raspberrypi:~ $ mode2 -d /dev/lirc0
Using driver default on device /dev/lirc0
Trying device: /dev/lirc0
Using device: /dev/lirc0
space 16777215
pulse 3387
space 1812
pulse 394
space 474
pulse 398
space 1347
pulse 399
space 472
pulse 397
space 475
pulse 396
space 476
pulse 396
space 475
```

Figure 5.12 Testing the IR communication

We now have to configure the handset so that the commands of the handset can be decoded. This requires the creation of a file called /etc/lirc/lircd.conf. A large number of configuration files for many models and types of handsets are available at the following web site under Browse Code. Note that you can usually find the handset code marked at the back of your handset (for example, Panasonic, N2QAYB000239, etc):

http://sf.net/p/lirc-remotes

or, at the following web site:

http://lirc.sourceforge.net/remotes/

Recording Commands
You may skip this section if you found your handset codes in the above web sites.

For demonstration purposes, we will now configure some of the buttons on our handset. Valid button names can be listed by entering the following command:

pi@raspberrypi:~$ **irrecord --list | less**

Make sure that LIRC is not running and then enter the following command to start the recording process:

- pi@raspberrypi:~$ **irrecord -d /dev/lirc0**
- enter a name for the file, e.g.**DEMO**. The configuration details will be stored in file **DEMO.lircd.conf**
- Press buttons randomly on your handset until you see two lines with dots. Do not press the same button for more than 10 dots
- Now, we will record the codes for keys 1,2,3, UP and DOWN.
- Enter **KEY_1**
- Keep pressing button 1
- Enter **KEY_2**
- Keep pressing button 2
- Enter **KEY_3**
- Keep pressing button 3
- Enter **KEY_UP**
- Keep pressing up button

- Enter **KEY_DOWN**
- Keep pressing down button
- Press Enter to FINISH recording
- Keep pressing the same button repeatedly, but do not hold down the button.
- The configuration data will be written into the named file

Figure 5.13 shows the configuration file **DEMO.lircd.conf** created in this demo.

```
# Please take the time to finish this file as described in
# https://sourceforge.net/p/lirc-remotes/wiki/Checklist/
# and make it available to others by sending it to
# <lirc@bartelmus.de>
#
# This config file was automatically generated
# using lirc-0.9.4c(default) on Mon May 13 09:04:42 2019
# Command line used: -d /dev/lirc0
# Kernel version (uname -r): 4.14.98-v7+
#
# Remote name (as of config file): DEMO
# Brand of remote device, the thing you hold in your hand:
# Remote device model nr:
# Remote device info url:
# Does remote device has a bundled capture device e. g., a
#     usb dongle? :
# For bundled USB devices: usb vendor id, product id
#     and device string (use dmesg or lsusb):
# Type of device controlled
#     (TV, VCR, Audio, DVD, Satellite, Cable, HTPC, ...) :
# Device(s) controlled by this remote:

begin remote

  name  DEMO
  bits           16
  flags SPACE_ENC
  eps            30
  aeps          100

  header       3459  1743
  one           421  1311
  zero          421   452
  ptrail        429
```

```
  pre_data_bits   32
  pre_data       0x40040100
  gap           74760
  toggle_bit_mask 0x0
  frequency     38000

      begin codes
          KEY_1                        0x0809
          KEY_2                        0x8889
          KEY_3                        0x4849
          KEY_UP                       0x2C2D
          KEY_DOWN                     0xACAD
      end codes

end remote
```

Figure 5.13 File DEMO.lircd.conf

- Now, copy file **DEMO.lircd.conf** to folder **/etc/lirc/lircd.conf**

  pi@raspberrypi:~$ **sudo cp DEMO.lircd.conf /etc/lirc/lircd.conf**

- Start **irw** and press the recorded keys on the handset. You should see the key codes displayed as shown in Figure 5.14.

  pi@raspberrypi:~$ **irw**

```
pi@raspberrypi:~ $ sudo cp DEMO.lircd.conf /etc/lirc/lircd.conf
pi@raspberrypi:~ $ irw
0000400401000809 00 KEY_1 DEMO
0000400401000809 01 KEY_1 DEMO
0000400401008889 00 KEY_2 DEMO
0000400401004849 00 KEY_3 DEMO
0000400401002c2d 00 KEY_UP DEMO
000040040100acad 00 KEY_DOWN DEMO
```

Figure 5.14 key codes displayed

Python Program

Before writing the Python program we need to install the **pylirc** package and also create a button configuration file. The steps are given below:

- Install pylirc:

  pi@raspberrypi:~$ **sudo apt-get install python-pylirc**

- Create a file called **lircrc** in your default folder (/home/pi):

  pi@raspberrypi:~$ **nano lircrc**

- Define the buttons to be used in this file. An example is shown in Figure 5.15, where buttons 1,2, UP and DOWN are defined. In this file, you should define a button name (**button**, e.g. KEY_1), program name (**prog**) that will be used during the initialization of LIRC in Python, and a **config** name which will b returned when the specified key is pressed.

```
begin
 button=KEY_1
 prog=myprogram
 config=ONE
end

begin
 button=KEY_2
 prog=myprogram
 config=TWO
end

begin
 button=KEY_UP
 prog=myprogram
 config=UP
end

begin
 button=KEY_DOWN
 prog=myprogram
 config=DOWN
end
```

Figure 5.15 file lircrc

The program listing (program: **rpiIRhandset.py**) is shown in Figure 5.16. At the beginning of the program, LIRC and time modules are imported to the program. LIRC is then initialized and **lirc.nextcode()** is called to return the code of the button pressed on the IR handset.

Figure 5.17 shows a run of the program and the codes displayed when buttons 1,2, UP and DOWN are pressed on the handset.

```
#--------------------------------------------------------------
#
#             DISPLAY CODES OF A COMMERCIAL IR HANDSET
#             ========================================
#
# In this pogram the KY-022 IR receiver module is used. The
# program receives the IR codes of a commercial handset and
```

```
# then displays them on the monitor. KY-022 is connected to
# GPIO port pin 23 of Raspberry Pi
#
# Program: rpiIRhandset.py
# Date   : April 2019
# Author : Dogan Ibrahim
#----------------------------------------------------------------
import time
import pylirc as lirc

lirc.init("myprogram")

#
# Program loop. Receive the codes from a commercial IR handset
# and displays them
#
while True:
   s = lirc.nextcode()              # Get IR code
   if s != None:                    # If code received
     print(s)                       # Display code
   time.sleep(0.1)                  # Wait a bit
```

Figure 5.16 Program listing

```
pi@raspberrypi:~ $ sudo python rpiIRhandset.py
['ONE']
['TWO']
['UP']
['DOWN']
```

Figure 5.17 Typical run of the program

Modified Arduino Uno Program – Displaying the Raw Data

The Arduino Uno program given in Figure 5.7 can be modified to display the IR code type as well as the raw data codes. The modified program is shown in Figure 5.18 (program: **IRhandset2**). Figure 5.19 shows a typical output from the program when the channel-up button is pressed on a commercial IR handset. The satellite IR handset TM-MINI-M2 was used to generate the code in Figure 5.19. The display shows the code, total number of raw data, and the raw data as mark (+) and space (-).

```
/**********************************************************************
 *             DISPLAY RAW CODES OF A COMMERCIAL IR HANDSET
 *             ============================================
 *
 * In this program the KY-022 IR LED receiver module is connected
 * to port pin 2 of the Arduino Uno. The program receives data from
 * a commercial IR handset and displays the raw codes on serial monitor
 *
```

```
 * Author: Dogan Ibrahim
 * Date  : April 2019
 * File  : IRhandset2
 *******************************************************************/
#include <IRremote.h>                              // Include IR header file

int RX_PIN = 2;                                    // KY-022 S pin at pin 2
IRrecv irrecv(RX_PIN);                             // Initialize library
decode_results results;

void setup()
{
  Serial.begin(9600);                              // Start serial monitor
  irrecv.enableIRIn();                             // Enable the IR receiver
}

//
// Display teh Raw codes
//
void display(decode_results *results)
{
  int count = results -> rawlen;                   // Raw data length
//
// If known, display the protocol type
//
  if (results->decode_type == NEC)
     Serial.print("NEC: ");
  else if(results->decode_type == SONY)
     Serial.print("SONY: ");
  else if(results->decode_type == RC5)
     Serial.print("RC5: ");
  else if(results->decode_type == RC6)
     Serial.print("RC6: ");
  else if(results->decode_type == JVC)
     Serial.print("JVC: ");
  else if(results->decode_type == PANASONIC)
     Serial.print("PANASONIC: ");
  else
     Serial.print("UNKNOWN: ");
//
// Display IR code and raw data
//
   Serial.println(results->value, HEX);
   Serial.print("Raw data count = ");
   Serial.println(count, DEC);
```

```
      for (int i = 1; i < count; i++)
      {
       if (i & 1)
       {
         Serial.print("+ ");
         Serial.println(results->rawbuf[i]*USECPERTICK, DEC);
       }
       else
       {
         Serial.print("- ");
         Serial.println((unsigned long) results->rawbuf[i]*USECPERTICK, DEC);
       }
     }
   }


   //
   // Inside the main program loop, display the received IR codes in
   // Raw format
   //
   void loop()
   {
    if (irrecv.decode(&results))                     // If code received
    {
       display(&results);                            // Display Raw codes
       irrecv.resume();                              // Wait for next value
    }
   }
```

Figure 5.18 Modified Arduino Uno program

```
NEC: 4040D02F
Raw data count = 68
+ 8950
- 4450
+ 550
- 550
+ 550
- 1700
+ 550
- 550
+ 550
- 550
+ 600
- 550
+ 550
- 550
```

Figure 5.19 Typical display from the program

5.3 Project 2 – Controlling 2 - Colour LEDs with a commercial IR handset

Description: In this project a 2-colour (red+green) LED is connected to the processor and the LED colour is controlled from the handset used in the previous project. Table 5.4 shows that buttons 1 and 2 are used on the handset to control the LED colour. Pressing button 1 on the handset (KEY_1) turns ON the red LED. Similarly, pressing button 2 turns ON the green LED.

Handset Button	LED Colour
1	Red
2	Green

Table 5.4 Buttons used to control the LED colours

Aim: The aim of this project is to show how we can control devices connected to a processor using a commercial IR handset. In this project, we are using a 2-colour LED, but this can easily be replaced with relays so that electrical devices such as lamps, electrical doors, appliances, etc can be controlled from the handset.

Sensor Used: In this project KY-022 sensor is used as in the previous project. Additionally, the KY-029 2-colour LED module is used. As shown in Figure 5.20, KY-029 is a 3-pin device with the pins ground, red, and green. The LED is active when its pins are set to logic HIGH.

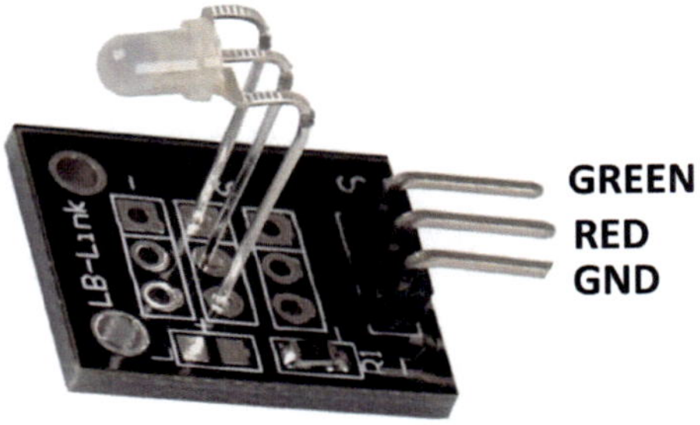

Figure 5.20 KY-029 2-colour LED

Block Diagram: Figure 5.21 shows the project block diagram.

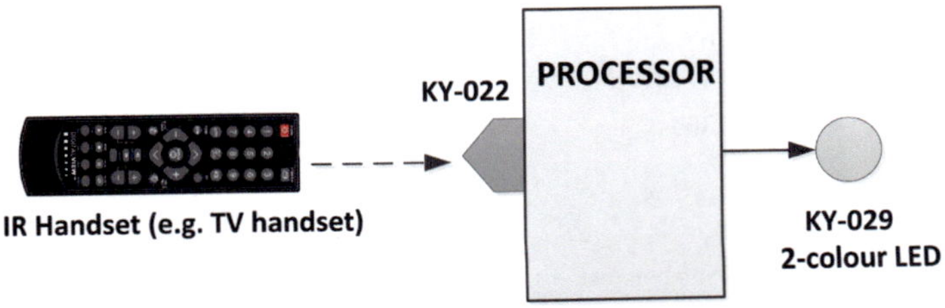

Figure 5.21 Block diagram of the project

Arduino Uno Circuit Diagram: The circuit diagram of the Arduino Uno version of the project is shown in Figure 5.22. KY-022 is connected to port pin 2 as before, and KY-029 red and green pins are connected to port pins 3 and 4 of the Arduino Uno respectively through 220 Ohm current limiting resistors.

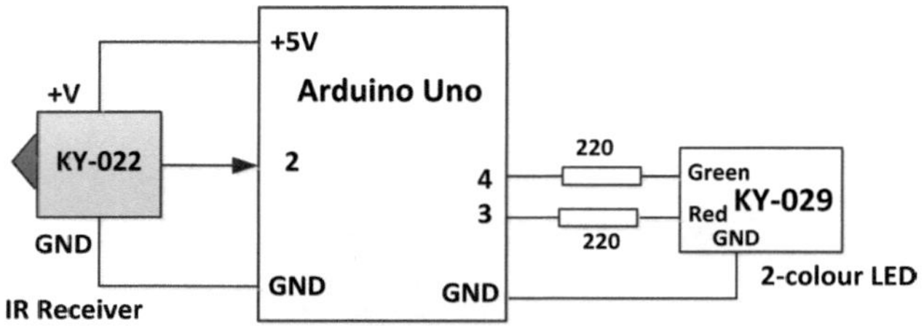

Figure 5.22 Arduino Uno circuit diagram of the project

Arduino Uno Program Listing: The Arduino Uno program listing (program: **IRLED**) is shown in Figure 5.23. At the beginning of the program, library **IRremote** is included, and the codes for buttons 1 and 2 are defined (see Table 5.3). Inside the setup routine red and green LED pins are configured as outputs and the LED is turned OFF. Inside the main program loop, the program waits until a button is pressed on the handset. If button 1 is pressed then the red LED is turned ON and the green one is turned OFF. If on the other hand button 2 is pressed then the green LED is turned ON and the red one is turned OFF.

```
/*****************************************************************
 *              CONTROL A 2-COLOUR LED WITH IR HANDSET
 *              ======================================
 *
 * In this program the KY-022 IR LED receiver module is connected
 * to port pin 2 of the Arduino Uno. Additionally, a KY-029 2-colour
 * LED is connected to port poins 3 (red) and 4 (green). The program
 * receives codes from a commercial IR handset and turns ON either
 * the red or the green LED. Pressing button 1 turns red ON, pressing
 * 2 turnd green ON
 *
 * Author: Dogan Ibrahim
 * Date  : April 2019
 * File  : IRLED
 *****************************************************************/
#include <IRremote.h>                          // Include IR header file
#define KEY1 4146609271                        // Code for button 1
#define KEY2 1971303647                        // Code for button 2

int RECV_PIN = 2;                              // KY-022 S pin at pin 2
int RedLED = 3;                                // KY-029 red pin
int GreenLED = 4;                              // KY-029 green pin

IRrecv irrecv(RECV_PIN);                       // Initialize library
decode_results results;
```

```
//
// Configure red and green LED pins as outputs and turn OFF the
// LED at the beginning of the program
//
void setup()
{
  pinMode(RedLED, OUTPUT);                    // Red LED is output
  pinMode(GreenLED, OUTPUT);                  // Green LED is output
  digitalWrite(RedLED, LOW);                  // Red LED OFF at start
  digitalWrite(GreenLED, LOW);                // Green LED OFF at start
  irrecv.enableIRIn();                        // Enable the IR receiver
}

//
// Inside the main program loop, decode and display the received
// IR codes from the handset and control the LED colours
//
void loop()
{
  if (irrecv.decode(&results))                // If code received
  {
    if(results.value == KEY1)                 // If KEY_1 pressed
    {
      digitalWrite(RedLED, HIGH);             // Red ON
      digitalWrite(GreenLED, LOW);            // Green OFF
    }
    else if(results.value == KEY2)            // If KEY_2 pressed
    {
      digitalWrite(GreenLED, HIGH);           // Green ON
      digitalWrite(RedLED, LOW);              // Red OFF
    }
    irrecv.resume();                          // Rcv next code
  }
}
```

Figure 5.23 Program listing

Figure 5.24 shows the project built on a breadboard.

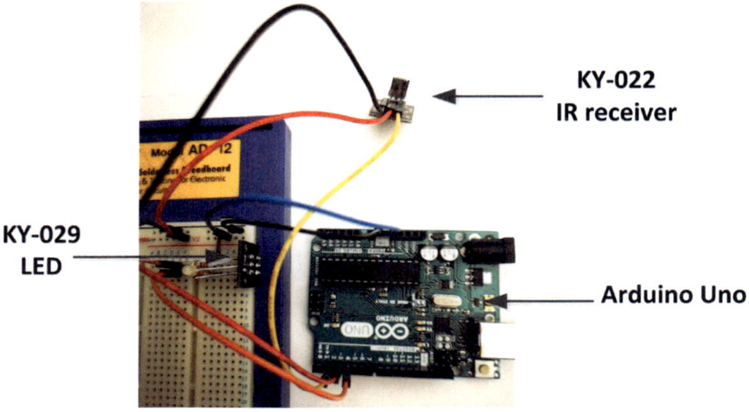

Figure 5.24 Project built on a breadboard

ESP32 DevKitC Program Listing: The ESP32 DevKitC version of the project is very similar to the Arduino Uno version, where KY-022 is connected to GPIO 2 of ESP32 DevKitC. Also, the +V pin of KY-022 should be connected to +3.3V pin of the ESP32 DevKitC. KY-029 red and green pins can be connected to GPIO 23 and 22 of the ESP32 DevKitC respectively through the same current limiting resistors. The same program as in Figure 5.21 can be used after making the above changes. Before compiling the program make sure that you change the Board type from **Arduino/Genuino Uno** to **ESP32 Dev Module**, using **Tools -> Board** in the Arduino IDE.

Raspberry Pi Program Listing: In the Raspberry Pi version of the program we will connect the S pin of KY-022 IR receiver module to GPIO 23 of the Raspberry Pi. Red and green pins of the KY-029 are connected to GPIO 17 and 27 respectively through 220 Ohm resistors as shown in Figure 5.25.

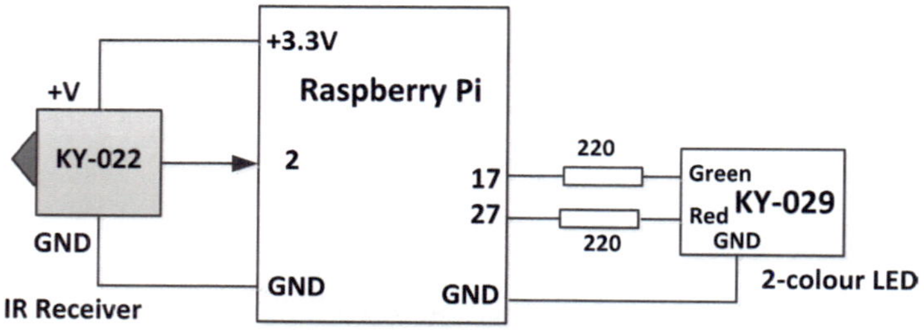

Figure 5.25 Raspberry Pi circuit diagram

Figure 5.26 shows the program listing (program: **rpiIRLED.py**). At the beginning of the program, **GPIO** and **pylirc** libraries are imported to the program, red and green LED connections are defined as 17 and 27 respectively. The LED pins are then configured as outputs and the LED is turned OFF. Inside the main program loop, the program waits to receive code from the IR handset. If button 1 is pressed then code **'ONE'** is received and the red LED is turned ON. If on the other hand button 2 is pressed then code **'TWO'** is received and the green LED is turned ON.

```
#--------------------------------------------------------------
#
#             CONTROL A 2-COLOUR LED WITH IR HANDSET
#             ======================================
#
# In this pogram the KY-022 IR receiver module is used. The
# program receives the IR codes of a commercial handset.
# Additionaly, a KY-029 2-colour LED is used. When button 1
# is pressed on the handset then the red LED is turned ON,
# when button 2 is pressed then the green LED is turned ON.
# S pi of KY-022 is connected to GPIO 23 of Raspberry Pi
#
# Program: rpiIRLED.py
# Date   : April 2019
# Author : Dogan Ibrahim
#---------------------------------------------------------------
import RPi.GPIO as GPIO                  # Import GPIO
import pylirc as lirc                    # Import LIRC

RedLED = 17                              # Red LED pin
GreenLED = 27                            # Green LED pin

GPIO.setmode(GPIO.BCM)
GPIO.setwarnings(False)
GPIO.setup(RedLED, GPIO.OUT)             # Configure red pin
GPIO.setup(GreenLED, GPIO.OUT)           # Configure green pin
GPIO.output(RedLED, GPIO.LOW)            # Turn OFF red LED
GPIO.output(GreenLED, GPIO.LOW)          # Turn OFF green LED

lirc.init("myprogram")
states = ['ONE', 'TWO']                  # Buttons 1,2 are used


#
# Program loop. Receive the codes from the commercial IR handset
# and control the LED colours as requested
#
while True:
   s = lirc.nextcode()                      # Get IR code
   if s != None:                            # If code received
     if s[0] == states[0]:                  # If 1 is pressed
       GPIO.output(RedLED, GPIO.HIGH)       # Red LED ON
       GPIO.output(GreenLED, GPIO.LOW)      # Green LED OFF
     elif s[0] == states[1]:                # If 2 is pressed
       GPIO.output(GreenLED, GPIO.HIGH)     # Green LED ON
       GPIO.output(RedLED, GPIO.LOW)        # Red LED OFF
```

Figure 5.26 Program listing

Figure 5.27 shows the project built on a breadboard.

Figure 5.27 Project built on a breadboard

5.4 Project 3 – Infrared transmitter - Scanning the TV channels using a commercial IR handset

Description: In this project, an infrared transmitter module is used to scan the TV channels. The program sends the correct code to the satellite receiver to increment the channels. Each channel is viewed for 5 seconds and then the next channel is selected. The handset used in Figure 5.19 is used in this project.

Aim: The aim of this project is to show how to use an IR transmitter module to transmit codes to a satellite receiver in order to increment the channel numbers.

Sensor Used: In this project, the KY-005 IR transmitter module is used. As shown in Figure 5.28, this is a 3-pin module consisting of an infrared LED. Only two pins of the module are used: GND and signal (S). The basic specifications of KY-005 are as follows:

- Operating voltage: 3.3V – 5V
- Forward voltage: 1.1V
- Forward current: 30mA – 60mA
- Power consumption: 90mW

Figure 5.28 KY-005 IR transmitter module

Block Diagram: Figure 5.29 shows the block diagram of the project.

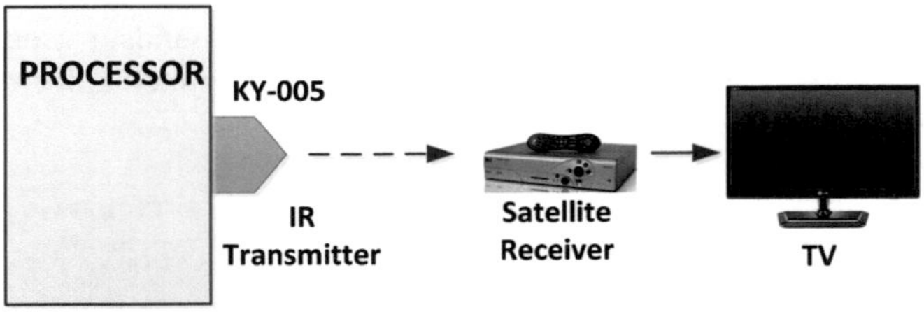

Figure 5.29 Block diagram of the project

Arduino Uno Circuit Diagram: KY-005 is simply an infrared LED and it must not be connected directly to an output port pin of a microcontroller without a current limiting resistor or some other circuitry. This is because the forward voltage of the LED is only 1.1V and it can be damaged if connected to a 5V output pin without any resistor. In addition, the forward current through the LED is specified as 30mA to 60mA. The maximum current output from an Arduino output port must not exceed 40mA and if connected directly to the LED, the output current at the port pin can exceed the recommended value. The range of the infrared module depends on the current through the LED and the higher the current the longer is the range. It may be worthwhile to use a transistor or a MOSFET to supply large current to the LED to increase its range. In this project, a transistor is used as a switch to supply current to the LED. The BC108 type NPN transistor is used in this project, although any other small NPN switching transistor could also be used instead.

Figure 5.30 shows the circuit diagram of the project. Port pin 3 of the Arduino Uno is connected to the base of the transistor through a resistor. A current limiting resistor is used in the collector circuit in series with the LED to provide 40mA current through the LED. The value of this resistor is calculated as follows:

R = (5V – 1.1V) / 40mA = 97.5, we have chosen to use 100 ohm resistor

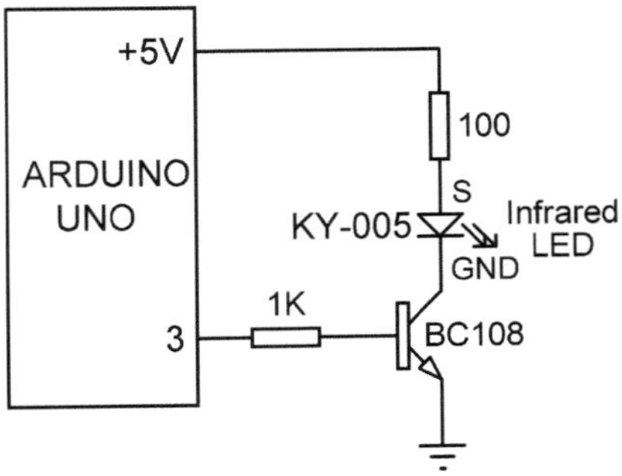

Figure 5.30 Arduino Uno circuit diagram of the project

Arduino Uno Program Listing: The Arduino Uno program listing (program: **TVscan**) is shown in Figure 5.31. Pin 3 of the Arduino is connected to pin S of the KY-005 module. The IR handset used in Figure 5.19 is used in this project. The IR code to increment the channel number has the value **0x4040D02F** which is a 32-bit number. The program is very simple where statement **irsend.sendNEC** is used to send the code to the satellite receiver to increment the channel number. As shown in Figure 5.19, the handset uses the NEC codes. This process is repeated continuously where the channel number is incremented after a delay of 5 seconds.

```
/*****************************************************************
 *                       SCAN TV CHANNELS
 *                       ================
 *
 * In this program the KY-005 IR LED transmitter module is connected
 * to port pin 3 of the Arduino Uno. The program scans the channels
 * with 5 seconds between each channel.
 *
 * Author: Dogan Ibrahim
 * Date  : April 2019
 * File  : TVscan
 ****************************************************************/
#include <IRremote.h>                              // Include IR header file
#include <IRremoteInt.h>

IRsend irsend;
int TX_PIN = 3;                                    // KY-005 S pin at pin 2

decode_results results;

void setup()
{
}

//
// Inside the main program loop send channel up codes every 5 seconds
//
void loop()
{
  irsend.sendNEC(0x4040D02F, 32);                  // Send IR code
  delay(5000);                                     // Wait 5 secs
}
```

Figure 5.31 Program listing

ESP32 DevKitC Program Listing: The ESP32 DevKitC version of the project is very similar to the Arduino Uno version, where KY-005 is connected to GPIO 3 of ESP32 DevKitC. Also, a transistor is used as a switch as in Figure 5.30. The same program as in Figure 5.31 can be used after making the above changes. Before compiling the program make sure that you change the Board type from **Arduino/Genuino Uno** to **ESP32 Dev Module**, using **Tools -> Board** in the Arduino IDE.

Raspberry Pi Program Listing: The block diagram of the Raspberry Pi version is the same as in Figure 5.29. Figure 5.32 shows the Raspberry Pi circuit diagram. Here, pin S of KY-005 is connected to GPIO 22 of Raspberry Pi through a transistor switch as in Figure 5.30.

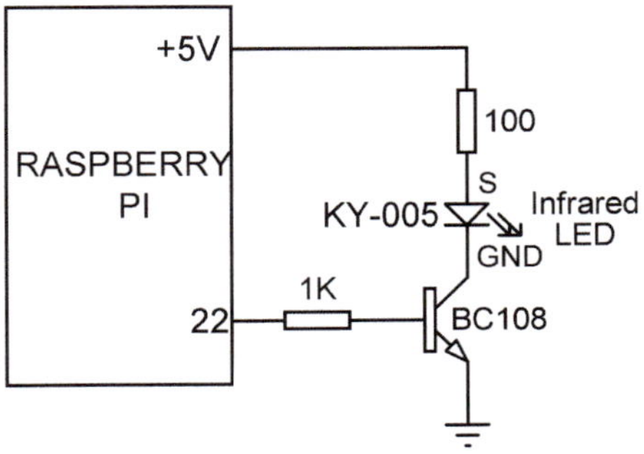

Figure 5.32 Raspberry Pi circuit diagram of the project

Before writing the Raspberry Pi version of the program, we have to install the package py_irsend as shown below:

pi@raspberrypi:~$ **sudo pip install py_irsend**

The general format of the **irsend** command is (see web site: http://lirc.org/html/irsend.html):

irsend [*options*] *sub-commands <remote> <code>* [*code...]*

The command options are:

-h --help	Display usage summary.
-v --version	Display version.
-d --device=*device*	Use given lircd socket [/usr/var/run/lirc/lircd].
-a --address=*host[*:port]	Connect to lircd at this address.
-# **--count**=*n*	Send command n times.

The sub-commands are:

send_once	- send one or more code(s) once
send_start	- start repeating a code.
send_stop	- stop repeating code.
list	- list configured remote items
set_transmitters	- set active transmitters
simulate	- simulate IR event

remote is the name of a remote, as described in the **lircd** configuration file.
code is the name of a remote control key of *remote*, as it appears in the **lircd.conf** configuration file.

num is the transmitter number of the hardware device.

list command lists the remotes or codes:

list_remotes()
list_codes()

The **simulate** command only works if it has been explicitly enabled in lircd using the --allow-simulate option.

Before writing the program, we have to find the list of the remotes and codes in our configuration file, shown in Figure 5.13. This is done interactively in Python as shown in Figure 5.33.

```
pi@raspberrypi:~ $ python
Python 2.7.13 (default, Sep 26 2018, 18:42:22)
[GCC 6.3.0 20170516] on linux2
Type "help", "copyright", "credits" or "license" for more information.
>>> from py_irsend import irsend
>>> irsend.list_remotes()
['DEMO']
>>> irsend.list_codes('DEMO')
['KEY_1', 'KEY_2', 'KEY_3', 'KEY_UP', 'KEY_DOWN']
>>>
```

Figure 5.33 Finding the remotes and codes in configuration file

Our database has one remotes item called **DEMO** and inside **DEMO** we have the codes **KEY_1**, **KEY_2**, **KEY_3**, **KEY_UP**, and **KEY_DOWN**. In this project, we will be using the code for **KEY_UP** to increment the channel numbers. Figure 5.34 shows the program listing (program: **rpiTVscan.py**). At the beginning of the program time and py_irsend are imported to the program. The remainder of the program runs in an endless loop where the TV channels are incremented every 5 seconds. Run the program by entering the following command:

pi@raspberrypi:~$ **sudo python rpiTVscan.py**

```
#---------------------------------------------------------------
#
#              SCAN TV CHANNELS
#              ================
#
# In this program the KY-005 infrared transmitter module is
# connected to GPIO 22 of Raspberry Pi through a transistor
# switch. The program sends codes to the TV to increment the
# channels every 5 seconds.
#
# Program: rpiTVscan.py
# Date   : May 2019
# Author : Dogan Ibrahim
#---------------------------------------------------------------
```

```
from py_irsend import irsend
import time

#
# Program loop. Send codes to teh TV to increment the channels
# every 5 seconds
#
while True:
    irsend.send_once('DEMO', ['KEY_UP'])
    time.sleep(5)
```

Figure 5.34 Raspberry Pi program listing

5.5 Project 4 – Two communicating Arduino Uno's using IR

Description: In this project, two Arduino Unos communicate using IR. The transmitting Arduino is called node TX and the receiving Arduino is called node RX. Node TX has a push-button switch module and an infrared transmitter module. Node RX has an active buzzer module and an IR receiver module. Every time the button is pressed a code is sent from node TX to node RX to activate the buzzer for 5 seconds.

Aim: The aim of this project is to show how two Arduino Unos can communicate using the IR.

Sensor Used: In this project the following modules are used from the sensor kit: KY-005 IR transmitter module, KY-022 IR receiver module, KY-004 button module, and KY-012 active buzzer module. All operation of all these modules has been described in earlier projects except the KY-004 button module. KY-012 active buzzer module is a 3-pin device but only the S pin and the GND pins are in use.

Figure 5.35 shows the KY-004 button module. This is a 3-pin module with a 10K pull-up resistor to +V. The switch output is normally at logic HIGH and goes to logic LOW when the button is pressed.

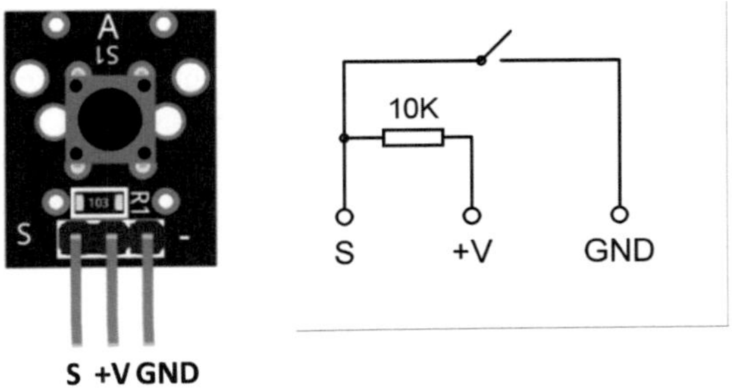

Figure 5.35 KY-004 button module

Block Diagram: Figure 5.36 shows the block diagram of the project.

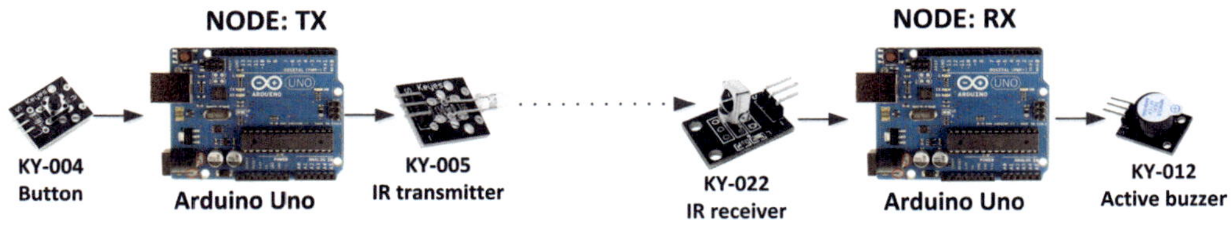

Figure 5.36 Block diagram of the project

Arduino Uno Circuit Diagram: The circuit diagram of the project is shown in Figure 5.37. Output S of the button module is connected to pin 4 of node TX. Pin 3 of this node drives the infrared transmitter through a transistor switch. Pin S of the infrared receiver is connected to pin 2 of node RX. Pin 3 of this node drives the buzzer. Notice that the current drawn by the buzzer is around 30mA and it may be necessary to connect a 100 Ohm resistor in series with the buzzer in order to limit the port output current, especially in circuits where other external devices are connected to the output ports.

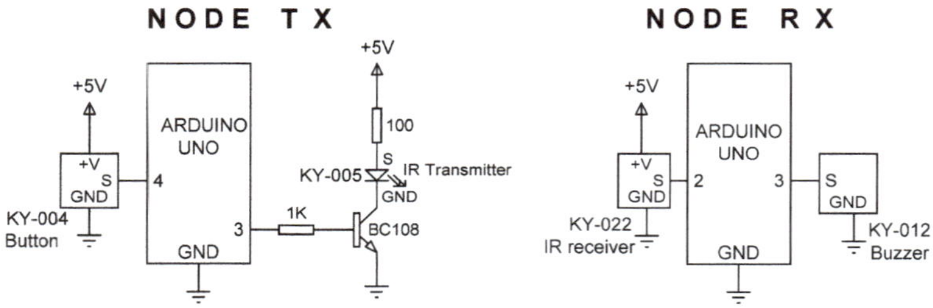

Figure 5.37 Circuit diagram of the project

Arduino Uno Program Listings

Node TX

Figure 5.38 shows the Node TX program listing (program: **TX**). At the beginning of the program, TX_PIN is assigned to port pin 3 and the button is assigned to pin 4. Inside the setup routine, the button is configured as an input. Inside the main program loop, the program waits until the button is pressed. Notice that the button state is normally at logic HIGH and goes to logic LOW when the button is pressed. After the button press is detected, hexadecimal code 0x100 is sent using the NEC IR protocol. At this stage, it does not matter which protocol we use and also what data we send since we will check the code received by node RX.

```
/*********************************************************************
 *              TRANSMIT DATA TO ANOTHER ARDUINO
 *              ================================
 *
 * In this program the KY-005 IR LED transmitter module is connected
 * to port pin 3 of the Arduino Uno. Additionaly. KY-004 button
 * module is connected to port pin 4. When the button is pressed, a
 * code is sent to the receiver Arduino to activate a buzzer for
```

```
 * 5 seconds
 *
 * Author: Dogan Ibrahim
 * Date  : April 2019
 * File  : TX
 *******************************************************************/
#include <IRremote.h>                         // Include IR header file
#include <IRremoteInt.h>

IRsend irsend;
int TX_PIN = 3;                               // KY-005 S pin at pin 2
int Button = 4;                               // Button pin

decode_results results;

void setup()
{
  pinMode(Button, INPUT);                     // Button is input
}

//
// Inside the main program loop send channel up codes every 5 seconds
//
void loop()
{
  while(digitalRead(Button) == HIGH);         // Wait for button LOW
  irsend.sendNEC(0x100, 12);                  // Send IR code
  delay(100);
  while(digitalRead(Button) == LOW);          // Wait for buton HIGH
                                              // Wait
}
```

Figure 5.38 Node TX program listing

Node RX

Initially, the program provided in Figure 5.7 (program **IRhandset**) was run and the button was pressed on node TX so that the code received could be displayed. The test showed that hexadecimal number 0xC2875BAA was received when the button was pressed.

Figure 5.39 shows the Node RX program listing (program: **RX**). At the beginning of the program, **RECV_PIN** and **Buzzer** are assigned to port pins 2 and 3 respectively. The code received when the button is pressed is assigned to **Code**. Inside the setup routine buzzer port is configured as an output and the buzzer is turned OFF. Inside the main program loop, the code received is compared with **Code** and if the correct code is received then the buzzer is activated for 5 seconds. At the end of 5 seconds, the buzzer is turned OFF and the above process repeats.

```
/*****************************************************************
 *             RECEIVE DATA FROM ANOTHER ARDUINO
 *             =================================
 *
 * In this program the KY-022 IR LED receiver module is connected
 * to port pin 2 of the Arduino Uno. Additionally, KY-012 active
 * buzzer is connected to pin 3. When the correct code is received,
 * the buzzer is activated for 5 seconds.
 *
 * Author: Dogan Ibrahim
 * Date  : April 2019
 * File  : RX
 ****************************************************************/
#include <IRremote.h>                       // Include IR header file

int RECV_PIN = 2;                           // KY-022 S pin at pin 2
int Buzzer = 3;                             // Buzzer pin
IRrecv irrecv(RECV_PIN);                    // Initialize library
decode_results results;

#define Code 0xC2875BAA
void setup()
{
  Serial.begin(9600);                       // Start serial monitor
  pinMode(Buzzer, OUTPUT);                  // Buzzer is output
  digitalWrite(Buzzer, LOW);                // Buzzer OFF
  irrecv.enableIRIn();                      // Enable the IR receiver
}

//
// Inside the main program loop, check if the received code is the
// correct code and if so activate the buzzer for 5 seconds
//
void loop()
{
  if (irrecv.decode(&results))              // Code received?
  {
    if(results.value == Code)               // Correct code ?
    {
      digitalWrite(Buzzer, HIGH);           // Activate buzzer
      delay(5000);                          // Wait 5 seconds
      digitalWrite(Buzzer, LOW);            // Stop buzzer
    }
    irrecv.resume();                        // Rcv next code
  }
}
```

Figure 5.39 Node RX program listing

Figure 5.40 shows the project built on breadboards.

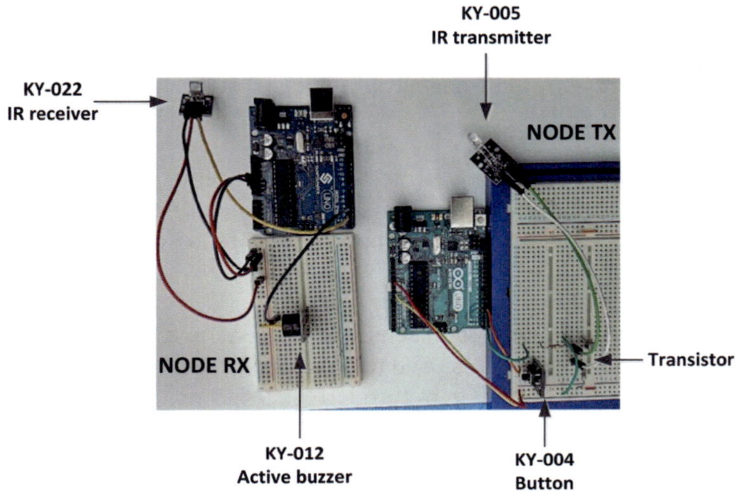

Figure 5.40 Project built on breadboards

5.6 Summary

In this Chapter, we have seen how to use the infrared transmitter-receiver modules in Arduino, ESP32 DevKitC and Raspberry Pi based projects. In the next Chapters, we will be seeing how to use the vibration and shock sensors in projects.

Chapter 6 • Vibration and shock projects

6.1 Overview

In the previous Chapter, we have seen how to develop projects for the Arduino Uno, Raspberry Pi, and ESP32 using infrared transmitter and receiver modules and some other modules in the sensor kit.

In this Chapter, we will be developing projects using the vibration and shock sensors. In general, vibration and shock sensors are similar in operation. Shock sensors are less sensitive and they are used to detect greater amounts of vibration or shock.

6.2 Project 1 – Target shooting detector

Description: In this project, a vibration sensor is attached to a loose target which is positioned at a distant place. The target is used for shooting practices. When the target is shot the sensor vibrates and causes a lamp to turn ON for 5 seconds to indicate that the target has been shot successfully.

Aim: The aim of this project is to show how a vibration or a shock sensor can be used in a project.

Sensors Used: In this project the following sensors are used: KY-002 vibration sensor (or the KY-031 shock sensor), and the KY-019 relay module.

KY-002 is a 3-pin sensor module that can be used to detect vibration or shock. The pins of the sensor are: GND, +V, and digital output S. As shown in Figure 6.1, the sensor module includes a switch which is vibration or shock activated and a 10K pull-up resistor to +V. Normally the output of the sensor is at logic HIGH and it goes to logic LOW when the module is subjected to vibration or shock.

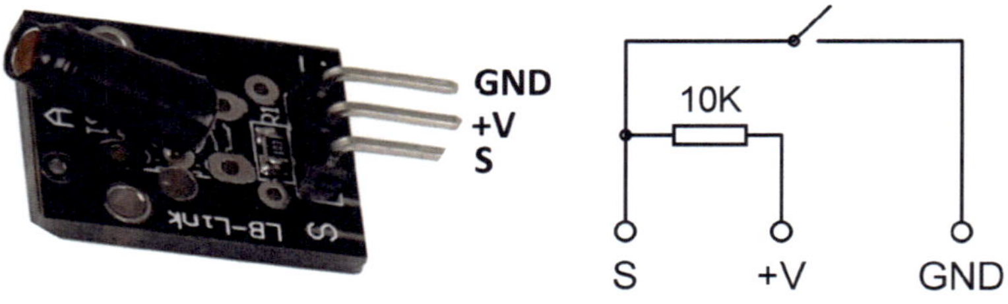

Figure 6.1 KY-002 vibration sensor

KY-031 is a shock sensor which is similar to KY-002 but it is less sensitive and requires larger vibration (or shock) to be activated. As shown in Figure 6.2, this sensor module also includes a 10K pull-up resistor to +V so that its output is normally at logic HIGH and goes to logic LOW when the sensor module is subjected to shock.

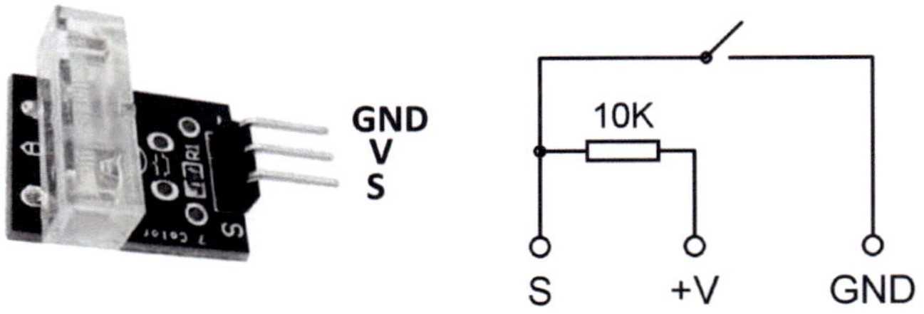

Figure 6.2 KY-031 shock module

Background Information: Vibration and shock sensors are used in applications where it is required to sense movement, vibration, or shock. Some typical application areas are in movement detection, automobile alarm circuits, door or window opening, target sensing, vibration monitoring and so on. KY-002 and KY-031 vibration and shock sensor modules are based on the Gaoxin SW-18010P type vibration switch. The switch assembly consists of a center post and a spring which surrounds this post. When sufficient force is applied to the sensor, the spring moves and shorts the terminals of the sensor. It is recommended that the sensor module should be placed as close as possible to the area where vibration or shock is to be monitored. These modules usually have open switch resistances greater than 10 Mega-ohm and closed switch resistance of less than 30 Ohms.

Block Diagram: Figure 6.3 shows the project block diagram. The vibration sensor is attached to the loose target so that it can vibrate when the target is shot.

Figure 6.3 Block diagram of the project

Arduino Uno Circuit Diagram: As shown in Figure 6.4, the output of KY-002 (or KY-031) is connected to port pin 2 of the Arduino Uno. S pin of the KY-019 relay module is connected to pin 3 of the Arduino Uno.

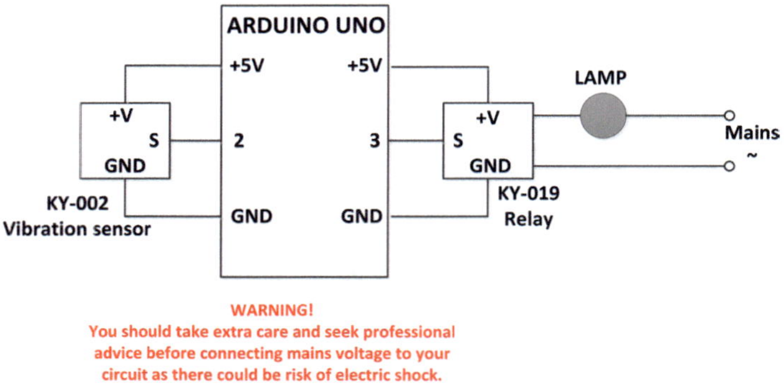

Figure 6.4 Arduino Uno circuit diagram

Arduino Program Listing: Figure 6.5 shows the program listing (program: **target**). At the beginning of the program, connections to the vibration sensor and the relay are defined. Inside the setup, routine relay module is configured as an output and it is turned OFF. Also, the vibration sensor module is configured as an input. Inside the main program loop, the program waits until there is vibration so that the vibration sensor is activated. When this happens, the relay is activated for 5 seconds which turns the lamp ON.

```
/*****************************************************************
 *                  TARGET SHOOTING DETECTOR
 *                  ========================
 *
 * In this program a KY-002 (or KY-031) vibration or shock sensor
 * module is connected to pin 2 of Arduino Uno. The sensor module is
 * attached to a loose target so that when the target is shot the sensor
 * module vibrates and is activated. As a result, a relay connected
 * to pin 3 is activated which in turn activates a lamp for 5 seconds
 * to indicate that the target has been shot.
 *
 * Author: Dogan Ibrahim
 * Date  : April 2019
 * File  : target
 *****************************************************************/
int Vibration = 2;                              // Vibration sensor
int Relay = 3;                                  // Relay pin

//
// Configure Relay as output and de-activate it to start with. Also,
// configure the vibration sensor as input
//
void setup ()
{
  pinMode(Relay, OUTPUT);                       // Relay output
  digitalWrite(Relay, LOW);                     // Relay OFF
```

```
  pinMode(Vibration, INPUT);                    // Vibration input
}

//
// This is the main program loop. Check if the vibration sensor is
// activated and if so activate the relay for 5 seconds
//
void loop ()
{
    while(digitalRead(Vibration) == 1);         // Wait if no vibration
    digitalWrite(Relay, HIGH);                  // Activate relay
    delay(5000);                                // Wait 5 seconds
    digitalWrite(Relay, LOW);                   // Stop relay
}
```

Figure 6.5 Arduino Uno program listing

Figure 6.6 shows the project built on a breadboard.

Figure 6.6 Project built on a breadboard

ESP32 DevKitC Program: The ESP32 DevKitC circuit diagram is similar to Figure 6.4 and for example, you can use GPIO pins 23 and 22 instead of 2 and 3. Also, the KY-051 voltage translator module (see Project 7 in section 4.2.7 on how to use the KY-051) is required to provide enough voltage to the relay for its reliable operation. The program given in Figure 6.5 can be used after the above simple changes.

Raspberry Pi Program: The Raspberry Pi program is straight forward and the readers should be able to write the program by studying the earlier projects. The KY-051 voltage translator nodule (see Project 6 in section 4.2.6, or see the Raspberry Pi section of the next project) is also required in the Raspberry Pi circuit in order to drive the relay reliably.

6.3 Project 2 – Vibration based toggle switch

Description: In this project, a vibration sensor is used as a toggle switch to control a relay. The state of the relay is toggled when the sensor is vibrated (e.g. touched) slightly.

Aim: The aim of this project is to show how a vibration sensor can be used in a project as a toggle switch.

Sensors Used: Same sensors as in the previous project are used in this project.

Block Diagram: Figure 6.7 shows the block diagram of the project.

Figure 6.7 Block diagram of the project

Arduino Uno Circuit Diagram: The circuit diagram of the project is the same as in Figure 6.4.

Arduino Uno Program Listing: Figure 6.8 shows the Arduino Uno program listing (program: **toggle**). The program is similar to the one in the previous project, but here the sensor is used to toggle the state of the relay module. A small delay is used to remove any contact bouncing problems.

```
/*****************************************************************
 *                VIBRATION BASED TOGGLE SWITCH
 *                =============================
 *
 * In this program a KY-002 (or KY-031) vibration or shock sensor
 * module is connected to pin 2 of Arduino Uno. A KY-019 relay module
 * is connected to pin 3. the state of teh relay is toggled when the
 * vibration module is vibrated (e.g. touched)
 *
 * Author: Dogan Ibrahim
 * Date  : April 2019
 * File  : toggle
*****************************************************************/
```

```
int Vibration = 2;                              // Vibration sensor
int Relay = 3;                                  // Relay pin

//
// Configure Relay as output and de-activate it to start with. Also,
// configure the vibration sensor as input
//
void setup ()
{
  pinMode(Relay, OUTPUT);                       // Relay output
  digitalWrite(Relay, LOW);                     // Relay OFF
  pinMode(Vibration, INPUT);                    // Vibration input
}

//
// This is the main program loop. Toggle teh state of the relay
// when the sensor is vibrated (e.g. touched)
//
void loop ()
{
     while(digitalRead(Vibration) == 1);        // Wait if no vibration
     digitalWrite(Relay, !digitalRead(Relay));  // Toggle the relay
     delay(200);                                // Small delay
}
```

Figure 6.8 Arduino Uno program listing

ESP32 DevKitC Program: The ESP32 DevKitC circuit diagram is similar to Figure 6.4 and for example, you can use GPIO pins 23 and 22 instead of 2 and 3. Also, the KY-051 voltage translator module (see Project 7 in section 4.2.7 on how to use the KY-051) is required to provide enough voltage to the relay for its reliable operation. The program given in Figure 6.8 can be used after the above simple changes.

Raspberry Pi Program: Figure 6.9 shows the Raspberry Pi circuit diagram. Pins 17 and 27 are used for the vibration sensor module and relay module interfaces respectively. A KY-051 voltage translator module is used to boost the +3.3V Raspberry Pi output voltage to +5V so that the relay module can be driven reliably.

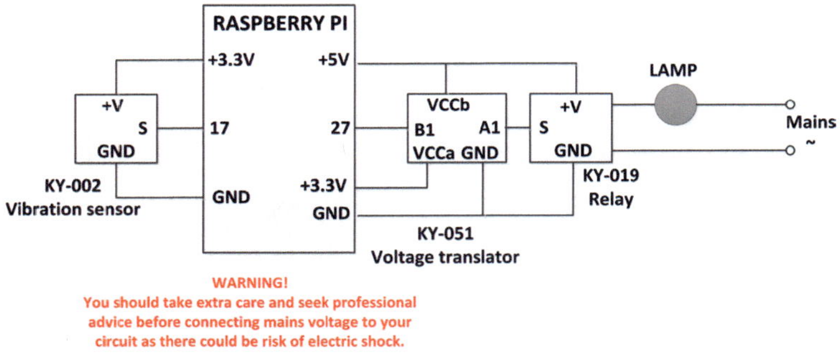

Figure 6.9 Raspberry Pi circuit diagram

Figure 6.10 shows the Raspberry Pi program (program: **rpitoggle.py**). At the beginning of the program modules, **time** and **GPIO** are imported into the program. Relay port is configured as an output and the relay is turned OFF at the beginning of the program. Also, the vibration sensor is configured as an input. Inside the main program loop, the state of the relay is toggled whenever the vibration sensor is touched. The program terminates when Cntrl+C is entered from the keyboard.

```
#---------------------------------------------------------------
#
#              VIBRATION BASED TOGGLE SWITCH
#              =============================
#
# In this program KY-002 (or KY-031) vibration or sensor module
# is connected to GPIo 17 of the Raspberry Pi. Additionally, a
# KY-019 relay is connected to GPIO 27 through a KY-051 voltage
# translator module. When the vibration sensor is touched the
# state of the relay module is toggled.
#
# Program: rpitoggle.py
# Date   : May 2019
# Author : Dogan Ibrahim
#----------------------------------------------------------------
import RPi.GPIO as GPIO
import time

Vibration = 17          # Vibration sensor
Relay = 27          # Relay

GPIO.setmode(GPIO.BCM)
GPIO.setwarnings(False)
GPIO.setup(Relay, GPIO.OUT)      # Relay is output
GPIO.output(Relay, GPIO.LOW)       # Turn OFF relay
GPIO.setup(Vibration, GPIO.IN)       # Vibration is input
```

```
#
# Program loop. Toggle the state of the relay if touched

RelayState = False
try:
 while True:
    while(GPIO.input(Vibration) == 1):
       pass
    RelayState = not RelayState
    GPIO.output(Relay, RelayState)
    time.sleep(0.5)

except KeyboardInterrupt:
    GPIO.cleanup()
```

Figure 6.10 Raspberry Pi program listing

6.4 Project 3 – No shock time duration measurement

Description: This project measures the duration of the time that there is no shock and displays it on the monitor (laptop or PC screen) in seconds.

Aim: The aim of this project is to show how the no shock time can be measured.

Sensors Used: In this project, the KY-031 shock sensor is used.

Block Diagram: The block diagram of the project is shown in Figure 6.11.

Figure 6.11 Block diagram of the project

Arduino Uno Circuit Diagram: Figure 6.12 shows the project circuit diagram. S pin of the sensor is connected to port pin 2 of the Arduino Uno.

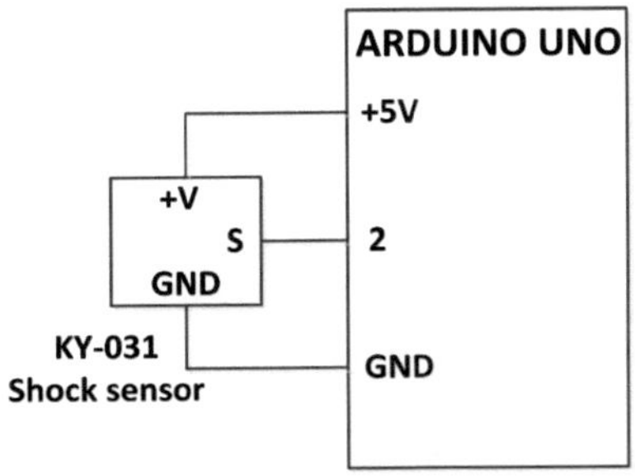

Figure 6.12 Circuit diagram of the project

Arduino Uno Program Listing: Figure 6.13 shows the Arduino Uno program listing (program: **shock**). The program waits until there is no shock and then reads and stores the processor time in **millis()**, where **millis()** returns the number of milliseconds passed since Arduino started running the current program. The duration of the no shock time is calculated in milliseconds and is divided by 1000 to convert into seconds. This value is then displayed on the monitor.

```
/*****************************************************************
 *                  SHOCK TIME MEASUREMENT
 *                  ======================
 *
 * In this program a KY-031 shock sensor module is connected to port
 * pin 2 of Arduino Uno. The program measures and displays the duration
 * of the time in seconds when there is no shock
 *
 * Author: Dogan Ibrahim
 * Date  : April 2019
 * File  : shock
 *****************************************************************/
int Shock = 2;                                    // Shock sensor
unsigned long NoShockTime, NoShockDuration, OldTime;

void setup ()
{
  Serial.begin(9600);
  pinMode(Shock, INPUT);                          // Shock input
}

void loop ()
{
     OldTime = 0;
     while(digitalRead(Shock) == 0);              // Wait for shock
     NoShockTime = millis();                      // Get time

     while(digitalRead(Shock) == 1)               // If no shock
```

```
        {
          NoShockDuration = (millis() - NoShockTime)/1000;
          if(NoShockDuration != OldTime)
          {
             Serial.print("No shock time(s) = ");
             Serial.println(NoShockDuration);
             OldTime = NoShockDuration;
          }
        }
        Serial.println("Shock detected");
}
```

Figure 6.13 Arduino Uno program listing

Figure 6.14 shows typical output from the program.

```
No shock time(s) = 12
No shock time(s) = 13
No shock time(s) = 14
No shock time(s) = 15
No shock time(s) = 16
No shock time(s) = 17
No shock time(s) = 18
No shock time(s) = 19
No shock time(s) = 20
No shock time(s) = 21
Shock detected
No shock time(s) = 1
No shock time(s) = 2
No shock time(s) = 3
No shock time(s) = 4
```

Figure 6.14 Typical output

6.5 Summary

In this Chapter, we have learned how to use the vibration and shock sensor modules. In the next Chapter, we will be using the ultrasonic transmitter-receiver pair in Arduino Uno, ESP32 DevKitC and Raspberry Pi based projects.

Chapter 7 • Ultrasonic sensor projects

7.1 Overview

In the previous Chapter, we have seen how to develop projects for the Arduino Uno, Raspberry Pi, and ESP32 using vibration and shock sensor modules and some other modules in the sensor kit.

In this Chapter, we will be developing projects using the ultrasonic sensor module and some other sensors in the sensor box.

7.2 Project 1 – Ultrasonic reverse parking with buzzer

Description: In this project, the ultrasonic sensor module is used together with an active buzzer to help while reverse parking our vehicle. As the distance to the objects gets smaller, the buzzer sounds faster to warn the driver that the objects at the rear of the vehicle are nearer.

Aim: The aim of this project is to show how the ultrasonic sensor module can be used in a project to measure distance.

Sensors Used: In this project, the following sensors are used: KY-050 ultrasonic sensor module and KY-012 active buzzer module are used.

KY-050 is a 4-pin module as shown in Figure 7.1. This module uses the HC-SR04 type ultrasonic transmitter/receiver hardware, and it has the following features:

- Operating voltage: 5V
- Operating current: 2mA
- Detection distance: 2cm – 450cm
- Input trigger signal: 10us TTL
- Sensor angle: not more than 15 degrees

Figure 7.1 KY-050 ultrasonic module

KY-050 has the following pin names and descriptions:

Vcc: Power input
Trig: Trigger input
Echo: Echo output
Gnd: Power ground

Background Information: The basic principle of operation of the KY-050 ultrasonic sensor module is as follows (see Figure 7.2):

- A 10μs trigger pulse is sent to the module
- The module then sends eight 40kHz square wave signals to the target and sets the echo pin HIGH
- The program starts a timer
- The signal hits the target and echoes back to the module
- When the signal is returned to the module the echo pin goes LOW
- The timer is stopped
- The duration of the echo signal is calculated and this is proportional to the distance to the target

The distance to the object is calculated as follows:

Distance to object (in metres) = (duration of echo time in seconds * speed of sound) / 2

The speed of sound is 340 m/s, or 0.034 cm/μs

Therefore,

Distance to object (in cm) = (duration of echo time in μs) * 0.034 / 2

or,

Distance to object (in cm) = (duration of echo time in μs) * 0.017

For example, if the duration of the echo signal is 294 microseconds then the distance to the object is calculated as follows:

Distance to object (cm) = 294 * 0.017 = 5cm

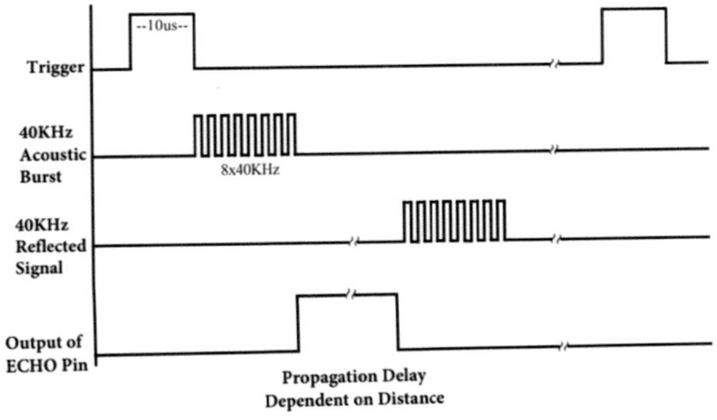

Figure 7.2 Operation of the ultrasonic sensor module

Block Diagram: Figure 7.3 shows the block diagram of the project.

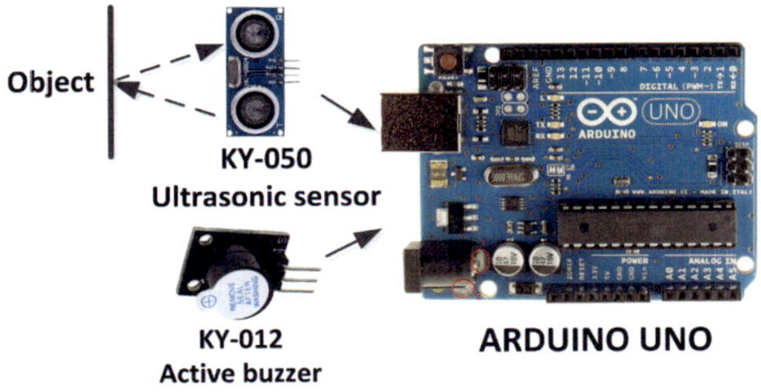

Figure 7.3 Block diagram of the project

Arduino Uno Circuit Diagram: Figure 7.4 shows the project circuit diagram. The following pins are connected between KY-050, KY-012 and Arduino Uno:

Arduino Uno Pin	KY-050 pin	KY-012 pin
2	trig	
3	echo	
4		S
GND	GND	GND
+5V	Vcc	

KY-012 buzzer module is directly connected to an Arduino Uno port pin 4. It is recommended to connect a 100 Ohm series resistor with this module in order to limit the port output current, especially if other devices also draw current from the port pins.

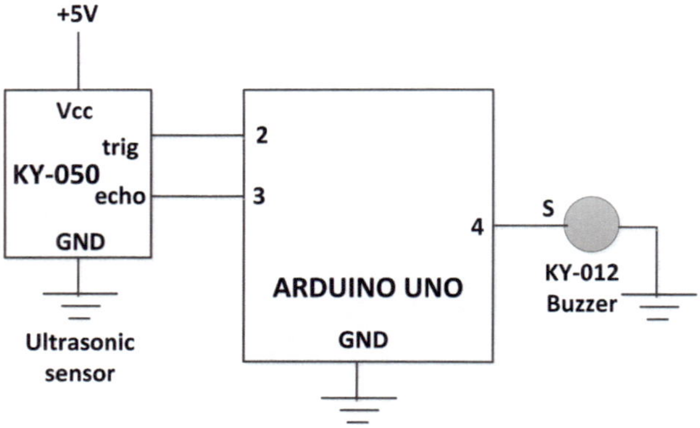

Figure 7.4 Circuit diagram of the project

Arduino Uno Program Listing: Figure 7.5 shows the Arduino Uno program listing (program: **ultrasonic**). At the beginning of the program, trig, echo, and buzzer are assigned port numbers 2, 3, and 4. Inside the setup routine buzzer is configured as an output and it is turned OFF. Also, trig and echo are configured as output and input respectively. Inside the main program loop, a trigger pulse is sent and statement **pulseIN** is used to read the echo signal. The distance to the object in front of the ultrasonic sensor is then calculated in centimeters and is stored in a variable called **distance**. Variable **dely** is set to different values depending on the calculated distance. **dely** gets smaller as the sensor gets nearer the object. Finally, the buzzer is activated with the duration set to variable **dely**. The net result is that the rate of the sound is increased as the sensor gets nearer the object. Notice that the distance is displayed on the serial monitor in Figure 7.5.

```
/****************************************************************
 *            ULTRASONIC REVERSE PARKING WITH BUZZER
 *            ======================================
 *
 * In this program a KY-050 ultrasonic sensor module is connected
 * to Arduino Uno. Additionally, a buzzer is connected to port pin
 * 4. The project can be used in revere parking a car. The buzzer
 * sounds at a faster rate when the vehicle gets closer to an object.
 *
 * Author: Dogan Ibrahim
 * Date  : May 2019
 * File  : ultrasonic
 ****************************************************************/
int trig = 2;                                  // trig pin
int echo = 3;                                  // echo pin
int buzzer = 4;                                // buzzer
int dely;

long tim;
float distance;

void setup ()
{
  Serial.begin(9600);
  pinMode(trig, OUTPUT);                       // trig is output
  pinMode(echo, INPUT);                        // echo is input
  pinMode(buzzer, OUTPUT);                     // buzzer is output
  digitalWrite(buzzer, LOW);                   // buzzer OFF
}

void loop ()
{
  digitalWrite(trig, LOW);                     // clear trig
  delayMicroseconds(5);                        // 5us delay
```

```
    digitalWrite(trig, HIGH);                    // set trigger HIGH for 10us
    delayMicroseconds(10);                       // 10us delay
    digitalWrite(trig, LOW);                     // remove trigger

    tim = pulseIn(echo, HIGH);                   // read the echo
    distance = tim * 0.034 / 2;                  // calculate distance
    Serial.println(distance);                    // display distance

    //
    // Set the delay depending on the distance to the object
    //
    if(distance > 100)
      dely = 0;
    else if(distance > 70 && distance < 90)
      dely = 600;
    else if(distance > 50 && distance < 70)
      dely = 400;
    else if(distance > 30 && distance < 50)
      dely = 300;
    else if(distance > 10 && distance < 30)
      dely = 200;
    else if(distance < 10)
      dely = 10;

    if(distance < 100)                            // if less than 100cm
    {
      digitalWrite(buzzer, HIGH);                 // buzzer ON
      delay(dely);                                // delay
      digitalWrite(buzzer, LOW);                  // buzzer OFF
      delay(dely);                                // delay
    }
}
```

Figure 7.5 Arduino Uno program listing

Figure 7.6 shows the circuit built on a breadboard.

Figure 7.6 Circuit built on a breadboard

ESP32 DevKitC Program: Figure 7.7 shows the ESP32 DevKitC circuit diagram of the project. trig, echo, and buzzer are connected to pins 23, 22 and 21 respectively. Notice that the KY-050 ultrasonic sensor requires +5V for its reliable operation. The output voltage of the ultrasonic sensor (echo) is 5V and this is too high for the ESP32 DevKitC where the maximum allowable input voltage is about +3.3V. A potential divider circuit was constructed using two resistors to lower the voltage from +5V to +3.3V. The voltage at the output of the potential divider circuit is given by:

V = (5V x R2) / (R1 + R2)

Where R1 = 1K, and R2 = 2K

Giving, V = (5V x 2) / 3 = 3.3V

The program listing is shown in Figure 7.8 (program: **esp32ultrasonic**) which is basically the same as in Figure 7.6 except that different port pins are used. Make sure that the board type is set to **ESP32 Dev Module**.

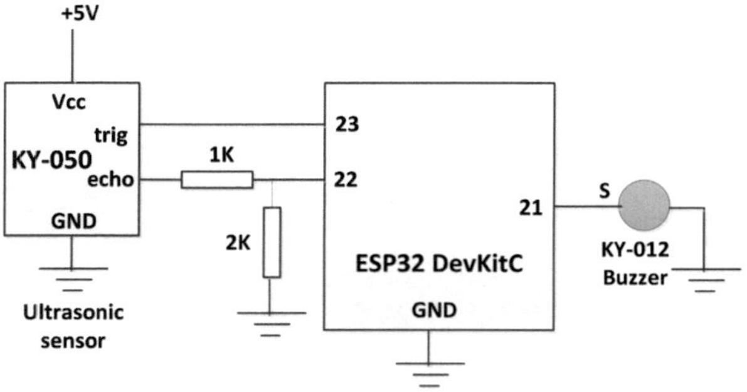

Figure 7.7 ESP32 DevKitC circuit diagram

```
/*****************************************************************
 *           ULTRASONIC REVERSE PARKING WITH BUZZER
 *           ======================================
 *
 * In this program a KY-050 ultrasonic sensor module is connected
 * to ESP32 DevKitC. Additionally, a buzzer is connected to port pin
 * 21. The project can be used in revere parking a car. The buzzer
 * sounds at a faster rate when the vehicle gets closer to an object.
 *
 * Author: Dogan Ibrahim
 * Date  : May 2019
 * File  : esp32ultrasonic
 *****************************************************************/
int trig = 23;                                    // trig pin
int echo = 22;                                    // echo pin
int buzzer = 21;                                  // buzzer
int dely;

long tim;
float distance;

void setup ()
{
  Serial.begin(9600);
  pinMode(trig, OUTPUT);                         // trig is output
  pinMode(echo, INPUT);                          // echo is input
  pinMode(buzzer, OUTPUT);                       // buzzer is output
  digitalWrite(buzzer, LOW);                     // buzzer OFF
}

void loop ()
{
  digitalWrite(trig, LOW);                       // clear trig
  delayMicroseconds(5);                          // 5us delay
```

```
    digitalWrite(trig, HIGH);                       // set trigger HIGH for 10us
    delayMicroseconds(10);                          // 10us delay
    digitalWrite(trig, LOW);                        // remove trigger

    tim = pulseIn(echo, HIGH);                      // read the echo
    distance = tim * 0.034 / 2;                     // calculate distance
    Serial.println(distance);                       // display distance

    //
    // Set the delay depending on the distance to the object
    //
    if(distance > 100)
      dely = 0;
    else if(distance > 70 && distance < 90)
      dely = 600;
    else if(distance > 50 && distance < 70)
      dely = 400;
    else if(distance > 30 && distance < 50)
      dely = 300;
    else if(distance > 10 && distance < 30)
      dely = 200;
    else if(distance < 10)
      dely = 10;

    if(distance < 100)                               // if less than 100cm
    {
      digitalWrite(buzzer, HIGH);                    // buzzer ON
      delay(dely);                                   // delay
      digitalWrite(buzzer, LOW);                     // buzzer OFF
      delay(dely);                                   // delay
    }
}
```

Figure 7.8 ESP32 DevKitC program listing

Figure 7.9 shows the project built on a breadboard.

Figure 7.9 Project built on a breadboard

Raspberry Pi Program: The circuit diagram of the Raspberry Pi version of the project is same as in Figure 7.7 (program: **rpiultrasonic**), but trig, echo, and buzzer pins are connected to GPIO pins 17, 27 and 22 respectively. The resistive potential divider circuit is also needed in the Raspberry Pi version of the project. The program listing is shown in Figure 7.10. At the beginning of the program, trig, echo and buzzer pins are defined. Trig and buzzer are configured as outputs and echo are configured as an input. Inside the main program loop, a trigger pulse is sent for 10 microseconds and the program waits to receive the echo signal. After receiving the echo signal its duration is calculated. Assuming that the speed of sound in air is 340m/s, the distance to the object is calculated and stored in variable **distancemetres** in meters. This value is then converted into centimeters in variable **distancecm**. The remainder of the program sets the buzzer delay depending on the distance of the object.

```
#-------------------------------------------------------------
#
#              ULTRASONIC REVERSE PARKING WITH BUZZER
#              ======================================
#
# In this program KY-050 ultrasonic sendor is connected to the
# Raspberry Pi. Additionally, KY-012 active buzzer is connected
# to GPIO 22. The program measurs the distance to the objects
# at the rear of the vehicle and activates the buzzer. The buzzer
# activation frequency is increased as the vehicle gets nearer the
# objects at the rear of the vehicle, thus helping the driver to
# park teh vehicle easily..
#
# Program: rpiultrasonic.py
```

```
# Date   : July 2018
# Author : Dogan Ibrahim
#------------------------------------------------------------
import RPi.GPIO as GPIO
import time

trig = 17                                  # trig pin
echo = 27                                  # echo pin
buzzer = 22                                # buzzer pin

GPIO.setmode(GPIO.BCM)
GPIO.setwarnings(False)
GPIO.setup(trig, GPIO.OUT)                 # trig is output
GPIO.setup(echo, GPIO.IN)                  # echo is input
GPIO.setup(buzzer, GPIO.OUT)               # buzzer is output
GPIO.output(buzzer, GPIO.LOW)              # buzzer OFF

#
# Program loop. Measure the distance to the objects at the rear
# of the vehicle and then activate the buzzer accordingly
#
while True:
   GPIO.output(trig, GPIO.LOW)             # wait until settled
   time.sleep(0.000005)                    # 5us delay

   GPIO.output(trig, GPIO.HIGH)            # send trigger
   time.sleep(0.00001)                     # wait 10us
   GPIO.output(trig, GPIO.LOW)             # remove trigger

   Tmr1 = time.time()                      # get time
   while GPIO.input(echo) == 0:            # wait no echo
     Tmr1 = time.time()                    # get time

   while GPIO.input(echo) == 1:            # echo
     Tmr2 = time.time()                    # get time

   Duration = Tmr2 - Tmr1                  # find duration
   distancemetres = (Duration * 340.0) / 2.0 # distance (m)
   distancecm = 100.0 * distancemetres     # distance (cm)
   print(distancecm)                       # display distance
#
#  Set the delay depending on distance of the object
#
   if distancecm > 100:
     dely = 0
   elif distancecm > 70 and distancecm < 90:
```

```
  dely = 600
elif distancecm > 50 and distancecm < 70:
  dely = 400
elif distancecm > 30 and distancecm < 50:
  dely = 300
elif distancecm > 10 and distancecm < 30:
  dely = 200
elif distancecm < 10:
  dely = 10

dely = dely / 1000.0
if distancecm < 100:
  GPIO.output(buzzer, GPIO.HIGH)              # buzzer ON
  time.sleep(dely)                            # delay
  GPIO.output(buzzer, GPIO.LOW)               # buzzer OFF
  time.sleep(dely)                            # delay
```

Figure 7.10 Raspberry Pi program listing

Figure 7.11 shows the project built on a breadboard.

Figure 7.11 Project built on a breadboard

7.3 Summary

In this Chapter, we have learned how to use the KY-050 ultrasonic sensor module in Arduino Uno, ESP32 DevKitC and Raspberry Pi projects. In the next Chapter, we will be learning how to use the sound sensor modules of the sensor kit.

Chapter 8 • Sound sensor projects

8.1 Overview

In the previous Chapter, we have seen how to develop projects for the Arduino Uno, Raspberry Pi, and ESP32 using the ultrasonic sensor module and the relay module in the sensor kit.

In this Chapter, we will be developing projects using the sound sensor modules and some other sensors in the sensor box.

8.2 Project 1 – Toggle lights by clapping hands

Description: In this project, the KY-037 sound sensor module is used together with the KY-019 relay module, where it is assumed that a mains operated lamp is connected to the normally open relay contacts. The state of the relay is toggled when we clap our hands near the microphone so that for example the lamp turns ON if it is OFF and vice versa.

Aim: The aim of this project is to show how a sound sensor module can be used in a project.

Sensors Used: In this project the following sensors are used: KY-037 sound sensor module and the KY-019 relay module. KY-037, a 4-pin module as shown in Figure 8.1 has the following pins:

- Digital output (D0)
- +V
- GND
- Analog output (A0)

Both digital and analog outputs are provided. Digital output goes to logic HIGH when the sound level is above a value which can be set by a potentiometer. Analog output provides a continuous analog signal proportional to the received sound level.

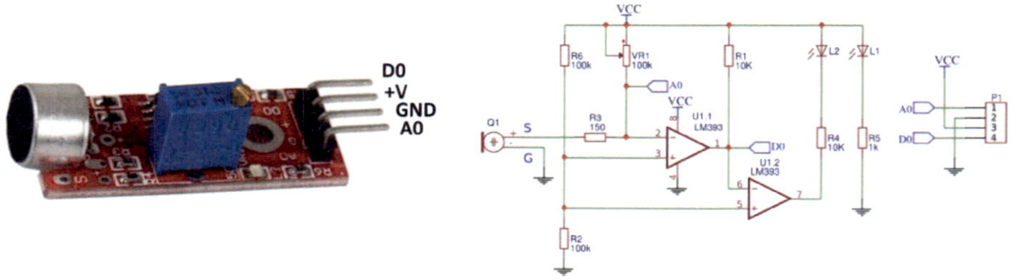

Figure 8.1 KY-037 sound sensor module

Notice that although the KY-037 module is used in this project, it is also possible to use the KY-038 sound sensor module instead without any hardware or software changes. KY-037 module is slightly more sensitive than the KY-038.

Background Information: As shown in Figure 8.1, the sound sensor module consists of an electret microphone, a potentiometer, an LM393 comparator chip, a power indicator LED, and another LED that is lit when the digital output is at logic HIGH. The potentiometer is used to adjust the sensitivity of the module, i.e. the gain of the electret microphone. There is no amplifier on the module and as such the module is not sensitive to low-intensity sounds. The comparator chip compares the sound output voltage of the electret microphone with half the supply voltage (e.g. 2.5V for 5V supply) and its output goes to the supply voltage (logic HIGH) if the output of the microphone is higher than half the supply voltage.

Block Diagram: Figure 8.2 shows the block diagram of the project.

Figure 8.2 Block diagram of the project

Arduino Uno Circuit Diagram: In this project, the digital output of the sound sensor module is used. This output is normally at logic LOW and goes to logic HIGH when the sound level is above the level set by the potentiometer. It is also possible to use the analog output and then activate the relay when the analog voltage goes above a certain value. Figure 8.3 shows the circuit diagram of the project.

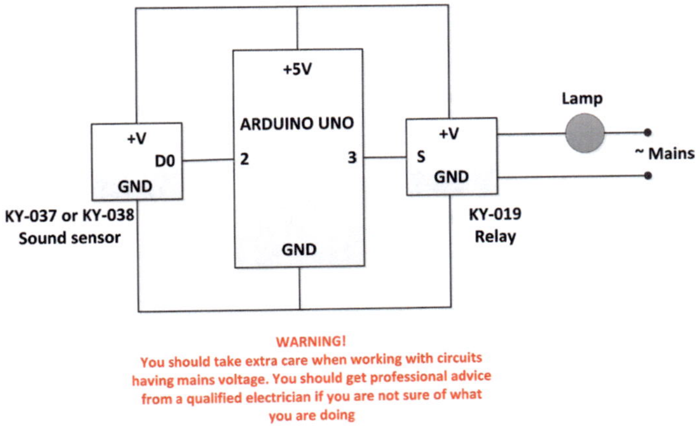

Figure 8.3 Arduino Uno circuit diagram

Setting the Sensitivity: The sensitivity for digital output can be set as follows:

- Apply power to the sound sensor module by connecting it to +5V and GND
- You should see the steady red power LED coming on
- Keep clapping your hands and at the same time adjust the potentiometer by turning its screw until the sound level LED flashes briefly after clapping
- Remove power from the sound sensor

Arduino Uno Program Listing: Figure 8.4 shows the program listing (program: **clap**). At the beginning of the program, variables **sound** and **relay** are assigned to port pins 2 and 3 respectively, with the sound being input and relay output. Inside the main program loop, the state of the relay is toggled whenever the sound sensor receives sound with intensity high enough to set its output to logic HIGH. Notice that the KY-037 sound sensor module has no built-in amplifier and therefore it is not very sensitive and you might have to clap your hands very close to the microphone to activate the circuit.

```
/****************************************************************
 *            TOGGLE LIGHTS BY CLAPPING HANDS
 *            ===============================
 *
 * In this program a KY-037 sound sensor module is used. Additionally,
 * a KY-019 relay module is used. The state of the relay is toggled
 * when we clap our hands near the microphone.
 *
 * Author: Dogan Ibrahim
 * Date  : May 2019
 * File  : clap
 ****************************************************************/
int sound = 2;                                  // sensor pin
int relay = 3;                                  // relay pin

void setup ()
{
  pinMode(sound, INPUT);                        // trig is output
  pinMode(relay, OUTPUT);                       // relay is output
  digitalWrite(relay, LOW);                     // relay OFF
}

//
// The output of the sound sensor will go to logic HIGH when we
// clap our hands near the microphone
//
void loop ()
```

```
    {
      if(digitalRead(sound) == 1)                    // sound received?
      {
        digitalWrite(relay, !digitalRead(relay));    // relay ON
        delay(100);
      }
    }
```

Figure 8.4 Program listing

ESP32 DevKitc Program Listing: The circuit diagram of the ESP32 DevKitC version of the project requires the KY-051 voltage translator module to be used since the relay requires +5V for its reliable operation. Figure 8.5 shows the circuit diagram. The program listing of the ESP32 DevKitC version is exactly the same as the program given in Figure 8.4, except that the GPIO pin numbers could be different.

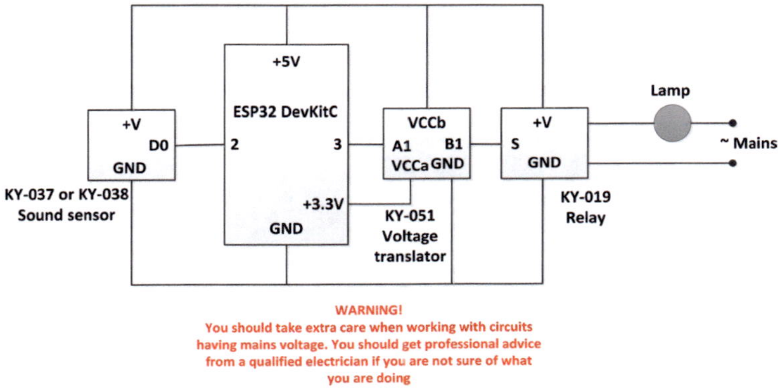

Figure 8.5 ESP32 DevKitC circuit diagram

Raspberry Pi Program Listing: The circuit diagram of the Raspberry Pi version is exactly the same as in Figure 8.5, except that the GPIO pin numbers could be different. The program is very simple and the readers should be able to write it with the experience gained from previous projects.

8.3 Summary

In this Chapter, we have seen how to use the sound sensor project with Arduino, ESP32 DevKitC and Raspberry Pi. In the next Chapter, we will be learning how to use the passive piezo buzzer module in projects.

Chapter 9 • Passive piezo buzzer sensor projects

9.1 Overview

In the previous Chapter, we have seen how to develop projects for the Arduino Uno, Raspberry Pi, and ESP32 using the sound sensor module and the relay module in the sensor kit. In this Chapter, we will be developing projects using the passive piezo buzzer module and some other sensors in the sensor box.

9.2 Project 1 – Playing melody

Description: In this project, the KY-006 passive piezo buzzer module is used to generate the well-known melody **Happy Birthday**. The melody is played continuously until stopped by the user.

Aim: The aim of this project is to show how the passive piezo buzzer can be used in projects.

Sensor Used: In this project, the KY-006 piezo buzzer sensor is used. As shown in Figure 9.1, this is a 3-pin sensor but only the two pins S (input) and GND are used.

Figure 9.1 KY-006 passive piezo buzzer module

Background Information: There are basically two types of piezo buzzers: active, and passive. Active buzzers are easy to use but they have the disadvantage that they can only generate a single fixed frequency of sound. Passive buzzer, on the other hand, can be used to generate sounds with different frequencies (or tones). This is usually achieved by sending PWM waveforms to the buzzer at the required sound frequency. KY-006 has the following basic specifications:

- Operating voltage: 1.5V to 15V
- Tone generation range: 1.5kHz to 2.5kHz
- 2-pin interface to host processor

There are basically three methods of generating sound on a passive buzzer:

- Perhaps the simplest way of generating sound is to use delays in a loop and toggle the state of the buzzer so that effectively a PWM waveform is generated and as a result, the buzzer sounds. The frequency of the sound can be adjusted by varying the delay in the loop.

- Generate PWM (or sine wave) directly from a processor using a software library
- Using piezo buzzer specific built-in tone generator library

Block Diagram: Figure 9.2 shows the block diagram of the project.

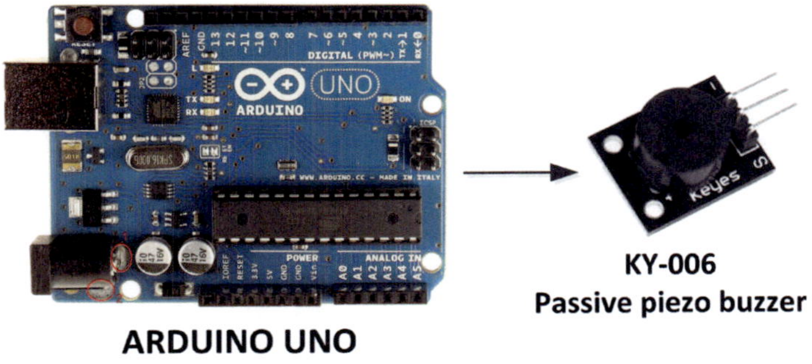

Figure 9.2 Block diagram of the project

Arduino Uno Circuit Diagram: Figure 9.3 shows the circuit diagram. Pin S of the buzzer is connected to pin 3 of the Arduino Uno.

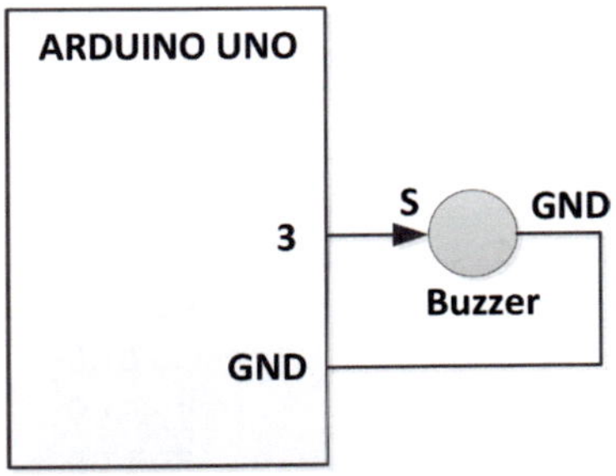

Figure 9.3 Circuit diagram of the project

Melody Tones: In this project the well-known Happy Birthday melody is played. Figure 9.4 shows the musical notes of this melody (see link: https://www.irish-folk-songs.com/happy-birthday-tin-whistle-sheet-music.html).

Figure 9.4 Musical notes of the Happy Birthday melody

The musical notes of this melody and their durations are as follows (here, the durations are given relative to each other). The frequency of each musical note is also shown below (see link: http://pages.mtu.edu/~suits/notefreqs.html):

Musical Note	**Duration**	**Frequency (Hertz)**
D	1	293.66
D	1	293.66
E	2	329.63
D	2	293.66
G	2	392.00
F	4	349.23
D	1	293.66
D	1	293.66
E	2	329.63
D	2	293.66
A	2	440.00
G	4	392.00
D	1	293.66
D	1	293.66
D	2	587.33
B	2	493.88
G	2	392.00
F	2	349.23
E	2	329.63
C	1	523.25
C	1	523.25
B	2	493.88
G	2	392.00
A	2	440.00
G	4	392.00

Arduino Uno Tone Library: The tone library helps to generate sounds on a passive piezoelectric buzzer with the required frequency and duration. The format of the tone statement is:

tone(pin, frequency, duration)

where **pin** is the pin where the passive piezoelectric buzzer is connected to, **frequency** is the frequency of the tone to be generated in Hertz (unsigned int), and **duration** is the duration of the tone in milliseconds (unsigned long, optional).

Program Listing: Figure 9.5 shows the program listing (program: **melody**). The program makes use of the Arduino Uno tone library. At the beginning of the program, the frequencies and the relative durations of the 25 musical notes in the melody are loaded into integer arrays called **Frequencies** and **Durations** respectively. Inside the setup routine buzzer is configured as an output port and is turned OFF. Inside the main program loop, the melody is played where the unit duration is set to be 150 milliseconds (can be changed if desired). The inter-note gap is set to be 1.3 times the duration of the note just played. The melody is repeated after 2 seconds delay.

```
/****************************************************************
 *                     PLAYING MELODY
 *                     ==============
 *
 * In this program a KY-006 passive piezoelectric sensor is used.
 * The well-known melody HAPPY BIRTHDAY is played by the program.
 *
 * Author: Dogan Ibrahim
 * Date  : May 2019
 * File  : melody
 ****************************************************************/
int buzzer = 3;                                  // buzzer pin
int Count = 25;                                  // No of notes
int k, DurationsMs;

int Frequencies[] =
{294,294,329,294,392,349,294,294,329,294,440,392,294,294,587,
494,392,349,329,523,523,494,392,440,392};

int Durations[] =
{1,1,2,2,2,4,1,1,2,2,2,4,1,1,2,2,2,2,2,1,1,2,2,2,4};

void setup ()
{
  pinMode(buzzer, OUTPUT);                       // buzzer is output
  digitalWrite(buzzer, LOW);                     // buzzer OFF
}


void loop ()
{
  for(k = 0; k < 25; k++)                       // Do for all notes
  {
    DurationsMs = Durations[k] * 150;           // Actual duration
    tone(buzzer, Frequencies[k], DurationsMs);  // Generate tone
    delay(DurationsMs*1.3);                     // inter-note space
  }

  delay(2000);                                  // 2 seconds delay
}
```

Figure 9.5 Arduino Uno program listing

ESP32 DevKitC Program: The hardware of the ESP32 DevKitC version of the project is same as the Arduino Uno version, where the buzzer can be connected to any pin of the ESP32 DevkitC except GPIO 1 and GPIO 3 which are reserved for the USB connection. In this version of the project, the buzzer is connected to GPIO 23.

Unfortunately, Arduino Uno IDE does not support the **tone()** library for the ESP32 DevKitC. For this reason, we have to generate the required frequencies by generating PWM waveforms. Figure 9.6 shows the program listing (program: **esp32melody**). At the beginning of the program, PWM parameters are specified where the resolution is set to 8 bits and channel 0 is selected. A function called **tone** is created which generates PWM waveform with the specified frequency and duration. The remainder of the program is the same as in Figure 9.5.

```
/*****************************************************************
 *                      PLAYING MELODY
 *                      ==============
 *
 * In this program a KY-006 passive piezoelectric sensor is used.
 * The well-known melody HAPPY BIRTHDAY is played by the program.
 *
 * Author: Dogan Ibrahim
 * Date  : May 2019
 * File  : esp32melody
 *****************************************************************/
int buzzer = 23;                                    // buzzer pin
int Count = 25;                                     // No of notes
int k, DurationsMs;
//
// PWM channel parameters
//
int freq = 2000;                                    // initial frequency
int channel = 0;                                    // use channel 0
int resolution = 8;                                 // resolution 8 bits

int Frequencies[] =
{294,294,329,294,392,349,294,294,329,294,440,392,294,294,587,
494,392,349,329,523,523,494,392,440,392};

int Durations[] =
{1,1,2,2,2,4,1,1,2,2,2,4,1,1,2,2,2,2,2,1,1,2,2,2,4};

void setup ()
{
  pinMode(buzzer, OUTPUT);                          // buzzer is output
  digitalWrite(buzzer, LOW);                        // buzzer OFF
  ledcSetup(channel, freq, resolution);             // setup PWM
```

```
  ledcAttachPin(buzzer, channel);                   // Attach to channel
}

//
// Generate tone with the specified frequency and duration, where
// the frequency is in Hz and duration is in milliseconds
//
void tone(int freq, int dur)
{
  ledcWriteTone(channel, freq);
  delay(dur);
}

void loop ()
{
  for(k = 0; k < 25; k++)                          // Do for all notes
  {
    DurationsMs = Durations[k] * 150;              // Actual duration
    tone(Frequencies[k], DurationsMs);             // Generate tone
    delay(DurationsMs*1.3);                        // inter-note space
  }

  delay(2000);                                     // 2 seconds delay
}
```

Figure 9.6 ESP32 DevkitC program listing

Raspberry Pi Program: The hardware of the Raspberry Pi version of the program is the same as the ESP32 DevKitC version where the buzzer is connected to GPIO 23. Sound is generated by generating PWM waveforms at the required frequency and duration. Figure 9.7 shows the program listing (program: **rpimelody.py**). At the beginning of the program modules, **time** and **GPIO** are imported to the program, frequencies of the melody and their durations are defined. GPIO 23, where the buzzer is connected to, is then configured as an output and the buzzer is turned OFF. The PWM parameters are then specified and the program enters the main program loop. Inside this loop, a **for** loop is set up to generate the 25 notes of the melody where function **tone** is called to generate the PWM waveforms. Built-in function **ChangeFrequency** changes the PWM frequency to the desired value.

```
#-------------------------------------------------------------
#
#                PLAY MELODY
#                ===========
#
# In this program a KY-006 passive piezoelectric sensor is
# connected to GPIO 23 of Raspberry Pi. The program plays the
# well-known melody HAPPY BIRTHDAY.
#
```

```
# Program: rpimelody.py
# Date   : May 2019
# Author : Dogan Ibrahim
#-------------------------------------------------------------
import RPi.GPIO as GPIO
import time

Frequencies = [294,294,329,294,392,349,294,294,329,294,440,392,294,
294,587,494,392,349,329,523,523,494,392,440,392]

Durations = [1,1,2,2,2,4,1,1,2,2,2,4,1,1,2,2,2,2,2,1,1,2,2,2,4]

buzzer = 23            # Buzzer pin
GPIO.setmode(GPIO.BCM)
GPIO.setwarnings(False)
GPIO.setup(buzzer, GPIO.OUT)        # Buzzer output
GPIO.output(buzzer, GPIO.LOW)       # Buzzer OFF

#
# PWM parameters
#
frequency = 10                      # Starting freq
pwm = GPIO.PWM(buzzer, frequency)   # PWM channelM

#
# This function generates PWW waveform with specified freq and dur
#
def tone(freq, dur):
  pwm.ChangeFrequency(freq)         # Change frequency
  time.sleep(dur/1000.0)            # Duration

#
# Program loop to play the melody
#
while True:
  for k in range(25):                     # Do for all notes
    pwm.start(50)                         # Start PWM
    DurationsMs = Durations[k] * 150      # Durations in ms
    tone(Frequencies[k], DurationsMs)     # Generate tone
    dely = (DurationsMs * 0.8) / 1000.0   # delay in ms
    pwm.stop()
    time.sleep(dely)                      # delay
```

Figure 9.7 Raspberry Pi program listing

9.3 Summary

In this Chapter, we have learned how to generate tones using a passive piezoelectric sensor module. In the next Chapter, we will be learning how to use the magnetic sensor modules.

Chapter 10 • Magnetic sensor projects

10.1 Overview

In the previous Chapter, we have seen how to develop projects for the Arduino Uno, Raspberry Pi, and ESP32 DevKitC using the passive piezo buzzer module.

In this Chapter, we will be developing projects using the magnetic sensor modules. We have already used some of the magnetic sensor modules in earlier projects, such as the KY-003 and KY-021.

10.2 Project 1 – Measuring magnetic field strength

Description: In this project, the KY-024 linear magnetic Hall sensor module is used to measure the magnetic field strength.

Aim: The aim of this project is to show how the linear magnetic Hall sensor module can be used in projects.

Sensor Used: Figure 10.1 shows the KY-024 linear magnetic Hall sensor module. This is a 4-pin module having the following pins:

- D0: digital output
- +V: power supply
- GND: power ground
- A0: analog output

Both digital and analog outputs are available from the module. The digital output is similar in operation to modules KY-003 or KY-021 and it changes state when the magnetic field is present near the module. The only difference here is that the sensitivity of KY-024 can be adjusted using the onboard potentiometer. When used in analog mode, the output voltage is linearly proportional to the magnetic field applied to the module and therefore in this mode, the module can be used to measure the magnetic field. KY-024 module consists of a Hall sensor chip, LM393 comparator chip, potentiometer, some resistors, and LEDs. The comparator compares the output of the Hall sensor with half the supply voltage and changes state if the Hall sensor output voltage is higher than half the supply voltage. It is recommended to adjust the sensitivity to the desired level in digital output applications.

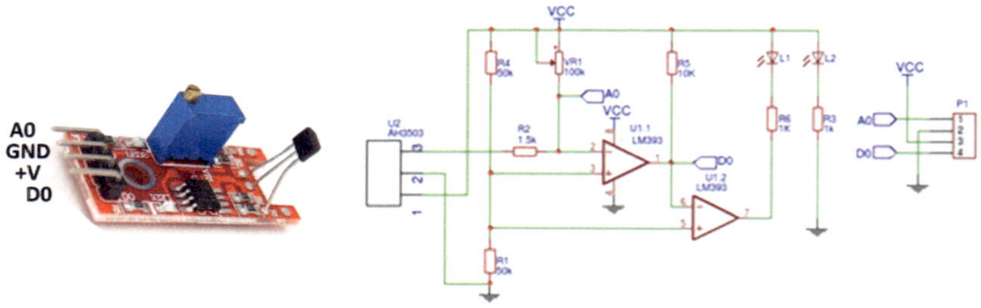

Figure 10.1 KY-024 linear magnetic Hall sensor

Background Information: Hall magnetic sensors are used to detect or measure magnetic fields. These sensors are used in applications such as measuring the magnetic field, magnetic switches, proximity sensing, motor shaft speed measurement, and so on. When used as a magnetic switch, the advantages of Hall sensors are:

- The cost is less than mechanical switches
- Hall sensor switches are more reliable than mechanical switches
- Hall sensor switches do not suffer from switch bouncing problems
- Hall sensor switches are faster than mechanical switches
- Hall sensor switches are not affected by environmental contaminants
- When used as linear analog sensors, these sensors are used to measure the magnetic field near the sensor. In this project, the analog output of the sensor module is used.

Block Diagram: Figure 10.2 shows the block diagram of the project.

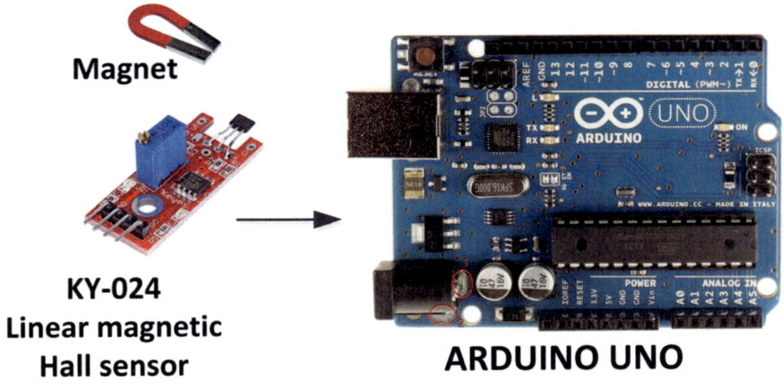

Figure 10.2 Block diagram of the project

Arduino Uno Circuit Diagram: Figure 10.3 shows the circuit diagram where the analog output of the sensor module is connected to analog input A0 of the Arduino Uno.

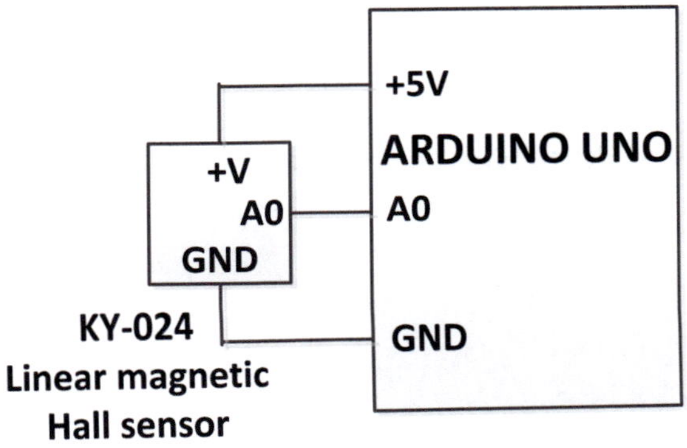

Figure 10.3 Circuit diagram of the project

Arduino Uno Program Listing: Figure 10.4 shows the Arduino Uno program listing (program: **magnetic**). The program reads the analog output of the sensor and converts this data into physical voltage in variable **mV**. This value is then plotted using the Arduino Uno serial plotter. Notice that using command **Serial.println** to display values also saves these values for the plotter. Figure 10.5 shows an output from the serial plotter when a magnet was moved close to the sensor. The vertical axis is the voltage output from the module in millivolts and the horizontal axis is the time. The output of the sensor can be calibrated to give the correct magnetic field strength.

```
/*****************************************************************
 *                  MEASURING MAGNETIC FIELD STRENGTH
 *                  =================================
 *
 * In this program a KY-024 linear Hall sensor module is used to
 * measure magnetic field.
 *
 * Author: Dogan Ibrahim
 * Date  : May 2019
 * File  : magnetic
 *****************************************************************/
int magnet = A0;                                // sensor pin
int reading;
float mV;

void setup ()
{
  Serial.begin(9600);
}

void loop ()
{
  reading = analogRead(magnet);                 // Read value
  mV = reading * 5000.0 / 1023.0;               // In mV
  Serial.println(mV);                           // Display and save
  delay(100);
}
```

Figure 10.4 Arduino Uno program listing

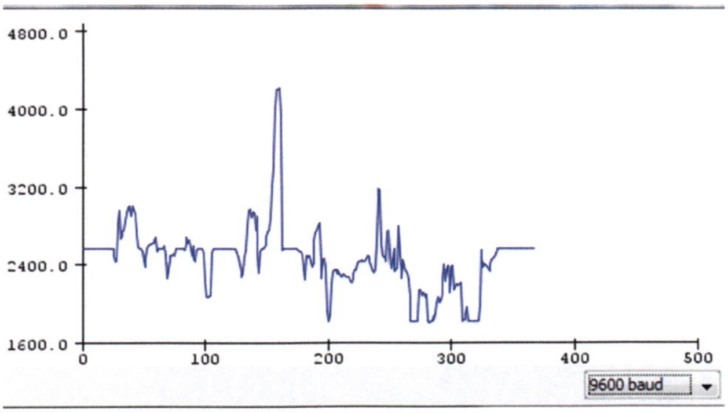

Figure 10.5 Plotting the magnetic field

ESP32 DevKitC Program Listing: The ESP32 DevKitC version of the program can easily be derived by examining the project in section 4.2.7 which uses one of the ADC channels, and also the program given in Figure 10.4. Connect the +V pin of the sensor module to +3.3V.

Raspberry Pi Program Listing: Raspberry Pi does not have on-board ADC, but KY-053 can be used as described in section 4.2.6 to read and display the analog output voltage of KY-024. Connect the +V pin of the sensor module to +3.3V.

10.3 Project 2 – Magnetic door alarm

Description: In this project, the KY-025 reed switch module is attached to the door frame and a magnet is attached to the door. When the door is closed the magnet is near the reed sensor module so that the output of the sensor module is at logic HIGH. When the door opens the magnet gets away from the sensor and the output of the sensor goes to logic LOW. The buzzer is then activated for 10 seconds.

Aim: The aim of this project is to show how the reed switch module can be used in projects.

Sensor Used: Two sensor modules are used in this project: KY-025 reed switch module, and KY-012 active buzzer module. Figure 10.6 shows the KY-025 reed switch module which has 4-pins:

- D0: digital output
- +V: power supply
- GND: power ground
- A0: analog output

As with the KY-024, both digital and analog outputs are available from the module. KY-025 module consists of a Hall sensor chip, LM393 comparator chip, potentiometer, some resistors, and LEDs. The comparator compares the output of the Hall sensor with half the supply voltage and changes state if the Hall sensor output voltage is higher than half the supply voltage. It is recommended to adjust the sensitivity to the desired level in digital output applications.

Figure 10.6 KY-025 reed switch module

Block Diagram: Figure 10.7 shows the block diagram of the project.

Figure 10.7 Block diagram of the project

Arduino Uno Circuit Diagram: The circuit diagram of the project is shown in Figure 10.8. In this project the digital output of the sensor is used, where D0 pin of the sensor module is connected to port pin 2 of Arduino Uno, and the buzzer is connected to pin 3.

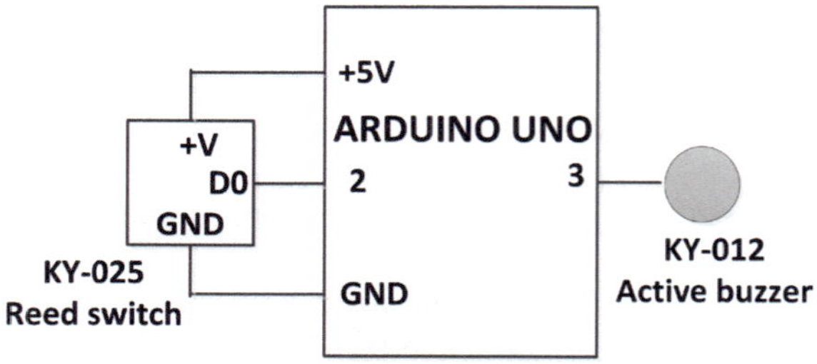

Figure 10.8 Arduino Uno circuit diagram

Arduino Uno Program Listing: Figure 10.9 shows the program listing (program: **reed**). Inside the setup routine, the sensor is configured as input and the buzzer as output. Inside the main program loop, the program waits until the door is opened. When the door is opened, the output of the reed switch goes to logic LOW and then the buzzer is activated for 10 seconds.

```
/*****************************************************************
 *                  MAGNETIC DOOR ALARM
 *                  ===================
 *
 * In this program a KY-025 reed magnetic switch is conencted to
 * port pin 2 and a KY-012 active buzzer is conencted to pin 3 of
 * the Arduino Uno. The buzzer sounds when the sensor is activated
 *
 * Author: Dogan Ibrahim
 * Date  : May 2019
 * File  : reed
 *****************************************************************/
int reed = 2;                                  // reed pin
int buzzer = 3;                                // buzzer pin

void setup ()
{
  pinMode(reed, INPUT);                        // reed is input
  pinMode(buzzer, OUTPUT);                     // buzzer is output
  digitalWrite(buzzer, LOW);                   // buzzer OFF
}

void loop ()
{
  while(digitalRead(reed) == 1);               // wait for door open
  digitalWrite(buzzer, HIGH);                  // buzzer ON
  delay(10000);                                // 10 secs delay
  digitalWrite(buzzer, LOW);                   // buzzer OFF
}
```

Figure 10.9 Arduino Uno program listing

ESP32 DevKitC Program Listing: The ESP32 DevKitC program is exactly the same as the one given in Figure 10.9. +V pin of the sensor module should be connected to +3.3V.

Raspberry Pi Program Listing: The Raspberry Pi version of the program is very simple and the reader should be able to drive it by studying the previous projects. +V pin of the sensor module should be connected to +3.3V.

10.4 Project 3 – Magnetic musical instrument

Description: In this project, the KY-035 analog magnetic sensor module is used together with a passive buzzer module. The buzzer makes sounds with different frequencies as a magnet is moved close to the sensor chip.

Aim: The aim of this project is to show how the KY-035 analog magnetic sensor module can be used in projects.

Sensor Used: Two sensor modules are used in this project: KY-035 magnetic sensor module and KY-006 passive piezo buzzer module. Figure 10.10 shows the KY-035 module which has 3-pins:

- Signal (S)
- +V
- GND

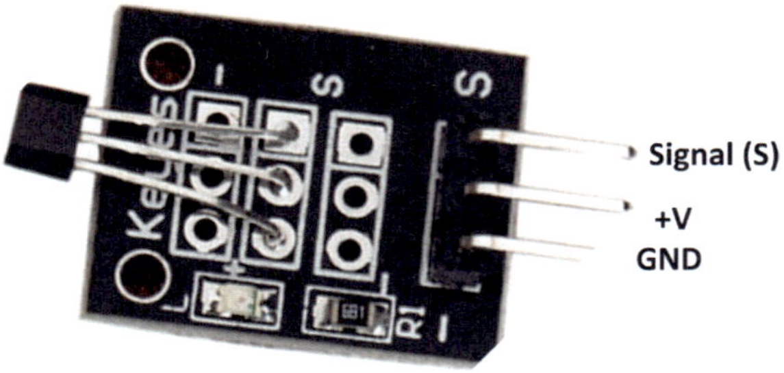

Figure 10.10 KY-035 module

KY-035 measures the magnetic field near its sensor chip and provides analog output.

Block Diagram: Figure 10.11shows the project block diagram.

Figure 10.11 Block diagram of the project

Arduino Uno Circuit Diagram: The circuit diagram of the project is shown in Figure 10.12. The analog output of the sensor is connected to analog input A0 of Arduino Uno. In addition, the passive piezo buzzer module is connected to port pin 2.

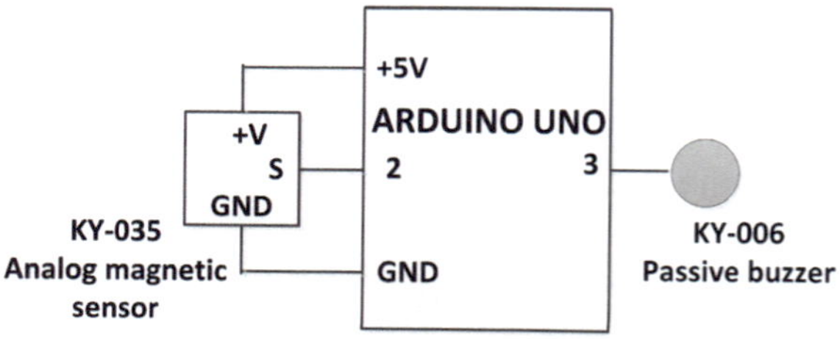

Figure 10.12 Arduino Uno circuit diagram

Arduino Uno Program Listing: Figure 10.13 shows the Arduino Uno program listing (program: **magtone**). Inside the setup routine buzzer is configured as an output and is turned OFF. Inside the main program loop, the analog output of the sensor is read and stored in variable **r**. If was found that without a magnet the output of the ADC had a value around 518. As this value will generate sound without a magnet, the output is modified such that sound is generated only if the ADC value is greater than 530. The value of **r** is used as the frequency in the built-in statement **tone**. As a magnet is brought close to the sensor chip sounds with different frequencies will be heard from the buzzer.

```
/****************************************************************
 *                    MAGNETIC MUSICAL INSTRUMENT
 *                    ===========================
 *
 * In this program a KY-035 analog magnetic sensor module is used
 * together with the KY-006 passive piezo buzzer module. The buzzer
 * generates sounds with different frequencies as a magnet is brought
 * close to the snesor chip.
 *
 * Author: Dogan Ibrahim
 * Date  : May 2019
 * File  : magtone
 ****************************************************************/
const int S = A0;                                // Signal pin
const int buzzer = 2;                            // Buzzer pin

void setup ()
{
  pinMode(buzzer, OUTPUT);                       // Buzzer is output
  digitalWrite(buzzer, LOW);                     // Buzzer OFF
}


void loop ()
{
  int r = analogRead(A0);                        // Read analog data
  if(r > 530)                                    // Suppress sound
     tone(buzzer, r, 100);                       // Generate sound
}
```

Figure 10.13 Arduino Uno program listing

10.5 Summary

In this Chapter, we have learned how to use the KY-024, KY-025, and KY-035 magnetic sensor modules in projects. In the next Chapter, we will be looking at the flame sensor module.

Chapter 11 • Flame sensor projects

11.1 Overview

In the previous Chapter, we have seen how to develop projects for the Arduino Uno, Raspberry Pi, and ESP32 DevKitC using the magnetic sensor modules.

In this Chapter, we will be developing projects using the flame sensor module.

11.2 Project 1 – Flame sensor with buzzer output

Description: In this project, the KY-026 flame sensor module is used to sense fire and activate a buzzer when a fire is detected.

Aim: The aim of this project is to show how the flame sensor module can be used in projects.

Sensor Used: In this project, the KY-026 flame sensor module and the KY-012 active buzzer module are used. Figure 11.1 shows the KY-026 flame sensor module. This is a 4-pin module having the following pins:

- D0: digital output
- +V: power supply
- GND: power ground
- A0: analog output

Both digital and analog outputs are available from the module. The digital output is normally at logic LOW and goes to logic HIGH when a flame is detected. KY-026 module consists of an infrared sensor chip that detects the infrared light emitted by fire, LM393 comparator chip, potentiometer, some resistors, and LEDs. The potentiometer is used to adjust the sensitivity of the module.

Figure 11.1 KY-026 flame sensor module

Background Information: Flame sensors consists of infrared LEDs that are sensitive to the infrared light emitted by a fire. KY-026 has the following basic features:

- Operating voltage: 3.3V to 5V
- Infrared detection wavelength: 760nm to 1100nm
- Sensor detect angle: 60º

Flame sensors are used with temperature and humidity sensors to detect forest fires. In this Chapter, we will develop a simple project that will activate a buzzer when a fire is detected.

Block Diagram: Figure 11.2 shows the block diagram of the project.

Figure 11.2 Block diagram of the project

Arduino Uno Circuit Diagram: The circuit diagram of the project is shown in Figure 11.3. In this project the digital output of the sensor is used, where D0 pin of the sensor module is connected to port pin 2 of Arduino Uno, and the buzzer is connected to pin 4.

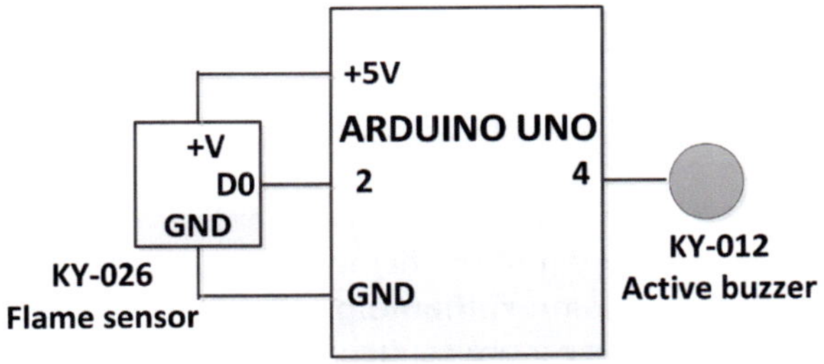

Figure 11.3 Arduino Uno circuit diagram

Arduino Uno Program Listing: Figure 11.4 shows the program listing (program: **flame**). Inside the setup routine, the sensor is configured as input and the buzzer as output. Inside the main program loop, the program waits until a fire is detected. When a fire is detected, the output of the sensor goes to logic HIGH and then the buzzer is activated.

```
/*****************************************************************
 *                  FLAME SENSOR WITH BUZZER OUPUT
 *                  ==============================
 *
 * In this program a KY-026 flame sensor module and a KY-012 active
 * buzzer module are used where the buzzer is activated when fire
 * is detected. Notice that the buzzer is activated until stopped
 * by the user
 *
 * Author: Dogan Ibrahim
```

```
 * Date   : May 2019
 * File   : flame
 ***************************************************************/
int flame = 2;                                   // flame sensor pin
int buzzer = 4;                                  // buzzer pin

void setup ()
{
  pinMode(flame, INPUT);                         // flame is input
  pinMode(buzzer, OUTPUT);                       // buzzer is output
  digitalWrite(buzzer, LOW);                     // buzzer OFF
}

void loop ()
{
  while(digitalRead(flame) == 0);                // wait if not fire
  digitalWrite(buzzer, HIGH);                    // buzzer ON
}
```

Figure 11.4 Arduino Uno program listing

ESP32 DevKitC Program Listing: The ESP32 DevKitC hardware is exactly the same as the one given in Figure 11.3, but +V pin of the flame sensor module should be connected to +3.3V. The ESP32 DevKitC program is exactly the same as the one given in Figure 11.4. Make sure you change the board type to ESP32 Dev Module before compiling the program.

Raspberry Pi Program Listing: The Raspberry Pi hardware is exactly the same as the one given in Figure 11.3, but +V pin of the flame sensor module should be connected to +3.3V. The program listing (program: **rpiflame.py**) is shown n Figure 11.5. At the beginning of the program flame and buzzer are configured as input and output respectively and the buzzer is turned OFF. The main program loop waits until a fire is detected and when this happens the buzzer is activated.

```
#----------------------------------------------------------------
#
#              FLAME SENSOR WITH BUZZER OUTPUT
#              ================================
#
# In this program the KY-026 flame sensor module and the KY-012
# active buzzer module are used. When fire is detected the buzzer
# is activated.
#
# Program: rpiflame.py
# Date   : May 2019
# Author : Dogan Ibrahim
#----------------------------------------------------------------
import RPi.GPIO as GPIO        # Import GPIO
```

```
flame = 2           # flame pin
buzzer = 4          # buzzer pin

GPIO.setmode(GPIO.BCM)
GPIO.setwarnings(False)
GPIO.setup(flame, GPIO.IN)      # flame is input
GPIO.setup(buzzer, GPIO.OUT)      # buzzer is output
GPIO.output(buzzer, GPIO.LOW)     # buzzer OFF

#
# Wait until fire is detected, and if so activate buzzer
#
try:
  while True:
     while GPIO.input(flame) == 0:    # wait for fire
       pass
     GPIO.output(buzzer, GPIO.HIGH)   # activate buzzer

except KeyboardInterrupt:
     GPIO.cleanup()
```

Figure 11.5 Raspberry Pi program listing

11.3 Summary

In this Chapter, we have learned how to use the flame sensor in a project. In the next chapter, we will be using the joystick module in a project.

Chapter 12 • Joystick module projects

12.1 Overview

In the previous Chapter, we have seen how to develop a project for the Arduino Uno, Raspberry Pi, and ESP32 DevKitC using the flame sensor module and the buzzer module.

In this Chapter, we will be developing projects using the joystick module.

12.2 Project 1 – Using the joystick

Description: This project shows how to use the KY-023 joystick module. The joystick is moved in various directions and the corresponding analog output value is read and displayed.

Aim: The aim of this project is to show how to use the KY-023 joystick module.

Sensor Used: In this project, the KY-023 joystick is used. As shown in Figure 12.1, KY-023 is a 5-pin module with the following pins:

- GND: power ground
- +V: power input
- VRx: x-axis potentiometer output
- VRy: y-axis potentiometer output
- SW: push-button switch output

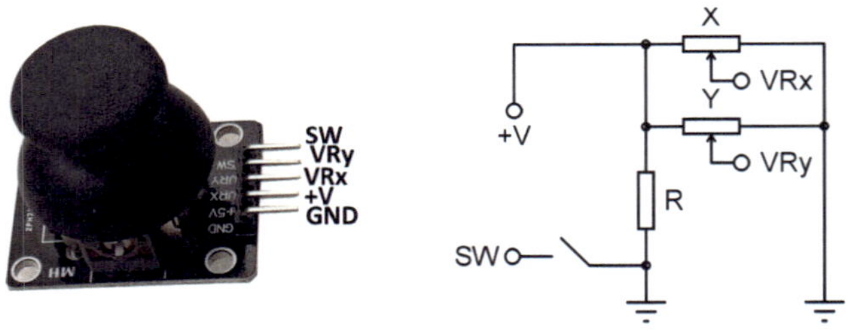

Figure 12.1 KY-023 joystick module

As shown in Figure 12.1, the module consists of two potentiometers, positioned at vertical planes to each other, and a push-button switch. When connected to a supply voltage of +V volts, the module produces an output of V/2 from X and Y potentiometers when in rest. Moving the joystick causes the output to vary from 0V to +V depending on its direction. If for example using a 10-bit ADC (0 to 1023 quantization levels) to read the analog output voltage of a potentiometer, the reading will be around 512 in resting position and will vary from 0 to 1023 as the joystick arm is moved in the same direction. Similar output is obtained in the other direction.

Background Information: Joysticks are commonly used in games and robotics. They are made of two or three potentiometers mounted at 90 degrees angle to each other. The potentiometers are connected to a short stick centered by springs. In resting mode, the stick is positioned such that the potentiometer arms are in the middle of the corresponding potentiometers. By moving the stick in one direction we effectively change the arm position of that potentiometer and this is read by the ADC of the processor.

Block Diagram: Figure 12.2 shows the block diagram of the project.

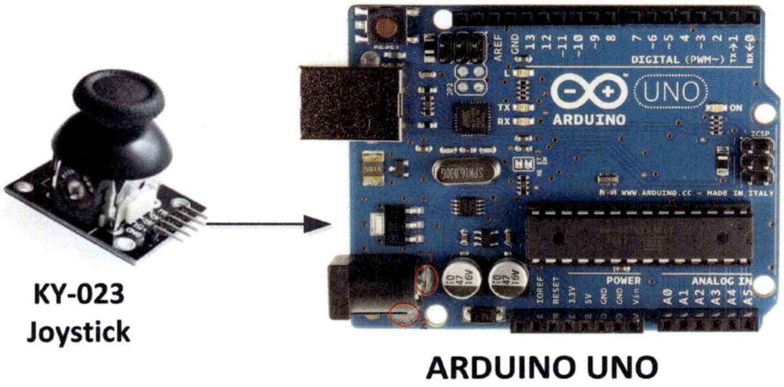

Figure 12.2 Block diagram of the project

Arduino Uno Circuit Diagram: Figure 12.3 shows the circuit diagram of the project. Pins VRx and VRy are connected to analog inputs A0 and A1 of Arduino Uno respectively. Also, the SW pin is connected to digital input 2.

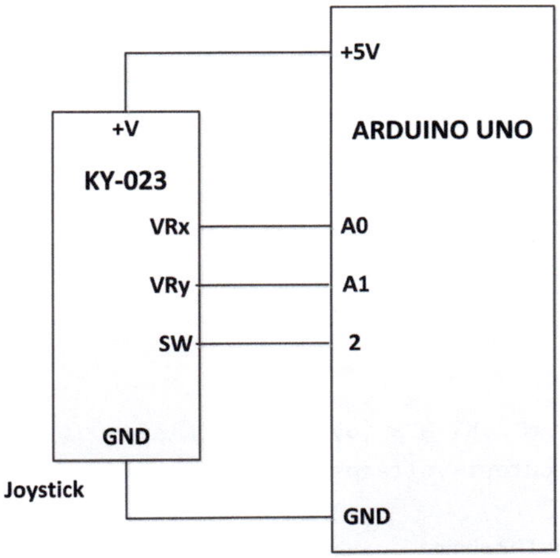

Figure 12.3 Arduino Uno circuit diagram

Arduino Uno Program: X-Y coordinates of the joystick are shown in Figure 12.4. With the 10-bit ADC of the Arduino, we expect to get the values as shown in the figure.

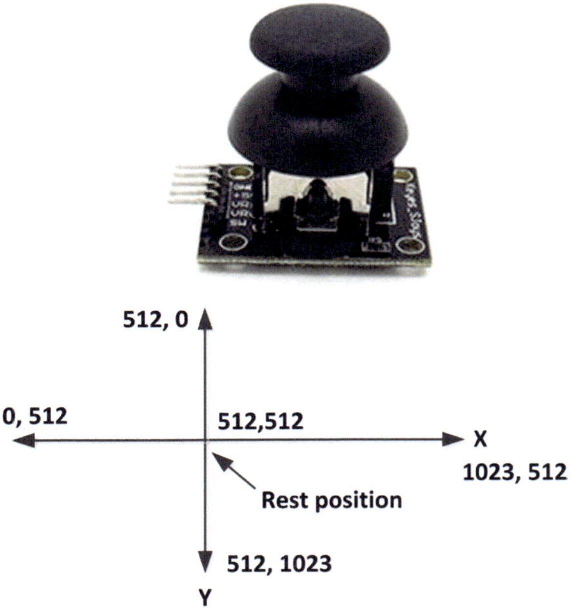

Figure 12.4 X-Y coordinates of the joystick

Figure 12.5 shows the Arduino Uno program listing (program: **joystick**). Pins **VRx** and **VRy** of the joystick are assigned to Arduino analog ports **A0** and **A1** respectively. Pin **SW** is assigned to port pin 2 and it is configured as an input with an internal pull-up resistor. The program reads the analog outputs of **VRx** and **VRy** and the state of switch **SW** and displays on the serial monitor. The switch output is normally at logic HIGH and goes to logic LOW when it is pressed. A typical output is shown in Figure 12.6.

```
/*****************************************************************
 *                          JOYSTICK
 *                          ========
 *
 * In this program a KY-023 joystick module is used. The program
 * displays the output voltages as the joystick stick is moved.
 *
 * Author: Dogan Ibrahim
 * Date  : May 2019
 * File  : joystick
 *****************************************************************/
const int VRx = A0;                                  // VRx pin
const int VRy = A1;                                  // VRy pin
const int SW = 2;                                    // SW pin

void setup ()
{
```

```
  Serial.begin(9600);
  pinMode(SW, INPUT_PULLUP);                     // SW is input
}

void loop ()
{
  Serial.print("X-axis value = ");               // Display text
  Serial.print(analogRead(VRx));                 // Display VRx
  Serial.print("     Y-axis value = ");          // Display text
  Serial.print(analogRead(VRy));                 // Display VRy
  Serial.print("     Switch = ");                // Display text
  Serial.println(digitalRead(SW));               // Display SW
  delay(1000);                                   // Wait a bit
}
```

Figure 12.5 Arduino Uno program listing

```
X-axis value = 516      Y-axis value = 507      Switch = 1
X-axis value = 517      Y-axis value = 507      Switch = 1
X-axis value = 517      Y-axis value = 507      Switch = 1
X-axis value = 517      Y-axis value = 507      Switch = 0
X-axis value = 517      Y-axis value = 507      Switch = 1
X-axis value = 516      Y-axis value = 507      Switch = 1
X-axis value = 517      Y-axis value = 507      Switch = 1
X-axis value = 517      Y-axis value = 507      Switch = 1
X-axis value = 517      Y-axis value = 507      Switch = 1
X-axis value = 518      Y-axis value = 1023      Switch = 1
X-axis value = 517      Y-axis value = 507      Switch = 1
```

Figure 12.6 Typical display of the joystick outputs

ESP32 DevKitC Program Listing: This circuit diagram of the ESP32 DevkitC version of the project is shown in Figure 12.7. ADC ports ADC2_0 (GPIO 4) and ADC2_1 (GPIO 0) are connected to joystick pins VRx and VRy respectively. Additionally, GPIO 23 is connected to pin SW.

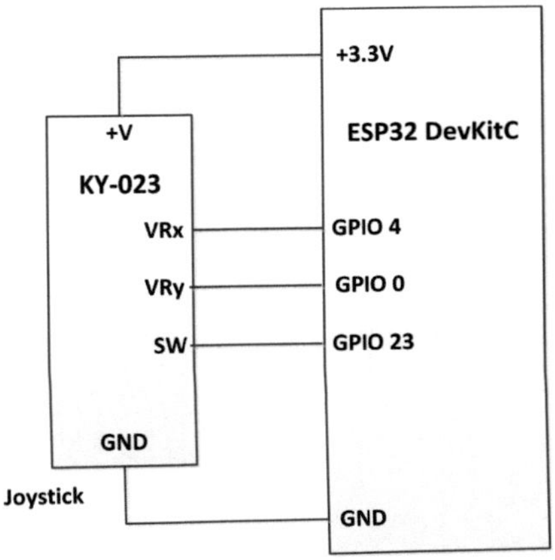

Figure 12.7 ESP32 DevKitC circuit diagram

Figure 12.8 shows the ESP32 DevKitC program listing (program: **esp32joystick**). Notice that the ADC is 12-bits wide having quantization levels from 0 to 4095. Therefore, we expect the joystick values at resting position to be 2048 and to vary between 0 and 4095. Make sure that you select the board type as ESP32 Dev Module before compiling the program.

```
/*****************************************************************
 *                         JOYSTICK
 *                         ========
 *
 * In this program a KY-023 joystick module is used. The program
 * displays the output voltages as the joystick stick is moved.
 *
 * Author: Dogan Ibrahim
 * Date  : May 2019
 * File  : esp32joystick
 *****************************************************************/
const int VRx = 4;                                  // VRx pin
const int VRy = 0;                                  // VRy pin
const int SW = 23;                                  // SW pin

void setup ()
{
  Serial.begin(9600);
  pinMode(SW, INPUT_PULLUP);                         // SW is input
}

void loop ()
{
  Serial.print("X-axis value = ");                   // Display text
  Serial.print(analogRead(VRx));                     // Display VRx
  Serial.print("     Y-axis value = ");              // Display text
  Serial.print(analogRead(VRy));                     // Display VRy
  Serial.print("     Switch = ");                    // Display text
  Serial.println(digitalRead(SW));                   // Display SW
  delay(1000);                                       // Wait a bit
}
```

Figure 12.8 ESP32 DevKitC program listing

A typical output is shown in Figure 12.9.

```
X-axis value = 1859      Y-axis value = 2911      Switch = 1
X-axis value = 1859      Y-axis value = 2907      Switch = 1
X-axis value = 1859      Y-axis value = 2907      Switch = 1
X-axis value = 1859      Y-axis value = 2906      Switch = 0
X-axis value = 1861      Y-axis value = 2911      Switch = 1
X-axis value = 1861      Y-axis value = 2910      Switch = 1
X-axis value = 1861      Y-axis value = 2907      Switch = 1
X-axis value = 4095      Y-axis value = 2903      Switch = 1
X-axis value = 4095      Y-axis value = 2911      Switch = 1
X-axis value = 1861      Y-axis value = 2907      Switch = 1
X-axis value = 1860      Y-axis value = 2907      Switch = 1
X-axis value = 1862      Y-axis value = 2907      Switch = 1
```

Figure 12.9 Typical display of the joystick outputs

Raspberry Pi Program Listing: Raspberry Pi has no onboard ADC and we have to use the 4-channel 16-bit KY-053 (see section 4.2.6) ADC module. Figure 12.10 shows the circuit diagram of the project. As described in Chapter 4, KY-053 operates using the I^2C bus. Pins VRx and VRy of the joystick are connected to pins A0 and A1 of the ADC. Also, pin SW of the joystick is connected to GPIO 17 of Raspberry Pi.

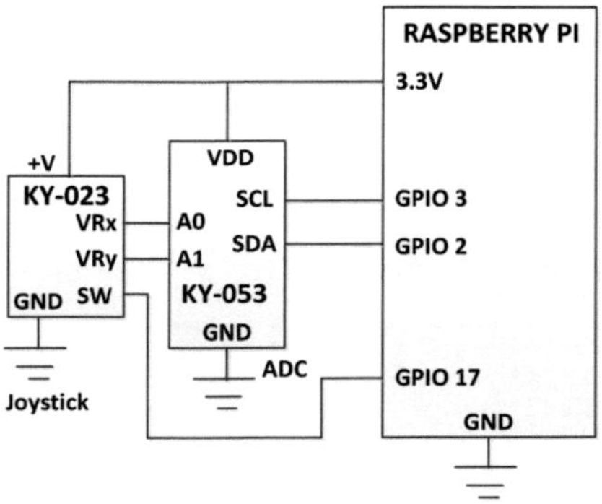

Figure 12.10 Raspberry Pi circuit diagram

Figure 12.11 shows the Raspberry Pi program listing (program: **rpijoystick.py**). Typical output from the program is shown in Figure 12.12.

```
#---------------------------------------------------------------
#
#                    JOYSTICK
#                    ========
#
# In this program a joystick (KY-023) is connected to the
# Raspberry Pi through the KY-053 ADC. The program displays
# the joystick values as the stick is moved.
#
# Program: rpijoystick.py
# Date   : May 2019
# Author : Dogan Ibrahim
#---------------------------------------------------------------
```

```
import RPi.GPIO as GPIO        # Import GPIOe
import time                    # Import time
import Adafruit_ADS1x15        # Import ADC

adc = Adafruit_ADS1x15.ADS1115()
GAIN = 1            # Set ADC gain

VRx = 0             # VRx at ADC 0
VRy = 1             # VRy at ADC 1
SW = 17             # SW at GPIO 17

GPIO.setmode(GPIO.BCM)
GPIO.setwarnings(False)
GPIO.setup(SW, GPIO.IN, pull_up_down=GPIO.PUD_UP)

while True:
    X = adc.read_adc(VRx, gain=GAIN)    # Read channel A0
    Y = adc.read_adc(VRy, gain=GAIN)    # Read channel A1
    switch = GPIO.input(SW)             # Read switch
    print "X = ", X, "   Y = ", Y, "   Switch = ",switch
    time.sleep(1)
```

Figure 12.11 Raspberry Pi program listing

```
X =  13356    Y =  13128    Switch =  0
X =  13349    Y =  13122    Switch =  1
X =  13351    Y =  13123    Switch =  1
X =  26420    Y =  13129    Switch =  1
X =  26420    Y =  13127    Switch =  1
X =  26420    Y =  13127    Switch =  1
X =  13374    Y =  13125    Switch =  1
X =  13373    Y =  13123    Switch =  1
X =  13373    Y =  13122    Switch =  1
X =  13373    Y =  13122    Switch =  1
X =  13373    Y =  13121    Switch =  1
X =  13372    Y =  13122    Switch =  1
X =  13374    Y =  13122    Switch =  1
X =  13373    Y =  13123    Switch =  1
X =  13373    Y =  13123    Switch =  1
X =  13372    Y =  13124    Switch =  1
X =  13373    Y =  13123    Switch =  1
X =  13371    Y =  13123    Switch =  1
X =  13381    Y =  13133    Switch =  1
X =  26418    Y =  19016    Switch =  1
X =  26417    Y =  19028    Switch =  1
X =  26417    Y =  19059    Switch =  1
X =  13374    Y =  13125    Switch =  1
```

Figure 12.12 Typical display of the joystick outputs

12.3 Project 2 – Joystick based musical instrument

Description: This project uses the KY-023 joystick module and the KY-006 passive piezo buzzer module. The project generates PWM based sounds with frequencies from 1000Hz to 2023Hz as the joystick is moved from the beginning of X-direction to its end.

Aim: The aim of this project is to show how the buzzer can be used with the joystick to generate sounds with different frequencies and different duty cycles.

Sensor Used: In this project, the KY-023 joystick and KY-006 passive piezo sensor module are used.

Block Diagram: Figure 12.13 shows the block diagram of the project.

Figure 12.13 Block diagram of the project

Arduino Uno Circuit Diagram: Figure 12.14 shows the project circuit diagram. Joystick pin VRx is connected to pin A0 of Arduino Uno, and the buzzer is connected to port pin 3.

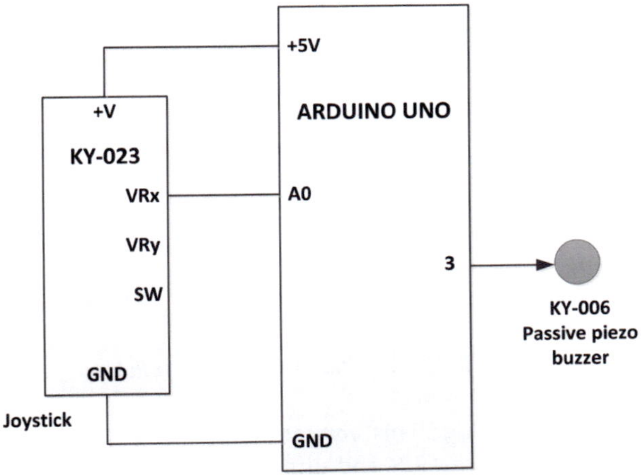

Figure 12.14 Arduino Uno circuit diagram

Arduino Uno Program Listing: The program listing (program: **joybuzzer**) is shown in Figure 12.15. Inside the setup routine **buzzer** is configured as an output and it is turned OFF. Inside the main program loop, analog output value of **VRx** potentiometer is read which should be between 0 and 1023. Then, 1000 is then added to this value so that the value is between 1000 and 2023. This value is then used as the frequency in Hertz in built-in function **tone**. As the joystick stick is moved in X-direction, you should hear sounds with different frequencies being generated.

```
/****************************************************************
 *              JOYSTICK BASED MUSICAL INSTRUMENT
 *              =================================
 *
 * In this program a KY-023 joystick module and a KY-006 passive
 * piezo buzzer is used. The program generates sounds with different
 * frequencies.
 *
 * Author: Dogan Ibrahim
 * Date  : May 2019
 * File  : joybuzzer
 *****************************************************************/
const int VRx = A0;                             // VRx pin
const int buzzer = 3;                           // Buzzer pin

void setup ()
{
  pinMode(buzzer, OUTPUT);                      // Buzzer is output
  digitalWrite(buzzer, LOW);                    // Buzzer OFF
}

//
// X takes values between 0 and 1023, where X is used to change the
// frequency. The frequency varies between 1000Hz and 2023Hz as the
// joystick arm is moved
//
void loop ()
{
  int X = analogRead(VRx);                      // Read X (0-1023)
  X = X + 1000;                                 // 1000Hz-2023Hz
  tone(buzzer, X, 100);                         // Generate tone
}
```

Figure 12.15 Arduino Uno program listing

ESP32 DevKitC Program Listing: This version of the program can easily be written by reference to the program in Figure 12.8 and Chapter 9.

Raspberry Pi Program Listing: This version of the program can easily be written by reference to the program in Figure 12.11 and Chapter 9.

12.4 Summary

In this Chapter, we have learned how to use the joystick module in projects. In the next Chapter, we will be using the obstacle sensor modules.

Chapter 13 • Obstacle sensor projects

13.1 Overview

In the previous Chapter, we have seen how to develop a project for the Arduino Uno, Raspberry Pi, and ESP32 DevKitC using the joystick module and the buzzer module.
In this Chapter, we will be developing projects using the KY-032 and KY-036 obstacle sensor modules.

13.2 Project 1 – Aid with car parking

Description: This project shows how to use the KY-032 obstacle detection module to aid in parking our car. The sensor is mounted in front of our car and a buzzer is activated if our car is close to the car in front of us. The detection range of the sensor is around 40cm.

Aim: The aim of this project is to show how to use the KY-032 obstacle detection module.

Sensor Used: In this project, the KY-032 and KY-012 active buzzer module are used. As shown in Figure 13.1, KY-032 is a 4-pin module with the following pins:

- EN (Enable)
- Out
- +V
- GND

Figure 13.1 KY-032 module

The specifications of this module are:

- Operating voltage: 3.3V to 5V
- Operating current: 20mA
- Detection distance: 2cm to 40cm
- Detection angle: ±35°

The module operates with 38kHz and consists of an infrared LED, an infrared receiver, two potentiometers, and a jumper. The light emitted by the LED is detected by the receiver which incorporates an optical 950nm IR filter to increase the sensitivity. One of the potentiometers (R6) is used to fine tune the signal so that it is exactly 38kHz, and this potentiometer can only be adjusted by using an oscilloscope (it is recommended to leave it at its center position). The other potentiometer (R5) is used to adjust the duty cycle of the signal which effectively controls the brightness and hence the range of the emitter LED. The EN pin must be set to logic HIGH to enable the module. If the EN pin is not used then the jumper must be installed. The EN function cannot be used if the jumper is in place, therefore you should remove the jumper in order to use the EN pin.

Background Information: Obstacle sensors are usually used in robotic applications to detect the distances to objects and change the direction of movement if objects are detected. These sensors are made using either ultrasonic transmitter/receiver pairs or infrared LED/receiver pairs. The advantage of using the ultrasonic method is that the detection range is much larger. Infrared sensors have the advantages that they are very cheap and are not affected by the visible light. In this project infrared LED/receiver pair is used to detect obstacles away from the front of our car.

Block Diagram: Figure 13.2 shows the block diagram of the project.

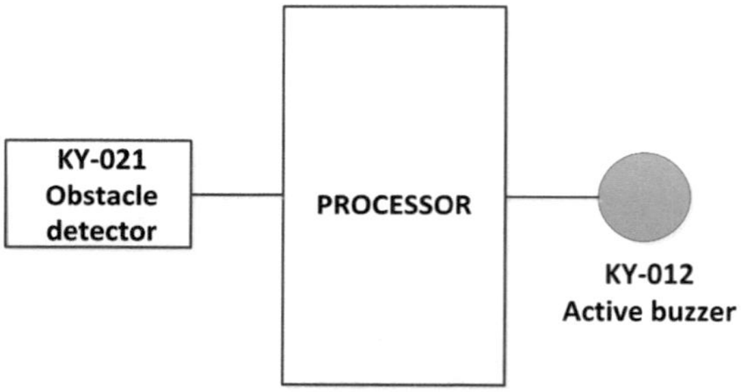

Figure 13.2 Block diagram of the project

Arduino Uno Circuit Diagram: The Arduino Uno circuit diagram of the project is shown in Figure 13.3. EN and OUT pins of the KY-032 sensor module are connected to pins 2 and 3 of Arduino Uno respectively. KY-012 active buzzer module is connected to port pin 4. The jumper is removed from the module.

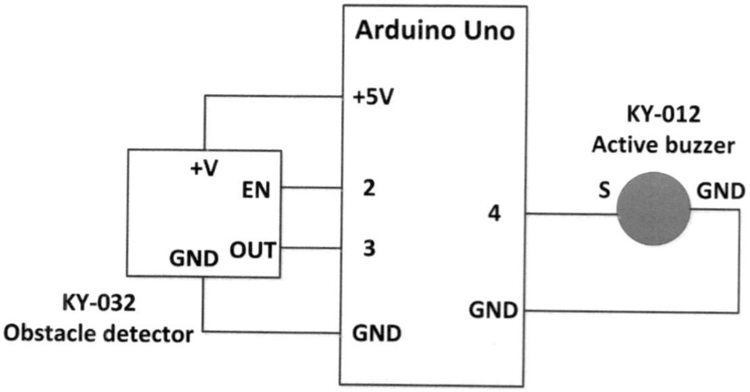

Figure 13.3 Arduino Uno circuit diagram

Arduino Uno Program Listing: Figure 13.4 shows the program listing (program: **park**). Inside the setup routine, **EN** and **buzzer** are configured as outputs, **EN** is enabled and **buzzer** is turned OFF. Also, the output signal of the sensor **(OUT**) is configured as an input. Inside the main program loop, the output of the obstacle sensor is checked and the buzzer is turned ON if an obstacle is detected, i.e. if the output of the obstacle sensor goes to logic LOW. You can set the sensitivity (i.e. the range) of the sensor module by adjusting potentiometer R5.

```
/****************************************************************
 *                      AID TO PARKING
 *                      ==============
 *
 * In this program a KY-032 obstacle detector module is used together
 * with the KY-012 active buzzer module. The buzzer is activated when
 * obstacle is detected in-front of the obstacle sensor.
 *
 * Author: Dogan Ibrahim
 * Date  : May 2019
 * File  : park
 ****************************************************************/
const int EN = 2;                                // EN pin
const int OUT = 3;                               // OUT pin
const int buzzer = 4;                            // Buzzer pin

void setup ()
{
  pinMode(buzzer, OUTPUT);                       // Buzzer is output
  digitalWrite(buzzer, LOW);                     // Buzzer OFF
  pinMode(EN, OUTPUT);                           // EN is output
  digitalWrite(EN, HIGH);                        // Enable module
  pinMode(OUT, INPUT);                           // OUT is input
}

//
//
//
void loop ()
{
  if(digitalRead(OUT) == LOW)                    // If obstacle
      digitalWrite(buzzer, HIGH);                // Buzzer ON
  else
      digitalWrite(buzzer, LOW);                 // Buzzer OFF
}
```

Figure 13.4 Arduino Uno program listing

ESP32 DevKitC Program Listing: The same circuit as in Figure 13.3 can be used, but you should avoid using GPIO 1 and GPIO 3 as these are used by the USB interface. The same program as in 13.4 can be used here with the modified GPIO pins.

Raspberry Pi Program Listing: The Raspberry Pi program is very simple and can very easily be derived by studying the previous projects.

13.3 Project 2 – Metal touch sensor

Description: This project shows how to use the KY-036 metal touch sensor in projects. This sensor is activated when the metal part in-front of the sensor is touched. The sensor module can be used in robotic projects to detect obstacles. It can also be used as a touch switch. In this project, a buzzer is activated when the sensor is touched by a finger.

Aim: The aim of this project is to show how to use the KY-036 metal touch sensor module in a project.

Sensor Used: In this project, the KY-036 and KY-012 active buzzer module are used. As shown in Figure 13.5, KY-036 is a 4-pin module with the following pins:

- Digital out (D0)
- +V
- GND
- Analog out (A0)

The sensor module consists of a pair of NPN Darlington transistors which are turned ON when touched. An LM393 comparator chip is used to compare half the supply voltage with the voltage at the output of the transistors. The output goes to logic HIGH when the voltage at the output of the transistors is above half the supply voltage. A power LED and a sensitivity LED are provided on the module. The sensitivity can be adjusted using the potentiometer. In addition to digital output, the module also provides analog output. In this project, the digital output is used.

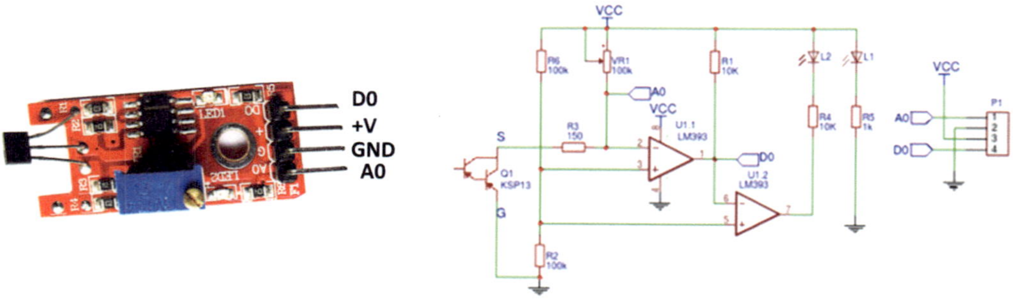

Figure 13.5 KY-036 metal touch sensor

Block Diagram: Figure 13.6 shows the project block diagram.

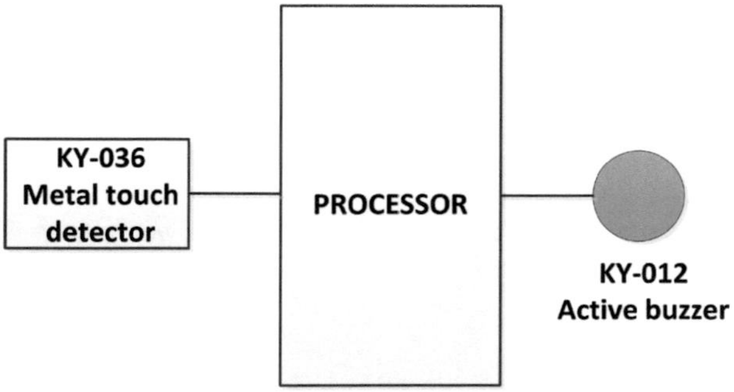

Figure 13.6 Block diagram of the project

Arduino Uno Circuit Diagram: Figure 13.7 shows the Arduino Uno circuit diagram of the project. D0 output of the sensor module is connected to port pin 2 of Arduino Uno. Additionally, the buzzer is connected to port pin 3.

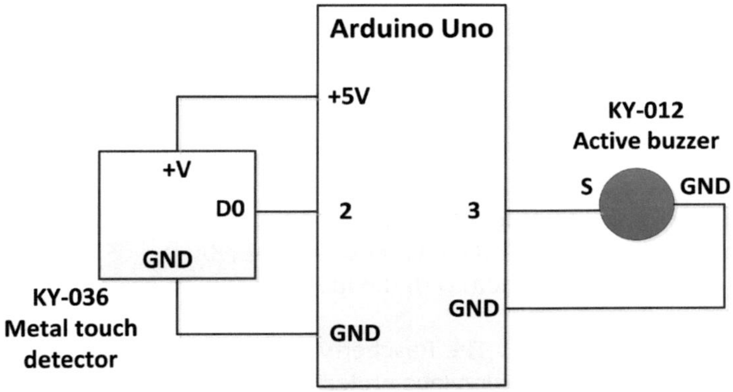

Figure 13.7 Circuit diagram of the project

Arduino Uno Program Listing: Figure 13.8 shows the program listing (program: **metal**). Inside the setup routine, **D0** is configured as input and **buzzer** is configured as an output. Inside the main program loop, the buzzer is activated whenever the sensor is touched.

```
/*****************************************************************
 *                       TOUCH SENSOR
 *                       ============
 *
 * In this program a KY-036 metal touch sensor module is used together
 * with the KY-012 active buzzer module. The buzzer is activated when
 * the sensor is touched.
 *
 * Author: Dogan Ibrahim
 * Date  : May 2019
 * File  : metal
*****************************************************************/
```

```
const int D0 = 2;                                    // D0 pin
const int buzzer = 3;                                // Buzzer pin

void setup ()
{
  pinMode(buzzer, OUTPUT);                           // Buzzer is output
  digitalWrite(buzzer, LOW);                         // Buzzer OFF
  pinMode(D0, INPUT);                                // D0 is input
}

//
// Activaet the buzzer when the sensor is touched by finger
//
void loop ()
{
  if(digitalRead(D0) == HIGH)                        // If touched
      digitalWrite(buzzer, HIGH);                    // Buzzer ON
  else
      digitalWrite(buzzer, LOW);                     // Buzzer OFF
}
```

Figure 13.8 Arduino Uno program listing

ESP32 DevKitC Program Listing: The same circuit as in Figure 13.7 can be used, but you should avoid using GPIO 1 and GPIO 3 as these are used by the USB interface. The same program as in 13.8 can be used here with the modified GPIO pins.

Raspberry Pi Program Listing: The Raspberry Pi program is very simple and can very easily be derived by studying the previous projects.

13.4 Summary

In this Chapter, we have learned how to use the metal touch sensor module KY-036 in projects. In the next Chapter, we will be developing projects using the tracking sensor module.

Chapter 14 • Tracking sensor module projects

14.1 Overview

In the previous Chapter, we have seen how to develop a project for the Arduino Uno, Raspberry Pi, and ESP32 DevKitC using the obstacle sensor modules together with the buzzer module.

In this Chapter, we will be developing projects using the KY-033 tracking sensor module.

14.2 Project 1 – Line tracking

Description: This project shows how to use the KY-033 tracking sensor module for line tracking. A dark line is drawn and it is shown how the output of the sensor module changes while tracking the line.

Aim: The aim of this project is to show how to use the KY-033 tracking module.

Sensor Used: In this project the KY-033 tracking sensor used. As shown in Figure 14.1, this is a 3-pin sensor with the pins:

- GND
- +V
- S

Where S is the digital output of the sensor module. KY-033 consists of an IR LED, IR receiver, LM393 comparator chip, a few resistors, a potentiometer, and an LED. IR LED emits infrared light which is reflected from a white surface and is received by the IR receiver. One input of the comparator chip is the potentiometer arm and the other input is the output of the IR receiver. If the IR receiver voltage is higher than the voltage at the arm of the potentiometer then the comparator produces a HIGH voltage at its output. When the IR LED and receiver are on a dark surface then there is no light reflection and as a result, the IR receiver is OFF. This makes the comparator output voltage HIGH. If on the other hand the IR LED and receiver are on a white surface then there is a light reflection and as a result, the IR receiver is ON. This makes the comparator output voltage LOW.

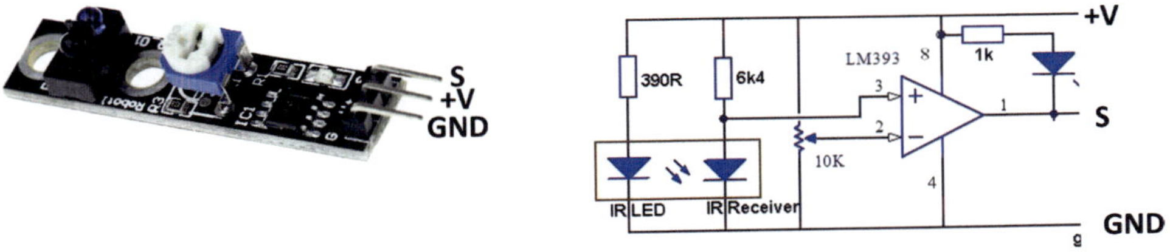

Figure 14.1 KY-033 module

Background Information: Line tracking sensors are used in robotic applications where the robot is programmed to follow a line (usually dark) drawn on the floor. Usually, two or more sensors are required to develop a line following robot. This is because with only one sensor if the robot moves outside the line there is no way to find out in which direction the robot has moved so that it can be placed back on the line. Figure 14.2 shows how a robot can be controlled to be on a dark line with two sensors.

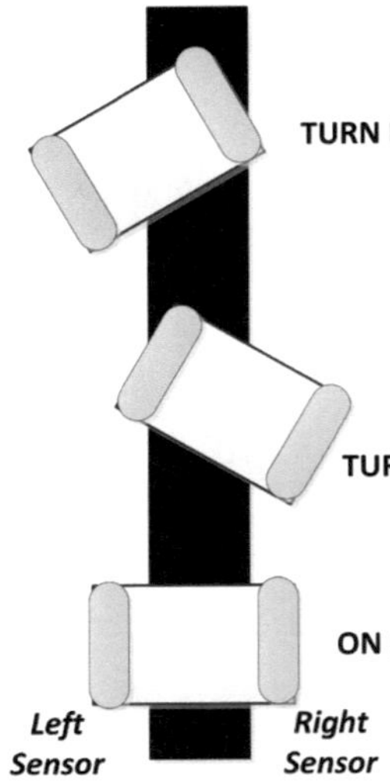

Figure 14.2 Controlling a robot with 2 sensors

Block Diagram: Block diagram of the project is shown in Figure 14.3.

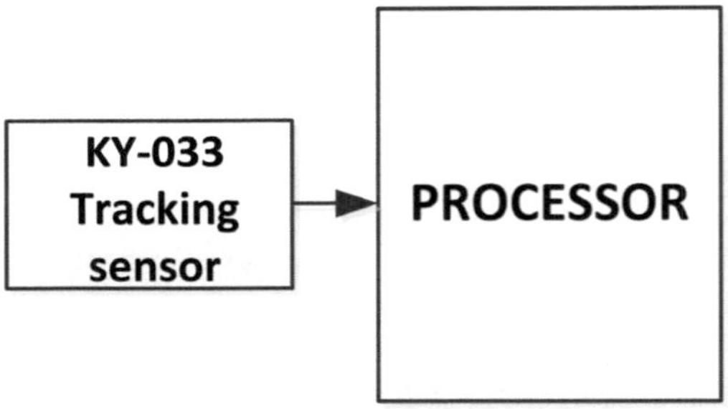

Figure 14.3 Block diagram of the project

Arduino Uno Circuit Diagram: Figure 14.4 shows the Arduino Uno circuit diagram. The output of the sensor module is connected to pin 2 of the Arduino Uno.

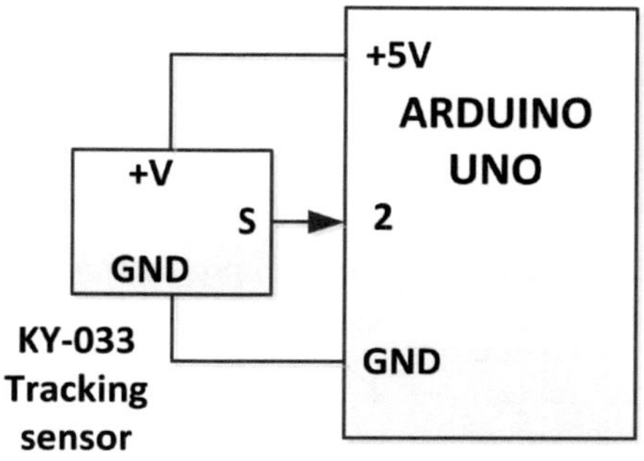

Figure 14.4 Circuit diagram of the project

Arduino Uno Program Listing: Figure 14.5 shows the program listing (program: **track**). The program reads the output of the sensor module and if it is dark under the sensors then the message **Tracker is online** is displayed. If the sensors are over a white medium (e.g. over a white paper) then the message **Tracker is NOT online** is displayed. Figure 14.6 shows output from the program.

```
/*****************************************************************
 *                   LINE TRACKING
 *                   =============
 *
 * In this program a KY-033 tracking sensor is used. A dark line is
 * drawn on a paper and the values obtained from the sensor are
 * displayed. Two such sensors can be used to navigate a robot to
 * follow a dark line.
 *
 * Author: Dogan Ibrahim
 * Date  : May 2019
 * File  : track
 *****************************************************************/
const int S = 2;                                  // Signal pin
int track;

void setup ()
{
  Serial.begin(9600);
  pinMode(S, INPUT);                              // Sensor is input
}


void loop ()
{
  track = digitalRead(S);
  if(track == HIGH)
    Serial.println("Tracker is on line");
```

```
  else
    Serial.println("Tracker is NOT on line");

  delay(500);
}
```

Figure 14.5 Arduino Uno program listing

```
Tracker is on line
Tracker is on line
Tracker is on line
Tracker is NOT on line
Tracker is NOT on line
Tracker is NOT on line
Tracker is NOT on line
Tracker is on line
Tracker is on line
Tracker is on line
Tracker is on line
Tracker is on line
Tracker is on line
```

Figure 14.6 Output from the program

ESP32 DevKitC Program: The circuit diagram of the ESP32 DevKitC version of the program is the same as in Figure 14.4, but the sensor pin +V is connected to +3.3V. The ESP32 DevKitC program is exactly the same as the one given in Figure 14.5.

Raspberry Pi Program Listing: The circuit diagram of the ESP32 DevKitC version of the program is the same as in Figure 14.4, but the sensor pin +V is connected to +3.3V. Raspberry Pi program listing is shown in Figure 14.7 (program: **rpitrack.py**).

```
#--------------------------------------------------------------
#
#                LINE TRACKING
#                =============
#
# In this program KY-032 tracking module is used. The program
# displays the values read by the sensor when it is above dark
# or white backgrounds.
#
# Program: rpitrack.py
# Date   : May 2019
# Author : Dogan Ibrahim
#--------------------------------------------------------------
import RPi.GPIO as GPIO
import time

track = 2          # sensor pin
```

```
GPIO.setmode(GPIO.BCM)
GPIO.setwarnings(False)
GPIO.setup(track, GPIO.IN)              # track is input

try:
 while True:
    r = GPIO.input(track)               # read tracker
    if r == 1:                          # if on line
       print("Tracker is on line")
    else:
       print("Tracker is NOT on line")  # if not on line
    time.sleep(0.5)

except KeyboardInterrupt:
    GPIO.cleanup()
```

Figure 14.7 Raspberry Pi program listing

14.3 Project 2 – Secret code lock

Description: In this project, the KY-033 tracking sensor is used together with the KY-019 relay module. A secret key is stored in the program. A key is set up by drawing dark lines on a piece of paper with varying thicknesses. The tracking sensor is moved across the paper at a constant speed where the sensor returns 0's for white places and 1's for dark places on the paper. The code read is compared with the secret code stored in the program. If the correct code is detected then the relay is activated, for example, to open a door.

Aim: The aim of this project is to show how the KY-033 tracking module can be used as a secret key.

Sensor Used: In this project, the KY-033 tracking sensor module and the KY-019 relay module are used.

Block Diagram: Figure 14.8 shows the block diagram of the project.

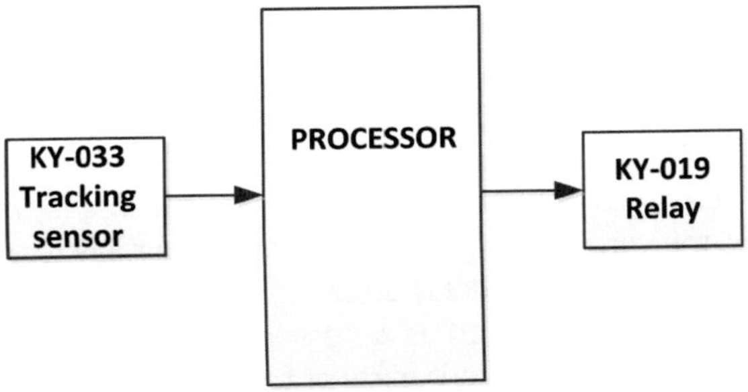

Figure 14.8 Block diagram of the project

Arduino Uno Circuit Diagram: Figure 14.9 shows the Arduino Uno circuit diagram. The sensor output is connected to port pin 2 of Arduino Uno as in the previous project. The relay is connected to port pin 3.

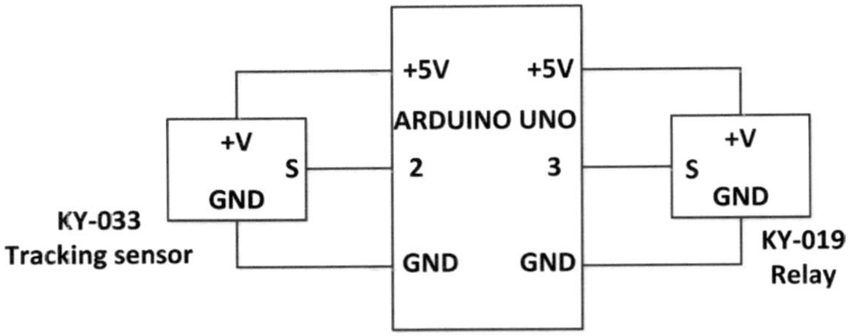

Figure 14.9 Arduino Uno circuit diagram

Secret Key on Paper: Dark lines were drawn on a piece of paper where a line 1cm wide is assumed to correspond to logic 1, 2 cm wide dark line corresponds to logic 11, etc, and white space of 1cm corresponds to logic 0. The secret code stored in the program is **10011001**. Figure 14.10 shows the correct code drawn on the paper.

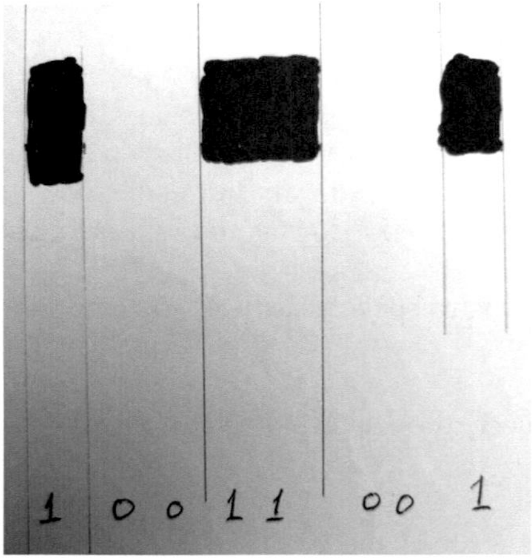

Figure 14.10 Secret key on the paper

Arduino Uno Program Listing: Figure 14.11 shows the program listing (program: **track-code**). Inside the setup routine sensor module is configured as input and the relay is configured as an output and is de-activated. Inside the main program loop, the program waits until the starting bit (i.e. 1) is detected. Then, the program reads the scanned code and looks for **0011001**. If the correct code is detected then the relay is turned ON for 10 seconds. Function **dly** introduces a small delay after reading each bit. This delay time depends on the scan rate and should be adjusted as necessary. It is advisable to turn on the serial printing and display messages at different parts of the program to make it easier to adjust the delay time. Function **ReadCode** returns 1 or 0 depending on whether or not the LED/receiver pair are on a dark line or on a white space respectively.

```
/****************************************************************
 *                    SECRET KEY
 *                    ===========
 *
 * In this program a KY-033 tracking sensor is used. Dark lines are
 * drawn on a piece of paper to represent a code where a dark line 1
 * cm wide corresponds to logic 1, and a white spaec of 1cm wide
 * corresponds to logic 0. If the code on the paper matches the secret
 * code stored inside the program then the relay is activated for
 * 10 seconds..
 *
 * Author: Dogan Ibrahim
 * Date  : May 2019
 * File  : trackcode
 ****************************************************************/
const int S = 2;                                // Signal pin
const int Relay = 3;                            // Relay pin

void setup ()
{
  pinMode(S, INPUT);                            // Sensor is input
  pinMode(Relay, OUTPUT);                       // Relay is output
  digitalWrite(Relay, LOW);                     // Deactivate
}

//
// Insert a small delay after reading each bit (adjust this delay to
// your reading speed)
//
void dly()
{
  delay(500);
}

//
// This function reads teh code from the paper
//
int ReadCode()
{
  int r = digitalRead(S);                       // Read code
  dly();                                        // Small delay
  return(r);                                    // Return code
}

//
// Read code from teh paper. If correct code is detected then activate
```

```
// the relay for 10 seconds. The secret code is 10011001
//
void loop ()
{
Bck:
  while(ReadCode() == 0);                    // Wait for 1
  if(ReadCode() != 0)goto Bck;               // If not 0
  if(ReadCode() != 0)goto Bck;               // If not 0
  if(ReadCode() != 1)goto Bck;               // If not 1
  if(ReadCode() != 1)goto Bck;               // If not 1
  if(ReadCode() != 0)goto Bck;               // If not 0
  if(ReadCode() != 0)goto Bck;               // If not 0
  if(ReadCode() != 1)goto Bck;               // If not 1
//
// Correct code detected, activate relay
//
  digitalWrite(Relay, HIGH);                 // Relay ON
  delay(10000);                              // Wait 10 seconds
  digitalWrite(Relay, LOW);                  // Relay OFF
}
```

Figure 14.11 Arduino Uno program listing

ESP32 DevKitC Program: The ESP32 DevKitC version of the project requires the KY-051 voltage translator module to be used since the KY-019 relay module requires +5V for its reliable operation. Also, the +V pin of KY-033 should be connected to +3.3V. The ESP32 DevkitC program is exactly the same as in Figure 14.11.

Raspberry Pi Program Listing: As with the ESP32 DevKitC version of the project, it is necessary to use the voltage translator module to activate the relay reliably. Figure 14.12 shows the Raspberry Pi circuit diagram. The program listing (program: **rpitrackcode.py**) is shown in Figure 14.13. As the beginning of the program, tracking sensor and relay pins are assigned to port pins 17 and 27 respectively. **Relay** is configured as an output and is turned OFF, tracking sensor is configured as an input. The secret code is **10011001** which is 8-bits wide. It may actually be much easier to use a shorter code (e.g. 4 bits) in order to make the system more reliable and have fewer trials to get the correct code. Inside the main program, the program waits until 1 is received. After this, a loop is formed to receive the remaining 7 bits of the code. The received code is compared with the secret code and if there is a match then the relay is activated for 10 seconds. Notice that the first bit of the secret code is 1 and this is not saved in variable **SecretCode**. The program displays comments **READY**, **Scanning**, and **Code Correct**. You should only scan the code when **READY** is displayed. When the LED/receiver of the tracking sensor is on white space, the onboard LED is ON, when they are on a dark line, the On-board LED is OFF.

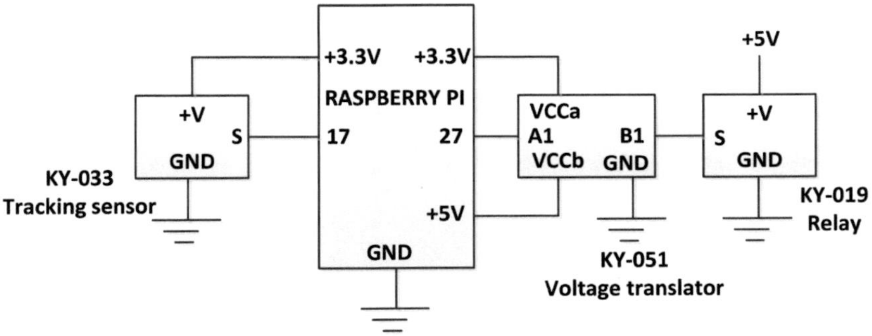

Figure 14.12 Raspberry Pi circuit diagram

```
#--------------------------------------------------------------
#
#                    SECRET KEY
#                    ==========
#
# In this project the KY-033 tracking sensor is used together
# with the KY-019 relay module and the KY-051 voltage translator
# module. Code is scanned from a paper by moving the tracking
# sensor module over the paper. When the correct code is detected
# the relay is turned ON for 10 seconds, for example to open a door.
#
# Program: rpitrackcode.py
# Date   : May 2019
# Author : Dogan Ibrahim
#---------------------------------------------------------------
import RPi.GPIO as GPIO          # Import GPIO
import time                      # Import time

track = 17                       # Tracker interface
Relay = 27                       # Relay interface interface

GPIO.setmode(GPIO.BCM)
GPIO.setwarnings(False)
GPIO.setup(Relay, GPIO.OUT)      # Relay is output
GPIO.setup(track, GPIO.IN)       # Tracker is input
GPIO.output(Relay, GPIO.LOW)     # Relay OFF

SecretCode = [0,0,1,1,0,0,1]     # Secret code
ReceivedCode = [None]*10


#
# This function reads a bit from the KY-033 tracker module
#
def Read():
```

```
        r = GPIO.input(track)
        return r

#
# This function generates delay (you should adjust this delay)
#
def Del():
     time.sleep(0.4)                        # 400ms delay

#
# Program loop. Read the code on the paper and compare with the
# secret key. If there is a match then activate the relay for 10
# seconds, for example to open a door.
#
while True:
  print("READY")
  while(Read() == 0):                      # Wait for 1
     pass
  Del()
  print("Scanning")

  for k in range(7):                       # Read the remainder
    ReceivedCode[k] = Read()               # Read code
    Del()

#
# Compare the received code and Secret Code. If flag=0 then
# correct code is received
#
  flag = 0
  for k in range(7):                       # Compare 7 bits
    if(ReceivedCode[k] != SecretCode[k]):
         flag = 1

  if flag == 0:                            # If correct code
     print("Code correct")
     GPIO.output(Relay, GPIO.HIGH)         # Turn ON relay
     time.sleep(10)                        # Wait 10 seconds
     GPIO.output(Relay, GPIO.LOW)          # Turn OFF relay
```

Figure 14.13 Raspberry Pi program listing

14.4 Summary

In this Chapter, we have learned how to use the tracking sensor in Arduino Uno, ESP32 DevKitC and Raspberry Pi projects. In the next Chapter, we will be developing projects using the rotary encoder module.

Chapter 15 • Rotary encoder module projects

15.1 Overview

In the previous Chapter, we have seen how to develop a project for the Arduino Uno, Raspberry Pi, and ESP32 DevKitC using the tracking sensor module together with the relay module.

In this Chapter, we will be developing projects using the KY-040 rotary encoder sensor module.

15.2 Project 1 – Rotary encoder evaluation

Description: This project shows how the KY-040 rotary encoder sensor module operates. Two LEDs are connected to the encoder to show how it operates.

Aim: The aim of this project is to show the rotary encoder sensor module operates.

Sensor Used: In this project, the KY-040 rotary sensor module is used. As shown in Figure 15.1, KY-040 is a 5-pin module with the pins:

- CLK (Encoder pin A)
- DT (Encoder pin B)
- SW (Normally open push-button switch)
- +V
- GND

The Keyes KY-040 rotary encoder is an input device that provides an indication of how much the arm has been rotated AND what direction it is rotating in. It is commonly used in servo and stepper motor control applications to determine how much the motor arm has rotated and also in which direction it has rotated. It is also used in digital potentiometers. KY-040 consists of two switches named CLK (also called Encoder pin A) and DT (also called encoder pin B) which are pulled-up to +V through 10K resistors, and a normally open independent push-button switch named SW. As the encoder arm is rotated the switches close one after the other one. In resting mode both switches are open and their outputs are pulled HIGH to the supply voltage. Closing a switch forces its output to go to logic 0, but the important point here is that in resting mode both switches are open. For example, rotating the arm in one direction will result switch CLK to close and just after that the second switch, DT closes. When the encoder comes to rest, again both switches become open. Rotating the encoder in the opposite direction will result switch DT to close first, followed by switch CLK to close. This sequence is repeated as the arm is rotated. We can, therefore, determine the direction of rotation by the switch closure pattern as shown in Figure 15.2. The number of arm rotations can also be determined by counting the edges of the switch closures.

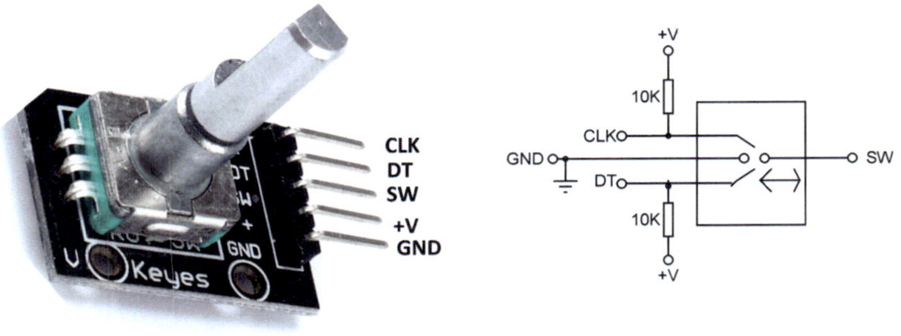

Figure 15.1 KY-040 module

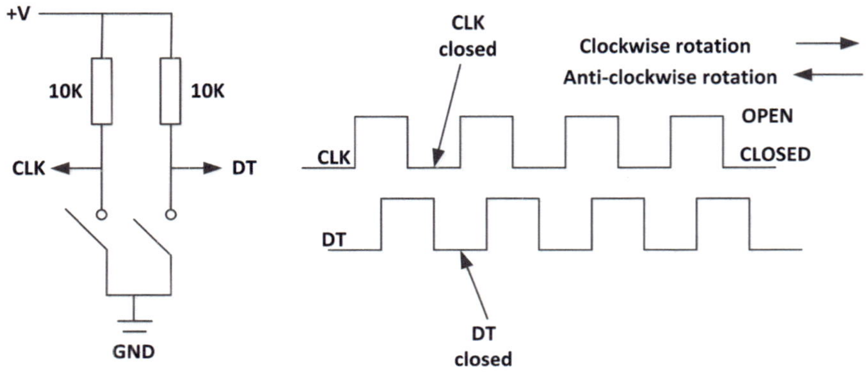

Figure 15.2 Determining the direction of rotation

Background Information: A rotary encoder (also called shaft encoder) is an electro-mechanical device with an arm that converts the angular position of a shaft to digital output signals. In general, there are two types of rotary encoders: incremental and absolute. Incremental encoders provide information about the current motion of the shaft and further processing is required to determine the direction and amount of rotation. Absolute encoders indicate the current shaft position directly. Both types of encoders are widely used in electrical motor applications to determine the direction of rotation and the amount that the shaft has rotated.

Block Diagram: Figure 15.3 shows the block diagram of the project.

Figure 15.3 Block diagram of the project

Circuit Diagram: The circuit diagram of the project is shown in Figure 15.4.

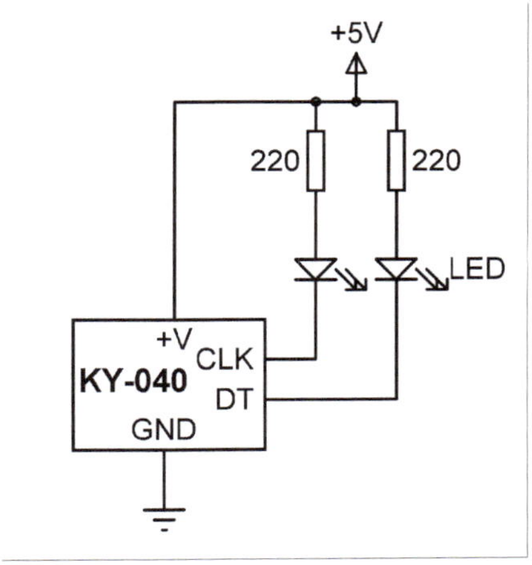

Figure 15.4 Circuit diagram of the project

Testing: Power up the circuit from the +5V of your Arduino Uno. You should see that at resting position both LEDs are OFF (both switches are open and pulled-up). Now, very slowly turn the encoder arm clockwise. You should see the LED connected to the CLK pin to turn ON. Immediately after this, the LED connected to DT pin will turn ON. Turn the arm slightly more so that the encoder is in its next resting position. You will see that both LEDs are OFF again. Now, turn the arm very slowly in an anticlockwise direction. This time you will see that the LED at the DT pin will come ON first, followed by the other LED. Both LEDs will be OFF again when the arm is in its next resting position.

15.3 Project 2 – Rotary encoder direction and position

Description: This project shows how the KY-040 rotary encoder sensor position and direction can be determined in a program.

Aim: The aim of this project is to show the rotary encoder sensor module can be used in a project.

Sensor Used: In this project, only the KY-040 rotary sensor module is used.

Arduino Uno Circuit Diagram: The circuit diagram of the Arduino Uno project is shown in Figure 15.5. CLK and DT pins of the encoder are connected to Arduino Uno pins 2 and 3 respectively. The SW pin is not used in this project.

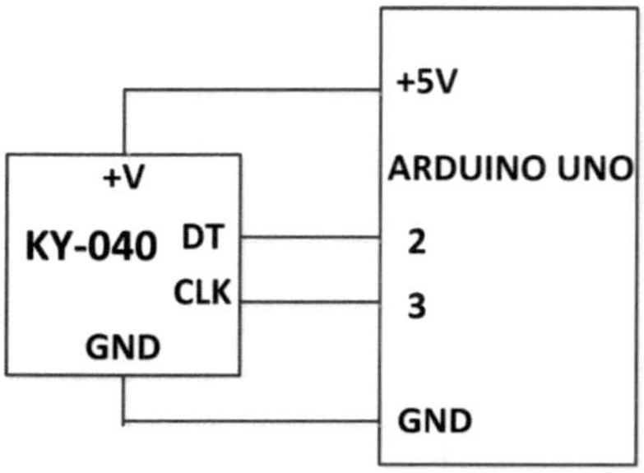

Figure 15.5 Arduino Uno circuit diagram

Arduino Uno Program Listing: Figure 15.6 shows the Arduino Uno program listing (program: **encoder**). At the beginning of the program, **CLK** and **DT** pins of the encoder are assigned to 2 and 3 respectively. Inside the setup routine, both **CLK** and **DT** are configured as inputs and the serial monitor is started with 115200 baud rate. Inside the main program loop, the current state of **CLK** pin is read. If this is not the same as its last state then it is assumed that the encoder arm has moved. The program then determines whether **CLK** or **DT** changed first and sets the direction accordingly. For clockwise direction, variable **Direction** is set to 1 and variable **EncoderCount** is incremented by one. Similarly, for anticlockwise direction, variable **Direction** is set to 0 and variable **EncoderCount** is decremented by one. The program finally displays the direction and the position of the encoder arm. It is recommended to use a 0.47uF capacitor from pin CLK to GND and also from DT to ground in order to suppress any noise and improve the reliability. Also, the speed of the serial monitor should be at least 115200, and the displayed message length should be kept to a minimum.

```
/****************************************************************
 *                    ROTARY ENCODER OPERATION
 *                    ========================
 *
 * In this program a KY-040 rotary encoder sensor module is used.
 * The program displays the direction and position of the encoder
 *
 * Author: Dogan Ibrahim
```

```
 * Date   : May 2019
 * File   : encoder
 **************************************************************/
int CLK = 2;                                      // CLK pin
int DT = 3;                                       // DT pin
int EncoderCount = 0;
int Direction;                                    // Encoder direction
int LastCLK, CurrentCLK;

void setup ()
{
  Serial.begin(115200);                           // Enable monitor
  pinMode(CLK, INPUT);                            // CLK is input
  pinMode(DT, INPUT);                             // DT is input
  LastCLK = digitalRead(CLK);
}


void loop ()
{
  CurrentCLK = digitalRead(CLK);                  // Read CLK
  if(CurrentCLK != LastCLK && CurrentCLK == 0)  // Encoder arm moved
// Arm rotated
  {
        if(digitalRead(DT) != CurrentCLK)         // CLK changed first
        {
          EncoderCount++;                         // Increment count
          Direction = 1;                          // CW
        }
        else                                      // DT changed first
        {
          EncoderCount--;                         // Decrement count
          Direction = 0;                          // CCW
        }

        if(Direction == 1)                        // If clockwise
            Serial.println("Rotated CW");         // Display msg
        else                                      // If anticlockwise
            Serial.println("Rotated CCW");        // Display msg

        Serial.print("Position: ");               // Display msg
        Serial.println(EncoderCount);             // Display position
    }
    LastCLK = CurrentCLK;
 }
```

Figure 15.6 Arduino Uno program listing

Figure 15.7 shows an output from the program as the encoder arm is rotated.

```
Position: 29
Rotated CW
Position: 30
Rotated CW
Position: 31
Rotated CW
Position: 32
Rotated CW
Position: 33
Rotated CCW
Position: 32
Rotated CCW
Position: 31
```

Figure 15.7 Output from the program

ESP32DevKitC Program Listing: For the ESP32 DevKitC version of the project you should connect +V pin of the sensor to +3.3V. Additionally, do not use GPIO 1 or GPIO 3 as they are reserved for the USB interface. The program given in Figure 15.6 can be used exactly as it is for the ESP32 DevKitC version after making the above changes.

Raspberry Pi Program Listing: For the ESP32 DevKitC version of the project you should connect +V pin of the sensor to +3.3V. **CLK** and **DT** pins can be connected to GPIO 2 and GPIO 3 of raspberry Pi respectively. The program listing is shown in Figure 15.8 (program: **rpiencoder.py**). Example output from the program is shown in Figure 15.9.

```
#------------------------------------------------------------
#   ROTARY ENCODER OPERATION
#   ========================
#
# In thiS project the KY-040 rotary encoder sensor module is
# used. The program displays the position of the encoder arm
# and its direction of rotation.
#
#
# Author: Dogan Ibrahim
# Date  : May 2019
# File  : rpiencoder.py
#-----------------------------------------------------------
import RPi.GPIO as GPIO           # import Rpi
GPIO.setwarnings(False)           # disable warnings
GPIO.setmode(GPIO.BCM)            # set BCM mode

CLK = 2                           # CLK pin
DT = 3                            # DT pin
```

```
GPIO.setup(CLK, GPIO.IN)                # configure as input
GPIO.setup(DT, GPIO.IN)                 # configure as input

LastCLK = GPIO.input(CLK)               # Read LastCLK
EncoderCount = 0                        # Set count to 0

try:
  while True:                           # Do FOREVER
    CurrentCLK = GPIO.input(CLK)
    if(CurrentCLK != LastCLK and CurrentCLK == 0):
        if GPIO.input(DT) != CurrentCLK:
           EncoderCount = EncoderCount + 1
           Direction = 1
        else:
           EncoderCount = EncoderCount - 1
           Direction = 0

        if Direction == 1:                     # if CW
           print("Rotated CW")                 # display msg
        else:         # if CCW
           print("Rotated CCW")                # display msg

        print "Position: ", EncoderCount       # display count
    LastCLK = CurrentCLK

except KeyboardInterrupt:
  GPIO.cleanup()
```

Figure 15.8 Raspberry Pi program listing

```
Position:  66
Rotated CW
Position:  67
Rotated CW
Position:  68
Rotated CW
Position:  69
Rotated CW
Position:  70
Rotated CW
Position:  71
Rotated CW
Position:  72
Rotated CW
Position:  73
Rotated CW
Position:  74
Rotated CCW
Position:  73
Rotated CCW
Position:  72
Rotated CCW
Position:  71
```

Figure 15.9 Output from the program

15.4 Summary

In this Chapter, we have learned how to use the rotary encoder module in projects. In the next Chapter, we will be developing projects using the Heartbeat sensor module.

Chapter 16 • Heartbeat sensor module projects

16.1 Overview

In the previous Chapter, we have seen how to develop a project for the Arduino Uno, Raspberry Pi, and ESP32 DevKitC using the rotary encoder sensor module.

In this Chapter, we will be developing a project using the KY-039 heartbeat sensor module.

16.2 Project 1 – Displaying heartbeat

Description: This project shows how the KY-039 heartbeat sensor module can be used to display the heartbeat.

Aim: The aim of this project is to show how the heartbeat sensor module can be used in projects.

Sensor Used: In this project, only the KY-039 heartbeat sensor module is used. As shown in Figure 16.1, this is a 3-pin module with the following pins:

- GND (gray cable)
- +V (white cable)
- S (black cable)

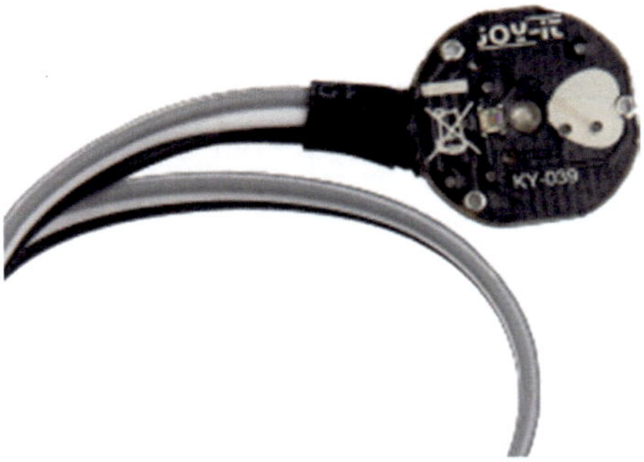

Figure 16.1 KY-039 module

The output of KY-039 is an analog signal and therefore ADC is required to read the signal. The module uses IR LED and a phototransistor. When a finger is placed between the LED and transistor we will get an analog output related to the light intensity passing through the finger which corresponds to the heart rate. The finger should be placed under the sensor as shown in Figure 16.2

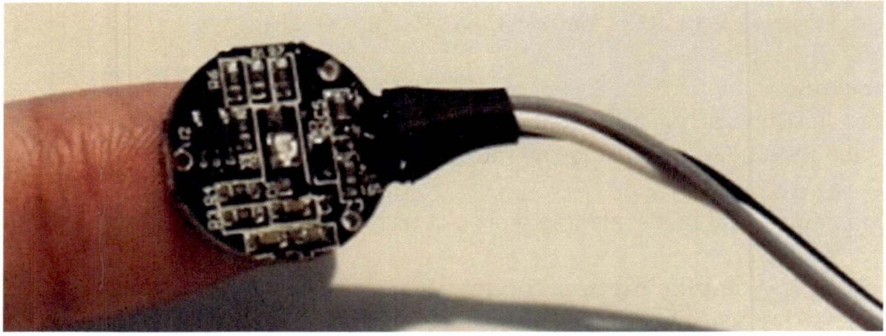

Figure 16.2 Placing the finger to read the heart beat

Background Information: A heartbeat sensor (or a heart rate sensor) is an electrical module used to measure the heartbeats either from the finger or from the wrist. There are many types of heartbeat sensors. They usually consist of an infrared LED and a phototransistor. Sticking the finger between the infrared diode and the phototransistor changes the amount of light received by the phototransistor as blood lows inside the finger. This change is detected and an analog voltage is produced at the output. The output signal is usually very noisy and may require filtering so that the heartbeats can easily be counted. In addition to measuring the heartbeats, the same technology is used to measure blood oxygen saturation (SpO2).

Arduino Uno Circuit Diagram: The circuit diagram of the project is shown in Figure 16.3. S pin of the sensor is connected to analog input A0 of the Arduino Uno.

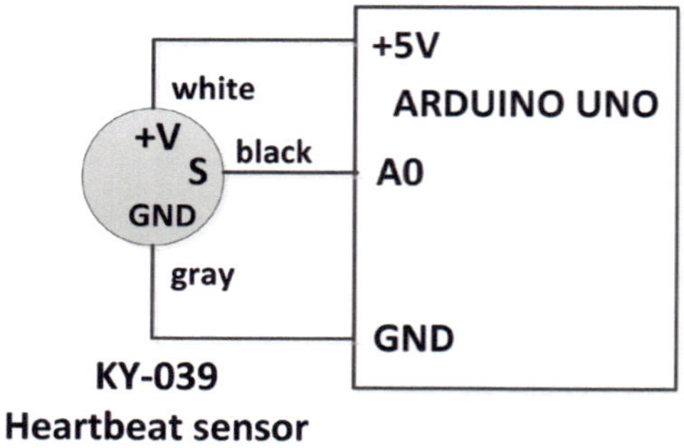

Figure 16.3 Circuit diagram of the project

Arduino Uno Program Listing: Figure 16.4 shows the Arduino program listing (program: **heartbeat**). The program simply reads the analog output of the sensor and plots the results on the serial plotter. You should place your finger on the sensor and then enable the serial plotter with **Tools -> Serial Plotter**. Figure 16.5 shows a typical display on the serial plotter.

```
/*****************************************************************
 *                     DISPLAY HEARTBEATS
 *                     ==================
 *
 * In this program a KY-039 heartbeat sensor module is used. The
 * program displays the heartbeat from the finger on serial plotter.
 *
 * Author: Dogan Ibrahim
 * Date  : May 2019
 * File  : heartbeat
 *****************************************************************/
int S = A0;                                      // S pin

void setup ()
{
  Serial.begin(115200);                          // Enable monitor
}


void loop ()
{
      Serial.println(analogRead(S));
      delay(5);
}
```

Figure 16.4 Arduino Uno program listing

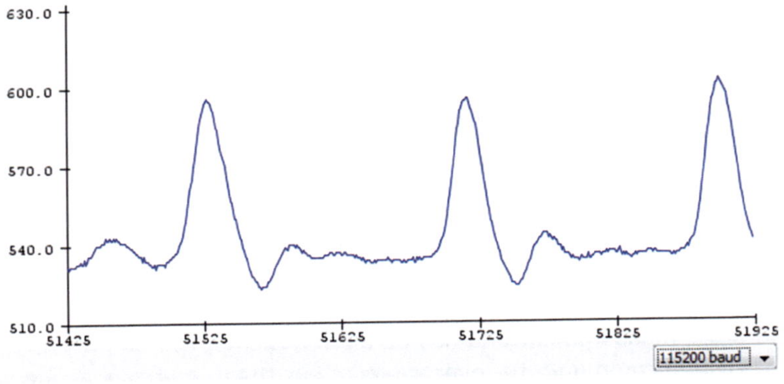

Figure 16.5 Typical display on serial plotter

ESP32 DevKitC Program Listing: The same program as in Figure 16.4 can be used, but make sure that you use an ESP32 DevKitC ADC channel (e.g. ADC2_0 or GPIO 4).

16.3 Summary

In this Chapter, we have seen how to use the heartbeat sensor module. In the next Chapter, we will be developing projects using temperature, humidity, and pressure sensor modules.

Chapter 17 • Temperature, humidity, and pressure sensor projects

17.1 Overview

In the previous Chapter, we have seen how to develop a project for the Arduino Uno, Raspberry Pi, and ESP32 DevKitC using the heartbeat sensor module.

In this Chapter, we will be developing projects using temperature, humidity, and pressure sensors.

17.2 Project 1 – Displaying and plotting the ambient temperature on the monitor

Description: In this project, we will be reading the ambient temperature and then display and also plot it on the serial monitor every second.

Aim: The aim of this project is to show how the ambient temperature can be read, displayed and also plotted using the serial monitor.

Sensor Used: In this project, the KY-001 temperature sensor module is used. As shown in Figure 17.1, this is a 3-pin digital output sensor module with the following pins:

- GND
- +V
- S (digital output)

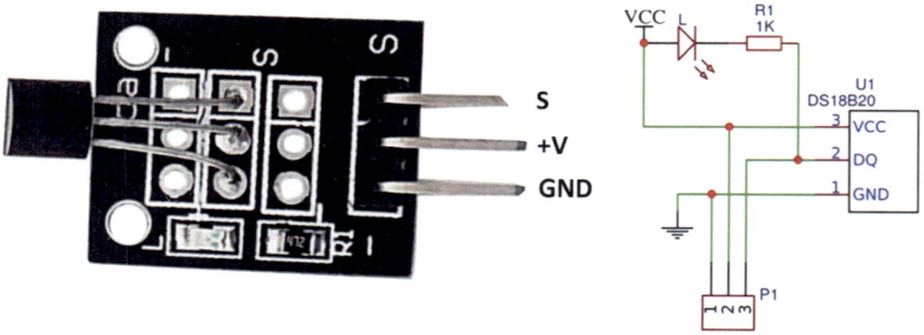

Figure 17.1 KY-001 module

KY-001 uses the DS18B20 digital temperature sensor chip. This chip provides 9-bit to 12-bit temperature measurement and has an alarm function with lower and upper trigger points. The DS18B20 communicates over a 1-Wire bus that requires only one data line and ground for communication with a processor. Each DS18B20 has a unique 64-bit serial code where multiple such devices can be connected to the same bus. A pull-up resistor from pin DQ to +V is required for proper operation of the sensor chip and this is provided on the board. Additionally, an LED is provided on the board which turns ON when data is output from the module. The key features of the DS18B20 are:

- Measures temperature from -55ºC to +125ºC
- Accuracy ±0.5º

- 750ms conversion time
- Operates with +3.3V to +5V
- Requires no external components
- Temperature alarm settings
- Zero standby power required

Background Information: DS18B20 temperature sensor chip is usually used to measure the ambient temperature. It has a resolution which is configurable between 9 to 12 bits, which equates to a temperature resolution of 0.5ºC, 0.25ºC, 0.125ºC, or 0.0625ºC. The temperature is stored in 16-bit, sign-extended two's complement format a shown in Table 17.1. Data is usually read from the module using library functions which are described in the relevant sections of this project. The library functions take care of the required data conversions. The unique feature of the DS18B20 sensor chip is that each chip has a unique ID and therefore many such chips can be connected on the same bus and then addressed uniquely.

TEMPERATURE	DIGITAL OUTPUT (Binary)	DIGITAL OUTPUT (Hex)
+125°C	0000 0111 1101 0000	07D0h
+85°C	0000 0101 0101 0000	0550h*
+25.0625°C	0000 0001 1001 0001	0191h
+10.125°C	0000 0000 1010 0010	00A2h
+0.5°C	0000 0000 0000 1000	0008h
0°C	0000 0000 0000 0000	0000h
-0.5°C	1111 1111 1111 1000	FFF8h
-10.125°C	1111 1111 0101 1110	FF5Eh
-25.0625°C	1111 1110 0110 1111	FF6Fh
-55°C	1111 1100 1001 0000	FC90h

*The power on reset register value is +85°C.

Table 17.1 DS18B20 data formats

Arduino Uno Circuit Diagram: Figure 17.2 shows the Arduino Uno circuit diagram. Pin S of the sensor module is connected to port pin 2 of Arduino Uno.

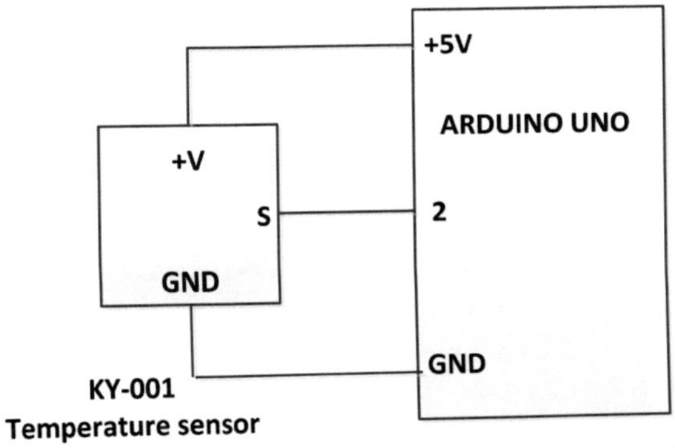

Figure 17.2 Arduino Uno circuit diagram of the project

Required Libraries: Before using the KY-001 module we have to download the OneWire library and Dallas Temperature library into our Arduino working environment. The steps are as follows:

- Go to the web site:

  https://github.com/PaulStoffregen/OneWire

- Click on **Clone or download** at the right-hand side (green button)
- Click on **Download ZIP** and save file **OneWire-master.zip** in a folder
- Start Arduino IDE and create a new file
- Click **Sketch -> Include Library** and select **Add .ZIP library**
- Browse to the folder where you saved the file, click on the file and click **Open**
- Click **Tools -> Manage Libraries**, enter **Dallas** and then click **Install** to install the Dallas Temperature library (see Figure 17.3)

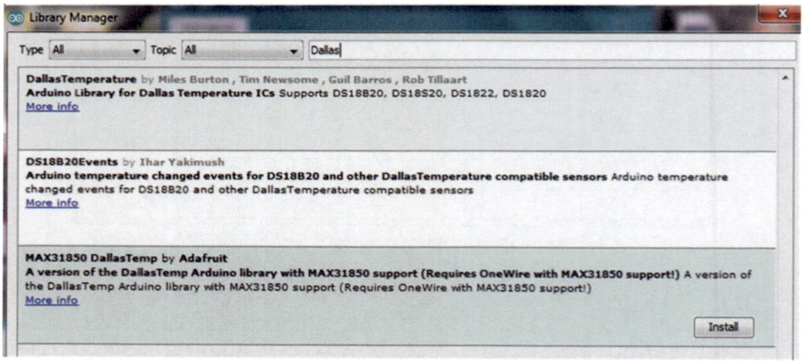

Figure 17.3 Install the Dallas Temperature library

Arduino Uno Program Listing: Figure 17.4 shows the Arduino Uno program listing (program: **DS18b20**). At the beginning of the program, the **OneWire** library and **DallasTemperature** library are included in the program. Inside the setup routine, the serial monitor is started with a 9600 baud rate. Inside the main program loop, the temperature is read every second.

```
/*****************************************************************
 *                     TEMPERATURE MEASUREMENT
 *                     =======================
 *
 * In this program a KY-001 temperature sensor module is used. The
 * ambient temperature is read and displayed and also plotted every
```

```
 * second on the serial monitor.
 *
 * Author: Dogan Ibrahim
 * Date  : May 2019
 * File  : DS18b20
 ***************************************************************/
#include <OneWire.h>                              // Include OneWire
#include "DallasTemperature.h"                    // Include Dallas

#define ONE_WIRE_BUS 2                            // Module on pin 2
OneWire S(ONE_WIRE_BUS);
DallasTemperature sensors(&S);

void setup()
{
  Serial.begin(9600);                             // Start monitor
  sensors.begin();                                // Start sensor
}

void loop(void)
{
  sensors.requestTemperatures();                  // Read temperature
  Serial.print("Temperature = ");                 // Display heading
  Serial.println(sensors.getTempCByIndex(0));     // Display temp
  delay(1000);                                    // WAit 1 second
}
```

Figure 17.4 Arduino Uno program listing

Displaying the Temperature: Click **Tools** -> **Serial Monitor** and set the baud rate to 9600. Figure 17.5 shows the temperature displayed on the serial monitor every second.

```
Temperature = 25.31
Temperature = 25.25
Temperature = 25.31
Temperature = 25.25
Temperature = 25.25
Temperature = 25.31
Temperature = 25.25
Temperature = 25.62
Temperature = 27.06
Temperature = 27.87
Temperature = 28.50
Temperature = 28.75
```

Figure 17.5 Displaying the temperature readings

Plotting the Temperature: Click **Tools -> Serial Plotter** and set the baud rate to 9600. Figure 17.6 shows the temperature plotted on the serial monitor every second. Here, the vertical axis is the temperature in Celsius and the horizontal axis is the time in seconds. Notice that you must close the serial monitor before starting the serial plotter.

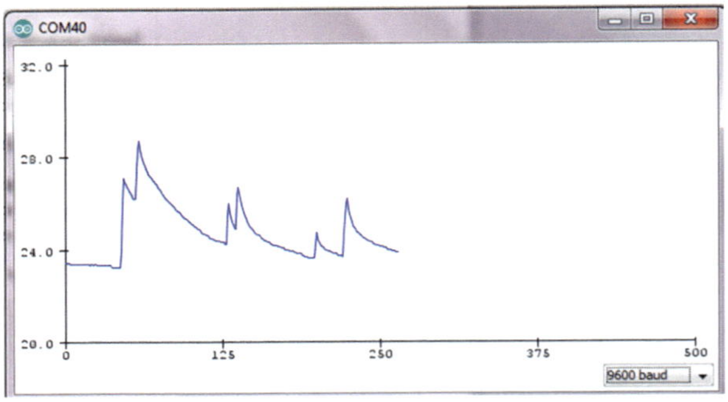

Figure 17.6 Plotting the temperature

ESP32 DevKitC Program Listing: The circuit diagram of the ESP32 DevKitC version of the project is exactly the same as in Figure 17.2, but the +V pin is connected to +3.3V. The program listing is exactly the same as in Figure 17.4, but remember to change the board type to Arduino Dev Module before compiling the program.

Raspberry Pi Program Listing: The circuit diagram of the Raspberry Pi version of the project is exactly the same as in Figure 17.2, but the +V pin is connected to +3.3V. Before writing the Raspberry Pi program we have to modify file **/boot/config.txt** as shown below:

- **pi@raspberrypi:~ $** sudo nano /boot/config.txt
- find the line with **dtoverlay** and replace with:

  ```
  dtoverlay=w1-gpio
  ```
- save and exit by entering **Cntrl+X** followed by **Y**
- reboot

We now have to find the unique address of our DS18B20 temperature sensor (this will be different for your sensor chip). Enter the commands shown in Figure 17.7. The unique address of the sensor used in this project is: **28-0316a141a4ff**

```
pi@raspberrypi:~ $ sudo modprobe w1-gpio
pi@raspberrypi:~ $ sudo modprobe w1-therm
pi@raspberrypi:~ $ cd /sys/bus/w1/devices
pi@raspberrypi:/sys/bus/w1/devices $ ls
00-200000000000  28-0316a141a4ff  w1_bus_master1
pi@raspberrypi:/sys/bus/w1/devices $ cd ~
pi@raspberrypi:~ $
```

Figure 17.7 Finding the sensor unique address

The program listing is shown in Figure 17.8 (program: **rpiDS18b20.py**). The program opens the sensor module as a file and reads the temperature data into variable **txt**. The data read at this stage is in two columns as follows:

```
5a 01 4b 46 7f ff 0c 10 44 : crc=44 YES
5a 01 4b 46 7f ff 0c 10 44 t=21625
```

The line starting with **t=** is the actual temperature read where the decimal point is after the first two digits. i.e. in the above example, the temperature is 21.625ºC. The **split** statement splits a string into a list of its words. In this program, the string is split with the carriage return ("\n") as the separator. Therefore, in this example, variable **dt** stores the following string in the second line of variable **txt**:

```
7f  01 4b 46 7f ff 0c 10 ba t=23937
```

Variable **data** then extracts the 9th field (starting from 0) which **is t=23937**. Variable **temp** extracts the numeric part of the data (starting from 0) which is in this case 23937.0 Finally, the data is divided by 1000 to give the actual physical temperature which is then displayed every second on the monitor. Figure 17.9 shows a typical output from the program.

```
#----------------------------------------------------------
#  DISPLAY TEMPERATURE
#  ===================
#
# In this project the KY-001 temperature sensor module is used.
# The program reads the ambient temperature every second and
# displays it on the monitor
#
# Author: Dogan Ibrahim
# Date  : May 2019
# File  : rpiDS18b20.py
#----------------------------------------------------------
import time                           # Import time library

try:
  while True:
     fl = open("/sys/bus/w1/devices/28-0316a141a4ff/w1_slave")
     txt = fl.read()                  # Read data
     fl.close()                       # Close file
     dt = txt.split("\n")[1]          # Split 2nd line
     data = dt.split(" ")[9]          # Extract temperature
     temp = float(data[2:])           # Extract numeric part
     temp = temp / 1000               # Actual temperature
     print "Temperature = ", temp     # Display temperature
     time.sleep(1)                    # Wait one second
```

```
except KeyboardInterrupt:
  exit(0)
```

Figure 17.8 Raspberry Pi program listing

```
pi@raspberrypi:~ $ python rpiDS18b20.py
Temperature =  23.812
Temperature =  23.875
Temperature =  23.937
Temperature =  23.937
Temperature =  24.0
Temperature =  24.0
Temperature =  24.062
Temperature =  24.25
```

Figure 17.9 Typical output from the program

Plotting in Raspberry Pi: There is no serial plotter type function in Raspberry Pi. In this section, we will learn how to plot the temperature variation in real time using the Raspberry Pi. For plotting, we can use the **matplotlib** library which is a sophisticated library with many functions and options. Because of the graphic nature of a plot, we have to use a desktop monitor or use the Raspberry Pi in desktop mode through the **vncserver**. The program listing is shown in Figure 17.10 (program: **rpiDS18b20plot.py**). At the beginning of the program, the **matplotlib** library is imported into the program. Function **animate** reads the temperature from the sensor module inserts a graph heading and y-axis title and draws the graph in real-time against time. If you are using the **vncserver,** start your desktop, click **Terminal**, and enter the command **python rpiDS18b20plot.py** to start the program. Figure 17.11 shows an output from the program.

```
#------------------------------------------------------------
#  PLOT TEMPERATURE
#  ================
#
# In this project the KY-001 temperature sensor module is used.
# The program reads the ambient temperature every second and
# plots it on the monitor
#
# Author: Dogan Ibrahim
# Date  : May 2019
# File  : rpiDS18b20plot.py
#-----------------------------------------------------------
import datetime

import matplotlib.pyplot as plt        # Import matplotlib
import matplotlib.animation as animation

fig = plt.figure()                     # Setup figure
ax = fig.add_subplot(1, 1, 1)
xs = []
```

```
ys = []


def animate(k, xs, ys):
     fl = open("/sys/bus/w1/devices/28-0316a141a4ff/w1_slave")
     txt = fl.read()                         # Read data
     fl.close()                              # Close file
     dt = txt.split("\n")[1]                 # Split 2nd line
     data = dt.split(" ")[9]                 # Extract temperature
     temp = float(data[2:])                  # Extract numeric part
     temp = temp / 1000                      # Actual temperature
     temp = str(round(temp,2))               # Round
     xs.append(datetime.datetime.now()) # time value (x)
     ys.append(temp)                         # temperature (y)

     ax.clear()
     ax.plot(xs,ys)                          # Plot x,y
     plt.xticks(rotation=45,ha='right') # 45 degree ticks
     plt.subplots_adjust(bottom=0.30)   # Bottom of plot
     plt.title("AMBIENT TEMPERATURE VARIATION")
     plt.ylabel("Temperature (C))")

#
# Start plotting in animation mode and refresh every second
#
ani = animation.FuncAnimation(fig, animate, fargs=(xs,ys),interval=1000)
plt.show()
```

Figure 17.10 Raspberry Pi plotting program

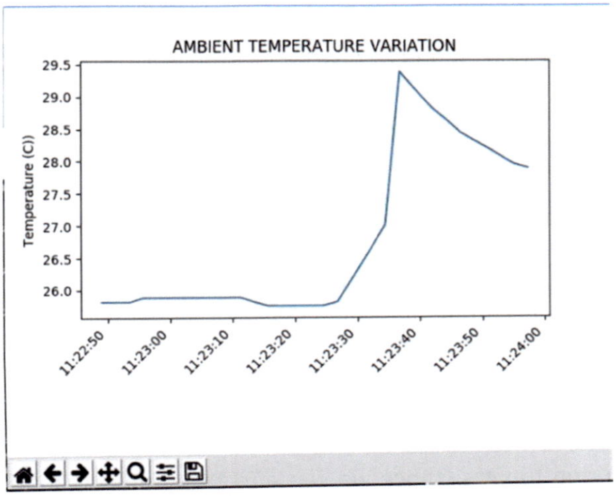

Figure 17.11 Output from the program

17.3 Project 2 – Temperature sensor with buzzer

Description: In this project, we will use a temperature sensor module to read the relative change in temperature. If the temperature goes above a certain value then a buzzer will be activated.

Aim: The aim of this project is to show how the relative temperature can be measured such that if it goes above a preset threshold value then a buzzer is activated.

Sensors Used: In this project, the KY-028 relative temperature sensor module is used together with the KY-012 active buzzer module. As shown in Figure 17.12, KY-028 is a 4-pin module with the following pins:

- D0 (digital output)
- GND (power ground)
- +V (power supply)
- A0 (analog output)

Figure 17.12 KY-028 module

The KY-028 module consists of an NTC thermistor, an LM393 comparator chip, a potentiometer, some resistors, and two LEDs. One of the LEDs indicates the power while the other one turns ON when the output of the module goes to logic HIGH. Both digital and analog outputs are provided. The analog output gives a voltage which depends on the temperature and the potentiometer setting. The analog pin is directly connected to the potentiometer and as a result, it is not possible to calculate the actual physical temperature. The digital output goes HIGH when the temperature goes above a preset threshold value and in this project, the digital output is used. Turning the potentiometer clockwise increases the temperature detection threshold of the module. The basic features of the KY-028 module are:

- operating voltage: +3.3V to +5V
- temperature measurement range: -55ºC to +125ºC
- measurement accuracy: ±0.5ºC

Background Information: Thermistors are temperature sensing components made of semiconductor materials. The resistance of a thermistor changes in proportion to temperature and by measuring the resistance we can effectively measure the temperature. NTC (Negative Temperature Coefficient) thermistors are non-linear components whose resistances decrease as the temperature increases. Thermistors are used in applications such as temperature measurement, temperature control, temperature compensation, and so on. The resistance of NTC thermistors can easily and accurately be calculated using the Steinhart-Hart equation. An example use of this equation is given in the next thermistor based project. The typical variation of the thermistor resistance with temperature is shown in Figure 17.13.

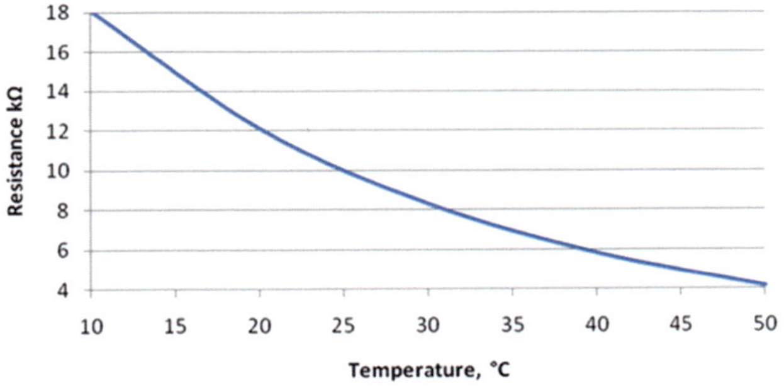

Figure 17.13 Typical thermistor characteristic

Arduino Uno Circuit Diagram: Figure 17.14 shows the circuit diagram of the project. Pin D0 of the sensor module is connected to Arduino port pin 2. The buzzer is connected to pin 4.

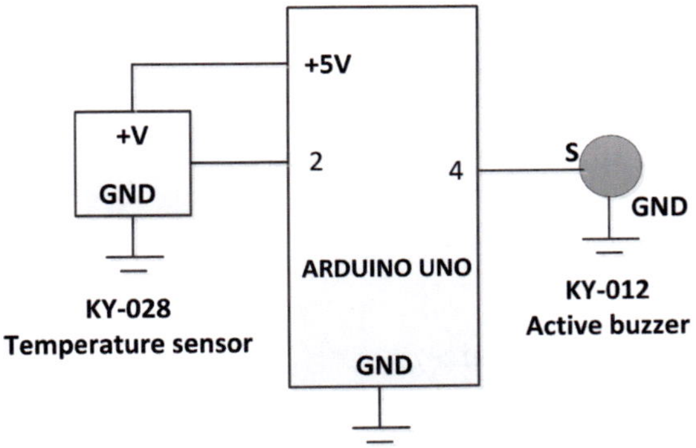

Figure 17.14 Circuit diagram of the project

Setting the Threshold Value: Make sure that the power LED is ON and the sense LED is OFF on the sensor module. If the sense LED is ON, turn the potentiometer anti-clockwise until the LED becomes OFF. You should now place the sensor in a higher temperature environment where the temperature is at the required threshold value. Then, turn the potentiometer screw slowly clockwise until the LED on the sensor module comes ON.

Arduino Uno Program Listing: The program listing is shown in Figure 17.15 (program: **reltemp**). Inside the setup routine, the sensor is configured as an input and the buzzer as an output. The program reads the digital output of the sensor and activates the buzzer id it is above the preset threshold value.

```
/****************************************************************
 *              TEMPERATURE MEASUREMENT WITH BUZZER
 *              ===================================
 *
 * In this program a KY-028 temperature sensor module and a KY-012
 * active buzzer module are used. KY-028 potentiometer is adjusted
 * such that if the temperature goes above a preset threshold value
 * then the output of the sensor goes HIGH. Thsi is detected by the
 * program which activates the buzzer when this happens.
 *
 * Author: Dogan Ibrahim
 * Date  : May 2019
 * File  : reltemp
 ****************************************************************/
int S = 2;                                  // Sensor S pin
int buzzer = 4;                             // Buzzer pin

void setup()
{
  pinMode(S, INPUT);                        // S is input
  pinMode(buzzer, OUTPUT);                  // Buzzer is output
  digitalWrite(buzzer, LOW);                // Buzzer OFF
}

//
// Activate teh buzzer if the temperature is above the preset value
//
void loop()
{
  if(digitalRead(S) == 1)                   // Wait
    digitalWrite(buzzer, HIGH);             // Buzzer ON
  else
    digitalWrite(buzzer, LOW);              // Buzzer OFF
}
```

Figure 17.15 Arduino Uno program listing

ESP32 DevKitC Program Listing: The circuit diagram of the ESP32 DevKitC version of the project is exactly the same as in Figure 17.14, but the +V pin is connected to +3.3V. The program listing is exactly the same as in Figure 17.15, but remember to change the board type to Arduino Dev Module before compiling the program.

Raspberry Pi Program Listing: The circuit diagram of the Raspberry Pi version of the project is exactly the same as in Figure 17.14, but the +V pin is connected to +3.3V. The Raspberry Pi program is very simple and can very easily be derived from the earlier programs.

17.4 Project 3 – Displaying the temperature on LCD – Arduino Uno

Description: In this project, we will be reading the ambient temperature every second using the KY-013 temperature sensor module and then display it on an LCD.

Aim: The aim of this project is to show how the temperature of an NTC thermistor temperature sensor can be read and also how to use an LCD in a project.

Sensor Used: In this project, the KY-013 analog output NTC thermistor type temperature sensor module is used. As shown in Figure 17.16 this is a 3-pin module with the following pins:

- GND
- +V
- S (analog output)

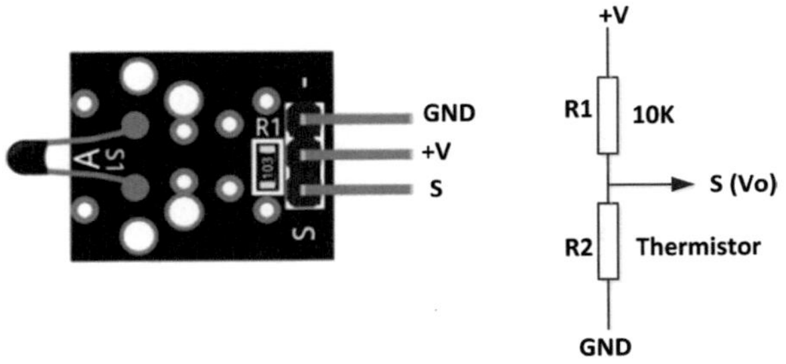

Figure 17.16 KY-13 module

The sensor module is connected to a 10K resistor as shown in the Figure to form a potential divider circuit. The voltage across the thermistor is read using an analog port of the processor. This voltage is proportional to the temperature where the temperature is calculated using the Steinhart-Hart equation. Different thermistors have different Steinhart-Hart coefficients and it is required to know these coefficients in order to calculate the temperature of the thermistor used. For the KY-013, these coefficients are specified as follows:

- c1 = 0.001129148
- c2 = 0.000234125
- c3 = 0. 0000000876741

Assuming the resistor is series with the thermistor, R1 = 10K (i.e. R1 = 10000 Ohm), and a 10-bit ADC is used (0 to 1023 quantization levels) to read the thermistor voltage, the temperature is calculated as follows (see Figure 17.16):

First, calculate the resistance of the thermistor. From the potential divider circuit, the output voltage Vo is given by:

$$Vo = V \times R2 / (R1 + R2) \quad (1)$$

Where V is the applied voltage. From this equation we find R2 as:

$$R2 = Vo \times R1 / (V - Vo) \tag{2}$$

With a 10-bit ADC, if Raw is the raw value read by the ADC then the actual physical voltage read, Vo, is given by:

$$Vo = Raw \times V / 1024 \tag{3}$$

From (3) and (2) we get:

$$R2 = [R1 \times Raw \times V / 1024] / (V - Vo] \tag{4}$$

Equation (4) is simplified to give:

$$R2 = R1 / (1024/Raw - 1) \tag{5}$$

or,

$$R2 = 10000 / (1024 / Raw - 1) \tag{6}$$

Knowing R2, the temperature is then given by:

$$T = \log(R2) \tag{7}$$

$$Tmp = 1 / (c1 + (c2 + (c3 \times T \times T)) \times T) \tag{8}$$

Now, we convert the temperature from Kelvin into Celsius:

$$Temp = Tmp - 273.15 \tag{9}$$

We will be using the above equations to calculate the temperature. Notice that the above calculations are only for 10K resistor. You should check to make sure that you have the correct resistor on the sensor module.

The LCD: In microcontroller systems, the output of a measured variable is usually displayed using LEDs, 7-segment displays, or LCD type displays. LCDs have the advantages that they can be used to display alphanumeric or graphical data. Some LCDs have 40 or more character lengths with the capability to display several lines. Some other LCD displays can be used to display graphics images. Some modules offer colour displays while some others incorporate backlighting so that they can be viewed in dimly lit conditions.

There are basically two types of LCDs as far as the interface technique is concerned: parallel LCDs and serial LCDs. Parallel LCDs (e.g. Hitachi HD44780) are connected to a microcontroller using more than one data line and the data is transferred in parallel form. It is common to use either 4 or 8 data lines. Using a 4 wire connection saves I/O pins but it is slower since the data is transferred in two stages. Serial LCDs are connected to the microcontroller using only one data line and data is usually sent to the LCD using the standard RS-232 asynchronous data communication protocol. Serial LCDs are much easier to use but they cost more than the parallel ones.

The programming of a parallel LCD is usually a complex task and requires a good understanding of the internal operation of the LCD controllers, including the timing diagrams. Fortunately, most high-level languages provide special library commands for displaying data on alphanumeric as well as on graphical LCDs. All the user has to do is connect the LCD to the microcontroller, define the LCD connection in the software, and then send special commands to display data on the LCD.

HD44780 LCD Module

HD44780 is one of the most popular alphanumeric LCD modules used in industry and also by hobbyists. This module is monochrome and comes in different sizes. Modules with 8, 16, 20, 24, 32, and 40 columns are available. Depending on the model chosen, the number of rows varies between 1, 2 or 4. The display provides a 14-pin (or 16-pin) connector to a microcontroller. Table 17.2 gives the pin configuration and pin functions of a 14-pin LCD module. Below is a summary of the pin functions:

Pin no	Name	Function
1	VSS	Ground
2	VDD	+ ve supply
3	VEE	Contrast
4	RS	Register select
5	R/W	Read/write
6	E	Enable
7	D0	Data bit 0
8	D1	Data bit 1
9	D2	Data bit 2
10	D3	Data bit 3
11	D4	Data bit 4
12	D5	Data bit 5
13	D6	Data bit 6
14	D7	Data bit 7
15	A	Anode (light)
16	K	Cathode (light)

Table 17.2 Pin configuration of HD44780 LCD module

V_{SS} is the 0V supply or ground. The V_{DD} pin should be connected to the positive supply. Although the manufacturers specify a 5V D.C supply, the modules will usually work with as low as 3V or as high as 6V.

Pin 3 is named V_{EE} and this is the contrast control pin. This pin is used to adjust the contrast of the display and it should be connected to a variable voltage supply. A potentiometer is normally connected between the power supply lines with its wiper arm connected to this pin so that the contrast can be adjusted.

Pin 4 is the Register Select (RS) and when this pin is LOW, data transferred to the display is treated as commands. When RS is HIGH, character data can be transferred to and from the module.

Pin 5 is the Read/Write (R/W) line. This pin is pulled LOW in order to write commands or character data to the LCD module. When this pin is HIGH, character data or status information can be read from the module.

Pin 6 is the Enable (E) pin which is used to initiate the transfer of commands or data between the module and the microcontroller. When writing to the display, data is transferred only on the HIGH to LOW transition of this line. When reading from the display, data becomes available after the LOW to HIGH transition of the enable pin and this data remains valid as long as the enable pin is at logic HIGH.

Pins 7 to 14 are the eight data bus lines (D0 to D7). Data can be transferred between the microcontroller and the LCD module using either a single 8-bit byte or as two 4-bit nibbles. In the latter case, only the upper four data lines (D4 to D7) are used. 4-bit mode has the advantage that four less I/O lines are required to communicate with the LCD. In this project, we will be using alphanumeric based LCD only and use a 4-bit interface only. For this interface, the required LCD pins are as follows (R/W is connected to ground):

- D4: D7
- E
- RS

Block Diagram: Figure 17.17 shows the project block diagram.

Figure 17.17 Block diagram of the project

Circuit Diagram: The circuit diagram of the project is shown in Figure 17.18. Pin S of the sensor module is connected to analog input A0 of the Arduino Uno. LCD pins RS and E are connected to pins 2 and 3. Also, D4-D7 are connected to pins 4-7 of Arduino Uno. A 10K potentiometer is used to control the contrast of the LCD.

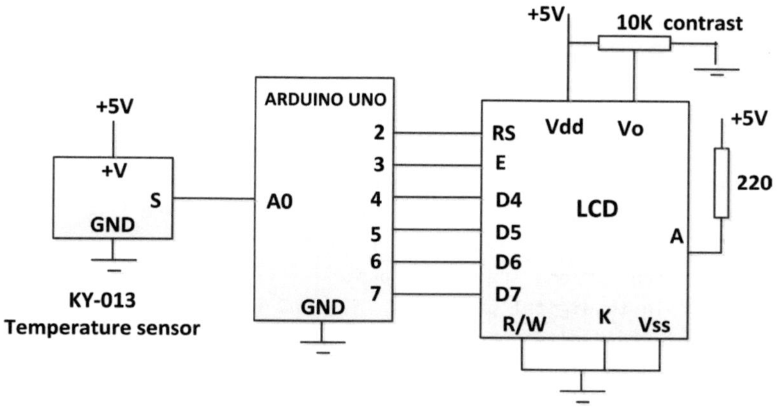

Figure 17.18 Circuit diagram of the project

Arduino Uno Program Listing: Before writing the program we have to install the LCD library for Arduino. The steps are as follows:

- Click **Tools -> Manage Libraries**
- Enter **Liquid crystal**
- Click **Install** to install the LCD library

The LCD library supports the following functions:

lcd.begin(col, row): initialize the LCD and specify number of columns and rows
lcd.print(data): displays data on LCD. We can optionally specify the base for numeric data
lcd.setCursor(col, row): position the cursor at the specified column and row, where (0,0) is the first row and first column
lcd.blink(): blink the cursor
lcd.noBlink(): do not blink
lcd.clear(): clear display and home the cursor (position 0,0)
lcd.home(): home the cursor (position 0,0)
lcd.rightToLeft(): go right for the enxt character
lcd.leftToRight(): go left for the next character
lcd.scrollDisplayRight(): scroll one position right
lcd.scrollDisplayLeft(): scroll one position left

Figure 17.19 shows the program listing (program: **lcdtemp**). At the beginning of the program, LCD library is included in the program and the thermistor coefficients are defined. The interface between the LCD and Arduino Uno is then defined. Inside the setup routine, the LCD is configured as having 16 columns and 2 rows. Inside the main program loop, the analog raw data of the sensor is read and function Temperature is called to calculate and return the temperature. The temperature is then displayed every second on the second row of the LCD in degrees Celsius.

```
/****************************************************************
 *                  DISPLAY TEMPERATURE ON LCD
 *                  ==========================
 *
 * In this program a KY-013 temperature sensor module is connected
 * to Arduino Uno. Additionally, a parallel LCD is connected. The
 * program displays the temperature every second on the LCD.
 *
 * The LCD connections are as follows:
 * LCD RS pin to digital pin 2
 * LCD E pin to digital pin 3
 * LCD D4 pin to digital pin 4
 * LCD D5 pin to digital pin 5
 * LCD D6 pin to digital pin 6
 * LCD D7 pin to digital pin 7
 * LCD R/W pin to ground
 * LCD VSS pin to ground
 * LCD VCC pin to 5V
 * 10K resistor: ends +5V and ground, wiper to LCD VO pin (pin 3)
 *
 * Author: Dogan Ibrahim
 * Date  : May 2019
 * File  : lcdtemp
 ****************************************************************/
#include <LiquidCrystal.h>                  // Include LCD library
int Sensor = A0;                            // Sensor pin

float c1 = 0.001129148;
float c2 = 0.000234125;
float c3 = 0.0000000876741;
float R1 = 10000.0;                         // For 10K resistor
float ADC_Res = 1023.0;                     // For 10 bit ADC

//
// Define the LCD interface to Arduino Uno
//
const int rs = 2, e = 3, d4 = 4, d5 = 5, d6 = 6, d7 = 7;
LiquidCrystal lcd(rs, e, d4, d5, d6, d7);

//
// Calculate and return the temperature
```

```
//
float Temperature(int RawValue)
{
  float R2, T, Tmp, Temp;
  R2 = R1 / ((ADC_Res / (float)RawValue - 1.0));
  T = log(R2);
  Tmp = 1 / (c1 + (c2 + (c3 * T * T)) * T);
  Temp = Tmp - 273.15;
  return Temp;
}

void setup()
{
  lcd.begin(16, 2);                          // LCD has 16 rows x 2
columns
  lcd.print("Temperature");                  // Display temperature
  delay(2000);
}

//
// Read the temperature every second and display on LCD
//
void loop()
{
   int Raw = analogRead(Sensor);             // Read ADC
   float temp = Temperature(Raw);            // Temperature in C
   lcd.clear();
   lcd.print("Temperature in C");
   lcd.setCursor(0, 1);                      // Second row
   lcd.print(temp);                          // Display temp
   delay(1000);                              // Wait one sec
}
```

Figure 17.19 Program listing

Figure 17.20 shows the project constructed on a breadboard. A typical display on the LCD is shown in Figure 17.21.

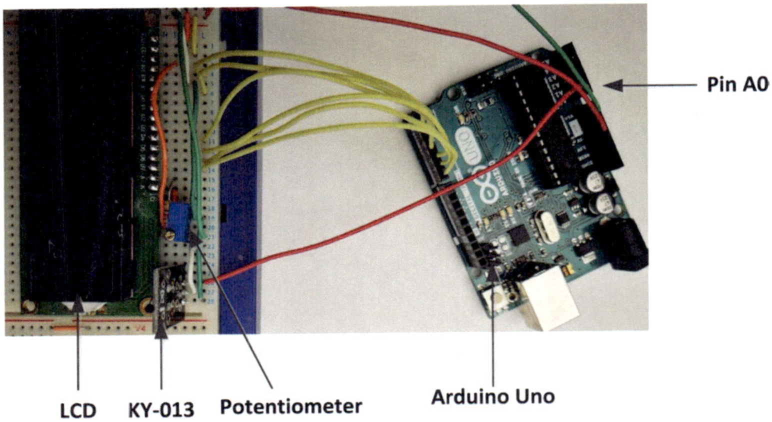

Figure 17.20 Project constructed on a breadboard

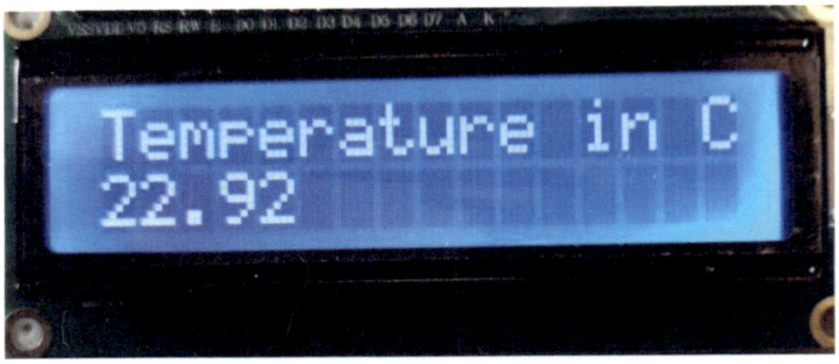

Figure 17.21 Typical display on LCD

17.5 Project 4 – Saving temperature as CSV file on PC with timestamp – Arduino Uno

Description: In this project, the temperature readings are saved in a file in comma-separated CSV format which is compatible with most spreadsheet programs such as Excel. The file can then be imported into Excel on the PC and plotted or statistically analyzed if required. The advantage of doing this is that we can use the extensive functions of Excel to plot the data in any format we like, and also statistically analyze the data, for example, find the mean, maximum, standard deviation, and so on. Up to 60 temperature data are read in one minute.

Aim: The aim of this project is to show how the temperature readings can be saved in a comma-separated CSV file and then how it can be imported into Excel.

Sensor Used: In this project, the KY-013 temperature sensor module as in the previous project is used.

Block Diagram: The block diagram of the project is the same as in Figure 17.17, but the LCD is not used in this project.

Circuit Diagram: The circuit diagram of the project is the same as in Figure 17.18, but the LCD is not used in this project.

Using the RealTerm Serial Capture Program: In this project, the PC based RealTerm serial capture program is used to capture the data received from the sensor module. By using the print or println statements we can normally display data on the Arduino IDE serial monitor. In this project, we direct the saved data to the **RealTerm** program and then save the received data in a file. It is also possible to insert commas and timestamp the received data so that it is in CSV format. The RealTerm program can be downloaded from the following link:

https://sourceforge.net/projects/realterm/files/latest/download

Arduino Uno Program Listing: Figure 17.22 shows the program listing (program: **tempcsv**). The program is basically the same as the one given in Figure 17.19, but in this project, the LCD is not used and therefore all the LCD related code is removed from the program. Additionally, the temperature is printed so that it can be captured by **RealTerm**.

```
/*****************************************************************
 *                 SAVE TEMPERATURE DATA IN CSV FORMAT
 *                 ===================================
 *
 * In this program a KY-013 temperature sensor module is connected
 * to Arduino Uno. Up to 60 temperature data is read in one minute
 * every and is stored in a file on the PC in CSV format.
 *
 * Author: Dogan Ibrahim
 * Date  : May 2019
 * File  : tempcsv
 *****************************************************************/
int Sensor = A0;                                // Sensor pin

float c1 = 0.001129148;                         // Thermistor coeff
float c2 = 0.000234125;
float c3 = 0.0000000876741;
float R1 = 10000.0;                             // For 10K resistor
float ADC_Res = 1023.0;                         // For 10 bit ADC

//
// Calculate and return the temperature
//
float Temperature(int RawValue)
{
  float R2, T, Tmp, Temp;
  R2 = R1 / ((ADC_Res / (float)RawValue - 1.0));
  T = log(R2);
  Tmp = 1 / (c1 + (c2 + (c3 * T * T)) * T);
  Temp = Tmp - 273.15;
  return Temp;
```

```
}

void setup()
{
  Serial.begin(9600);                               // Start monitor
}

//
// Read 60 temperature data in one minute (one every second).
//
void loop()
{
  for(int k = 0; k < 60; k++)
  {
    int Raw = analogRead(Sensor);                   // Read ADC
    float temp = Temperature(Raw);                  // Temperature in C
    Serial.println(temp);                           // Display temp
    delay(1000);                                    // Wait one sec
  }
  while(1);                                         // Stop the program
}
```

Figure 17.22 Program listing

Capturing the Temperature Data: The steps to capture the data and import into Excel are given below:

- Connect the sensor module to your Arduino
- Compile and upload the program to your Arduino
- Start the **RealTerm** program
- Click **Capture** and choose a name for the file in a textbox named **File** where the data is to be saved (e.g. **C:\temp\capture.txt**)
- Click Tools and find out the Port number (e.g. **Port: "COM40"**)
- Click the radio button called **comma** under tab **Delimiter**
- Click **YMDHS** under tab **TimeStamp** (see Figure 17.23)

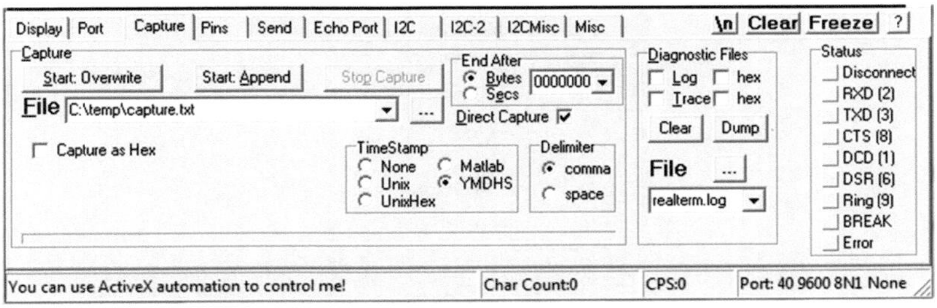

*Figure 17.23 RealTerm **Capture** settings*

- Click tab **Port** and set the **Baud** rate to 9600, and the **Port** number to 40 as found earlier. Set **Parity** to None, **Data Bits** to 8, **Stop Bits** to 1, and **Hardware Flow Control** to None as shown in Figure 17.24.

- Click tab **Change** to activate the changes

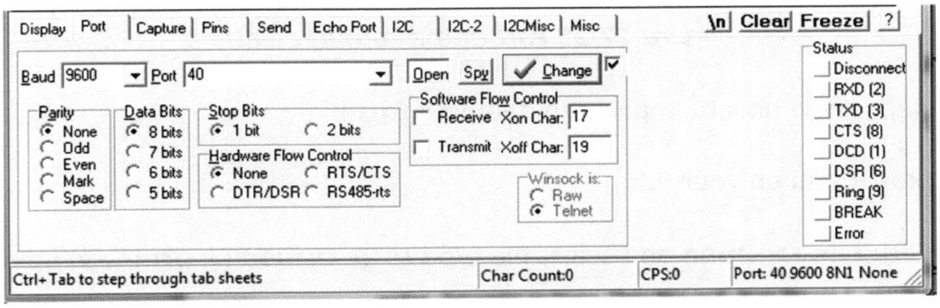

*Figure 17.24 RealTerm **Port** settings*

- Click tab **Capture**

- Push the Arduino Uno Reset button and keep it pushed down. Click **Clear** to clear the screen. Click tab **Start: Overwrite** and then release the Reset button to start capturing the data

- You should see the data being captured (lower part of the screen turns red colour and the character count is incremented automatically at the bottom of the screen). Wait for a minute until all the data is captured and then click **Stop Capture.** The character counter should stop when there is no more data.

We now have the temperature data in CSV format in file **C:\temp\capture.txt**. Figure 17.25 shows part of the captured data.

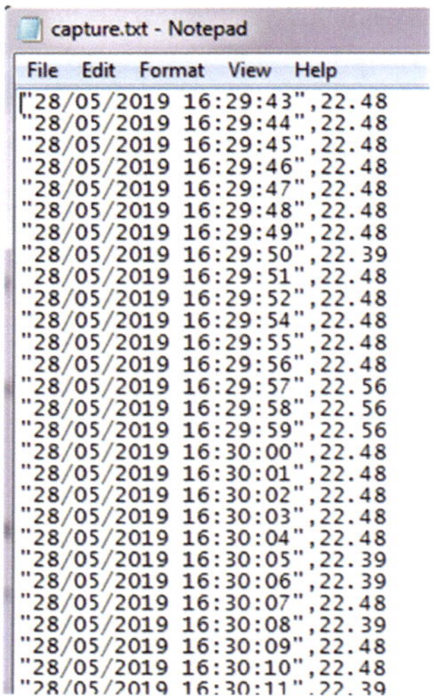

Figure 17.25 Part of the captured data

Following steps show how to import the data into Excel:

- Start Excel on your PC
- Click **File -> Open** and select file type as **Text files (*.prn;*.txt;.csv)**
- Browse for file **C:\temp\capture.txt** and click **Open**
- Select file type as **Delimited** and click **Next**
- Select Comma as the delimiter as shown in Figure 17.26 and click **Next**

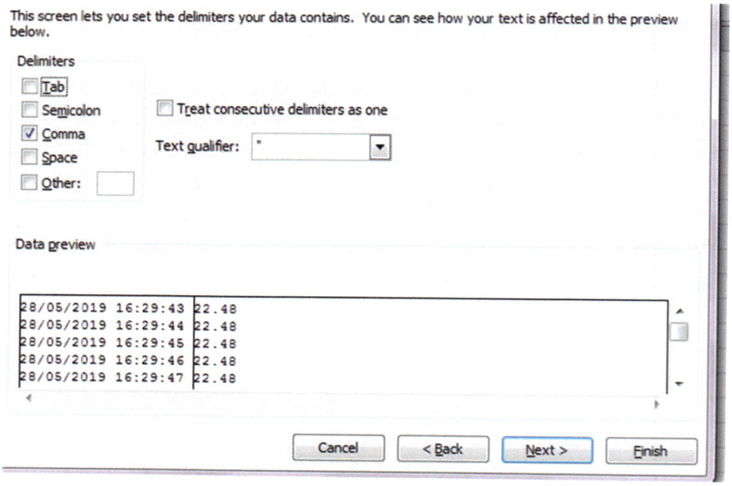

Figure 17.26 Select comma as the delimiter

• Select Date as the column format as shown in Figure 17.27 and click **Finish**

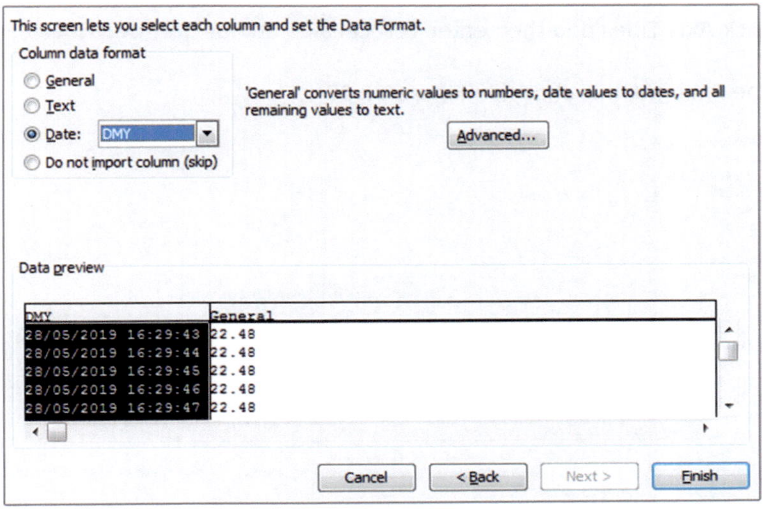

Figure 17.27 Select column format

• You should see the data in Excel form. You can expand column **A** so that the date can be seen clearly

• Click **Insert** and select **Scatter** as the graph type.

• Click on X-axis, right click and select **Format Axis**

• Click Number at the left pane and select **Time** at the right-hand side textbox as shown in Figure 17.28

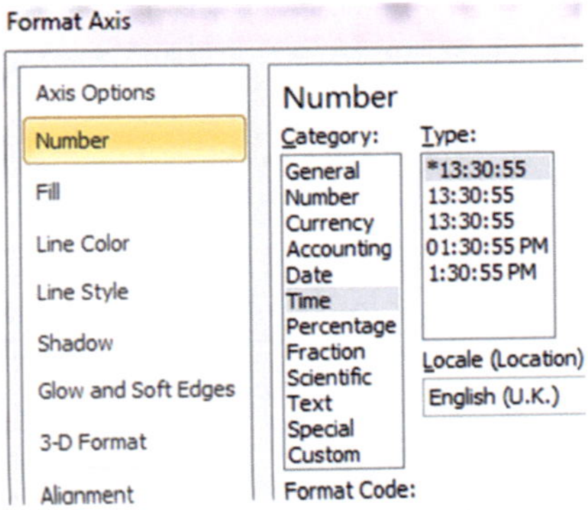

Figure 17.28 Select X axis format

• Click on **Chart Tools** and then **Layout**

• Select **Gridlines** and insert vertical grid lines

- Click Axis Titles and then enter horizontal axis title as **Time**
- Click Axis Titles and then enter vertical axis title as **Temperature**
- The final graph is shown in Figure 17.29

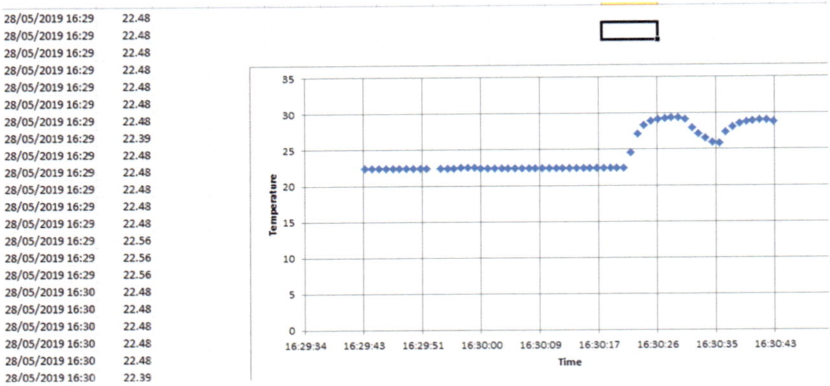

Figure 17.29 Final graph

17.6 Project 5 – Displaying the temperature on LCD – ESP32 DevKitC

Description: This project is the same as Project 3, but here the ESP32 DevKitC processor is used.

Aim: The aim of this project is to show how an LCD can be used with the ESP32 DevKitC to display the ambient temperature.

Circuit Diagram: The circuit diagram of the project is shown in Figure 17.30. The connections between the LCD and the processor are as shown in the Figure.

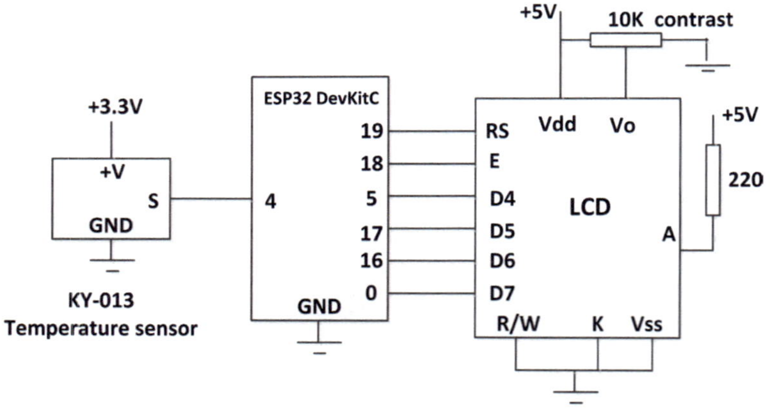

Figure 17.30 Circuit diagram of the project

Program Listing: The ESP32 DevKitC version of the program is very similar to the one given in Figure 17.19, but here the LCD connections are different, and also the ADC is 12-bits wide (0 to 4095 quantization levels). Figure 17.31 shows the program listing (program: **esp32lcdtemp**).

```
/****************************************************************
 *                DISPLAY TEMPERATURE ON LCD
 *                ==========================
 *
 * In this program a KY-013 temperature sensor module is connected
 * to ESP32 DevKitC. Additionally, a parallel LCD is connected. The
 * program displays the temperature every second on the LCD.
 *
 * The LCD connections are as follows:
 * LCD RS pin to digital pin 19
 * LCD E pin to digital pin 18
 * LCD D4 pin to digital pin 5
 * LCD D5 pin to digital pin 17
 * LCD D6 pin to digital pin 16
 * LCD D7 pin to digital pin 0
 * LCD R/W pin to ground
 * LCD VSS pin to ground
 * LCD VCC pin to 5V
 *
 * KY013 S pin is connected to GPIO 4 (ADC2_0) of ESP32 DevKitC
 *
 * 10K resistor: ends +5V and ground, wiper to LCD VO pin
 *
 * Author: Dogan Ibrahim
 * Date  : May 2019
 * File  : esp32lcdtemp
 ****************************************************************/
#include <LiquidCrystal.h>                   // Include LCD library
int Sensor = 4;                              // Sensor pin

float c1 = 0.001129148;
float c2 = 0.000234125;
float c3 = 0.0000000876741;
float R1 = 10000.0;                          // For 10K resistor
float ADC_Res = 4095.0;                      // For 12 bit ADC

//
// Define the LCD interface to Arduino Uno
//
const int rs = 19, e = 18, d4 = 5, d5 = 17, d6 = 16, d7 = 0;
LiquidCrystal lcd(rs, e, d4, d5, d6, d7);
```

```
//
// Calculate and return the temperature
//
float Temperature(int RawValue)
{
  float R2, T, Tmp, Temp;
  R2 = R1 / ((ADC_Res / (float)RawValue - 1.0));
  T = log(R2);
  Tmp = 1 / (c1 + (c2 + (c3 * T * T)) * T);
  Temp = Tmp - 273.15;
  return Temp;
}

void setup()
{
  lcd.begin(16, 2);                          // LCD has 16 rows x 2
columns
  lcd.print("Temperature");                  // Display temperature
  delay(2000);
}

//
// Read the temperature every second and display on LCD
//
void loop()
{
   int Raw = analogRead(Sensor);             // Read ADC
   float temp = Temperature(Raw);            // Temperature in C
   lcd.clear();
   lcd.print("Temperature in C");
   lcd.setCursor(0, 1);                      // Second row
   lcd.print(temp);                          // Display temp
   delay(1000);                              // Wait one sec
}
```

Figure 17.31 Program listing

17.7 Project 6 – Displaying the temperature on LCD – Raspberry Pi

description: This project is the same as Project 3, but here the Raspberry Pi processor is used.

Aim: The aim of this project is to show how an LCD can be used with the Raspberry Pi to display the ambient temperature.

Circuit Diagram: The circuit diagram of the project is shown in Figure 17.32. In this project, the KY-053 ADC module is used to read the sensor voltage, where the sensor output is connected to channel 0 of the ADC. The connections between the LCD and the processor are as shown in the Figure.

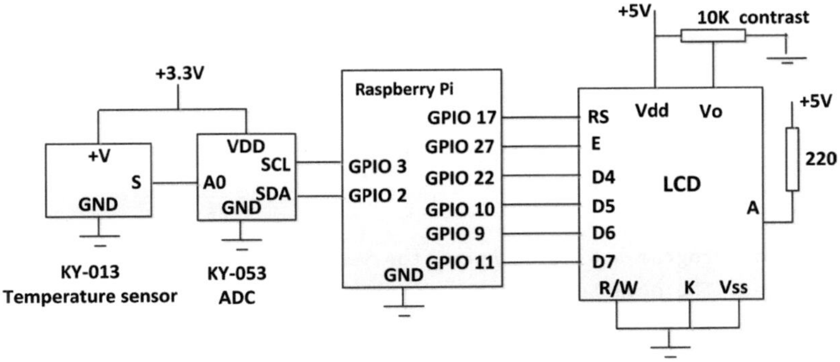

Figure 17.32 Circuit diagram of the project

Program Listing: Before writing the program we have to install a Raspberry Pi LCD library. The library used in this project is installed with the following command:

```
pi@raspberrypi:~ $ sudo pip install RPLCD
```

Some of the functions supported by this library are:

lcd.cursor_pos(row, col): position the cursor at the given row and column. Top left corner is (0,0)
lcd.clear(): clear screen
lcd.cursor_mode=CursorMode.blink: set blinking block
lcd.cursorMode=CursorMode.line: set line cursor
lcd.cursorMode=CursorMode.hide: set cursor off
lcd.write_string(data): display data

The LCD library RPLCD must be imported to the program before the LCD functions can be used. Also, the interface between the LCD and Raspberry Pi should be defined using the CharLCD statement.

Figure 17.33 shows the program listing (program: **rpilcdtemp.py**). At the beginning of the program the libraries used in the program are imported. The ADC library is called **Adafruit_ADS1x15** and its use has already been described in section 4.2.6. The interface between the LCD and the Raspberry Pi is defined as follows:

```
lcd =CharLCD(numbering_mode=GPIO.BCM,cols=16,rows=2,pin_rs=17,
pin_e=27,pins_data=[22,10,9,11])
```

By default, the pin numbering mode is board numbering and it must be set to BCM. The LCD has 16 columns and 2 rows. Then the connections between the LCD and Raspberry Pi are defined. Connections to LCD pins D4, D5, D6, and D7 are defined in a list called **pins_**

data. Function **Temperature** calculates the temperature of the thermistor and returns it as Celsius to the main program. Text **Temperature in C** is displayed at the first row of the LCD and the value of the measured temperature is then displayed at the second row of the LCD every second.

```
#--------------------------------------------------------------
#
#             DISPLAY TEMPERATURE ON LCD
#             ==========================
#
# In this program a KY-013 thermistor temperature sensor module
# is used. The program reads and displays the temperature every
# second on the LCD. A KY-053 ADC module is used to read the data
#
# Program: rpilcdtemp.py
# Date   : May 2019
# Author : Dogan Ibrahim
#---------------------------------------------------------------
#
# Import libraries used
#
import RPi.GPIO as GPIO                   # Import GPIO
import time                               # Import time
import Adafruit_ADS1x15                   # Import ADC
from RPLCD.gpio import CharLCD            # Import LCD
import math                               # Import math

GPIO.setwarnings(False)

#
# Configure LCD interface
#
lcd = CharLCD(numbering_mode=GPIO.BCM,cols=16,rows=2,pin_rs=17,\
pin_e=27,pins_data=[22,10,9,11])

adc = Adafruit_ADS1x15.ADS1115()
GAIN = 1                                  # Set ADC gain
ch = 0                                    # Channel 0

#
# Temperature sensor coefficients
#
c1 = 0.001129148
c2 = 0.000234125
c3 = 0.0000000876741
R1 = 10000.0
```

```
ADC_Res = 26399.0

#
# Calculate and return the temperature
#
def Temperature(RawValue):
  R2 = R1 / ((ADC_Res / RawValue - 1.0))
  T = math.log(R2)
  Tmp = 1 / (c1 + (c2 + (c3 * T * T)) * T)
  Temp = Tmp - 273.15
  return Temp

lcd.write_string("TEMPERATURE")
time.sleep(2)

#
# Read and display the temperature on LCD
#
while True:
     Raw = adc.read_adc(ch, gain=GAIN)
     temp = Temperature(Raw)
     lcd.clear()
     lcd.write_string("Temperature in C")
     lcd.cursor_pos = (1, 0)
     lcd.write_string(str(temp)[:5])
     time.sleep(1)
```

Figure 17.33 Program listing

Notice that the gain of the ADC is set to 1 which corresponds to ±4.096V full-scale. This corresponds to raw ADC value of ±32767. Therefore, the full-scale raw ADC value with +3.3V is 26399. i.e. when the voltage applied to the ADC is +3.3V then the ADC will output a digital value of 26399. This value is used in the program as a variable **ADC_Res**.

Other ADC values for different gain setting are as follows (see links: https://learn.adafruit.com/raspberry-pi-analog-to-digital-converters/ads1015-slash-ads1115 and http://www.ti.com/lit/ds/symlink/ads1115.pdf):

Gain	**ADC full-scale voltage**	**ADC Raw Value for +3.3V**
2/3	±6.144V	17600
1	±4.096V	26399
2	±2.048V	52798
4	±1.024V	105597
8	±0.512V	211193
16	±0.256V	422387

It may be useful to start the program automatically every time the Raspberry Pi is re-started. This can be done by editing file **etc/rc.local** using, for example, the **nano** text editor and entering the following statement at the end of the file. Remember to enter **Cntrl+X** followed by **Y** to save and exit the file:

```
python /home/pi/rpilcdtemp.py &
```

17.8 Project 7 – Saving temperature as CSV file on PC with timestamp – Raspberry Pi

Description: In this project, the temperature readings are saved in a file in comma-separated CSV format as in section 17.5 so that the file can then be imported into Excel on the PC and plotted or statistically analyzed if required. Up to 60 temperature data are read in one minute as in Project 4. The circuit diagram of the project is the same as in Figure 17.32, but here the LCD is not used.

Program Listing: Figure 17.34 shows the program listing (program: **rpitempcsv**). The file where the data is to be saved is called **temperature.csv** and this is saved in variable **csvfile**. Function**Temperature** is same as in the previous project and it returns the temperature. The main program loop is executed 60 times with one-second delay between each iteration. The current time and temperature are stored temporarily in list **csvdata**. File **temperature.csv** is then opened in append (**a**) mode with the delimiter set to comma and the line terminator set to carriage-return. **csvdata** is then written to the file. The above process is repeated every second for 60 seconds.

```
#--------------------------------------------------------------
#
#               CREATE CSV FILE OF THE TEMPERATURE DATA
#               =======================================
#
# In this program a KY-013 thermistor temperature sensor module
# is used. The program reads and saves the temperature data in
# csv format so that it can be imported to Excel
#
# Program: rpitempcsv.py
# Date   : May 2019
# Author : Dogan Ibrahim
#---------------------------------------------------------------
#
# Import libraries used
#
import time                             # Import time
import Adafruit_ADS1x15                 # Import ADC
import math                             # Import math
import csv                              # Import csv

csvfile = "temperature.csv"             # CSV file
```

```
adc = Adafruit_ADS1x15.ADS1115()
GAIN = 1                           # Set ADC gain
ch = 0                             # Channel 0

#
# Temperature sensor coefficients
#
c1 = 0.001129148
c2 = 0.000234125
c3 = 0.0000000876741
R1 = 10000.0
ADC_Res = 26399.0

#
# Calculate and return the temperature
#
def Temperature(RawValue):
  R2 = R1 / ((ADC_Res / RawValue - 1.0))
  T = math.log(R2)
  Tmp = 1 / (c1 + (c2 + (c3 * T * T)) * T)
  Temp = Tmp - 273.15
  return Temp

#
# Read the data and save in csv format
#
for k in range(60):                          # Do for 60 seconds
     Raw = adc.read_adc(ch, gain=GAIN)       # Read temperature
     temp = Temperature(Raw)                 # Temperature in C
     tempstr = str(temp)[:5]                 # Convert to string
     Tim = time.strftime("%H:%M:%S")         # Current time
     csvdata = [Tim, tempstr]                # Time, Data
#
# Now save the data in in CSV format with comma delimited
#
     with open(csvfile, "a") as output:
       dat = csv.writer(output, delimiter=",",lineterminator='\n')
       dat.writerow(csvdata)
     time.sleep(1)
```

Figure 17.34 Program listing

Figure 17.35 shows part of the data created in temperature.csv.

```
pi@raspberrypi:~ $ cat temperature.csv
14:11:24,22.43
14:11:25,22.43
14:11:26,22.44
14:11:27,22.44
14:11:28,22.45
14:11:29,22.45
14:11:30,22.45
14:11:32,22.45
14:11:33,22.45
14:11:34,22.45
```

Figure 17.35 Part of the created data

The created CSV formatted file can be imported and analyzed in Excel as described in section 17.5 (Project 4).

17.9 Project 8 – ON/OFF temperature control – Arduino Uno

Description: This is an ON/OFF type temperature control project used to control the temperature in a room. A temperature set-point is specified and a temperature sensor is used to read the ambient temperature in the room. If the temperature is below the set-point then a heater is switched ON. If on the other hand, the temperature goes above the set-point then the heater is switched OFF. The heater is controlled with a relay.

Aim: The aim of this project is to show how the ON/OFF type temperature control project can be designed to control the temperature in a room.

Sensors Used: In this project, the KY-052 temperature and pressure sensor module are used. Additionally, a KY-019 relay module is used. Although the sensor measures both the temperature and the pressure, in this project only the temperature measurement is used. As shown in Figure 17.36, KY-052 is a 6-pin module with the following pins:

- GND
- VCC
- SCL
- SDA
- CSB
- SDO

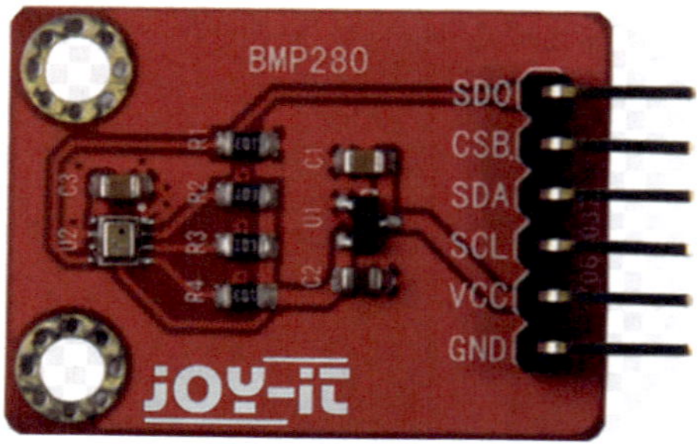

Figure 17.36 KY-052 module

KY-052 module is based on the BMP280 sensor chip which can be used to measure the absolute atmospheric pressure as well as the ambient temperature. The module communicates with the processor over the SPI bus. The basic specifications of this module are:

- Operating voltage: 3.3V to 5V
- Pressure sensing range: 300hPa to 1100hPa
- Absolute Pressure accuracy: ±1hPa
- Pressure resolution: 0.01hPa
- Temperature sensing range: -40ºC to +85ºC
- Average measurement time: 5.5ms
- Interface: I^2C and SPI

Background Information: ON/OFF type temperature control is the simplest type of automatic control where there is no need to know the dynamic characteristics of the plant which is under control. Although this method is very simple, it has some disadvantages. Firstly, it is not possible to keep the plant temperature at a constant value and there are usually fluctuations. The lifetime of the relay is limited since it is switched ON and OFF many continuously. Despite these disadvantages, ON/OFF type control is still used in many control applications.

The BMP280 chip can be interfaced to a processor using either the I^2C or the SPI (Serial Peripheral Interface) bus. In this project, the SPI bus is used. This bus consists of the following 4 lines:

- **MOSI**: Master Out Slave In
- **MISO**: Master In Slave Out
- **SCLK**: Clock
- **SS**: Slave Select

SPI devices communicate in full-duplex mode using a master-slave architecture with a single master and one or many slaves. Slaves are selected using the Slave Select line where only one slave is enabled at any time.

Arduino Uno supports only one SPI bus with the following port pins:

- **MOSI**: pin 11
- **MISO**: pin 12
- **SCLK**: pin 13
- **SS**: pin 10

Block Diagram: Figure 17.37 shows the project block diagram.

Figure 17.37 Block diagram of the project

Circuit Diagram: The circuit diagram of the project is shown in Figure 17.38. The connections between the Arduino Uno and KY-052 are as follows:

KY-052 pin	SPI pin name	Arduino Uno pin
GND		GND
VCC		+5V
SCL	SCLK	13
SDA	MOSI	11
CSB	SS	10
SDO	MISO	12

S pin of the KY-019 relay is connected to port pin 4.

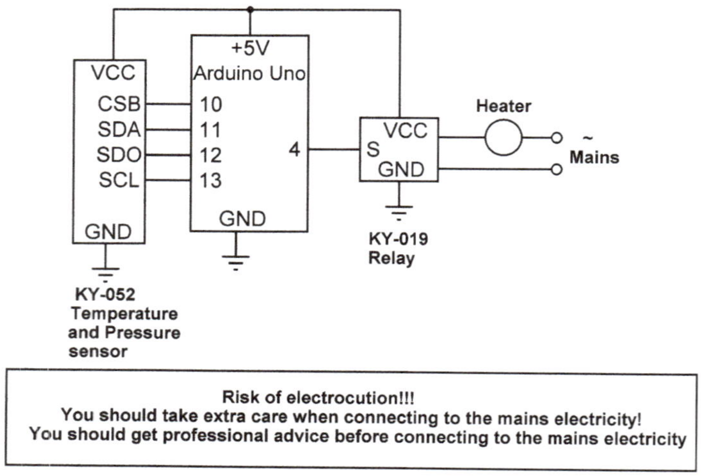

Figure 17.38 Circuit diagram of the project

Program Listing: Before writing the program, we have to install the BMP280 library. The steps are as follows:

- Go to the web site:

  https://github.com/adafruit/Adafruit_BMP280_Library

- Click **Clone or download**, and
- Click **Download ZIP** and store file **Adafruit_BMP280_Library-master.zip** in a folder
- Start Arduino IDE and click **Sketch-> Include Library**
- Click **Add .ZIP Library** and browse to find the saved file
- Click **Open**

Figure 17.39 shows the program listing (program: **onoffcontrol**). At the beginning of the program, the libraries used in the program are included. Then, the connections between the sensor module and Arduino Uno are defined. The required temperature **SetPoint** value is set to 27ºC. Inside the setup routine, the relay is configured as an output and is de-activated. Inside the main program loop, the temperature is read every second and compared with the **SetPoint** value. If the measured temperature is below the **SetPoint** then the relay is turned ON so that the heater is also ON, otherwise, the relay is turned OFF. Notice that, although not used in this project, the program also shows how to read the atmospheric pressure and convert it into millibars.

```
/*****************************************************************
 *                  ON/OFF TEMPERATURE CONTROL
 *                  ==========================
 *
 * In this program a KY-052 temperature/pressure sensor module is
 * used. Additionally, a KY-019 relay module is used and is wired
 * to an electric heater. The program controls the temperature
 * by turning the relay ON and OFF so that the temperature is
 * within the requiered set-point.
 *
 * Author: Dogan Ibrahim
 * Date  : May 2019
 * File  : onoffcontrol
 *****************************************************************/
#include <Wire.h>
#include <SPI.h>
#include <Adafruit_Sensor.h>
#include <Adafruit_BMP280.h>

#define CS 10
#define MOSI 11
```

```
#define MISO 12
#define SCK 13

Adafruit_BMP280 Sensor(CS, MOSI, MISO, SCK);

int Relay = 4;                                  // Relay at pin 4
#define SetPoint 27                             // Set point

void setup()
{
  Serial.begin(9600);                           // Start monitor
  pinMode(Relay, OUTPUT);                       // Relay is output
  digitalWrite(Relay, LOW);                     // Relay OFF
  Sensor.begin();                               // Start sensor
}

//
// Read the temperature and compare it with the set-point. Then, control
// the relay so that the heater is turned ON and OFF to achieve the
// set-point temperature
//
void loop()
{
  float T = Sensor.readTemperature();
  //float P = Sensor.readPressure();          // in Pascals (not used)
  //P = P * 0.01;                             // in mbars (not used)

  Serial.print(SetPoint);                     // Set point
  Serial.print(",");
  Serial.println(T);                          // Temperature

  if(T < SetPoint)
    digitalWrite(Relay, HIGH);                // Relay ON
  else
    digitalWrite(Relay, LOW);                 // Relay OFF

  delay(1000);                                // Wait one secs

}
```

Figure 17.39 Program listing

Figure 17.40 shows both the **SetPoint** temperature (here fixed at 27ºC) and the actual measured temperature, both plotted on the same graph. This is done first printing the **SetPoint** value, followed by a comma, and then the temperature value, followed by a carriage return. As can be seen from the figure, the measured temperature fluctuates around the required **SetPoint** value.

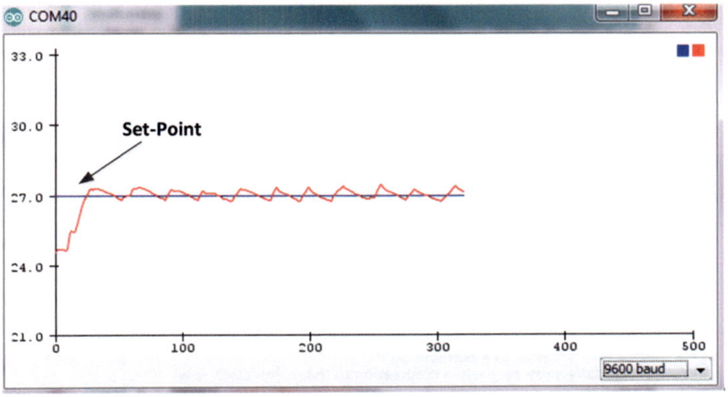

Figure 17.40 Graph of the SetPoint and actual measured temperature

17.10 Project 9 – ON/OFF temperature control – ESP32 DevKitC

The ESP32 DevKitC version of the project requires the KY-051 voltage translator module to be used to activate the relay reliably. Also, the sensor module must be connected to the SPI pins of the ESP32 DevKitC which are as follows:

- **MOSI**: GPIO 23
- **MISO**: GPIO 19
- **SCLK**: GPIO 18
- **SS**: GPIO 5

Figure 17.41 shows the circuit diagram of the project. The connections between the sensor module and the ESP32 DevKitC are as follows:

KY-052 pin	SPI pin name	ESP32 DevKitC pin
GND		GND
VCC		+3.3V
SCL	SCLK	18
SDA	MOSI	23
CSB	SS	5
SDO	MISO	19

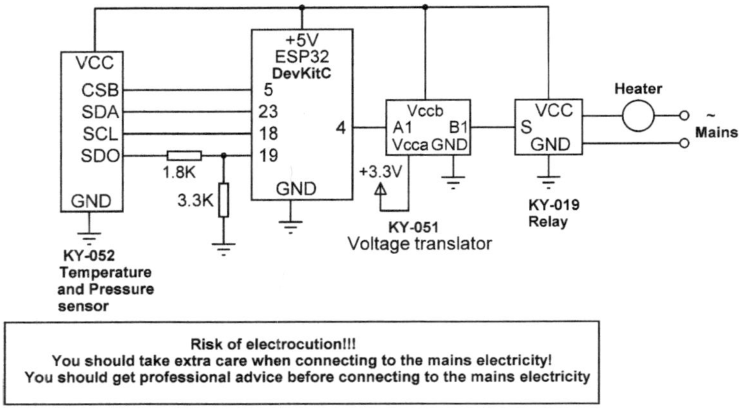

Figure 17.41 Circuit diagram of the project

Pin 2 of ESP32 DevKitC is connected to the relay through the KY-051 voltage translator module. The only output from the sensor module is from pin MISO (Master-In-Slave-Out). Therefore, a resistor divider circuit is used to drop the voltage from 5V to around 3.3V for the ESP32 DevKitC input.

The program listing of the ESP32 DevKitC version of the project is exactly the same as in Figure 17.39, except for the following changes. Remember to set the board type to ESP32 Dev Module before compiling the program. The serial plotter can be used to plot the **Set-Point** and the measured temperature as in the Arduino Uno version of the program:

```
#define CS 5
#define MOSI 23
#define MISO 19
#define SCK 18
```

17.11 Project 10 – ON/OFF temperature control – Raspberry Pi

Raspberry Pi Program Listing: As with the ESP32 DevKitC version, the Raspberry Pi version of the project requires the KY-051 voltage translator module to be used to activate the relay reliably. In Raspberry Pi version of the program, the sensor module is used in I^2C mode, and not in SPI mode. The I^2C pins of the Raspberry Pi are:

GPIO 2 SDA
GPIO 3 SCL

Figure 17.42 shows the circuit diagram of the project. The connections between the sensor module and the ESP32 DevKitC are as follows:

KY-052 pin	**I^2C pin name**	**Raspberry Pi pin**
GND		GND
VCC		No connection
SCL	SCL	3

SDA	SDA	2
CSB	SS	+3.3V
SDO	MISO	23

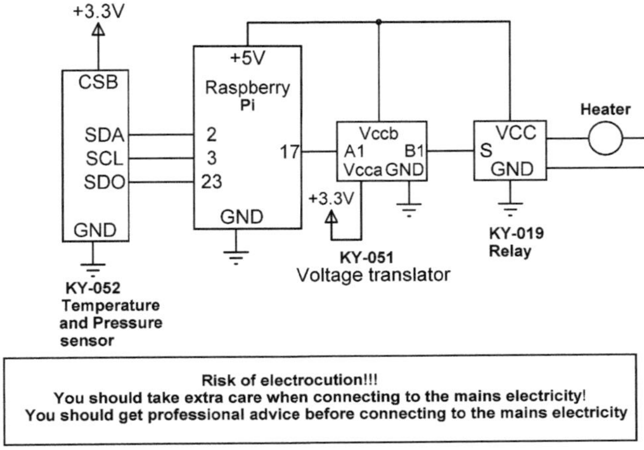

Figure 17.42 Circuit diagram of the project

The relay module is connected to GPIO 17 through the KY-051 voltage translator module. The use and operation of the I^2C interface are described in detail in Section 4.2.6 and the necessary software must be installed before using the I^2C interface. Additionally, the BMP280 library must be installed before using the sensor module. Make sure that your Raspberry Pi is connected to a network and then enter the following:

```
pi@raspberrypi:~ $ sudo apt-get install git

pi@raspberrypi:~ $ git clone https://github.com/bastienwirtz/
Adafruit_python_BMP

pi@raspberrypi:~ $ cd Adafruit_Python_BMP/

pi@raspberrypi:~ $ sudo python setup.py install
```

The program listing is shown in Figure 17.43 (program: **rpionoffcontrol.py**). At the beginning of the program, the BMP280 library is included in the program. The address of the sensor module (0x76) is defined, the relay is configured as an output and is turned OFF. The temperature is then read and if it is lower than the **SetPoint** then the relay is turned ON which turns ON the heater to increase the temperature. The program displays the **SetPoint** and the measured temperature as shown in Figure 17.44. Notice that, although not used in this program, it is also shown how to read the atmospheric pressure.

```
#   ON/OFF TEMPERATURE CONTROL
#   ==========================
#
# In thiS project the KY-052 pressure/temperature sensor module
# is used. Additionally, a KY-019 relay module and a KY-051
# voltage translator module is used. An electric heater is
# connected to the relay. The program controls the heater so
# that the SetPoint temperature is acheived.
#
# Author: Dogan Ibrahim
# Date  : April 2019
# File  : rpionoffcontrol.py
#-----------------------------------------------------------
import RPi.GPIO as GPIO                    # import Rpi library
import time                                # import time library
import Adafruit_BMP.BMP280 as BMP280       # import bmp280

sensor = BMP280.BMP280(address=0x76)       # sensor address

GPIO.setwarnings(False)                    # disable warnings
GPIO.setmode(GPIO.BCM)                     # set BCM mode

SetPoint = 27.0                            # SetPoint temperature
Relay = 17                                 # relay

GPIO.setup(Relay, GPIO.OUT)                # configure as output
GPIO.output(Relay, GPIO.LOW)               # relay OFF

try:
  while True:
    Temp = float(sensor.read_temperature())
    print "SetPoint=",SetPoint,"  Measured Temperature = ",Temp
#   P = sensor.read_pressure()

    if Temp < SetPoint:
      GPIO.output(Relay, GPIO.HIGH)        # turn relay ON
    else:
      GPIO.output(Relay, GPIO.LOW)         # turn relay OFF
    time.sleep(1)                          # wait one second

except KeyboardInterrupt:
    GPIO.output(Relay, GPIO.LOW)           # relay OFF
    GPIO.cleanup()                         # Cleanup
```

Figure 17.43 Program listing

```
pi@raspberrypi:~ $
pi@raspberrypi:~ $ python rpionoffcontrol.py
SetPoint= 27.0   Measured Temperature =  24.0
SetPoint= 27.0   Measured Temperature =  23.0
SetPoint= 27.0   Measured Temperature =  23.0
SetPoint= 27.0   Measured Temperature =  23.0
SetPoint= 27.0   Measured Temperature =  23.0
SetPoint= 27.0   Measured Temperature =  23.0
SetPoint= 27.0   Measured Temperature =  23.0
SetPoint= 27.0   Measured Temperature =  23.0
SetPoint= 27.0   Measured Temperature =  23.0
SetPoint= 27.0   Measured Temperature =  23.0
SetPoint= 27.0   Measured Temperature =  23.0
SetPoint= 27.0   Measured Temperature =  23.0
SetPoint= 27.0   Measured Temperature =  23.0
```

Figure 17.44 Display of SetPoint and measured temperature

17.12 Summary

In this Chapter, we have seen how to develop projects using the temperature and pressure sensors of the sensor kit. In the next few Chapters, we will be developing projects using a temperature and humidity sensor module together with Wi-Fi or Bluetooth connectivity.

Chapter 18 • Wi-Fi and Bluetooth based projects using sensors – ESP32 DevKitC

18.1 Overview

In the previous Chapter, we have seen how to develop projects for the Arduino Uno, Raspberry Pi, and ESP32 DevKitC using the temperature and pressure sensor modules.

In this Chapter, we will be developing projects using a temperature and humidity sensor module with Wi-Fi or Bluetooth connectivity on an ESP32 DevKitC.

18.2 Project 1 – Displaying temperature and humidity on a mobile phone using Wi-Fi

Description: In this project, we will be reading the ambient temperature and humidity from a sensor module and then send the data to a mobile phone over the ESP32 DevKitC on-board Wi-Fi link.

The data will be sent in the following format where T and H are the temperature and humidity readings:

```
T=nn  H=nn
```

A request for data is made by the mobile phone when it sends the character **S** to the ESP32 DevKitC. This project uses two way UDP communications to receive and send data.

Aim: The aim of this project is to show how the temperature and data can be read using a combined sensor module and also it shows how to send data to a mobile phone using the ESP32 DevKitC Wi-Fi connectivity.

Sensor Used: In this project, the KY-015 temperature and humidity sensor module are used. As shown in Figure 18.1, this is a 3-pin module with the following pins:

- GND
- +V
- S (digital output)

Figure 18.1 KY-015 sensor module

KY-015 gives digital output and it has the following basic specifications:

- Supply voltage: 3.3V to 5.5V DC
- 2.5mA current consumption (during a conversion)
- Humidity range: 20-90% RH, Temperature range: 0 to 50 ^{0}C
- Humidity accuracy: + -5% RH, temperature accuracy: + -2 ^{0}C
- Humidity resolution: 1% RH, temperature resolution: 1 ^{0}C
- Signal transmission range: 20 meters

Background Information: There are two sensors in the DHTxx family. DHT22 is more expensive and has a wider temperature range (-40ºC to +125ºC) than the DHT11 with better accuracy (±0.5ºC). Additionally, DHT22 has a better humidity range (0% to 100%) and better humidity accuracy (2-5%) than the DHT11. The advantage of DHT11 is that it has a sampling rate of 1Hz which means that the data can be read every second, while DHT22 sampling rate is 0.5Hz, meaning that the data is available every 2 seconds. The temperature is measured using an NTC thermistor, and the humidity is measured using a humidity sensing element.

Block Diagram: Figure 18.2 shows the block diagram of the project. Communication is established through a Wi-Fi router where the ESP32 DevKitC and an Arduino mobile phone are both connected through the same router.

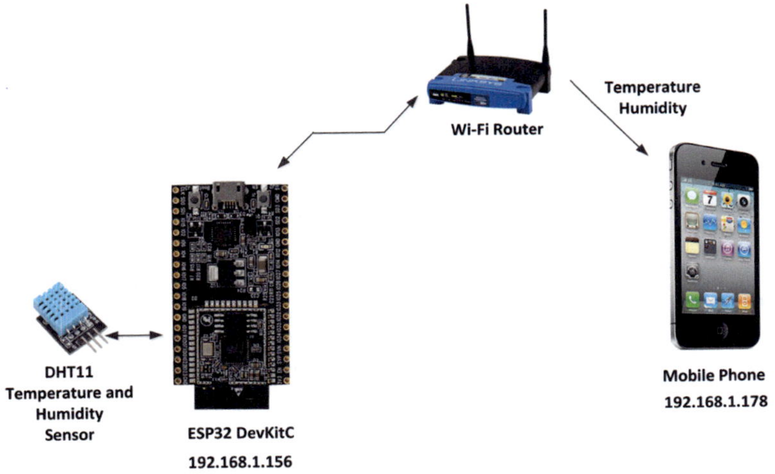

Figure 18.2 Block diagram of the project

Circuit Diagram: The connections between the sensor module and ESP32 DevKitC are shown in Figure 18.3. Pin S of DHT11 is connected to GPIO 23 of the processor. Pins +V and GND are connected to +3.3V and GND pins of the processor respectively.

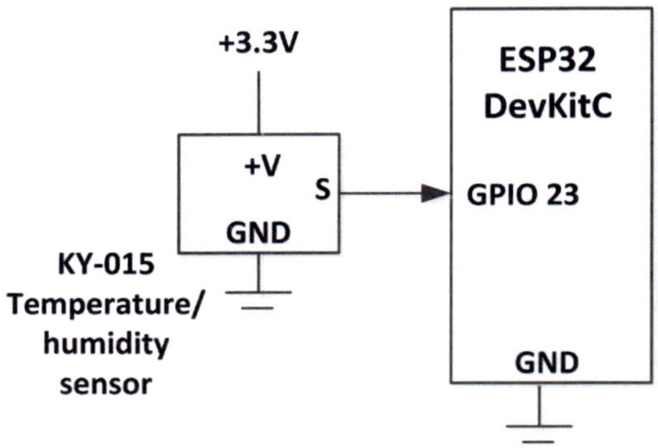

Figure 18.3 Circuit diagram of the project

Before writing the program we have to install the DHT11 sensor library. The steps to install the library into the Arduino IDE environment are given below:

- Start a new Arduino IDE session with the board type set to ESP32 Dev Module
- Click **Sketch -> Include Library -> Manage Libraries**
- Search for library **DHT-sensor-library** as shown in Figure 18.4 and click **Install** to install the library.

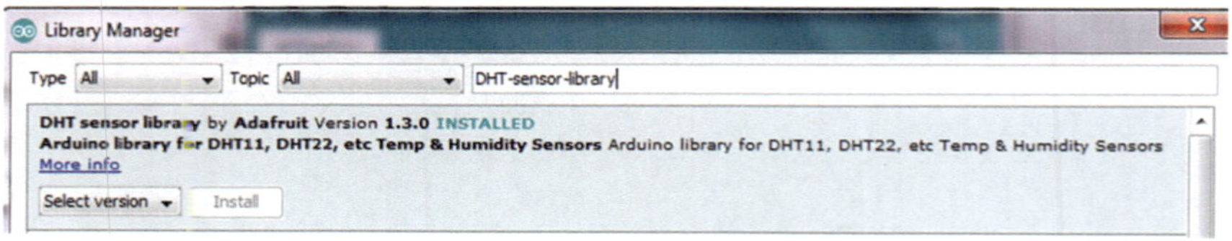

Figure 18.4 Install the DHT-sensor-library

- We now have to install the **Adafruit Unified Sensor** library. Click **Sketch -> Include Library -> Manage Libraries**
- Search for library **Adafruit Unified Sensor** as shown in Figure 18.5 and click to install the library

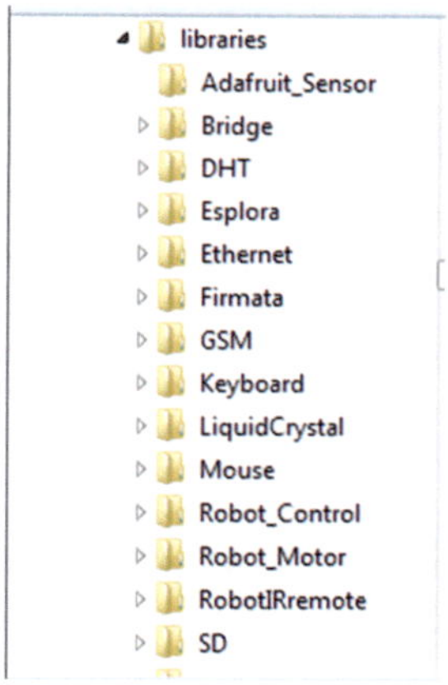

Figure 18.5 Install the Adafruit Unified Sensor library

- Make sure that you have the following two folders under your **Libraries** folder inside the Arduino main folder: **DHT_Sensor_Library** and **Adafruit_Unified_ Sensor**

- Re-start the Arduino IDE

- We are now ready to develop our program to read the relative humidity and the temperature.

The program to send the temperature and humidity data to the mobile phone is based on UDP communications which use the socket library. Socket library is mainly used in network-based communications. UDP and TCP/IP are the two most commonly used protocols to send and receive data over a network. TCP/IP is a reliable protocol which includes handshaking and thus guarantees the delivery of packets to the required destination. UDP on the other hand is not so reliable, but is a fast protocol.

Table 18.1 shows a comparison of the UDP and TCP/IP type communications.

TCP/IP	UDP
Connection-oriented protocol	Connectionless protocol
Slow	Fast
Highly reliable data transmission	Not so reliable
Packets arranged in order	No ordering of packets
20-byte header size	8-byte header size
Error checking and re-transmission	No error checking
Data received acknowledgment	No acknowledgment
Used in HTTP, HTTPS, FTP etc	Used in DNS, DHCP, TFTP etc

Table 18.1 Comparison of UDP and TCP/IP

UDP and TCP/IP protocol based programs are server-client based where one node sends data and the other node receives it and vice-versa. Data is transferred through ports where the server and the clients must use the same port numbers.

UDP is a connectionless protocol and thus there is no need to make a connection to the destination node before a packet can be sent to it. The communication between a server and a client are basically as follows:

Server

- Define the destination node IP address and port number
- Construct the data packet
- Create a socket
- Bind the socket to the local port
- Receive data from the client
- Send data to the client
- Close the connection

Client

- Define the destination node IP address and port number
- Create a socket
- Send data to the server
- Receive data from the server
- Close the connection

Notice that both the server and the client can send and receive data packets from each other.

Mobile Phone Application: In this project, an Android-based mobile phone is used to receive the UDP packets from the ESP32 DevKitC. Android apps named **UDP RECEIVE and SEND** by Wezzi Studios (version 4.0) is used in this project. This app can be installed from the **Play Store**. This application can send and receive UDP packets from any other device running the UDP protocol. The screen is in two parts: the upper Sender part and the lower Receiver part (see Figure 18.6). Before sending a packet the user must enter the destination IP address, port number, and the message to be sent. Clicking the **SEND UDP MESSAGE** button will send the packet to its destination. In the Receiver part, the local IP address is given The user must specify the local port number as well. Received packets will then be displayed on the screen. The ESP32 DevKitC and the mobile phone IP addresses are: 192.168.1.156 and 192.168.1.178 respectively. The IP address of the mobile phone can be seen on the screen when the UDP apps are started.

Figure 18.6 Android UDP send/receive apps

Program Listing: The program listing is shown in Figure 18.7 (program: **esp32toarduino**). Make sure that the board type is set to ESP32 Dev Module before compiling the program. At the beginning of the program, the Wi-Fi and the DHT11 library headers are included in the program, the local port number is defined, and the local Wi-Fi name and password are defined. Function **Connect_WiFi** connects to the local Wi-Fi network. Function **TempHum** reads the ambient temperature and humidity and stores in variables **T** and **H** respectively using the following commands:

```
H = dht.readHumidity();                    // Read humidity
T = dht.readTemperature();                 // Read temperature
```

Inside the setup routine function **Connect_WiFi** is called to connect to local Wi-Fi and UDP and DHT11 are started. Connecting to the local Wi-Fi is very easy and requires only the following commands:

```
WiFi.begin(ssid, password);
while(WiFi.status() != WL_CONNECTED)
{
  delay(1000);
}
```

The remainder of the program is executed in an endless loop. Inside this loop, the program waits to receive a packet (command to return the temperature and humidity readings) from the UDP server (mobile phone here). The request is identified by character **S** and when this character is received, the temperature and humidity are read and a packet is formed using character array **Packet**. This array stores the temperature and humidity readings in the required format. The packet is then sent to the mobile phone over port 5000.

Character array **Packet** is formed as follows:

```
Packet[0] = 'T';              // Display T
Packet[1] = '=';              // Display =
int msd = T/10;               // Extract high digit
int lsd = T - msd*10;         // Extract low digit
Packet[2] = msd + '0';        // Convert msd to ASCII character
Packet[3] = lsd + '0';        // Convert lsd to ASCII character
Packet[4] = ' ';              // Space character
Packet[5] = ' ';              // Space character
Packet[6] = 'H';              // Display H
Packet[7] = '=';              // Display =
msd = H/10;                   // Extract high digit
lsd = H - msd*10;             // Extract low digit
Packet[8] = msd + '0';        // Convert msd to ASCII character
Packet[9] = lsd + '0';        // Convert lsd to ASCII character
Packet[10] = 0;               // NULL terminator
```

```
/****************************************************************
 *          SEND TEMPERATURE AND HUMIDITY TO A MOBILE PHONE
 *          ================================================
 *
 * This is an UDP based monitoring program where a DHT11 type
 * temperatrue and humidity sensor chip is connected to GPIO
 * port 23 of the ESP32 DevKitc. The program reads the ambient
 * temperatrue and humidity and sends the readings to an Android
 * mobile phone using UDP packets. The data on the mobile phone
 * is displayed using an UDP apps, available on the Play Store.
 * The data is sent to the mobile phone whenever it is requested.
 *
 * A request for data is made to the ESP32 DevKitc when character
 * S is sent over the UDP link. The ESP32 DevKitC sends the data
 * to the device that made the request. Port 5000 is used for
 * the communication
 *
 *  The IP addresses of the ESP32 DevKitc and mobile phone are:
 *  192.168.1.56 and 192.168.1.125 respectively.
 *
 *  File:   esp32toarduino
 *  Author: Dogan Ibrahim
 *  Date:   June, 2019
 ****************************************************************/
#include "WiFi.h"
#include <WiFiUdp.h>
//
// DHT11 sensor library includes
```

```
//
#include <Adafruit_Sensor.h>
#include "DHT.h"
#define DHT11_PIN 23
#define DHTTYPE DHT11
DHT dht(DHT11_PIN, DHTTYPE);

WiFiUDP udp;

//
// Use local port 5000
//
const int Port = 5000;
char Packet[20];

//
// Local Wi-Fi SSID and password (Enter your own SSID and password)
//
const char* ssid = "BTHomeSpot-XNH";
const char* password = "49345jbaeb";
int T, H;

//
// Read the ambient temperature and humidity and store in variables
// T and H respectively
//
void TempHum()
{
   H = dht.readHumidity();                    // Read humidity
   T = dht.readTemperature();                 // Read temperature
}

//
// This function connects the ESP32 DevKitc to the local Wi-Fi
// network. The network name and passwors are as specifed earlier
//
void Connect_WiFi()
{
      WiFi.begin(ssid, password);
      while(WiFi.status() != WL_CONNECTED)
      {
        delay(1000);
      }
}

//
```

```
// Connect to the local Wi-Fi. Also, UDP is started in local
// port, and DHT11 is started
//
void setup()
{
    Connect_WiFi();                             // Connect to WiFi
    udp.begin(Port);                            // Start UDP
    dht.begin();                                // Start DHT
}

//
// This is the main program loop. Inside the main program we read
// the temperature and humidity an send them as a packet to the
// mobile phone when a request is made by the mobile phone.
// A request is made when character S is sent by the mobile
// phone.
//
// The packet format is:
//
//  T=nn H=nn
//
void loop()
{
    int PacketSize = udp.parsePacket();
    if(PacketSize)                              // PAcket received
    {
        udp.read(Packet, PacketSize);
        if(Packet[0] == 'S')                    // Request S?
        {
           TempHum();
           Packet[0] = 'T';                     // Header T
           Packet[1] = '=';                     // Text =
           int msd = T/10;                      // MSD of temperature
           int lsd = T - msd*10;                // LSD of temperature
           Packet[2] = msd + '0';
           Packet[3] = lsd + '0';
           Packet[4] = ' ';                     // Space
           Packet[5] = ' ';                     // Space
           Packet[6] = 'H';                     // Header H
           Packet[7] = '=';                     // Text =
           msd = H/10;                          // MSD of humidity
           lsd = H - msd*10;                    // LSD of humidity
           Packet[8] = msd + '0';
           Packet[9] = lsd + '0';
           Packet[10] = 0;
           udp.beginPacket(udp.remoteIP(), Port);
```

```
                udp.print(Packet);
                udp.endPacket();
            }
        }
    }
```

Figure 18.7 Program listing

Figure 18.8 shows the temperature and humidity displayed on the Android mobile phone (T=24 H=55) after command **S** is sent from the mobile phone.

Figure 18.8 Displaying the temperature and humidity

18.3 Project 2 – Remote control from mobile phone using Wi-Fi

Description: In this project, two KY-019 relay modules are connected to the ESP32 DevkitC. The relays are controlled remotely by entering commands on a mobile phone. The idea here is that the DevKitC will be configured as a UDP client. Then, UDP packets will be sent from the mobile phone to control these relays which can then control the electrical apparatus if desired.

Valid commands are as follows (any other commands are ignored by the program):

0=ON	Turn ON Relay0
0=OFF	Turn OFF Relay0
1=ON	Turn ON Relay1
1=OFF	Turn OFF Relay1

Note: There is only one relay module in the sensor kit.

Block Diagram: The block diagram of the project is shown in Figure 18.9.

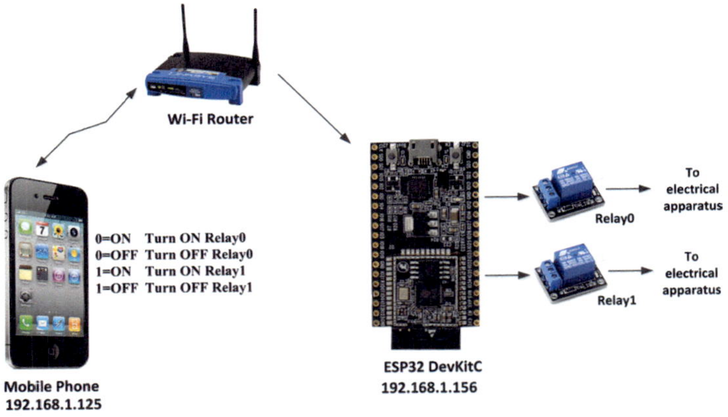

Figure 18.9 Block diagram of the project

Circuit Diagram: The circuit diagram of the project is shown in Figure 18.10. Relay0 and Relay1 are connected to GPIO 23 and GPIO 22 respectively. A KY-051 voltage translator is used to operate the relays reliably.

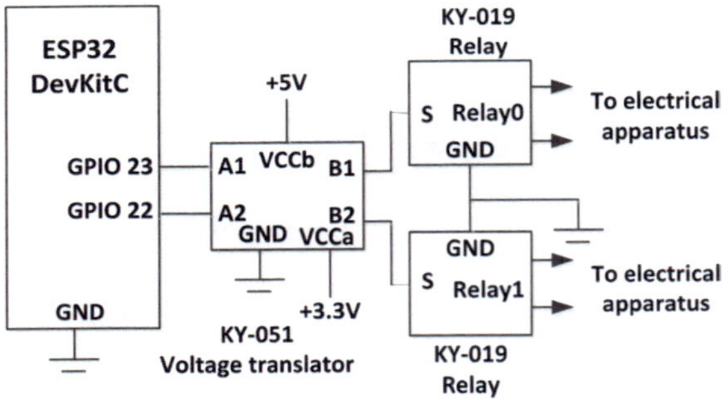

Figure 18.10 Circuit diagram of the project

Program Listing: Figure 18.11 shows the program listing (program: **relayard**). At the beginning of the program, the Wi-Fi library headers are included in the program, **Relay0** and **Relay1** are assigned to GPIO ports 23 and 22 respectively, the local port number is defined, and the local Wi-Fi name and password are defined. Function **Connect_WiFi** connects to the local Wi-Fi network.

Inside the setup routine, the relay ports are configured as outputs and both relays are turned OFF to start with. Then function **Connect_WiFi** is called to connect to local Wi-Fi and UDP is started on the local port.

The remainder of the program is executed in an endless loop. Inside this loop, the program waits to receive a packet (command) from the UDP server (mobile phone here). The received packet is stored in character array **Packet** and the program checks the command and if this is a valid command, turns ON/OFF the relays as required.

The following code is used to decode the received command:

```
if(Packet[1] == '=')
 {
    if(Packet[0] == '0')
    {
      if(Packet[2] == 'O' && Packet[3] == 'N')
      {
           digitalWrite(Relay0, HIGH);
      }
      else if(Packet[2] == 'O' && Packet[3] == 'F' && Packet[4] == 'F')
      {
           digitalWrite(Relay0, LOW);
      }
    }
    else if(Packet[0] == '1')
    {
      if(Packet[2] == 'O' && Packet[3] == 'N')
      {
          digitalWrite(Relay1, HIGH);
      }
      else if(Packet[2] == 'O' && Packet[3] == 'F' && Packet[4] == 'F')
      {
          digitalWrite(Relay1, LOW);
      }
    }
```

```
/*************************************************************
 *          UDP BASED CONTROL FROM MOBILE PHONE
 *          ===================================
 *
 * This is an UDP based control program where 2 relays are connected
 * to GPIO ports 23 and 22 of the ESP32 devkitc board, and named
 * as Relay0 and Relay1. Commands are sent from an Android type
 * mobile phone to turn the relays ON/OFF. The ESP32 DevKitC is
 * configured as an UDP client in this application.
 *
 *  File:   relayard
 *  Author: Dogan Ibrahim
 *  Date:   June, 2019
 *
 *************************************************************/
#include "WiFi.h"
#include <WiFiUdp.h>
//
// Relay oins
```

```
//
#define Relay0 23
#define Relay1 22
WiFiUDP udp;
//
// Use local port 5000
//
const int Port = 5000;
char Packet[80];

//
// Local Wi-Fi name and password
//
const char* ssid = "BTHomeSpot-XNH";
const char* password = "49345ajaeb";

//
// This function connects the ESP32 Devkitc to the local Wi-Fi
// network. The network name and passwors are as specifed earlier
//
void Connect_WiFi()
{
      WiFi.begin(ssid, password);
      while(WiFi.status() != WL_CONNECTED)
      {
        delay(1000);
      }
}



//
// Configure relays as outputs, turn OFF the relays to start with,
// Connect to the local Wi-Fi. Also, UDP is started in local port
//
void setup()
{
    pinMode(Relay0, OUTPUT);
    pinMode(Relay1, OUTPUT);
    digitalWrite(Relay0, LOW);
    digitalWrite(Relay1, LOW);
    Connect_WiFi();
    udp.begin(Port);
}

//
// This is the main program loop. Inside the main program we read
```

```
// UDP packets and then control the relays as requested. The format
// of the control commands are:
//
// 0=ON or 0=OFF for Relay0
// 1=ON or 1=OFF for Relay1
//
// Any other commands are simply ignored by the program
//
void loop()
{
   int PacketSize = udp.parsePacket();
   if(PacketSize)
   {
     udp.read(Packet, PacketSize);

     if(Packet[1]=='=')
     {
        if(Packet[0]=='0')
        {
          if(Packet[2]=='O' && Packet[3]=='N')
          {
             digitalWrite(Relay0, HIGH);
          }
          else if(Packet[2]=='O' && Packet[3]=='F' && Packet[4]=='F')
          {
             digitalWrite(Relay0, LOW);
          }
        }
        else if(Packet[0]=='1')
        {
          if(Packet[2]=='O' && Packet[3]=='N')
          {
            digitalWrite(Relay1, HIGH);
          }
          else if(Packet[2]=='O' && Packet[3]=='F' && Packet[4]=='F')
          {
            digitalWrite(Relay1, LOW);
          }
        }
     }
   }
}
```

Figure 18.11 Program listing

As an example, Figure 18.12 shows the command sent from the mobile phone application to turn on relay1 (command: **1=ON**). In this project, the ESP32 DevKitC and the mobile phone IP addresses are: 192.168.1.156 and 192.168.1.125 respectively

Figure 18.12 Command to turn ON Relay1

Note: You must take extra care and get professional advice to avoid electric shock if you are connecting the relays to mains equipment.

18.4 Project 3 – Sending temperature and humidity to mobile phone using Bluetooth classic

Description: In this project, the ambient temperature and humidity are read from a sensor as in section 18.2, and are then sent to a mobile phone using Bluetooth classic every 5 seconds.

The Aim: The aim of this project is to show how data can be sent to a mobile phone using the ESP32 DevKitC Bluetooth connectivity.

The Block Diagram: The block diagram of the project is shown in Figure 18.13. A DHT11 type temperature and humidity sensor are used in this project.

Figure 18.13 Block diagram of the project

Circuit Diagram: The circuit diagram of the project is as in Figure 18.3, where the output of sensor DHT11 is connected to GPIO port 23.

Program Listing: The program listing is shown in Figure 18.14 (program: **blueard**). The DHT11 temperature and humidity sensor chip used in project 1 (see Section 18.2). At the beginning of the program, **DHT** and **BluetoothSerial** header files are included in the program. Make sure that you have the latest version of the ESP32 software for Arduino since the Bluetooth Serial Library has been added recently to the ESP32 Arduino IDE. Inside the **setup** routine, the DHT11 and BluetoothSerial are initialized where the ESP32 is given the name **ESPDHT11**. The main program runs in an endless loop where the temperature and humidity readings are read from the DHT11 sensor chip every 5 seconds and are then sent to the mobile phone over a Bluetooth classic link using **printf** statements.

```
/***************************************************************************
* SENDING TEMPERATURE & HUMIDITY TO MOBILE PHONE USING BLUETOOTH CLASSIC
* ======================================================================
*
* In this program a DHT11 type temperature and humidity sensor chip
* is connected to the ESP32 DevKitC. The program sends the temperature
* and humidity readings to a Bluetooth classic compatible mobile phone
* every 5 seconds
*
* Program: blueard
* Date   : June, 201
* Author : Dogan Ibrahim
 **************************************************************************/
#include "Adafruit_Sensor.h"
#include "DHT.h"
#define DHT11_PIN 23                                        // DHT11 on pin 23
#define DHTTYPE DHT11

#include"BluetoothSerial.h"
BluetoothSerial BT;
DHT dht(DHT11_PIN, DHTTYPE);

//
// Initialize the DHT11 and BluetoothSerial
//
void setup()
{
    dht.begin();                                            // Initialize DHT11
    BT.begin("ESPDHT11");                                   // Initialize
}


void loop()
```

```
{
    while(1)
    {
      float humidity = dht.readHumidity();                 // Read humidity
      float temperature = dht.readTemperature();           // Read temperature
      BT.printf("Temperature=%5.2f\n\r", temperature);     // Send temperature
      BT.printf("Humidity=%5.2f\n\r", humidity);           // Send humidity
      delay(5000);                                         // Wait 5 seconds
    }
}
```

Figure 18.14 Program listing

Testing the Program on Mobile Phone

The program can be tested on an Android mobile phone as follows:

- Add a Bluetooth classic app to your Android mobile phone. In this project, the free of charge apps called **Serial Bluetooth Terminal** (by Kai Morich) shown in Figure 18.15 is used

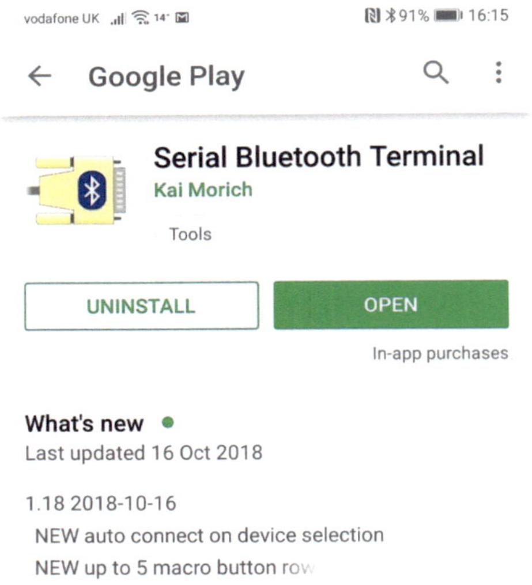

Figure 18.15 Serial Bluetooth Terminal

- Connect your ESP32 DevKitC to a power supply (e.g. PC USB port or portable power supply)

- Open the Bluetooth folder on your mobile phone and pair with **ESPDHT11** if requested. Delete any older pairings if not needed.

- Install and open the **Serial Bluetooth Terminal** on your mobile phone

- Click **Devices** from the menu and then click on device **ESPDHT11**. You should see the **Connected** message displayed

- Select **Terminal** from the menu in your apps. You should see the temperature and humidity displayed every 5 seconds as shown in Figure 18.16.

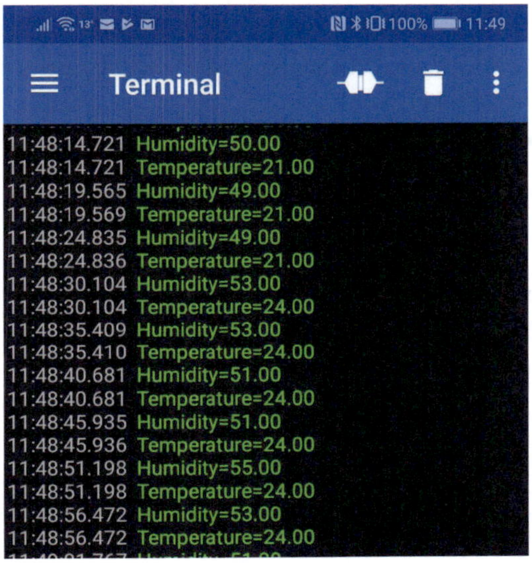

Figure 18.16 Displaying the temperature and humidity

Chapter 19 • Wi-Fi and Bluetooth based projects using sensors – Raspberry Pi

19.1 Overview

In this Chapter, we will be developing projects using a temperature and humidity sensor module with Wi-Fi or Bluetooth connectivity on a Raspberry Pi.

19.2 Project 1 – Displaying temperature and humidity on a mobile phone using Wi-Fi

Description: In this project, we will be reading the ambient temperature and humidity from a sensor module and send to a mobile phone when command **S** is received from the mobile phone. Wi-Fi connectivity of Raspberry Pi is used in this program and it is assumed that the Raspberry Pi is already connected to a Wi-Fi router.

Aim: The aim of this project is to show how to use the Wi-Fi connectivity on Raspberry Pi, and also how to use the temperature and humidity sensor.

Sensor Used: In this project, the KY-015 temperature and humidity sensor (see section 18.2) is used.

Block Diagram: The block diagram of the project is shown in Figure 19.1. The IP addresses of the mobile phone and Raspberry Pi are 192.168.1.178 and 192.168.1.164 respectively.

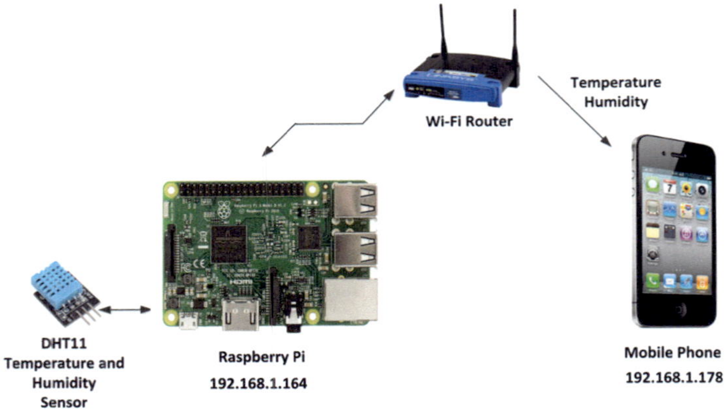

Figure 19.1 Block diagram of the project

Circuit Diagram: The circuit diagram of the project is same as in Figure 18.3, but ESP32 DevKitC should be replaced with Raspberry Pi, and GPIO 23 should be replaced with GPIO 2 since pin S of the sensor is connected to GPIO 2 of Raspberry Pi.

Program Listing: Before writing the program, we have to install the DHT11 library to our Raspberry Pi. The steps are given below:

- pi@raspberrypi:~ $ **git clone https://github.com/adafruit/Adafruit_Python_DHT.git**
- pi@raspberrypi:~ $ **cd Adafruit_Python_DHT**
- pi@raspberrypi:~ /Adafruit/Python_DHT $ **sudo apt-get install build-essential python-dev**
- pi@raspberrypi:~ /Adafruit/Python_DHT $ **sudo python setup.py install**
- pi@raspberrypi:~ /Adafruit/Python_DHT $ **cd ~**
- pi@raspberrypi:~ $

Figure 19.2 shows the program listing (program: **rpitoandroid.py**). At the beginning of the project, the DHT library and socket library are imported to the program. The program uses the UDP communication where the port number is set to 5000 and a UDP socket is created. Inside the main program loop, the program checks if a packet has been received from the mobile phone and if so the command is checked. If the command is **S** then the temperature and humidity are read by calling function **TempHum**. These values are converted into a string and sent to the mobile phone.

```
#------------------------------------------------------------
#  SEND TEMPERATURE AND HUMIDITY READINGS TO MOBILE PHONE
#  ======================================================
#
# In thiS project the KY-015 temperature and humidity sensor
# module is used. The temperature and humidity are sent to
# a mobile phone (Android) over the Wi-Fi link when command
# S is  entered on the mobile phone.
#
# Author: Dogan Ibrahim
# Date  : June 2019
# File  : rpitoandroid.py
#-----------------------------------------------------------
import Adafruit_DHT                    # import DHT library
Sensor = 2                             # sensor pin
import socket                          # import socket library


#
# Function returns the  temperature and humidity
#
def TempHum():
  h,t = Adafruit_DHT.read_retry(Adafruit_DHT.DHT11,Sensor)
  return t,h
```

```
#
# Strat of MAIN program
#
port = 5000
UDP = ("", port)
sock = socket.socket(socket.AF_INET, socket.SOCK_DGRAM)
sock.bind(UDP)

try:
  while True:
    data, addr = sock.recvfrom(80)                  # receive packet
    if(data.decode() == 'S'):                       # S ?
       T,H=TempHum()                                # get temp and hum
       dat = str(T) + " " + str(H)                  # form a string
       tup = (addr[0], port)                        # send to mobile
       sock.sendto(dat, tup)

except KeyboardInterrupt:
  exit(0)
```

Figure 19.2 Program listing

Mobile Phone Application: The mobile application (UDP RECEIVE and SEND) used in section 18.2 can be used to receive UDP based data from the Raspberry Pi. Before sending a packet the user must enter the destination IP address, port number, and the message to be sent. Clicking the **SEND UDP MESSAGE** button will send the packet to its destination. In the Receiver part, the local IP address is given. The user must specify the local port number as well. Figure 19.3 shows the temperature and humidity data received on the mobile phone as 26.0 and 54.0 respectively.

Figure 19.3 Android UDP send/receive apps

19.3 Project 2 – Sending the temperature and humidity data to the Cloud using Wi-Fi

Description: In this project, the ambient temperature and the humidity data are read and sent to the cloud so that they can be accessed from anywhere on Earth.

Aim: The aim of this project is to show how the ambient temperature and humidity readings can be sent to the Cloud through the Wi-Fi of the Raspberry Pi.

Sensor Used: Sensor Used: In this project the KY-015 temperature and humidity sensor (see section 18.2 and also previous project).

Block Diagram: The block diagram of the project is shown in Figure 19.4.

Figure 19.4 Block diagram of the project

The Cloud

There are several free cloud services that can be used to store sensor data (for example **SparkFun**, **Thingspeak,** etc). In this project, the **Thingspeak** is used. This is a free Cloud service where sensor data can be stored and retrieved using simple HTTP requests. ThingSpeak was originally launched by ioBridge in 2010 as a service in support of IoT applications. You can send data to ThingSpeak from your devices, create instant visualizations of live data, and send alerts using web services. In summary, ThingSpeak enables engineers and scientists to prototype and build IoT systems without setting up expensive servers or developing web software. The collected data can be pre-processed and analyzed using various tools, such as MATLAB. More information on Thingspeak can be obtained from the web site:

https://thingspeak.com/

Before using the Thingspeak, we have to create an account from their web site and then log in to this account. You can create a new account by giving your email address and choose a password by opening the following link:

https://thingspeak.com/login

You should get an email to verify and activate your account. Give yourself a **User ID** and accept the **Online Service Agreement**. Click your intent as **Personal, non-commercial projects** and click **OK**.

(next time you log in, specify your email address and click **Next** (see Figure 19.5). Enter your password and click **Sign In).**

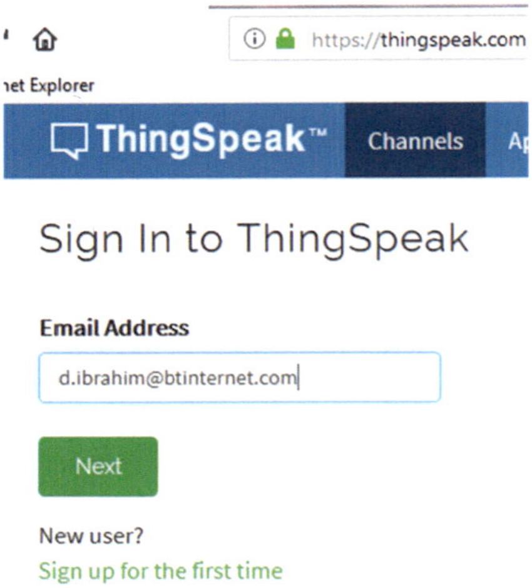

Figure 19.5 Successful sign-up to Thingspeak

Then, you should create a New Channel by clicking on **New Channel**. Fill in the form as shown in Figure 19.6. Give the name **Raspberry Pi 3 Weather** to the application and create two channels called **TEMPERATURE** and **HUMIDITY**. Click **Save Channel** at the bottom of the form.

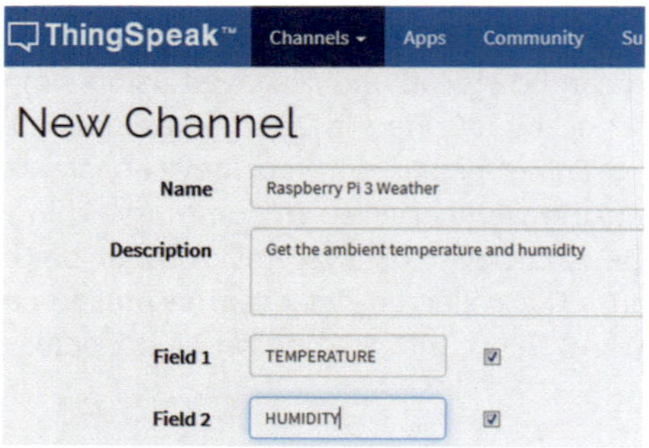

Figure 19.6 Create a New Channel (only part of the form shown)

Now click the **Public View** and then click **Share** and make the channel shearable by every-one so that it is public (see Figure 19.7)

Figure 19.7 Make the channel shearable

Click on **Public View** and you should see your channel details as shown in Figure 19.8.

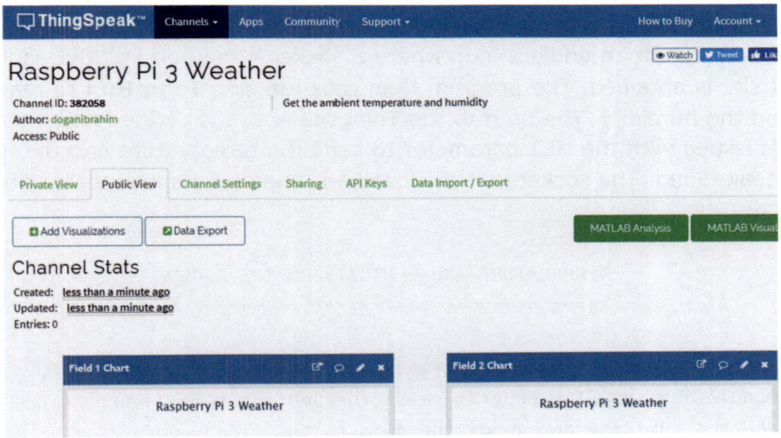

Figure 19.8 Channel details

Your channel is now ready to be used with your data. You should click the **API Keys** tab and save your unique **Write API** and **Read API** keys and the **Channel ID** in a safe place (see Figure 19.9). The **Channel ID** can be displayed by clicking the Channel Details tab. In this example, the Channel ID was 382054.

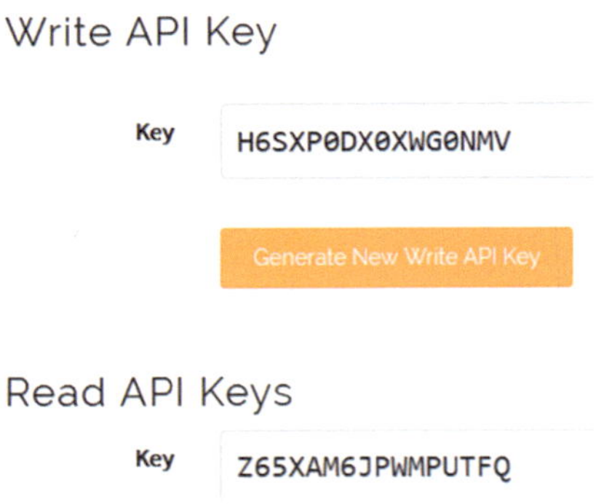

Figure 19.9 API keys

Program Listing: Figure 19.10 shows the program listing (program: **rpicloud.py**). At the beginning of the program, modules **DHT**, **time**, and **socket** are imported into the program and the write API key is defined. Function **TempHun** is created to read and return the ambient temperature and the humidity rounded to one decimal point. The remainder of the program is executed in an endless loop where a socket is created and the address of the Thingspeak site is obtained. The program then calls function **TempHun** to read the temperature and the humidity. The path to the Thingspeak site is defined and a socket **send** command is issued with the GET parameter to send the temperature and the humidity to the Thingspeak Cloud. The socket is then closed and the process is repeated after 30 seconds of delay.

```
#                TEMPREATURE AND HUMIDITY ON THE CLOUD
#                =====================================
#
# In this project the KY-015 temperature and humidity sensor
# module is used. The program reads the ambient temperature
# and the humidity and sends the data to the cloud every 30
# seconds. The data can be displayed or plotted on the Cloud.
# In this project the free Thingspeak Cloud is used to store and
# display the weather data
#
# Author: Dogan Ibrahim
# File  : rpicloud.py
# Date  : June, 2019
#-----------------------------------------------------------------
import time                                   # import time
import Adafruit_DHT                           # import DHT
import socket                                 # import socket

Sensor = 2                                    # Sensor pin

#
# Read and return the temperature and humidity to main program
```

```
#
def TempHum():
  h,t = Adafruit_DHT.read_retry(Adafruit_DHT.DHT11,Sensor)
  H = round(h, 1)
  T = round(t, 1)
  return T,H


#
# Define the Write API key
#
APIKEY = "H6SXP0DX0XWG0NMV"

# Start of main program loop. Read the ambient temperature and
# the humidity and then send to the Thingspeak Cloud every 30
# seconds.
#
while True:
  sock = socket.socket()
  addr = socket.getaddrinfo("api.thingspeak.com",80)[0][-1]
  sock.connect(addr)
  (t, h) = TempHum()
  host = "api.thingspeak.com"
  path = "api_key="+APIKEY+"&field1="+str(t)+"&field2="+str(h)
  sock.send(bytes("GET /update?%s HTTP/1.0\r\nHost: %s\r\n\r\n"
   %(path, host)))
  sock.close()                          # close socket
  time.sleep(30)                        # wait 30 seconds
```

Figure 19.10 Program listing

Figure 19.11 shows the temperature and the humidity data plotted in real-time. The graphs can be configured by clicking the **Chart Options** on each graph. Figure 19.12 shows the two graphs configured by giving titles to the axes.

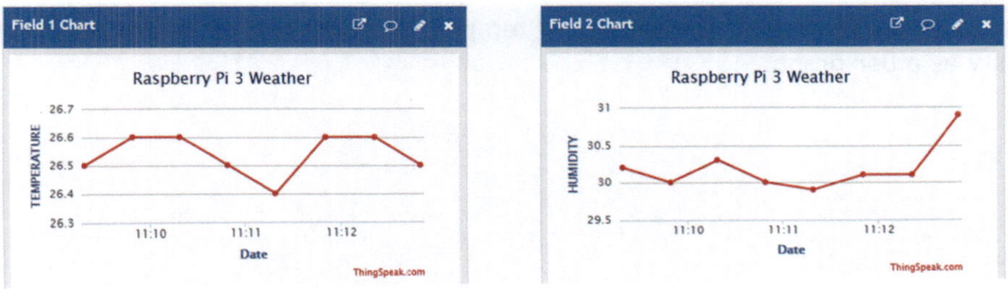

Figure 19.11 Plotting the temperature and the humidity

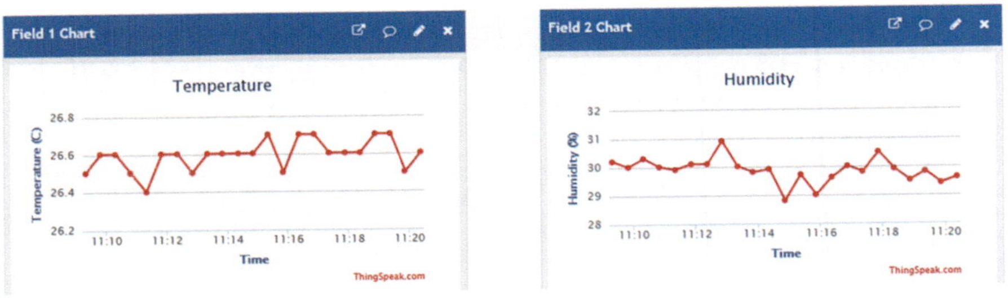

Figure 19.12 Graphs configured by giving titles to axes

The type of plotting can also be changed. In Figure 19.13, data is shown as column charts.

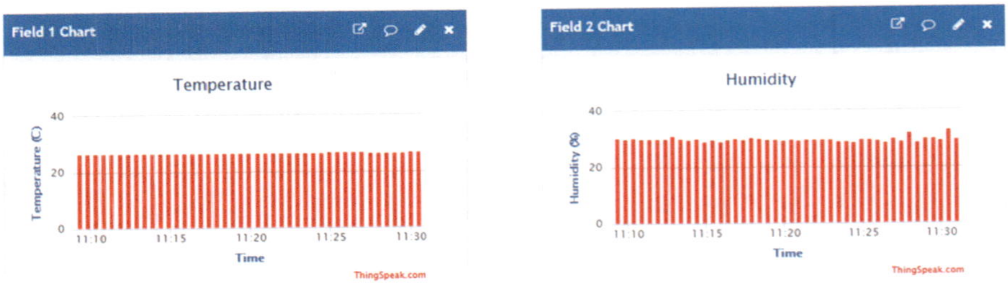

Figure 19.13 Showing the data as a column chart

The collected data can be exported to other software packages (e.g. Excel). This is done by clicking the **Data Export** tab.

The following link can be used to access the plotted data externally:

https://api.thingspeak.com/channels/YOUR_CHANNEL_ID

where, for example for this project the channel ID is: 382054. Therefore, the link to the data in this project is:

https://api.thingspeak.com/channels/382054

Figure 19.14 shows the graphs where the temperature is drawn as a line-graph and the humidity as a bar-graph.

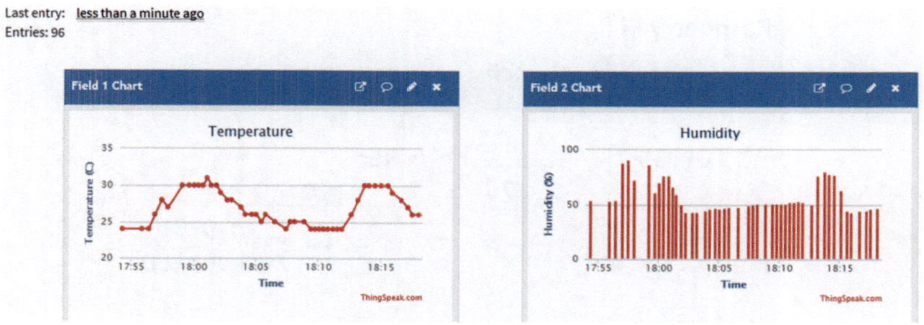

Figure 19.14 Graph outputs from Thingspeak

19.4 Project 3 – Bluetooth based remote control from mobile phone

Description: In this project, a KY-029 2-colour LED is connected to Raspberry Pi. The green or the red LED is turned ON by sending commands from a mobile phone. Valid commands are:

G1	Turn the Green LED ON
G0	Turn the Green LED OFF
R1	Turn the Red LED ON
R0	Turn the Red LED OFF

The Bluetooth connectivity of Raspberry Pi is used in this project.

Aim: The aim of this project is to show how the Bluetooth connectivity of Raspberry Pi can be used in a project.

Sensor Used: Sensor Used: In this project, the KY-029 2-colour LED module is used.

Block Diagram: Figure 19.15 shows the project block diagram.

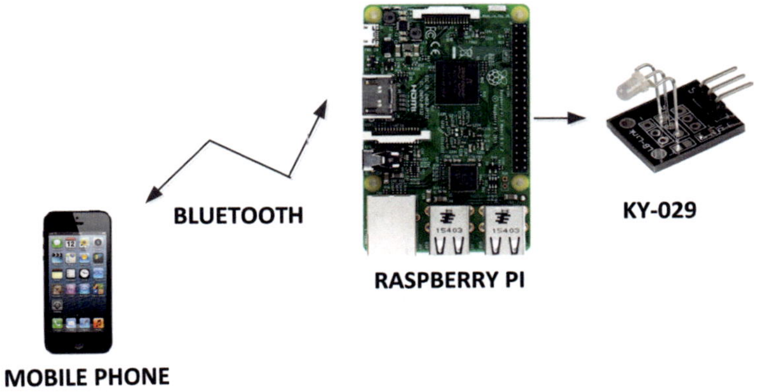

Figure 19.15 Block diagram of the project

Circuit Diagram: Figure 19.16 shows the circuit diagram of the project. The LED module is connected to Raspberry Pi through current limiting resistors.

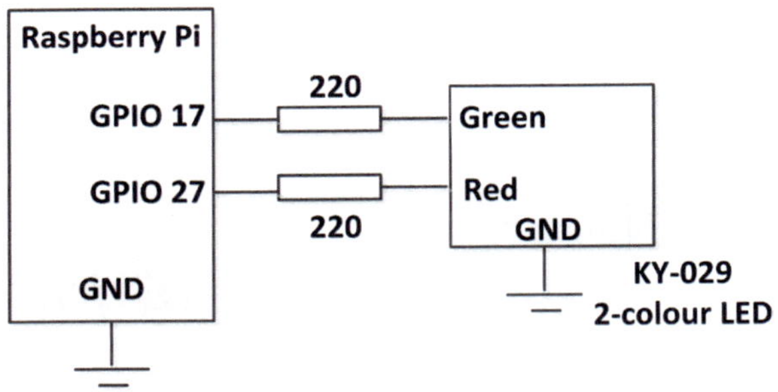

Figure 19.16 Circuit diagram of the project

Bluetooth On Raspberry Pi: In this project, we will be sending commands from an Android mobile phone to our Raspberry Pi. We must, therefore, first of all, enable Bluetooth from the Settings menu on our Android device. In this example, the Android Bluetooth device name is set to **MyAndroid**.

There are two ways you can enable Bluetooth on the Raspberry Pi: using graphical desktop (GUI mode) or using the command mode. We will look at both methods in the following sections.

Using the Graphical Desktop

The steps for enabling Bluetooth on the Raspberry Pi using the graphical desktop are given below:

- Start the VNC server on your Raspberry Pi and log in using the VNC Viewer.
- Click on the Bluetooth icon on your Raspberry Pi screen at the top right-hand side, and turn Bluetooth ON. Then, select **Make Discoverable.** You should see the Bluetooth icon flashing (Figure 19.17)

Figure 19.17 Enable Bluetooth on your Raspberry Pi

- Click **scan** on your mobile phone Bluetooth settings and click **raspberrypi** under **Available Devices** to pair with the Raspberry Pi (**raspberrypi** is the default Bluetooth name of your Raspberry Pi). Accept the pairing request on your Raspberry Pi. You should see **raspberrypi** under **PAIRED DEVICES** on your mobile phone (Figure 19.18).

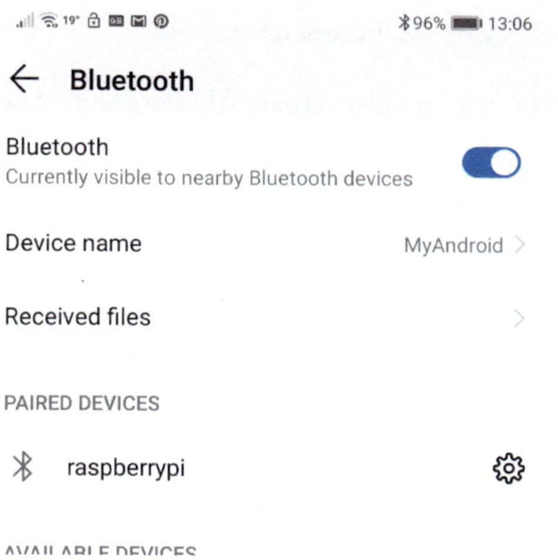

Figure 19.18 Mobile phone paired with Raspberry Pi

- Click on Bluetooth icon and you should see **MyAndroid** in green colour (Figure 19.19).

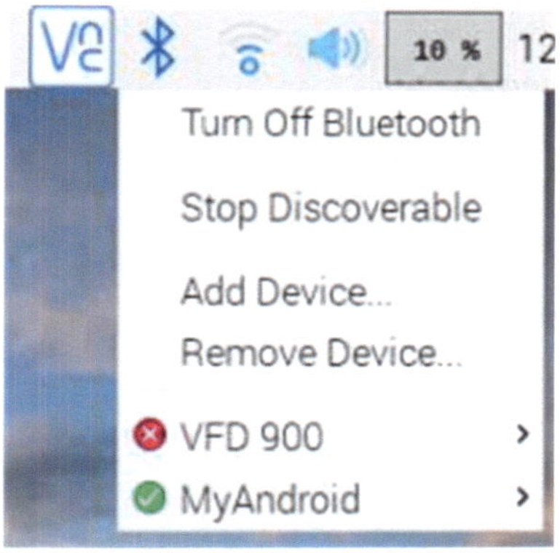

Figure 19.19 Bluetooth connection on Raspberry Pi

Using Command Mode

You can enable Bluetooth on your Raspberry Pi using the command mode. Additionally, you can make Bluetooth discoverable, scan for nearby Bluetooth devices and then connect to a Bluetooth device. The steps are given below (characters types by the user are in bold for clarity):

- Make your Bluetooth discoverable with the following command:

```
pi@raspberrypi: ~ $ sudo hciconfig hci0 piscan
```

- Start the Bluetooth tool on your Raspberry Pi from the command mode:

```
pi@raspberrypi:~ $ bluetoothctl
```

You should see the mobile phone (MyAndroid) MAC address displayed as shown in Figure 19.20. In this example, the mobile phone MAC address is: **B4:CD:27:15:68:7B**

```
pi@raspberrypi:~ $ bluetoothctl
[NEW] Controller B8:27:EB:19:CB:E7 raspberrypi [default]
[NEW] Device 41:E8:5C:9C:E8:3D 41-E8-5C-9C-E8-3D
[NEW] Device B4:CD:27:15:68:7B MyAndroid
[NEW] Device 28:BE:03:7A:53:F5 VFD 900
[CHG] Device 41:E8:5C:9C:E8:3D RSSI: -73
```

Figure 19.20 MyAndroid MAC address

- Turn Bluetooth ON:

```
[bluetooth]# power on
```

- Configure Bluetooth to run:

```
[bluetooth]# agent on
[bluetooth]# default-agent
```

- Make device discoverable:

```
[bluetooth]# discoverable on
```

- Scan for nearby Bluetooth devices. You should see the nearby Bluetooth devices listed with their MAC addresses.

```
[bluetooth]# scan on
```

- Pair the mobile phone with Raspberry Pi:

```
[bluetooth]# pair B4:CD:27:15:68:7B
```

- Connect to our mobile phone:

```
[bluetooth]# connect B4:CD:27:15:68:7B
```

- Exit from the Bluetooth tool by entering Cntrl+Z

- You can find the Bluetooth MAC address of your Raspberry Pi by entering the following command:

```
pi@raspberrypi:~ $ hciconfig | grep "BD Address"
```

The Bluetooth MAC address of our Raspberry Pi is: **B8:27:EB:19:CB:E7**

- You can change the Bluetooth broadcast name by the following command:

```
pi@raspberrypi:~ $ sudo hciconfig hci0 name "new name"
```

- To see your Bluetooth broadcast name, enter:

```
pi@raspberrypi:~ $ sudo hciconfig hci0 name
```

Some other useful Raspberry Pi 3 Bluetooth commands are:

- To reset Bluetooth adapter: **sudo hciconfig hci0 reset**
- To restart Bluetooth: **sudo invoke-rc.d bluetooth restart**
- To list Bluetooth adapters: **hciconfig**

You can find the Bluetooth MAC address of your Android phone as follows:

- Go to the **Settings** menu
- Tap **About Phone**
- Tap **Status**
- Scroll down to see your **Bluetooth address** (see Figure 19.21)

```
pi@raspberrypi:~ $ bluetoothctl
[NEW] Controller B8:27:EB:19:CB:E7 raspberrypi [default]
[NEW] Device B4:CD:27:15:68:7B raspberrypi
[NEW] Device 28:BE:03:7A:53:F5 VFD 900
[bluetooth]# power on
Changing power on succeeded
[bluetooth]# agent on
Agent registered
[bluetooth]# default-agent
Default agent request successful
[bluetooth]# discoverable on
Changing discoverable on succeeded
[bluetooth]# scan on
Discovery started
[CHG] Controller B8:27:EB:19:CB:E7 Discovering: yes
[NEW] Device 73:08:4E:17:F1:14 73-08-4E-17-F1-14
[NEW] Device 59:60:1C:20:32:4F 59-60-1C-20-32-4F
[NEW] Device 61:15:51:BF:CD:CE 61-15-51-BF-CD-CE
[CHG] Device 73:08:4E:17:F1:14 RSSI: -69
[CHG] Device 73:08:4E:17:F1:14 RSSI: -79
[bluetooth]#
```

Figure 19.21 Bluetooth MAC address of the mobile phone

Python Bluetooth Library

You will need to install the Python Bluetooth library before developing your program. This is done by entering the following command in the command mode:

```
pi@raspberrypi:~ $ sudo apt-get install python-bluez
```

Accessing From the Mobile Phone

In order to be able to access the Raspberry Pi from mobile phone apps make the following changes to your Raspberry Pi from the command line:

- Start **nano** to edit the following file:

```
pi@raspberrypi:~ $ sudo nano /etc/systemd/system/dbus-org.bluez.
service
```

- Add **–C** at the end of the **ExecStart= line**. Also add another line after the **ExecStart** line. The final two lines should look like:

```
ExecStart=/usr/lib/bluetooth/bluetoothd -C
ExecStartPost=/usr/bin/sdptool add SP
```

- Exit and save the file by entering **Ctrl+X** followed by **Y**

- Reboot Raspberry Pi:

```
pi@raspberrypi:~ $ sudo reboot
```

Android Bluetooth Apps

In this project, we will be sending commands to the Raspberry Pi from an Android-based mobile phone. We, therefore, need an application on our mobile phone where we can send data through Bluetooth. There are many such applications free of charge in the Android **Play Store**. The one chosen by the author is called **Arduino Bluetooth Controller – All in One** by **Apps valley** (see Figure 19.22). You should install this application (or a similar one) on your Android phone so that you can send commands to the Raspberry Pi.

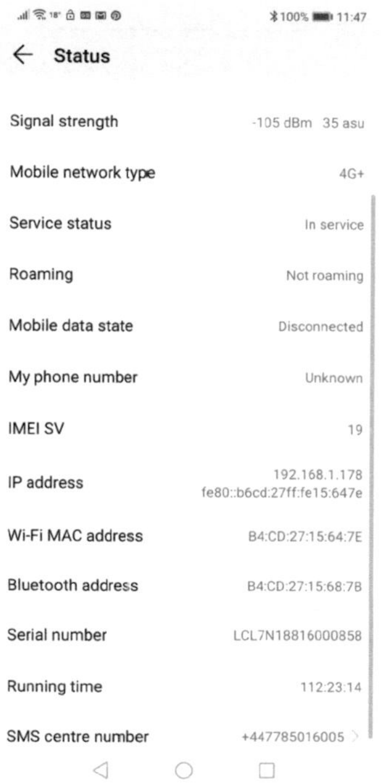

Figure 19.22 Android Bluetooth apps

Program Listing: Figure 19.23 shows the program listing of the project (program: **rpi-bluet.py**). At the beginning of the program modules **socket**, **RPi.GPIO** and **bluetooth** are imported to the program. The two KY-29 LED ports are defined and both configured as outputs. The program then creates a Bluetooth socket, binds and listens on this socket, and then waits to accept a connection. The remainder of the program is executed in a loop where the program issues statement **ClientSock.recv** and waits to receive commands from the mobile phone. The received command is decoded and the green or the red LED is turned ON as requested.

```
#--------------------------------------------------------------
#               BLUETOOTH BASED 2-COLOUR LED CONTROL
#               ====================================
#
# In this project a KY-029 2-colour LED module is connected to
# the Raspberry Pi GPIo ports 17 and 27. The green and red LEDs
# are controlle by sedning comamnds from an Android mobile phone
# using the Bluetooth communication. The commands are sent using
# a Bluetooth apps on the Android mobile phone.
#
# Author: Dogan Ibrahim
# File  : rpibluet.py
# Date  : June, 2019
```

```
#------------------------------------------------------------
import socket                         # Import socket
import RPi.GPIO as GPIO               # Import GPIO
GPIO.setwarnings(False)
GPIO.setmode(GPIO.BCM)
import bluetooth                      # Import bluetooth

#
# Green LED is on GPIO 17, Red is on GPIO 27
#
GreenLED = 17                         # Green LED on GPIO 17
RedLED = 27                           # Red LED on GPIO 27

#
# Configure LEDs as outputs
#
GPIO.setup(GreenLED, GPIO.OUT)
GPIO.setup(RedLED, GPIO.OUT)

#
# Turn OFF LEDs to start with
#
GPIO.output(GreenLED, 0)
GPIO.output(RedLED, 0)

#
# Start of main program loop. Read commands from the Android
# mobile phone, decode them, and control the LEDs
#
#
Port = 1
ServerSock = bluetooth.BluetoothSocket(bluetooth.RFCOMM)
ServerSock.bind(("", Port))
ServerSock.listen(1)
ClientSock, addr = ServerSock.accept()

#
# Turn ON the Green LED if the command is: G1
# Turn OFF the LED if the command is:      G0
# Turn ON the Red LED if the command is:   R1
# Turn OFF the Red LED if the command is:  R0
#
while True:
  data = ClientSock.recv(1024)
  if data[0] == 'G':                            # G received
    if data[1] == '1':                          # 1 received
```

```
        GPIO.output(GreenLED, 1)                # Green LED ON
      else:
        GPIO.output(GreenLED, 0)                # Green LED OFF
    elif data[0] == 'R':                        # R received
      if data[1] == '1':                        # 1 received
        GPIO.output(RedLED, 1)                  # Red LED ON
      else:
        GPIO.output(RedLED, 0)                  # Red LED OFF
```

Figure 19.23 Program listing

Figure 19.24 shows the mobile application sending commands to turn the two LEDs ON and OFF in different order. The steps to use the mobile apps is as follows:

- Run your program:

```
pi@raspberrypi:~ $ python rpibluet.py
```

- Start the mobile apps and click the button at the bottom right-hand side to refresh the Bluetooth scan list
- Click on **raspberrypi B8:27:EB:19:CB:E7** to connect to the Raspberry Pi
- Click on the **TERMINAL** icon (icon of a keyboard) to get into terminal mode
- Enter the required command. e.g. **G1** to turn ON Green LED, **G0** to turn OFF Green LED, etc.

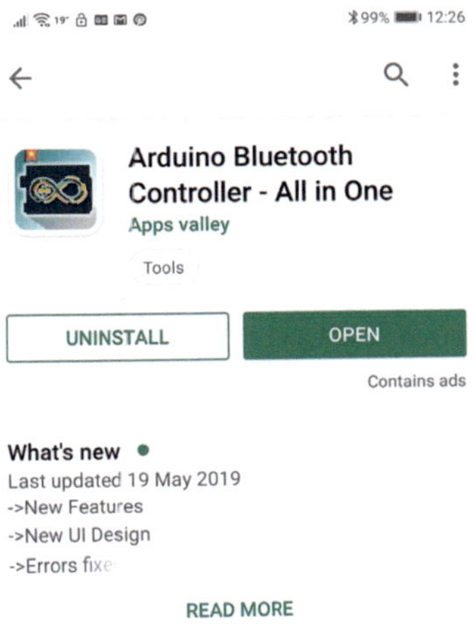

Figure 19.24 Mobile application

You could enter the program name in the following format inside file **/etc/rc.local** so that the program starts automatically after the Raspberry Pi re-starts:

```
python /home/pi/rpibluet.py &
```

When you finish your project don't forget to remove the above line from file **/etc/rc.local**, otherwise the program will run every time your Raspberry Pi is re-started. You should also shut down your Raspberry Pi orderly instead of just removing the power cable. The command to shutdown orderly is:

```
pi@raspberrypi:~ $ sudo shutdown -h now
```

Chapter 20 • Wi-Fi and Bluetooth based projects using sensors – Arduino Uno

20.1 Overview

In this Chapter, we will be developing projects using a sensor module and a Wi-Fi link to establish communication between an Android Uno and a mobile phone.

20.2 Project 1 – Controlling a relay from mobile phone using Wi-Fi

Description: In this project, we will be sending commands over the Wi-Fi link from a mobile phone to control a relay connected to the Arduino Uno. Valid commands are (character **#** is used as the command terminator):

RON#	Turn Relay ON
ROFF#	Turn Relay OFF

Aim: The aim of this project is to show how to use the Wi-Fi connectivity on Arduino Uno together with a sensor module.

Sensor Used: In this project, the KY-019 relay module is used.

Arduino Uno Wi-Fi Connectivity: Arduino Uno has no built-in Wi-Fi module and as such, it cannot be connected to a Wi-Fi network without interfacing an external Wi-Fi module to it. There are several Arduino Wi-Fi shields available in the market that can be plugged on top of the Arduino Uno to provide Wi-Fi capability to the basic board. Perhaps the easiest and the cheapest way of providing Wi-Fi capability to an Arduino Uno is by using an ESP-01 processor board. This is a tiny board (see Figure 20.1), measuring only 2.7cm x 1.2cm, and based on the ESP8266 processor chip, and costing around $3 USD. ESP-01 has the following features:

- Operating voltage: +3.3V
- Interface: using simple AT commands over serial port/UART
- Integrated TCP/IP protocol stack. 802.11 b/g/n
- No external components required

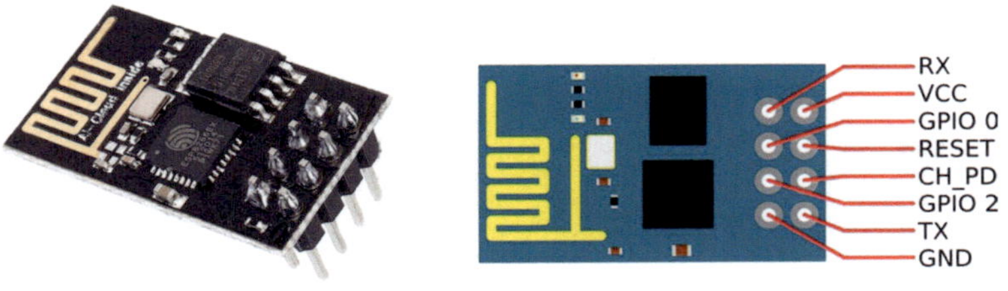

Figure 20.1 ESP-01 processor board

ESP-01 is used in the Wi-Fi projects in this Chapter. ***Note that ESP-01 is not included in the standard sensor kit.***

ESP-01 communicates with the host processor through its TX and RX serial port pin. It is an 8-pin board, having the pin names:

VCC:	+3.3V power supply pin
GND:	Power supply ground
GPIO0:	I/O pin. This pin must be connected to +3.3V for normal operation, and to GND for uploading firmware to the chip
GPIO2:	General purpose I/O pin
RST:	Reset pin. Must be connected to +3.3V for normal operation
CH_PD:	Enable pin. Must be connected to +3.3V for normal operation
TX:	Serial output pin
RX:	Serial input pin

ESP-01 pins are not standard breadboard compatible and an adaptor is required if the board is to be attached to a breadboard (see Figure 20.2).

Figure 20.2 ESP-01 breadboard adapter

Block Diagram: Figure 20.3 shows the project block diagram.

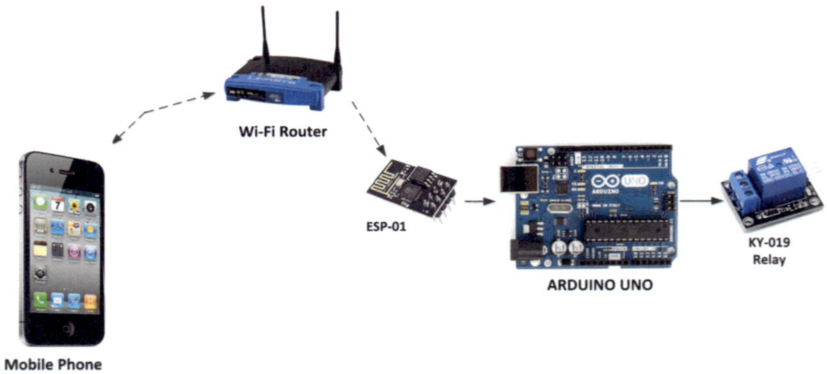

Figure 20.3 Block diagram of the project

Circuit Diagram: Figure 20.4 shows the circuit diagram of the project. Pins 0 and 1 of Arduino Uno are used as the serial UART RX and TX functions respectively. ESP-01 pins are not +5V tolerant and because of this, a potentiometer divider resistive network is set up to drop the voltage from 5V to about 3.3V for the ESP-01. S pin of the KY-019 relay module is connected to port pin 5 of Arduino Uno. You should make sure that the power supply voltage of ESP-01 is +3.3V.

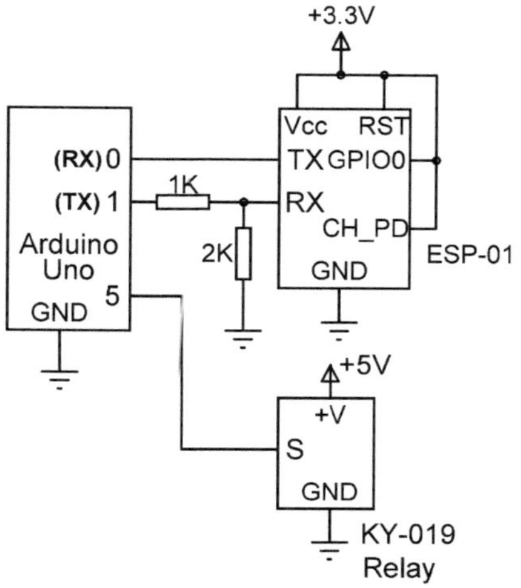

Figure 20.4 Circuit diagram of the project

Program Listing: Figure 20.5 shows the program listing (program: **ardwifi**). Inside the setup routine serial communication speed is set to 115200 which is the default Baud rate for ESP-01, and the relay is configured as an output and turned OFF. Function **Connect-ToWiFi** is called to connect to the Wi-Fi. The remainder of the program runs in an endless loop formed using a **while** statement. Inside this loop data is received from the mobile device and the relay is controlled accordingly. Commands **RON#** and **ROFF#** turn the relay ON and OFF respectively. Data packet is received from the mobile phone using statement readBytesUntil. This statement takes three arguments: the terminator character, buffer address where the data is to be stored, and the length of the data. The program waits until the specified number of characters are received, or the terminator is received, or until the statement times out (set by function **SetTimeout** in milliseconds). Function **strstr** looks for a sub-string in a string and returns a non-zero value if the sub-string is found. The reason for using the **strstr** function is because the data received from the mobile device is in the following format **+IDO,n: data** (e.g. **+IDO,4:RON#**) where 0 is the link ID and n is the number of characters received. Using the **strstr** function we can easily search for the strings **RON** or **ROFF** in the received data packet.

Function **ConnectToWiFi** sends the following commands to the ESP-01 to connect to the Wi-Fi:

AT+RST - reset ESP-01
AT+CWMODE - set ESP-01 mode (here it is set to Station mode)
AT+CWJAP - set Wi-Fi ssid name and password
AT+CPIMUX - set connection mode (here it is set to multiple connection)
AT+CIFSR - returns the IP address (not used here)
AT+CIPSTART - set TCP or UDP connection mode, destination IP address, and port number (here, UDP is used with port number set to 5000.
destination IP address is set to "0.0.0.0" so that any device can connect and send data over Port 5000).

```
/*****************************************************************************
            CONTROLLING A RELAY FROM MOBILE PHONE
            =====================================

  In this program an ESP-01 module is used to provide Wi-Fi functions.
  A KY-019 relay is connected to Arduino Uno. The program controls the
  relay by receiving commands from the mobile phone.

  Author: Dogan Ibrahim
  Date  : June 2019
  File  : ardwifi
*****************************************************************************/
int Relay = 5;                                  // Relay pin

void setup()
{
  pinMode(Relay, OUTPUT);                       // Relay is output
  digitalWrite(Relay, LOW);                     // Relay OFF
  Serial.begin(115200);                         // Set speed
  Serial.setTimeout(3600000);                   // Wait 1 hour
  ConnectToWiFi();                              // Connect to Wi-Fi

}

//
// This function connects to the Wi-Fi
//
void ConnectToWiFi()
{
  Serial.print("AT+RST\r\n");
  delay(2000);

  Serial.print("AT+CWMODE=1\r\n");
  delay(3000);
```

```
  Serial.print("AT+CWJAP=\"BTHomeSpot-XNH\",\"49346ajaeb\"\r\n");
  delay(8000);

  Serial.print("AT+CPIMUX=1\r\n");
  delay(3000);

  Serial.print("AT+CIFSR\r\n");
  delay(3000);

  Serial.print("AT+CIPSTART=\"UDP\",\"192.168.1.178\",0,5000,2\r\n");
  delay(3000);
}

void loop()
{
  //
  // Receive data packets over UDP and activate/de-activate the
  // relay. Function strstr(a,"b") returns a value greater than
  // 0 if string a contains sub-string "b". The command sent by the
  // mobile device must be terminated with a # character key
  //
  while (1)
  {
    char buf[]="             ";

    Serial.readBytesUntil('#', buf, 15);          // Wait for data
    if(strstr(buf, "RON") >0)                     // RON?
      digitalWrite(Relay, HIGH);                  // Relay ON
    else if(strstr(buf, "ROFF") > 0)              // ROFF?
      digitalWrite(Relay, LOW);                   // Relay OFF
  }
}
```

Figure 20.5 Program listing

Notice that small delays are used after each command. Command **AT+CWJAP** requires a longer delay. The program can easily be modified such that the delays can be removed and the responses from ESP-01 can be checked. This way as soon as the correct response is received the program can continue.

Testing the Program

The program can easily be tested with a mobile phone. You should install a **UDP Server** apps on your Android mobile phone before starting the test. There are many freely available UDP apps in the **Play Store**. The one installed and used in this project is called the **UDP Sender** by *hastarin* (hastarin@gmail.com) as shown in Figure 20.6.

Figure 20.6 UDP Server apps for Android

The steps to test the program are as follows:

- Construct the circuit
- Compile and download the program to your development board
- Start the **UDP Server** apps on your mobile phone and set the Port number to 5000 and the destination IP address (ESP-01 IP address, which was 192.168.1.160 in this project). Enter command **RON#** on the mobile phone. Click **Send** to send the command to Arduino Uno. The relay should now become active and the red LED on the relay module will turn ON. Figure 20.7 shows the command entered on the mobile phone.

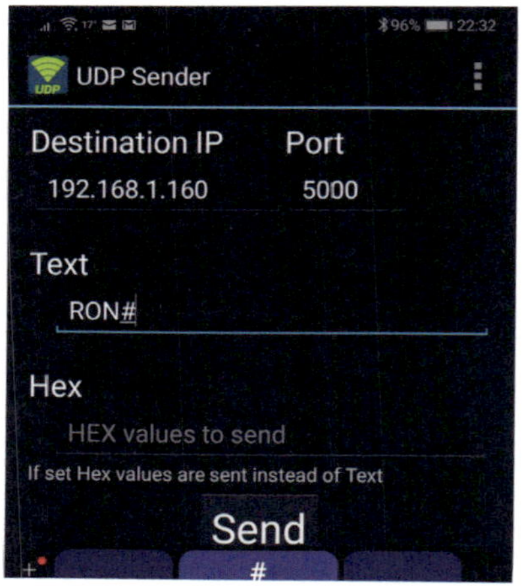

Figure 20.7 Command to activate the relay

Notice that the IP address of the ESP-01 can be obtained by scanning all the devices on the local Wi-Fi router. For example, Android apps called **Wifi Watch** by *Riverdevs* (riverdevs@gmail.com) can be used to see the IP addresses of all the devices connected to the router. The ESP-01 is listed as shown in Figure 20.8 (IP: **192.168.1.160**).

Figure 20.8 Finding the IP address of the ESP-01

Note: Because there is only one hardware UART on Arduino Uno, you will have to disconnect the RX line on your Arduino Uno before uploading the program from Arduino IDE.

20.3 Project 2 – Displaying temperature and humidity on a mobile phone using Wi-Fi

Description: In this project, we will be reading the ambient temperature and humidity from a sensor module and then send the data to a mobile phone over a Wi-Fi link.
The data will be sent in the following format where T and H are the temperature and humidity readings respectively:

```
T=nn   H=nn
```

A request for data is made by the mobile phone when it sends the characters **TH#** to Arduino Uno, where **#** is the terminator character. This project uses two way UDP communications to receive and send data.

Aim: The aim of this project is to show how the temperature and data can be read using a combined sensor module and also it shows how to send data to a mobile phone using an Arduino Uno with the ESP-01 Wi-Fi connectivity.

Sensor Used: In this project, the KY-015 temperature and humidity sensor module is used (see section 18.2).

Block Diagram: Figure 20.9 shows the block diagram of the project.

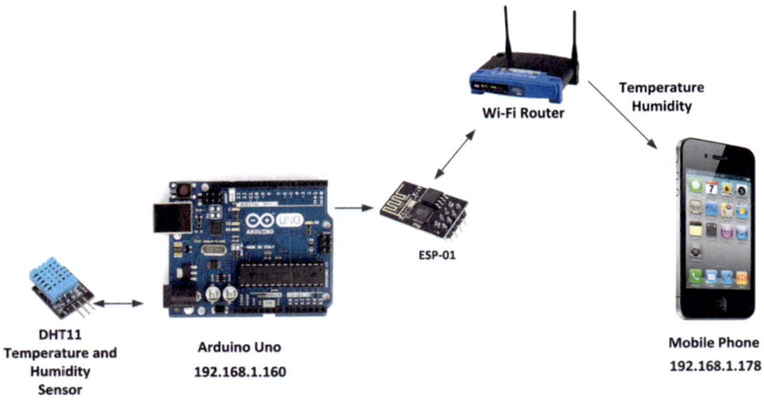

Figure 20.9 Block diagram of the project

Circuit Diagram: The connections between the sensor module, ESP-01, and Arduino Uno are shown in Figure 20.10. Pin **S** of DHT11 is connected to pin 5 of Arduino Uno and pins +V and GND are connected to +5V and GND pins respectively. ESP-01 is connected to Arduino Uno as in Figure 20.4.

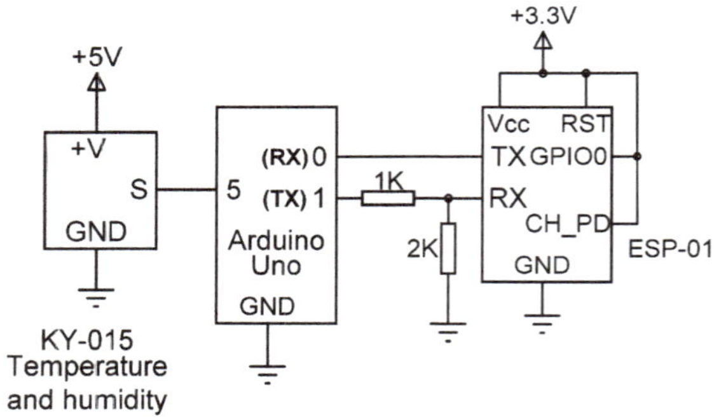

Figure 20.10 Circuit diagram of the project

Note that ESP-01 is not included in the standard sensor kit.

The DHT11 library must be installed in the Arduino Uno environment before the program can be developed. The steps are the same as described in section 18.2.

Program Listing: The program listing is shown in Figure 20.11 (program: **ardwifidht**). At the beginning of the program, the DHT11 library header is included in the program. Inside the setup routine serial port baud rate is set, and function **ConnectToWiFi** is called to connect to the local Wi-Fi router. Inside the main program loop, the program waits to receive command **TH#** and when this command is received, the temperature and humidity are read from the sensor. Variable **MyData** stores the temperature and humidity in the following format: **T=nn H=mm**. The length of this string is then extracted. Sending data through the Wi-Fi UDP link involves sending command **AT+CIPSEND** to ESP-01, followed by the number of bytes to be sent (i.e. the length of the data). The actual data is then sent after a short delay. This process is repeated until stopped by the user.

```
/***********************************************************************
          SEND TEMPERATURE AND HUMIDITY TO MOBILE PHONE
          =============================================

  In this program an ESP-01 module is used to provide Wi-Fi functions.
  A KY-015 temperature and humidity sensor module is used to read
  and send the temperature and humidity readings to a mobile phone

  Author: Dogan Ibrahim
  Date  : June 2019
  File  : ardwifidht
***********************************************************************/
#include "Adafruit_Sensor.h"
#include "DHT.h"
#include "string.h"

#define DHT11_PIN 5                                  // DHT11 on pin 5
#define DHTTYPE DHT11

DHT dht(DHT11_PIN, DHTTYPE);
String temp, hum, data;
char buf[30];

void setup()
{
  dht.begin();
  Serial.begin(115200);                             // Set speed
  Serial.setTimeout(3600000);                       // Wait 1 hour
  ConnectToWiFi();                                  // Connect to Wi-Fi
}

//
// This function connects to the Wi-Fi
//
void ConnectToWiFi()
{
  Serial.print("AT+RST\r\n");
  delay(2000);

  Serial.print("AT+CWMODE=1\r\n");
  delay(3000);
```

```
  Serial.print("AT+CWJAP=\"BTHomeSpot-XNH\",\"49346ajaeb\"\r\n");
  delay(10000);

  Serial.print("AT+CPIMUX=1\r\n");
  delay(3000);

  Serial.print("AT+CIFSR\r\n");
  delay(3000);

  Serial.print("AT+CIPSTART=\"UDP\",\"192.168.1.178\",5000,5000,2\r\n");
  delay(3000);
}


void loop()
{
  int Temperature, Humidity;
  String MyData, Dt;
  int l;
  //
  // Receive data packets over UDP as commands. If the comamnd is
  // S then read and send the temperaqture and humidity data to the
  // mobile phone that sent the command
  //
  while (1)
  {
    for(int k=0; k<30; k++)buf[k]=0x0;                      // Clear buffer

    Serial.readBytesUntil('#', buf, 30);                    // Wait for data
    if(strstr(buf, "TH") > 0)                               // S?
    {
        Humidity = dht.readHumidity();                      // Read humidity
        Temperature = dht.readTemperature();                // Read temp and hum
        MyData="T="+String(Temperature)+" H=" + String(Humidity);
        l = MyData.length();
        Dt = "AT+CIPSEND="+String(l);
        Serial.print(Dt);
        Serial.print("\r\n");
        delay(2000);
        Serial.print(MyData);
    }
  }
}
```

Figure 20.11 Program listing

Figure 20.12 shows the project built on a breadboard.

Figure 20.12 Project built on a breadboard

Note: Because there is only one hardware UART on Arduino Uno, you will have to disconnect the RX line on your Arduino Uno before uploading the program from Arduino IDE.

20.4 Project 3 – Controlling a relay from mobile phone using Bluetooth

Description: In this project, we will be sending commands over the Bluetooth link from a mobile phone to control a relay connected to the Arduino Uno. Valid commands are:

R1	Turn Relay ON
R0	Turn Relay OFF

Aim: The aim of this project is to show how to use the Bluetooth connectivity on Arduino Uno together with a sensor module.

Sensor Used: In this project, the KY-019 relay module is used. Additionally, the HC-06 Bluetooth module is used (***Note that HC-06 is not included in the standard sensor kit).*** HC-06 is a 4-pin module with the following pins (see Figure 20.13):

Figure 20.13 HC-06 Bluetooth module

HC-06 is a serially controlled module, having the following basic specifications:

- +3.3V to +6V operation
- 30mA unpaired current (10mA matched current)
- Built-in antenna
- Default communication: 9600 baud, 8 data bits, no parity, 1 stop bit
- Signal coverage 30 feet

Block Diagram: Figure 20.14 shows the block diagram of the project.

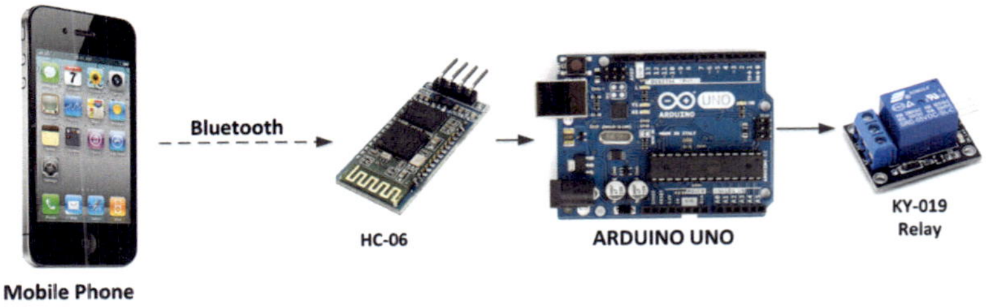

Figure 20.14 Block diagram of the project

Circuit Diagram: Figure 20.15 shows the project circuit diagram. TXD and RXD pins of the Bluetooth module are connected to UART pins RX (0) and TX (1) of Arduino Uno. Relay is connected to pin 5.

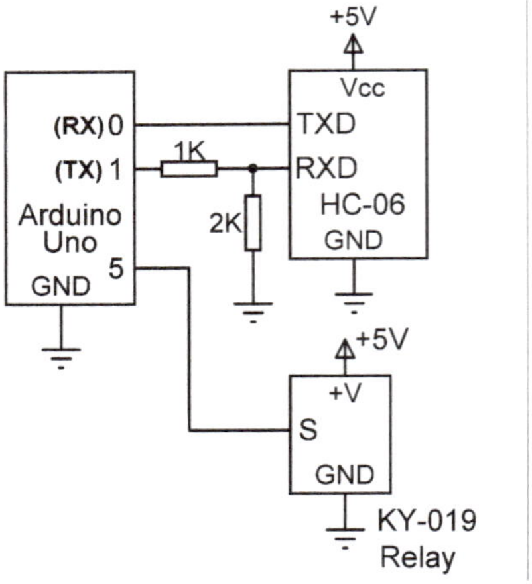

Figure 20.15 Circuit diagram of the project

Program listing: The program listing of the project is shown in Figure 20.16 (program: **bluerelay**). At the beginning of the program, the hardware UART interface is set to baud rate 9600 which is the default speed of HC-06 and the relay is configured as an output and is turned OFF. The remainder of the program runs in an endless loop. Inside this loop data (commands) are received from the Bluetooth device using the **readBytes** function. This function reads characters from the serial port where the second argument specified the number of characters to be read. The read characters are stored in a character array Buffer. The program then controls the relay based on the received command. e.g. **R1** turns the relay ON, **R0** turns it OFF and so on.

```
/**********************************************************************
            CONTROLLING A RELAY USING BLUETOOTH
            ====================================

  In this program a HC-06 type Bluetooth module is used to control
  a KY-019 relay module. The program controls the relay by receiving
  commands from the mobile phone.

  Author: Dogan Ibrahim
  Date  : June 2019
  File  : bluerelay
*********************************************************************/
int Relay = 5;                                        // Relay pin
char Buffer[10];

void setup()
{
  Serial.begin(9600);                                 // Bluetooth serial
  pinMode(Relay, OUTPUT);                             // Relay is output
  digitalWrite(Relay, LOW);                           // Relay OFF
}


void loop()
{
        Serial.readBytes(Buffer, 2);
        if(Buffer[0] == 'R' && Buffer[1] == '1')
            digitalWrite(Relay, HIGH);
        else if(Buffer[0] == 'R' && Buffer[1] == '0')
            digitalWrite(Relay, LOW);
}
```

Figure 20.16 Program listing

Testing the Program

The program can be tested by using an Android mobile phone to send commands through a Bluetooth communication interface. There are many freely available Bluetooth communication programs in the Play Store. The one chosen by the author was called the **Bluetooth Controller** by *mightyIT* (it@memighty.com) as shown in Figure 20.17. You should install this app on your Android mobile phone so that you can send commands to the development board.

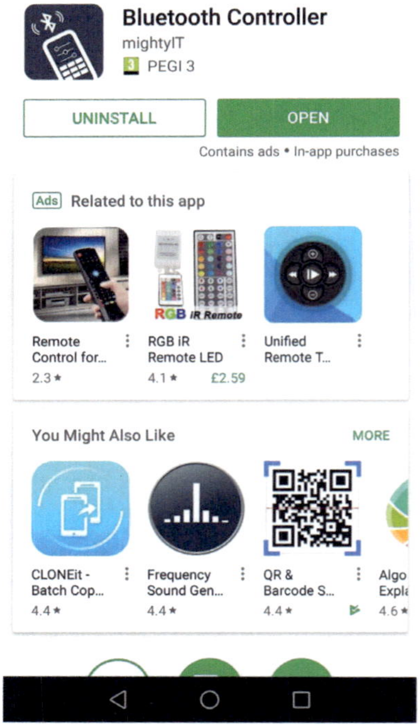

Figure 20.17 Bluetooth Controller apps

The steps to test the application are as follows:

- Construct the project
- Compile and download the program to your Arduino Uno (remember to disconnect the RX line when uploading your program)
- Active the **Bluetooth Controller** apps on your mobile phone
- The apps will look for nearby Bluetooth devices. Click on **HC-06** when displayed on the mobile phone screen (you may have to scan for devices).
- You will now be asked to enter the password to pair the mobile phone with the development board. Enter the default password of **1234.** You should see a green colour dot at the top right-hand side of the screen when a connection is made to the development board. Also, HC-06 with its address (e.g. HC-06 [98:D3:31:FB:5E:B6] should be displayed at the top left side of the screen.
- To turn the relay ON enter command **R1** and click **Send ASCII**. You should see the relay turning ON. Enter command **R0** to turn OFF the relay. Figure 20.18 shows an example screen.

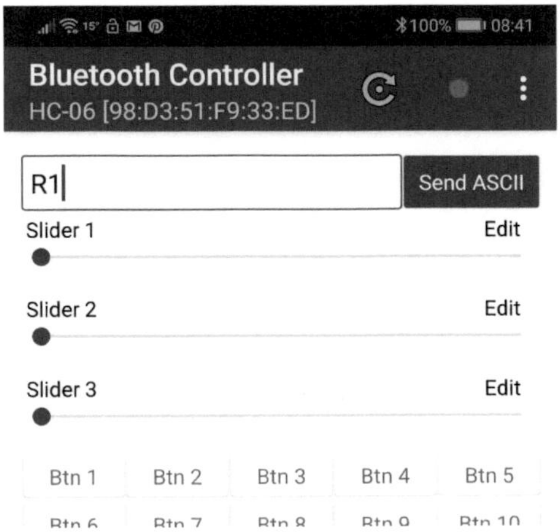

Figure 20.18 Example command to turn the relay ON

We can modify the program in Figure 20.16 by sending a confirmation to the mobile phone when there is a change in the relay status. The required modifications are shown below:

```
void loop()
{
        Serial.readBytes(Buffer, 2);
        if(Buffer[0] == 'R' && Buffer[1] == '1')
        {
            digitalWrite(Relay, HIGH);
            Serial.println("Relay is ON");
        }
        else if(Buffer[0] == 'R' && Buffer[1] == '0')
        {
            digitalWrite(Relay, LOW);
            Serial.println("Relay is OFF");
        }
}
```

For example, as shown in Figure 20.19, the text Relay is ON is displayed on the screen after the command **R1** is sent.

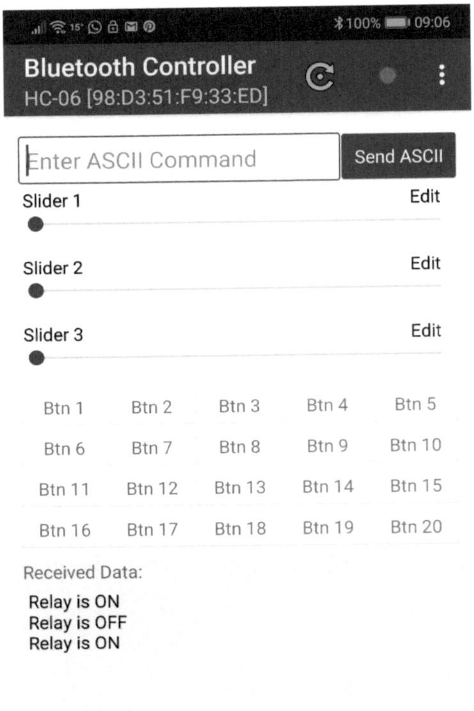

Figure 20.19 Example display

Appendix A - Sensor kit contents (JOY-iT Sensor-Kit X40)

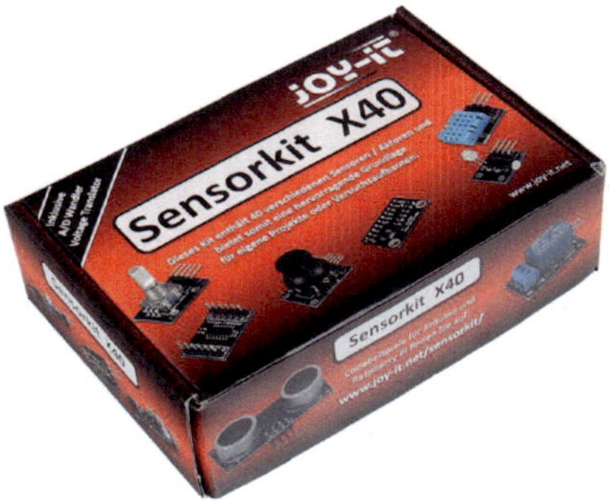

KY-001 Temperature sensor module
KY-002 Vibration switch module
KY-003 Hall magnetic field sensor module
KY-004 Button module
KY-005 Infrared transmitter module
KY-006 Passive Piezo buzzer module
KY-009 RGB LED SMD module
KY-010 Light barrier module
KY-011 2-colour 5mm LED module
KY-012 Active piezo buzzer module
KY-013 Temperature sensor module
KY-015 Combi temperature+humidity sensor module
KY-016 RGB 5mm LED module
KY-017 Tilt switch module
KY-018 Photoresistor module
KY-019 5V relay module
KY-020 Tilt switch module
KY-021 Mini magnetic reed module
KY-022 Infrared receiver module
KY-023 Joystick module
KY-024 Linear magnetic Hall sensor
KY-025 Reed module
KY-026 Flame sensor module
KY-027 Magic light cup module
KY-028 Temperature sensor module
KY-029 2-colour 3mm LED module
KY-031 Knock sensor module
KY-032 Obstacle detect module
KY-033 Tracking sensor module
KY-034 7-colour LED flash module
KY-035 Bihor magnetic sensor module
KY-036 Metal touch module
KY-037 Microphone sensor module
KY-038 Microphone sound sensor module
KY-039 Heartbeat sensor module
KY-040 Rotary encoder module
KY-050 Ultrasonic distance sensor module
KY-051 Voltage translator module
KY-052 Pressure+temperature sensor module
KY-053 Analog-to-digital converter module

Appendix B – Projects and sensor modules used

Section	Sensor Module Used
1.4, 2.10, 3.4, 4.2.1	KY-011
4.2.2	KY-009
4.2.3	KY-016, KY-017, KY-020
4.2.4	KY-021, KY-034
4.2.5	KY-018, KY-019
4.2.6	KY-018, KY-019, KY-051, KY-053
4.2.7	KY-018, KY-019, KY-051
4.2.8	KY-003, KY-018, KY-019
4.2.9	KY-010, KY-012
4.2.10	KY-027
5.2	KY-022
5.3	KY-022, KY-029
5.4	KY-005
5.5	KY-004, KY-005, KY-012, KY-022
6.2	KY-002, KY-019, KY-031, KY-051
6.3	KY-002, KY-019, KY-031, KY-051
6.4	KY-031
7.2	KY-012, KY-050
8.2	KY-019, KY-037
9.2	KY-006
10.2	KY-024
10.3	KY-012, KY-025
10.4	KY-006, KY-035
11.2	KY-012, KY-026
12.2	KY-023
12.3	KY-006. KY-023
13.2	KY-012, KY-032
13.3	KY-012, KY-036
14.2	KY-033
14.3	KY-019, KY-033
15.2	KY-040
15.3	KY-040
16.2	KY-039
17.2	KY-001
17.3	KY-012, KY-028
17.4	KY-013
17.4	LCD
17.5	KY-013
17.6	KY-013
17.7	KY-013, KY-053
17.8	KY-013, KY-053
17.9	KY-019, KY-052
17.10	KY-019, KY-051, KY-052

17.11	KY-019, KY-051, KY-052
18.2	KY-015
19.2	KY-015
19.4	KY-029
20.2	KY-019
20.3	KY-015
20.4	KY-019

Additional Components Used (not included in the basic sensor kit):

17.6	LCD
17.7	LCD
17.8	LCD
20.2	ESP-01
20.3	ESP-01
20.4	HC-06
7.2	1K resistor, 2K resistor
2.10, 3.4, 15.2	2 x 220 Ohm resistors
15.2	Small LED (any colour)
1.4	2 x 330 Ohm resistors
17.7	Small 10K trimmer potentiometer

Appendix C – Sensor modules and projects using them

Sensor Module	Section Used
KY-001	17.2
KY-002	6.2, 6.3
KY-003	4.2.8
KY-004	5.5
KY-005	5.4, 5.5
KY-006	9.2, 12.3, 10.4
KY-009	4.2.2
KY-010	4.2.9
KY-011	1.4, 2.10, 3.4, 4.21
KY-012	4.2.9, 5.5, 7.2, 10.3, 11.2, 13.2, 13.3, 17.3
KY-013	17.4, 17.5, 17.6, 17.7, 17.8
KY-015	18.2, 19.2, 20.3
KY-016	4.2.3
KY-017	4.2.3
KY-018	4.2.5, 4.2.6, 4.2.7, 4.2.8
KY-019	4.2.5, 4.2.6, 4.2.7, 4.2.8, 6.2, 6.3, 8.2, 14.3, 17.9, 17.10, 17.11, 20.2, 20.4
KY-020	4.2.3
KY-021	4.2.4
KY-022	5.2, 5.3, 5.5
KY-023	12.2, 12.3
KY-024	10.2
KY-025	10.3
KY-026	11.2
KY-027	4.2.10
KY-028	17.3
KY-029	5.3, 14.4
KY-031	6.2, 6.3, 6.4
KY-032	13.2
KY-033	14.2, 14.3
KY-034	4.2.4
KY-035	10.4
KY-036	13.3
KY-037	8.2
KY-038	8.2
KY-039	16.2
KY-040	15.2, 15.3
KY-050	7.2
KY-051	4.2.6, 4.2.7, 6.2, 6.3, 17.10, 17.11
KY-052	17.9, 17.10, 17.11
KY-053	4.2.6, 17.7, 17.8

Additional components used (not included in the basic sensor kit):

LCD	17.4, 17.6, 17.7, 17.8
ESP-01	20.2, 20.3
HC-06	20.4
2 x 330 Ohm resistors	2.10, 3.4, 15.2
2 x 330 Ohm resistors	1.4
1K resistor	7.2
2K resistor	7.2
Small LED (any colour)	15.2
10K trimmer potentiometer	17.7

Index